Tourism and National Parks
Issues and Implications

Edited by

RICHARD W. BUTLER AND STEPHEN W. BOYD

JOHN WILEY & SONS, LTD
Chichester · New York · Weinheim · Brisbane · Toronto · Singapore

National   01243 779777
International   (+44) 1243 779777
email (for orders and customer service enquiries): cs-books@wiley.co.uk
Visit our Home Page on http://www.wiley.co.uk
or http://www.wiley.com

Other Wiley Editorial Offices

John Wiley & Sons, Inc., 605 Third Avenue,
New York, NY 10158-0012 USA

WILEY-VCH Verlag GmbH, Pappelallee 3,
D-69469 Weinheim, Germany

Jacaranda Wiley Ltd, 33 Park Road, Milton
Queensland 4064, Australia

John Wiley & Sons (Asia) Pte Ltd, 2 Clementi Loop #02-01,
Jin Xing Distripark, Singapore 129809

John Wiley & Sons (Canada) Ltd, 22 Worcester Road,
Rexdale, Ontario M9W 1L1, Canada

British Library Cataloguing in Publication Data
A catalogue record for this book is available from the British Library

ISBN 0-471-98894-4

Typeset in 10/12pt Times by BookEns Ltd, Royston Herts
Printed and bound in Great Britain by Bookcraft (Bath) Ltd, Midsomer Norton, Somerset
This book is printed on acid-free paper responsibly manufactured from sustainable forestry, in which at
least two trees are planted for each one used for paper production.

To Margaret and Carla, our long-suffering wives

Contents

Contributors

Stephen Boyd is Senior Lecturer in the Geography Division, Staffordshire University, UK

Richard Butler is Professor of Tourism in the School of Management Studies at the University of Surrey, UK

C. Michael Hall is Associate Professor in the Centre for Tourism, Otago University, Dunedin, New Zealand

Kay Booth is a Research Associate and **David Simmons** Professor in the Department of Parks and Tourism, Lincoln University, New Zealand

Sanjay Nepal is a Research Associate at the Centre for Development and Environment, University of Bern, Switzerland

Gavin Parker is Lecturer and **Neil Ravenscroft** Reader in the School of Management Studies, University of Surrey, UK

David Weaver is Senior Lecturer in the School of Tourism and Hotel Management, Griffith University, Queensland, Australia

John Marsh is Professor of Geography at Trent University, Peterborough, Ontario, Canada

Robert Lilieholm is Associate Professor and **Lisa Romney** a Research Assistant in the College of Natural Resources, Utah State University, Logan, Utah, USA

Phillip Dearden is Professor of Geography, University of Victoria, BC, Canada

Jerry Vaske is Professor, **Maureen Donnelly** is Associate Professor and **Doug Whittaker** a Research Assistant in the Department of Natural Resource, Recreation and Tourism, Colorado State University, Fort Collins, Colorado, USA

Philippa Sowman is Survey Design Statician with Statistics New Zealand in Christchurch, New Zealand, and **Douglas Pearce** is Professor of Tourism Management School of Business and Public Management, Victoria University, New Zealand

Harold Goodwin is Director of Tourism and Conservation at the International Centre for Protected Landscapes and affiliated with the University of Greenwich, UK

Dallen Timothy is Assistant Professor in the Sport Management, Recreation and Tourism Division, Bowling Green State University, Ohio, USA

Carolyn Cresswell is a Consultant with the UK government and development agencies and is based in England, and **Fergus Maclaren** is a Consultant with Definitive Development and Canadian government agencies, and is based in Calgary, Canada

J. Gordon Nelson is Distinguished Professor Emeritus at the University of Waterloo, Ontario, Canada

Acknowledgements

As all editors know, assembling contributions and producing a complete volume is not an easy task and a great deal of support and cooperation is needed from many people. This volume has been no exception. Our first acknowledgements are to the contributors of the chapters. They responded to our often unrealistic requests with good humour and even promptness in some cases, and have genuinely tried to follow our somewhat optimistic suggestions in good faith. We take responsibility for any shortcomings and errors in the finished result.

We would also like to thank Claire Plimmer, and before her, Iain Stevenson, at John Wiley and Sons for their support and patience. Between the four of us the volume has had a rather long history before making its appearance, but we hope they feel their support has been justified.

Acknowledgement is also made to DFID, DETR and IIED for permission to use material from their reports in Chapter 15 and to M. Brosnan for use of his imagery in Chapter 14.

Finally, we owe a great deal of thanks to Margaret Williamson, School of Management Studies, University of Surrey, for her skill and patience in producing the finished manuscript.

Part One:
Historical Context

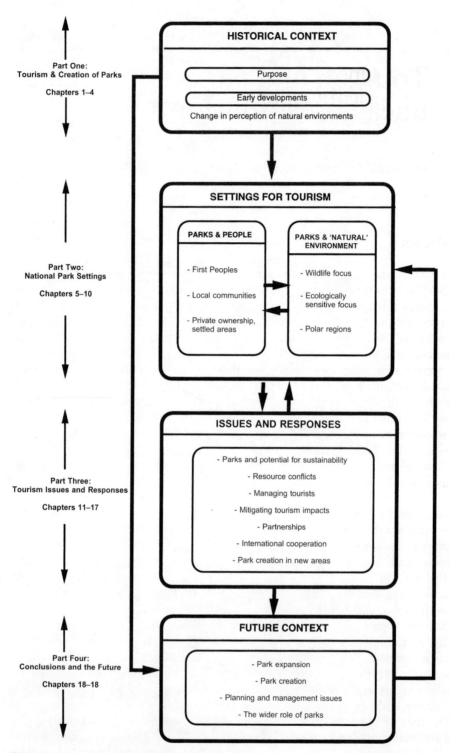

Figure I. Conceptual framework

1 Tourism and parks – a long but uneasy relationship

RICHARD W. BUTLER AND STEPHEN W. BOYD

Introduction

In the century and a quarter since their establishment, national parks have played a significant role as tourist attractions in many countries. In some they are the major set of tourist attractions and the foundation of small but often important tourism industries. Despite this, the relationship between tourism and national parks is not always a satisfactory one, and there is often considerable and vocal opposition to the continuance and particularly the expansion of tourism in many national parks. This may appear somewhat surprising given the fact that tourism has been strongly associated with national parks from the earliest days of their establishment and is often placed firmly in legislation and park policies as a major function of parks systems (see Boyd and Butler, Hall, and Booth and Simmons, this volume).

The nature of the relationship between national parks and tourism has not been reviewed or discussed at length, although there is a plethora of literature on national parks and on tourism individually. Works on national parks have often included some discussion on the issues and problems associated with the presence of tourism in the parks, as the bibliographies of the chapters in this book bear witness, and over the last three decades the literature on tourism has become even more voluminous. While an increasing proportion of the tourism literature has addressed environmental matters, particularly sustainable tourism and the impacts of tourism (see, for example, Mathieson and Wall, 1982; Hall and Lew, 1998; Mowforth and Munt, 1998; Wahab and Pigram, 1997; Butler, 1999) relatively little has dealt specifically with national parks, or indeed tourism in any form of park or reserve, apart from some specific case studies (for example, Dearden and Rollins, 1993; Pigram and Sundell, 1997).

The focus of this book is first and foremost on tourism in national parks. It does not discuss the full range of issues facing national parks, nor does it deal with all aspects of tourism. Where it deals with issues such as park origins and functions, management issues and future problems, it does so from the perspective of tourism and the benefits and problems which accrue from that activity. Where chapters examine the effect of tourism on local populations and indigenous peoples, or on wildlife, they do so in the context of national parks specifically. It is recognised that there are some problems with this approach. One, as mentioned above, is that not all aspects of either national parks nor tourism can be explored. Another is that there is no attempt made to provide a global coverage of national parks. The contributions which follow use examples from six continents, but the emphasis is upon the relationships between park systems and tourism in a variety of contexts, rather than an analysis of specific park systems.

A broad general framework illustrating this relationship is proposed (Figure I) and is discussed in more detail later in this chapter. The framework provides the overall structure for the volume. It begins with the historical development of the concept of national parks and the place of tourism and recreation within the national parks ideal and the systems which have been created. The discussion which is contained in the following three chapters is focused on the first systems which were established, the USA, and after that, Australia, New Zealand and Canada. All these systems have a great deal in common in terms of their establishment, the role which tourism was expected to play, and the importance given to tourism and visitation of the early parks. Despite major changes in emphasis and focus for parks over the following decades, many of these early principles still apply. It is not difficult to understand how, the dynamics of both parks and tourism notwithstanding, many of the issues are essentially the same as they were over a century ago, although the scale of the problems and the range of possible responses have broadened very considerably.

National parks

The image of national parks and their acceptability appears to be generally high, with a few exceptions where local populations have been or feel disadvantaged by the establishment of parks. While the establishment of the first parks was generally supported, as Hall (this volume) notes, in some cases this was because they were seen as otherwise worthless and thus the opportunity cost in establishing them was low. There are still concerns in some quarters over issues such as the necessity to preserve large areas of environment when large, apparently untouched other areas exist (a common complaint in North America), the loss of revenue and jobs by not extracting resources from parks, the impacts which result in and around parks from tourism, and conflicts between national and other levels of government over the operation of parks. Despite these issues, which have been present almost from the establishment of national parks, the movement has grown and is now represented in most countries of the world. National parks today represent only one type from of a range of protected areas (for example, Biosphere Sites, Marine Reserves, RAMSAR sites and World Heritage Sites), although at the time of their establishment, with a few exceptions, they represented the only extensive protected environments.

A global definition of national parks received finalisation and approval in 1969 at a General Assembly of the International Union for the Conservation of Nature, held in New Delphi, India. The Assembly identified three essential characteristics of a national park and defined it as:

> a relatively large area where
>
> 1. one or several ecosystems are not materially altered by human exploitation and occupation, where plant and animal species, geomorphological sites and

habitats of special scientific, educative and recreative interest or which contains a natural landscape of great beauty and

2. the highest competent authority of the country has taken steps to prevent or to eliminate as soon as possible exploitation or occupation in the whole area and to enforce effectively the respect of ecological, geomorphological or aesthetic features which have led to its establishment and

3. visitors are allowed to enter, under special conditions, for inspirational, educative, cultural and recreative purposes (quoted in van Osten, 1972, p. 5).

National parks can, therefore, be expected to be large, untouched (or relatively so) areas of natural environment, with significant features, protected at the highest level, and allowing among other uses, that of recreation (tourism). There are exceptions to this image in the cases discussed in this book. Some of the parks in Australia and other countries (Hall, Weaver) are relatively small, some international parks (Timothy) have other functions, there are as yet no formal parks in Antarctica (Marsh), and the national parks in England and Wales (Parker and Ravenscroft) have long been recognised as not fitting this definition in a number of elements. However, all are termed national parks by the respective governments involved, and including a varied collection of parks provides a better indication of the range of issues and problems facing national parks and their managers in the context of tourism than confining discussion to the traditional 'old' North American model. In the future, if the global system of national parks is to be completed appropriately, an even wider range of national park types and functions is likely to have to be utilised as a result of an increasingly competitive and complex set of demands on the global environment.

Tourism, recreation and leisure in national parks

While, as noted earlier, the focus of this book is specifically tourism within national parks, it is impossible not to acknowledge that a real problem exists in attempting to differentiate between tourist and recreational uses of areas such as national parks. Discussion of the often subtle and semantic differences between tourism, recreation and leisure is not appropriate here, and can be found in a number of sources in the relevant tourism, recreation and leisure literature (for example, see, Jackson and Burton, 1999). Suffice it to say here that tourism in general, can be regarded as vacation or holiday travel, where the primary motivation is pleasure or enjoyment. Recreation normally is taken to imply non-vacation visitation for pleasure, often of a domestic nature, i.e. not travelling beyond the boundaries of one's own country. None of the authors in this book specifically address the distinction between tourist and recreational use of national parks, and they were not asked to do so by the editors. Rather, they have focused on pleasure-based use of the parks, and thus throughout the book tourism should be taken to include recreational use of the parks unless a specific distinction is made. While it is acknowledged that this may be somewhat imprecise and introduce a measure of generalisation about use which is not always accurate, for the reasons noted below, it is felt that the problems resulting from tourist and recreational use of parks are closely related and often dealt with in the same manner.

As discussed in the other chapters in this part of the book, those establishing the first national parks saw a very real and distinct role for tourism within those parks. Tourism was seen not only as a valid and appropriate use of the parks, but also as a

significant source of revenue for the parks themselves and the infrastructure involved
in visiting them, including railroads and hotels. There was little differentiation
between tourism and any other form of pleasure use of the parks at that time, and
the public and private sectors worked together, or at least did not often work in
opposing directions, with respect to development of tourism related facilities in the
parks and their promotion (Brown, 1970; Hart 1983). The disagreements over the
nature and scale of tourism-related development in national parks which have
characterised much of the recent history of national parks, especially in 'Western'
countries, were rarely an issue in the first two decades or more of most parks'
establishment. Parks were seen as places for people to visit and enjoy.

For reasons discussed below (Boyd and Butler and Hall, this volume) most of the
parks established in early years were considerable distances from major population
centres, and thus anyone visiting the parks had to be a tourist in the sense that they
were travelling considerable distances and spending a good many overnights on their
visits. Early definitions of tourism are as uncertain as are many present-day ones, but
the general impression of tourists visiting parks at the end of the nineteenth century
was of affluent, privileged individuals, frequently foreign, often on long trips of
several months' duration, with visits to the new parks as one feature of an
exploratory journey to the 'New Worlds' (North America and Australia in
particular). The provision of accommodation and other facilities was essential,
and often the trains served as travelling hotels (Hart, 1983). Recreational use of
national parks was rare, if only because initially there was little, if any, local
population in areas surrounding the new parks. In the case of the Canadian national
parks, for example, the only recreational use of the parks in the early years was by
the rail crews of the Canadian Pacific and Canadian National Railroads as they
constructed and maintained the railroad track and facilities.

This pattern of use has changed dramatically in many countries, particularly in
North America, Europe and Australia, and recreational as opposed to tourist use of
the parks is now the major form of visitation. In many respects there is little
difference between the actual activities engaged in by tourists and recreationists
within many national parks; they walk, observe wildlife, camp, fish, and relax, and
use the same facilities, accommodation, restrooms, interpretive facilities, transport
facilities, and trails. Observation of behaviour may fail to note any difference
between these two groups of users in many contexts. There are, however, some
important differences and implications for park management and operations. By
definition, recreationists are (relatively) local residents and their length of stay in
parks is short, often not involving an overnight visit. They tend to have their own
transport, be more familiar with the setting and be repeat visitors. Tourists, on the
other hand, tend to have a wider range of characteristics, living further away from
the parks (often in other countries), generally staying overnight and often many
nights, tend to use commercial accommodation more and camp less, are much less
likely to be repeat visitors, and travel more by public or commercial transport. At
one end of a continuum of use, therefore, are recreationists who live on the edge of
the park, at the other are international tourists from the other side of the world.
There can be significant differences in needs, experiences, and expectations, if less so
in actual behaviour between these two groups.

In some systems, of which North America is a good example, recreational use, particularly combined with domestic tourist use, now far outweighs conventional tourism use in many parks, although the best-known parks (Banff, Grand Canyon, Yellowstone, for example) are major international icons and attractions used extensively in tourist promotional literature. Others, the African game parks for example, are used almost exclusively by foreign tourists (see Lilieholm and Romney, Chapter 10 and Goodwin, Chapter 15), although in South Africa domestic use has always been significant and is increasing. In the United Kingdom (see Parker and Ravenscroft, Chapter 7) the national parks are extremely heavily used by domestic visitors (recreationists and tourists alike) but almost incidentally by international tourists, partly because they are somewhat inaccessible without private transport, and partly because they are lacking major tourism icons to attract international visitors. This reflects in part the *raison d'être* of the parks' establishment, the protection of a developed landscape and the provision of access for the UK population, a pattern which may be repeated in other areas where the designation of large untouched areas is not possible for a variety of reasons, including the lack of such areas in some countries.

National parks have experienced, therefore, not only vastly increased levels of use since their establishment, but in many cases the addition of a related but different user population; in the case of the earliest parks, very heavy use from more local populations, while in other cases, heavy use from international tourists as different countries have 'opened up' for tourism (see Cresswell and Maclaren, Chapter 17). As is discussed later, the range of pressures on parks which has resulted from this increased and diversified pleasure-related use has correspondingly grown and intensified. In the future (see Butler, Chapter 19), the continued blurring between the boundaries of tourism and recreation is likely to mean that the differences between these two user groups become even less for most users, although the extreme ends of the user continuum are likely to be as far apart as currently is the case.

Structure of the book

As noted above, the focus of this book is on tourism and national parks and the relationship between these elements. To this end, a conceptual framework consisting of four sections (historical context, settings, issues and responses, and future context) has been developed to examine this relationship, and it is around this framework that the book is structured. Unlike many edited volumes, this book is not the product of a conference on a particular topic, where a collection of papers are selected and then edited. Instead, each contributor was invited to write on a specific aspect of the relationship between tourism and national parks, based on their expertise on the topic(s) in question, as recognised from the tourism literature. Topics were chosen that represented elements making up the framework, and as such each contribution adds something specific to the overall discussion. Given that each contributor discussed a specific aspect, the end product has been an edited volume that has a high degree of continuity present throughout. Introductory linkages are provided, at the start of each section, which not only provide continuity, but also serve to introduce each chapter within that section. Given this, the focus here is to outline the basic elements that make up the conceptual framework and the linkages that exist between them (see Figure I).

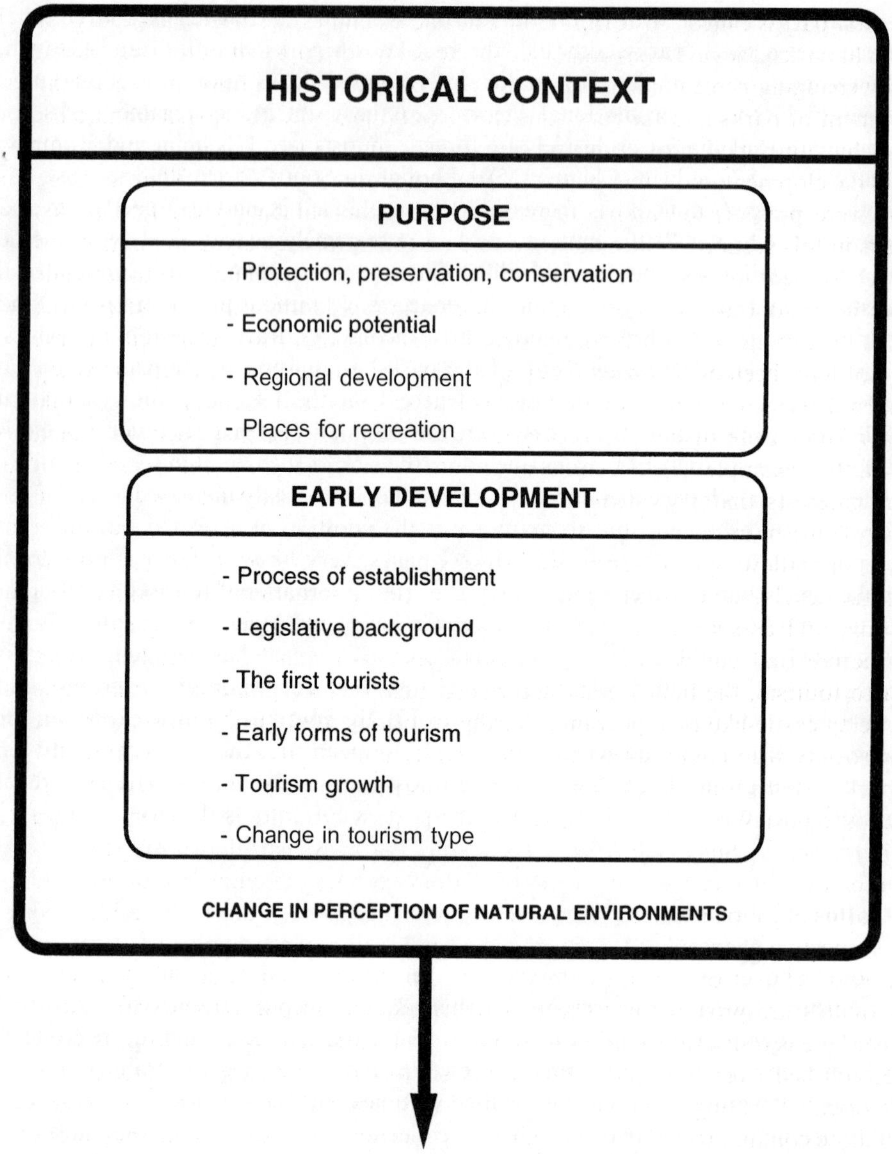

HISTORICAL CONTEXT

PURPOSE

- Protection, preservation, conservation

- Economic potential

- Regional development

- Places for recreation

EARLY DEVELOPMENT

- Process of establishment

- Legislative background

- The first tourists

- Early forms of tourism

- Tourism growth

- Change in tourism type

CHANGE IN PERCEPTION OF NATURAL ENVIRONMENTS

Figure 1.1.   Historical context

The first part is called 'Historical Context' and examines the origins and purpose of national parks, the role tourism played in the early development of the first parks, and how changing perceptions towards the natural environment have influenced the development of parks and the functions they should provide. Purposes behind park creation have included protection, preservation, conservation, economic potential, regional development and being places for recreation (see Figure 1.1). While all these reasons were present, to varying degrees, in the establishment of the first parks, emphasis in this section is placed deliberately on the influence played by tourism on the establishment of the first parks. This is justified on the basis that while preservation and romantic notions of safeguarding wilderness places were often stated as *the* driving forces behind early park establishment, many of the first parks would not have been established if they had offered no potential for tourism. Many have been described as being situated on 'worthless lands' and therefore not suitable for other human use or development (Hall, this section). The first parks in North America, for example, Yellowstone and Banff, benefited from the presence of railroad interests that provided not only initial access to the parks but also the necessary tourism infrastructure within the parks for the first tourists.

In the 'early development' content of this part, discussion is provided to illustrate that initial developments within parks preceded the introduction of National Park legislation, and as such few, if any, restrictions were placed on the type of built infrastructure that could be erected or activities that could be undertaken. With respect to tourism, the built infrastructure often emphasised grandeur, for example hotels being castle-like in appearance; hardly surprising as the first tourists were the elite of society who could afford to travel. Description is also offered on how the early park systems were developed, and how tourism growth remained incremental prior to the post-World War II period and the democratisation of leisure within Western societies. Since the 1960s, the earlier park systems have struggled to accommodate ever-increasing numbers of visitors expecting to enjoy and participate in new forms of tourism and recreational activity. The reality of this is also addressed within respective chapters that comprise the first section of the book.

The next element of the framework is entitled 'Settings for Tourism'. Again, as details of this are provided elsewhere in the book (see introduction to Part Two), comment here is restricted to noting that as national parks and systems of parks have been established over time, they have done so within a diversity of 'natural' and 'people-oriented' settings. Each has been marketed for tourism, from the exotic and wild to those containing distinctive peoples and places within them. As the framework shows, natural settings range from those environments that are virtually free from human presence (e.g. polar areas) to those where parks have been developed in settings which have a long-established history of permanent settlement and use. In many cases, the natural setting cannot be divorced from the people present, hence the arrows within the framework between both subsets. Few settings are rarely 'natural', as they have been, and will continue to be, influenced by human presence. In addition, the 'people' elements within environments play an important role in how parks are used for tourism, as well as influencing how parks are managed and the degree to which the interests of various peoples are considered and accommodated.

The third part of the framework is labelled 'Issues and Responses'. The link between the previous part and this one is clear, namely that issues arise from the type of setting in which parks are situated, as well as their historical development. The focus here is with tourism issues within parks, although some non-tourism issues are also explored (e.g. resource conflicts). It is also suggested within the framework that there exist backward linkages to the previous section. Responses made to tourism issues within parks can alter the settings in terms of the degree to which they remain 'natural', as well as affecting the relationships, both positive and negative, that exist between tourism and 'peoples' linked to parks. The extent of linkages forward and back, as well as descriptions of each of the issues and responses are provided in detail in an introductory discussion at the start of the third section of the book.

The fourth and final part of the conceptual framework is labelled 'Future Context'. Here attention is directed at the present and future relationships between tourism and national parks, how these will be affected by ongoing park expansion, new park creation, and changes in both the nature of tourism and types of tourists visiting parks. Once again, there are a number of forward and backward linkages present. The early historical context of the establishment of the tourism–park relationship has implications for the future, in that the ongoing expansion of the early park systems will most likely continue in an incremental manner. At the same time, future developments both in terms of new parks and new forms of tourism and tourists have implications which can cause changes to the settings in which the relationship between tourism and national parks takes place.

Conclusion

Tourism research has come of age. This maturing is evidenced in the proliferation of books that are appearing on the subject, as well as the growth of new journals (e.g. *Journal of Sustainable Tourism, Current Issues in Tourism, Tourism Geographies*) devoted to tourism research. Early books examined tourism in a general way, (Pearce, 1989, 1995) and while there has been a departure from this towards a more thematic approach, some emphasis on the general still remains popular (e.g. Shaw and Williams, 1994) today. While this approach has merits of providing an overview of subject material, the majority of recent publications on tourism have addressed the subject by themes (e.g. Public Policy; Hall, 1994; Transport; Page, 1997; Indigenous Peoples; Butler and Hinch, 1996). Others have examined tourism or types of tourism within a particular geographical location (e.g. The Developed World; Weaver, 1998 or Australia; Hall, 1995). National parks have been a less popular area examined by tourism researchers. While chapters in books and journal papers have been written on the topic, there has been an absence of books on the topic. Those that have been published have either focused on a particular park system (e.g. Canada; Dearden and Rollins, 1993) or have addressed issues such as delimitation, planning and management (e.g. Pigram and Sundell, 1997). This book differs from the above by combining the two broad topics of tourism and national parks, and examining the relationships and issues involved when these two phenomena interact, and this fills an apparent and important lacunae that has existed within the current tourism literature.

References

Brown, R.C., 1970, The doctrine of usefulness: natural resource and national park policy in Canada, 1887–1914. In *Canadian parks in perspective*, G. Nelson, ed., pp. 46–62. Harvest House, Montreal

Butler, R.W., 1999, Sustainable tourism: a state of the art, *Tourism Geographies*, **1**(1): 7–25

Butler, R.W. and Hinch, T., 1996, *Tourism and Indigenous Peoples*, Thompson International Press, London

Dearden, P. and Rollins, R., eds, 1993, *Parks and protected areas in Canada: Planning and management*, Oxford University Press, Toronto

Hall, C.M., 1994, *Tourism and politics: Policy, power and place*, Wiley, Chichester

Hall, C.M., 1995, *An introduction to tourism in Australia: Impacts, planning and development*, Longman, Melbourne

Hall, C.M. and Lew, A., eds, 1998, *Sustainable tourism: Geographical Perspectives*, Longman, Harlow

Hart, E.J., 1983, *The selling of Canada: The CPR and the beginnings of Canadian tourism*, Altitude Press, Banff

Jackson, E. and Burton, T.L., eds, 1999, *Recreation and leisure in the millennium*, Venture Publishing, Philadelphia

Mathieson, A. and Wall, G., 1982, *Tourism: Economic, physical and social impacts*, Addison-Wesley Longman, London

Mowforth, M. and Munt, I., 1998, *Tourism and sustainability: New tourism in the Third World*, Routledge, London

Page, S., 1997, *Transport for tourism*, Routledge, London

Pearce, D.G., 1989, *Tourist development*, Longman, Harlow

Pearce, D.G., 1995, *Tourism today: A geographical analysis*, Longman, Harlow

Pigram, J.J. and Sundell, R.C., eds, 1997, *National parks and protected areas: Selection, delimitation, and management*, Centre for Water Policy Research, UNE, Armidale, Australia

Shaw, G. and Williams, A., 1994, *Critical issues in tourism: A geographical perspective*, Blackwell, Oxford

van Osten, R., 1972, *World national parks: Progress and opportunities*, Hayez, Brussels

Wahab, S. and Pigram, J.J., eds, 1997, *Tourism, development and growth: the challenge of sustainability*, Routledge, London

Weaver, D.B., 1998, *Ecotourism in the developed world*, CAB International, Wallingford

2 Tourism and national parks: the origin of the concept

STEPHEN W. BOYD AND RICHARD W. BUTLER

Introduction

An innovation, in almost every field, tends to set the pattern of expectations and to serve as a model for subsequent developments in that area. The establishment of the first national park system was no exception, and because tourism was present in most of the early national parks in North America from the very onset of the two systems there (USA and Canada), the expectation that tourism would be associated with national parks has continued in every subsequent system. As will be discussed below, this chapter has two foci, the ideals and settings relating to the establishment of national parks, and the role that tourism played, and was expected to play, in those first parks. Together these two foci throw considerable light on the current problems and issues discussed in the two principal parts of this book.

National park systems, like many other phenomena, have grown incrementally, often in an *ad hoc* fashion. This applies both to individual systems, and to the set of national park systems throughout the world. There has been little pattern to the spatial spread of national parks systems throughout the world, although it would be naive to ignore the fact that Canada borders the USA and was obviously influenced by developments there. The adjacent states of New Zealand and Australia, as other British colonies at the end of the nineteenth century, also learned some lessons from North America. Beyond that, however, the pattern of development is somewhat haphazard. The nature of the systems however, the type of lands put aside for parks, the principles on which they have been established and the functions which they are expected to fulfil, are very similar the world over and very close in many respects, and most cases, to the first model, that of the USA.

This chapter proceeds by examining first the establishment of the US and then the Canadian national park systems. The discussion follows to a limited degree the general model discussed in the previous chapter, that is, the historical context in which the systems were founded, the settings for the parks and tourism, the issues and responses which this establishment produced, and the anticipated future directions, which themselves become the remaining chapters of the book. We argue strongly that it is impossible to understand, and hope to be able to resolve, many of the current issues facing national parks in the context of tourism without understanding the origins of the parks and their links with tourism. The incremental and *ad hoc* growth referred to above, has meant that most systems have added functions, particularly in the areas of tourism and leisure, and because tourism is such a dynamic feature, have had inevitably to deal with problems quickly and in an adaptive manner. Equally inevitably, this has often resulted in *ad hoc* solutions to long term issues.

National park establishment in North America

Historical context

Parks have a long, if indistinct, history, dating back several thousand years (Shephard, 1967). The images of the great hunting parks of the past found expression in art from the seventeenth century onwards, and associated activities such as hunting were a frequent element in many pictures. The landscaping of large estates in England, in particular in the eighteenth century, captured this image, with large trees, a mixture of woodlands and pasture, wild and domesticated animals, and often stylised castles and elaborate buildings, with hills or mountains as a backdrop. This ideal image of ancient privilege, nobility and land management found fertile ground in both the Old and New Worlds. Several authors have commented on the development in America of national images of nature, wilderness and man's activities in such settings (see, for example, Nash, 1967; Shephard, 1967; Huth, 1972). In the American psyche of the time, there was a great desire for cultural equality or superiority with the Old World, but acknowledgement that in the early and mid-nineteenth century this was not easily possible in terms of antiquities or the urban environment. However, the natural environment, particularly as it was being captured by North American artists and writers such as George Catlin and James Fennimore Cooper, provided an alternative. Despite some major variations in their works, many of their contemporaries evoked images building on the 'park' themes noted above.

At the same time, the impact of development and the 'opening up' of North America was being appreciated in terms of such phenomena as urbanisation, deforestation, overuse of land and drainage of rivers and marshes. Writers such as Thoreau and George Perkins Marsh drew the attention of influential politicians and others to the loss of the natural environment in many of the settled parts of eastern North America. In particular, Marsh's *Man and nature: or, physical geography as modified by human action* (1864) can be regarded as an early call for a rethinking of the then-current approach to the environment, and a need for the introduction of the concept of conservation, although that term was not then in use. His and Thoreau's writings were reflecting themes elucidated some decades earlier by others such as Catlin.

Catlin, in the 1830s, had argued the case for the protection of much of the Great Plains, then being crossed and subdivided at a great rate. In 1841, while writing on the North American Indians on the Great Plains, he may well have been the first to call for a national park:

in his classic attire, galloping his wild horse ... amid the fleeing herds of elk and buffaloes. What a beautiful and thrilling specimen for America to preserve and hold up to the views of her refined citizens and the world, in future ages. *A nation's Park* [author's emphasis] containing man and beast, in all the wild and freshness of their nature's beauty (Catlin, 1841, pp. 261–262).

The imagery in that quotation sums up much of the commentary made above: 'refined citizens and the world', 'nature's beauty', 'preserve ... in future ages' and 'wild and freshness'.

By the middle of the nineteenth century, therefore, one can identify concerns over the impact of settlement and expansion on the natural landscape and its inhabitants (human and non-human), a growing interest in landscape design and preservation, the realisation of the need for open 'natural' areas for people to use for relaxation, and the emergence of more modern science, related especially to Darwin and others' ideas on evolution. The efforts of people such as Olmstead, the great park designer, were influential in the establishment of the forerunner of the national parks, Yosemite Park in 1864 (Huth, 1972). Yosemite had been explored during the early period of the great geological expeditions into the American west, and its impressive features captured in paint by Ayers in the 1850s. Ewers (1965) notes the images of Ayers' work: the geology, dramatised as the overall setting, the flat valley floor of grassland, reminiscent of the English landscaped scene, and the presence of animals and men around the campfire. Yosemite was seen as a suitable opportunity to preserve both the image of awesome nature, and a landscape suitable for human relaxation.

Similar influences were found in the case of the first national park, Yellowstone, established in 1872. Coulter had returned to the area after the Lewis–Clarke expedition to the Northwest in 1805–6 and discovered Yellowstone, although it was not until 1870, when the Washburn–Langford–Doane party explored the region that its true grandeur was revealed. The combination of the images of Moran, who painted Yellowstone during the Hayden expedition in 1871, and the earlier work of the Washburn–Langford–Doane expedition, did much to influence Congress to establish the park. The Yellowstone Act of 1 March 1872, withdrew more than 1 million acres of land from settlement, occupancy and sale, for the dedication and setting apart 'as a public park or pleasuring-ground for the benefit and enjoyment of the people'. The language used is echoed in the introduction to the legislation establishing Banff National Park a few years later, as noted below.

Shephard (1967) argues strongly that the English landscape idea was of great significance in the establishment of both Yosemite and Yellowstone, writing at length on the North American fascination with old European images and the desire to match these images with creations of their own. He comments that the Washburn–Langford–Doane expedition members saw Yellowstone:

> with all the momentum of American tourists unleashed in Rome or in the Rhineland. While Hudson Valley aristocrats were copying old Gothic or wishing that they could import Scottish castles intact, Langford, Hedges, and Doane were discovering an unchartered [sic] heritage of castles, fortresses, and ramparts already in the American landscape. Minarets, water towers, turrets, line the canyon the Yellowstone ... [the geysers were perceived as fountains and the terraced hot springs as] exactly the kind of adjunct that one might expect in a Villa garden (Shephard, 1967, pp. 248–249).

(Shephard's comment on importing Scottish castles finds an echo some three decades later in the building of the Banff Springs Hotel in Canada's first national park, modelled after early nineteenth-century Scottish baronial-style castles.)

There were clearly a number of other factors involved in the establishment of these early parks, and two of the major influences were directly related to tourism (and recreation). One was the growing need for space to be put aside for relaxation. This activity could take many forms, from simple passive enjoyment of scenery, to hunting and fishing, mountaineering (becoming popular in the European Alps), amateur scientific endeavours, painting and writing, or simply travel, often by train, to see the splendours of nature. While it was clear that numbers of visitors were never envisaged to reach current levels of several million to some individual parks, there was perceived a growing need for the provision of such space, and not just for the elite who were the early visitors to these parks. Olmstead in particular, was a strong proponent of the need to either bring people to the outdoors, or, as he did in Central Park in New York, to bring the outdoors to all people.

The second influence, and a major factor in the establishment of national parks in Canada (as discussed below) was the perceived economic benefits which could accrue from the development of tourism to these newly established parks. As railroads were pushed further and further west, not only were areas becoming accessible to travellers other than those on expeditions, but the railroads needed income to finance their endeavours. The early market for these parks were affluent Americans and Europeans who had not only time but money available for exotic travel into the new wilderness to engage in a variety of activities, not all of which would be acceptable in national parks today, particularly the big-game hunting.

In the Canadian context, attitudes were some decades behind the USA (Nash, 1967), although in the final scheme of things only a little over a decade separates the establishment of the two systems. In Canada, much less impact had been experienced by the environment through human activities, although the evidence from south of the border was obvious to those who travelled there. Canada was much more of a frontier than the USA, but the push west by the railroads was almost contemporary. Political factors were important here, as it was clearly felt and expressed that a railroad from the east coast to the west would be a strong unifying force for the emerging country. The then Canadian prime minister strongly encouraged the Canadian Pacific Railroad to push to the west and the government of British Columbia provided land and routes through the Rockies for the railroad in perpetuity. These lands were to prove key in the establishment of subsequent parks, since under the Canadian constitution, national parks can only be established on Crown (Federal) land. If such land is within any of the established provinces, it has to be deeded free of all rights and encumbrances to the federal government.

The impetus for the establishment of the first Canadian park in Banff came by accident, with the discovery of hot springs by engineers working for the Canadian Pacific Railroad. Their attempts to commercialise the hot springs caused concern in the nation's capital and resulted in the establishment of a federal reserve of 10 square miles around the hot springs in 1885. From this nucleus emerged Banff National Park. Although there is great similarity in the phrasing of the legislation to establish the first reserve at Banff with that used to establish Yellowstone, Lothian (1977) argues that in the case of the Reserve at Banff, the initial wording was based on regulations governing Arkansas Hot Springs, a public spa reserved by Congress considerably earlier, in 1832. It is clear from the wording of the various pieces of legislation which followed that, while preservation of the hot springs area was the initial stimulus for the establishment of the reserve and subsequent park, economic gain from tourism and the provision of recreation opportunity for Canadians were of equal importance. As Nelson (1973) has commented, the three threads of preservation, economics and recreation were strongly and obviously linked in the establishment and early expansion of the Canadian system.

Ironically the reason given for the establishment of the reserve around the hot springs was public sanitation, as Nicol notes when quoting the original dedication:

> whereas, near the station of Banff ... there have been discovered several hot mineral springs which promise to be of great sanitary advantage to the public, and in order that proper control of the lands surrounding these springs may remain vested in the Crown, the said lands...are hereby reserved from sale or settlement or squatting. (Nicol, 1970, pp. 21–22)

The actual establishment of a national park came two years later with the expansion of the area to 260 square miles and the passing of legislation creating the Rocky Mountains National Park, the preamble noting that the area was reserved 'as a public park and pleasure ground for the benefit, advantage and enjoyment of the people of Canada'. The Rocky Mountains Park Act (1887) continued the emphasis on recreation and enjoyment by stating that there would 'not be issued any leases, licences or permits' that would 'impair the usefulness of the park for the purposes of public enjoyment and recreation' (Chapter 32). There can be few clearer statements of the importance of the place of recreation (tourism) in a new park.

Early park settings (1872–1933)

The creation of Yellowstone, the world's first national park, provided the precedent for other national parks. As noted by Zinser (1995), it was important for a number of reasons. First, it established the political feasibility of setting aside large areas to be protected and enjoyed as part of national heritage. Second, it demonstrated that private exploitation of natural resources was not necessarily the best public policy. Third, it set down the principle that responsibility for the park was to be national (federal government) and not regional (state government), and fourth, it paved the way for the development of early systems of parks in the USA, Canada, Australia, New Zealand and the creation of parks further afield.

Following the establishment of Yellowstone, the early history of US national park development took on a particular geographical focus. All eight parks that were established by 1915 were located within western states, including Sequoia and Yosemite (1890) in California, Mount Rainer (1899) in Washington, and Rocky Mountain (1915) in Colorado. Park development maintained this geographical focus until 1933, witnessing the establishment of parks in the west such as Grand Canyon (Arizona, 1919), Zion (Utah, 1919), and Grand Teton (Wyoming, 1929). However there was limited development in the east, including Lafayette (Maine, 1919), Great Smoky Mountains (North Carolina/ Tennessee, 1926), Shenandoah (Virginia, 1926)

Figure 2.1. US national parks: geographic distribution

and Mammoth Cave (Kentucky, 1926). By the close of the period, the USA had a 'system' of 18 national parks (see Figure 2.1). A similar pattern of establishment took place in Canada, which by 1930, had fourteen national parks. Again the majority were located in the west including Glacier and Yoho in the Province of British Columbia, both being established one year after Banff. These were followed by Waterton Lakes (1895), Elk Island (1906) and Jasper (1907) in Alberta, and Mount Revelstoke (1914) and Kootenay (1920) in British Columbia. Only three of the early Canadian parks were established in the east, all within the Province of

Ontario: St Lawrence Islands, established in 1904 from crown (federal) land that had been initially under Indian ownership, Point Pelee converted from a naval reserve in 1918, and Georgian Bay Islands established in 1929 (Nelson, 1982) (see Figure 2.2).

Examination of the early parks in the USA and Canada reveals a number of similarities. First, a similar location bias existed in park establishment, displaying an early spatial disparity between supply (parks) and demand (population). Reports of the early parks noted that the majority of visitors came from the built-up areas along the eastern American seaboard, the metropolitan centres in eastern Canada, and as far afield as Europe and Australasia. Second, as a result of this, visitor numbers to the early parks remained small. For instance, only 120 000 recreation visits were recorded in the American parks by 1904 (Zinser, 1995). Reasons for this were the distance travelled and time spent by early visitors to reach parks, the limited tourism infrastructure that had been built in parks by this time, and the extent to which parks were generally accessible. Marsh (1982) notes these factors in his discussion of the early recreation development of Glacier National Park in Canada, commenting on

Figure 2.2. Canadian national parks: geographic distribution

the primary role the railway (Canadian Pacific Railroad, CPR) played in both developing a hotel within the park, and providing access for the early tourists. Over the remainder of this time period, visits to national parks in the USA continued to grow in an incremental fashion. A million visits were recorded by 1920, reaching 3.3 million by 1930 (Zinser, 1995). The rise in numbers in the latter part of the period was accounted for by the growth in car ownership, and developments in road infrastructure to and within the early parks. In Canada, Nelson (1982) notes that from 1910 onwards, the automobile was influential in visitors travelling from Calgary and further afield in North America, to Banff and other western parks.

Third, attractions were focused on nature and the spectacles it offered, ranging from the spouting geysers of Yellowstone, the towering granite towers of Yosemite, to the alpine environments of the western Canadian parks. Banff, to an extent, was an early exception. Developed as a spa in the European tradition, it offered the early tourists hot baths, albeit against a spectacular natural backdrop. The emphasis in promoting the park was on the hot springs, the grand hotel and the therapeutic 'powers' and attraction the waters were believed to hold. While many of the early parks were established on 'worthless' land, in the sense that they could not be developed for other human uses, these early visitors did not view them as being worthless. Apart from the opportunity to enjoy the majesty of nature, visits to the early parks had deeper and higher meanings attached to them. In the writings of early visitors to Glacier national park in Canada, for example, the mountains take on a spiritual dimension, where the 'peaks were inspiring, dangerous, close to God and a reminder of His power and achievements' (as quoted in Nelson 1982, p. 44).

Fourth, both park 'systems' benefited from early legislation to assist in national park creation and early park management. In the USA, following the Yellowstone Act of 1872, the Antiquities Act of 1906 (8 June) gave presidential blanket authority to proclaim and reserve historic landmarks, historic and prehistoric structures and other objects of historic or scientific interest. Mesa Verde National Park in Colorado was one of the earliest parks to be set aside under the Act (29 June 1906), and the powers under the Act were responsible for the establishment of almost a quarter of the national park system that exists in the USA today. A second piece of American legislation, the National Park Service Act of 1916, set in place the mandate of:

> conserving the scenery and the natural and historic objects and the wildlife therein and to provide for the enjoyment of the same in such manner ... as will leave them unimpaired for the enjoyment of future generations (as quoted from Zinser, 1995, p. 72).

The wording of the Act confirmed the dual mandate of parks, namely the conservation of park resources as well as providing for the enjoyment of the public. In so doing, it established the basis of conflict within parks between protection and use, a conflict that continues to exist today. The Act also brought into being the National Park Service (NPS), which assumed overall responsibility for the park units that had been developed up to this time. However, the existing units of 1916, comprising the US National Park System, were not national in the truest sense of the word. The 'system' had developed in a piecemeal fashion, with the absence of a single administration overseeing developments. No common management structure existed to ensure that parks would be protected from other resource users, no single budget existed and poor relations existed between units within the 'system'. Under the Act, the NPS took charge of the affairs of the existing park units, both national parks and national monuments, to protect park resources from utilitarian conservation interests. Earlier, the Hetch Hetchy affair (1913) had pitted the interests of preservationists against conservationists supporting a wise use of resources: the interests of the former lost out and the Hetch Hetchy Dam was constructed on the Tuolumne River within Yosemite national park. In Canada, a number of Acts had important implications for the development of the early parks. First was the Dominion Lands Act of 1883, that placed management of public lands under the auspices of the Minister of the Interior and allowed government to reserve forest lands and forest parks in a state of preservation. It was under this legislation that Waterton Lakes, Elk Island and Jasper National Parks in Alberta were established. A second piece of legislation was the Dominion Forest Reserve and Parks Act of 1911. This too, had strong preservationist tones, providing the necessary legislation to protect large areas from mining and timbering activities. As a consequence, Mount Revelstoke, Kootenay in British Columbia, Wood Buffalo bordering Alberta and the Northwest Territories, Prince Albert in Saskatchewan and Riding Mountain in Manitoba were developed (Nelson, 1973; Markle, 1975). Two other developments took place in 1930, at the close of this time period, that had long-lasting implications for future park developments. The first of these was that after 1930 the federal government no longer had control over the natural resources within the crown (federal) lands within the Canadian Prairie Provinces. By handing over control to the individual provinces, expansion of the park 'system' in the west would be halted until the 1970s. The second significant development, also occurring in 1930, was the passing of the National Parks Act. This defined the function of Canadian National Parks and read as follows:

> The Parks are hereby dedicated to the people of Canada for their benefit, education and enjoyment, subject to the provisions of the Act and Regulations, and such parks shall be maintained and made use of so as to leave them unimpaired for the enjoyment of future generations (as quoted in Lothian, 1977, p. 8).

Although the early policy makers in Canada felt they had explicitly stated the function and purpose of national parks, problems in the wording chosen and the ambiguity within the Act allowed for varying interpretations of 'unimpaired', 'enjoyment' and 'benefit' to develop. These in turn saw the emergence of a dual mandate of protection and use to develop, a problem which would only be addressed by amendments to the Act in 1989.

A fifth and final similarity between the two countries was the presence of leading park officials who had the insight to encourage the development of travel to the parks. In the USA, S.T. Mather was appointed as the first director of the NPS. From the very early days of the NPS, balancing preservation against use, he recognised the need for the development of infrastructure (roads and hotels) within the parks to encourage travel, along with programmes of park interpretation, and education for visitors. Cars were to be permitted within parks, and private concessionaires were allowed to provide a range of accommodation from camps to luxury hotels. He also set down guidelines regarding appropriate types of recreation for the parks (Ise, 1961). In Canada, under the Dominion Forest

Reserve and Parks Act (1911), the Dominion Parks Branch was established to oversee management of all national parks, and to establish a 'national parks system'. J.B. Harkin was its first commissioner, holding office from 1911 to 1936. His insight was responsible for the development of recreation and tourism within the early parks. A strong promoter of preservation and keeping parks in a true state of wilderness, he also recognised the potential that lay in encouraging recreational developments within parks as a viable means to provide the interest and funding needed to develop the Canadian national park 'system'. According to Nelson (1976), the original reserve at Banff had rapidly expanded by 1910, as entrepreneurs moved into the Rocky Mountain park to promote and 'exploit' recreation. From 1910 onwards, the early parks experienced increased tourism from a more mobile society benefiting from developments in the automobile industry. Associated developments such as further road expansion and upgrading occurred in the 1920s and 1930s, all at the expense of preservation.

As this time period drew to a close, the initial form of a national park systems had started to emerge in both countries. Early legislation assisted the advance of tourism within the parks. For example, over this time period, the Army Corps of Engineers built the road networks within US parks, and the army was used to protect visitors. The reorganisation in the US national park system of 10 August 1933 saw the development of a single national federal system of park lands, comprising historic and natural places. As a result, further development of parks systems would continue at a greater pace in the USA as compared to Canada, as the next section illustrates.

Development of park systems (1934–1972)

With respect to the establishment of a formal system of parks, the USA differed considerably from Canada. The passing of the Antiquities Act of 1906 saw the establishment of units within the system entitled 'national monuments', as opposed to units named as 'national parks', with attention directed at landmarks of historic interest, including both natural and cultural features. By the end of this time period, a range of new types of 'park' within the overall national park system would emerge, including Parkways, National Recreation Areas, National Military sites, National Battlefield Parks, National Seashores, National Historic Parks and National Memorials. Towards the end of this time period, other 'park' additions included National Lakeshores, Rivers and Trails.

Despite the proliferation of this new type of 'park' unit, the overall parks system still comprised three basic groups: parks that had natural value (national parks being included here), those that had historical value and parks that had recreational value. By 1951, 60 new units had been added to the existing system: 41 historical, 11 natural and eight recreational (Zinser, 1995). The increasing number of historical units was the result of the passing of the Historic Sites Act of 1935, giving emphasis to historic preservation. A number of new national parks, were added within the natural category including, Everglades, Florida in 1934, Big Bend, Texas in 1935, Olympic, Washington in 1938, and Kings Canyon, California in 1940. The period from 1951 to 1972 saw increased pressure being placed on parks to accommodate a growing interest in recreational and tourism use. From 6 million users of parks in 1942, growth in the early post-war years was phenomenal. By 1950, visitor numbers had risen to 33 million, only to more than double to 72 million by 1960. The NPS was quick to respond to this surge of interest to use parks for recreation and tourism. Conrad Wirth, who had held the position of director of the NPS since 1951, launched the Mission 66 programme in 1956. This was a ten-year programme to upgrade park facilities to help meet this new demand, and to have a system that was suitable to celebrate 50 years since the creation of the NPS in 1916. Between 1951 and 1972, an additional 100 units were added to the existing National Parks System: 56 were historical units, 32 recreational units (half of which were reservoir-related or formed seashore and parkway units), and 12 were natural. Of the 12 natural units added, seven were national parks, including Haleakala, Hawaii in 1960 and Redwoods, California in 1968 (Zinser, 1995). An important legislative development that had bearing on the development of the National Parks System was the passing of the Wilderness Act of 1964, which established national wilderness preserves as areas absent of human occupancy. Nelson (1982) viewed this development, and additions to the existing National Parks System, as a response to accommodating increased demand of use of back-country areas for passive recreational use, providing the mechanism by which the system could expand.

In contrast to the USA, a stop–go policy was present as the Canadian national park system expanded over the 1934–72 time period. With the constitution denying the federal government control over public land in the Prairie Provinces, the opportunity for expansion was severely curtailed. By the outbreak of World War II, only two new parks had been created, Cape Breton Highlands, Nova Scotia in 1936 and Prince Edward Island (PEI) in 1937. The post-war decades heralded new opportunities for expansion. The 1950s through to the early 1970s were a time that brought increasing economic prosperity to a larger segment of the population than had previously been the case. An expanding population (a consequence of the baby boom) increased urban growth, and a buoyant economy (fuelled by automation and service-related occupations, better working conditions, more paid vacations, improved transportation, better road networks and more disposable incomes), all resulted in parks, once the domain of the elite elements of society, becoming destinations areas where summer vacations could be spent and where camping and picnicking activities could be enjoyed by the general public on a more frequent basis. Evidence of this is cited by Nelson (1976) who states that during this period the western parks came to be visited by more easterners and Americans who had travelled west and north, respectively.

The Canadian national park system was slow to meet this new demand. By the early 1960s, only two more parks had been established, Fundy National Park, New Brunswick in 1948 and Terra Nova National Park, Newfoundland in 1957. Under Jean Chrétian (then Minister of Indian Affairs and Northern Development), a new phase of Canadian national park expansion occurred between 1969 and 1972 with ten new parks being created. These were Kejimkujik (Nova Scotia), Kouchibouguac (Quebec) in 1969; Pacific Rim (British Columbia), Gros Morne (Newfoundland), Forillon and La Maurice (Quebec) in 1970; Pukaskwa (Ontario) in 1971; Kluane (Yukon) and, Nahanni and Baffin Island (Northwest Territories) in 1972. The intention behind the development of some parks, particularly in Maritime Canada, was to act as regional economic growth poles. Parks developed in the north of the country (partly a political gesture of sovereignty) saw the start of inclusive areas where native peoples were present. This brought new challenges as to how these parks were to be managed in line with park philosophy. At the same time, numbers of visitors increased threefold from 5 million to 15 million between 1960 and 1972, with the majority of this increase within the existing western parks. There was a clear need to develop institutional arrangements to safeguard the parks from this increased level of use.

As with other developments, the USA led the way and Canada followed. Under the Mission 66 programme, aspects of capacity and recreational use within national parks were reviewed in the light of concerns that if the trends of the 1950s continued (increased mechanisation of recreation and increased growth in attendance, at an annual rate of 15–25 per cent), many recreational facilities would be destroyed by overuse (Clawson, 1959; the Outdoor Recreation Resources Review Commission, 1962). The latter multi-volume report underscored the growing concern for conservation of the natural resource base. One specific outcome from the Outdoor Recreation Resources Review Commission (ORRRC) was the establishment of a zoning system to allocate land to different classes of use according to the nature and intensity of demand and the land character (Nelson, 1982). Canada responded in the 1960s by proposing an early form of zoning for winter activities in Banff. However, it would not be until the early 1970s that a more comprehensive zoning scheme was developed within Canadian parks that allocated land-use priorities to different areas of a park (Murphy, 1985). It nevertheless provided a broad framework for land management, attempting to balance the system's twin mandates of preservation and visitor enjoyment by setting aside some areas for primarily preservation purposes and others for recreation and visitor facilities.

Other institutional arrangements introduced in the 1960s included the introduction of public hearings in the form of public participation in master planning for national parks. In Canada, public pressure against plans to develop Lake Louise (in Banff) saw the rejection of a proposed village service centre concept. Within the US parks system, separate management concepts and principles were developed for units classed as natural, historical and recreational, with the first policy being produced for each in 1968. In Canada, the first official policy was produced in 1964, in which the concept of systems planning was first introduced (Eidsvik, 1983). Prior to the issuing of the policy, each national park was managed as an individual unit; with a systems approach, each park became part of the national whole. The first National Park System Plan (Parks Canada, 1966) was based on physiographic regions of Canada. Like developments in the USA, by the late 1960s specific management plans had been developed for individual parks, and public participation (in the form of public hearings) was used as the principal mechanism to control developments within parks (Nelson, 1973). At the close of this time period, a more elaborate Canadian National Parks System Plan (Parks Canada, 1971) was introduced whereby terrestrial natural regions were identified and evaluated as potential sites for future parks management, to achieve representation of all regions (Eidsvik, 1983). While a diverse range of units had been acquired in the USA since before the 1930s, it was not until 1972 that a National Parks System Plan was officially published.

Recent developments (1973 to 1990s)

In the USA, between 1973 and the 1990s, 97 new park units were added. Emphasis was on historical units (51), with over a third of these being military and presidential sites. Twenty-nine units were natural, seventeen of these being established in Alaska as the result of Acts such as the Alaska National Interest Land Conservation Act of 1980. The remaining units were recreational, including national rivers and scenic trails. By 1990, the National Parks System in the USA comprised a total of 357 units (Zinser, 1995). With the ongoing expansion of the parks system, recreational use continued to increase from 72 million in 1960 to 190 million by 1970, 220 million by 1980, and 268 million by 1990. Recreational and tourism use is not spread evenly throughout the system, but is concentrated within a number of national parks, parkways, national seashores and national recreation areas. While only 50 units are classed as national parks, this category comprises 60 per cent of the entire acreage within the system, in part, because of the large national parks formed in Alaska since 1980.

Since 1973, the national parks system in Canada has expanded into areas in the North (Ivvavik, Ellesmere Island, Vuntut and Aulavik), western (South Moresby) and eastern peripheries (Mingan Archipelago). One exception has been the establishment of Bruce Peninsula in Ontario, within a few hours' drive of metropolitan Toronto. To date, only slightly over half of the terrestrial regions are represented, requiring more parks to be established both in the north and in various ecoregions in the west and east. The establishment of new parks in terrestrial regions not yet represented will follow a detailed systems plan produced by Parks Canada in 1980.

A comparison between the US and Canadian park policies shows a high degree of similarity in terms of criteria used for inclusion of new national parks to the system, and generally how planning and management of parks is undertaken. For example, the revised policy in the USA in 1975 reoriented park policies to be more in line with preservation, with management planning ensuring that recreational use did not threaten scenic beauty and wildlife. In Canada, the revised policy of 1979 stressed ecological integrity over use, and introduced policy on a range of issues pertaining to park environments (Parks Canada, 1979). The Environmental Assessment and Review Process (EARP) set out earlier (1973) required that Environmental Impact Assessments (EIAs) were undertaken prior to the establishment of new parks. With the increased use of national parks, institutional arrangements have needed to keep pace. The Parks Canada Master Planning Process (Parks Canada, 1985), states that the public will be involved in the early stages of park planning. While management Policies for the US system of parks have remained unchanged since 1988, a new policy for Canadian parks was produced in 1994. It emphasises ecological integrity, in keeping with amendments of the National Parks Act in 1989 reflecting this shift of thinking (Parks Canada, 1994). As such, management has shifted to focus on ecosystem-based management and protection within parks, where individual park plans must follow this new thinking. Emphasis in the current policy is on heritage and the potential within parks to offer sustainable forms of tourism. The latter aspect has important implications for an expanding park system, where ecological integrity takes priority over use (see Boyd, Chapter 11).

Conclusions

The focus of this chapter has been the role of tourism in the development of the national park concept and the way the early parks in the USA and Canada developed into complex park systems. The chronology behind the development of these park systems has been discussed, as it provides the context against which parks became viewed increasingly as places of recreation and tourism. Continuing tourism use of the parks will depend on existing institutional arrangements being updated to accommodate a growing and increasingly diverse recreation and tourism market. Since the creation of Yellowstone, the world's first park in the USA, the concept of national parks has spread to all continents, with the exception of Antarctica. The initial expansion and development of other park systems was concentrated in Australia and New Zealand, and it is to Australasia that the following chapters in this section turn.

References

Catlin, G., 1841, *Letters and notes on the manners, customs and conditions of the North American Indians*, Wiley and Putnam, New York

Clawson, M., 1959, The crisis in outdoor recreation. *American Forests*, **65**(3): 22–31

Eidsvik, H.K., 1983, Parks Canada, conservation and tourism: A review of the seventies – a preview of the eighties. In *Tourism in Canada – selected issues and options*, P.E. Murphy, ed., pp. 241–269, Western Geographical Series, 21, Department of Geography, University of Victoria, Victoria,

Ewers, J.C., 1965, *Early artists of the Old West*, Doubleday and Co., New York

Huth, H., 1972, *Nature and the American*, University of Nebraska Press, Lincoln

Ise, J., 1961, *Our national park policy: A critical history*, Johns Hopkins Press, Baltimore

Lothian, W.F., 1977, *A History of Canada's national parks*, Parks Canada, Ottawa

Markle, B.R., 1975, *A perception study of Canada's national parks system*, unpublished masters thesis, University of Western Ontario, London, Canada.

Marsh, G.P., 1864, *Man and nature; or, physical geography as modified by human action*, Scribner, New York

Marsh, J.S., 1982, The evolution of recreation in Glacier national park, British Columbia, 1880 to present. In *Recreational land use: Perceptions on its evolution in Canada*, G. Wall and J.S. Marsh, eds, pp. 62–76, Carleton University Press, Ottawa

Murphy, P.E., 1985, *Tourism: A community approach*, Methuen, New York

Nash, R., 1967, *Wilderness and the American mind*, Yale University Press, New Haven

Nelson, J.G., 1973, Canada's national parks: past, present and future. *Canadian Geographical Journal*, **86**: 69–89

Nelson, J.G., 1976, *Man's impact on the western Canadian landscape*, McClelland and Stewart Limited, Carleton University

Nelson, J.G., 1982, Canada's national parks, past, present and future. In *Recreational land use: Perspectives on its evolution in Canada*, G. Wall and J.S. Marsh, eds, pp. 41–61, Carleton University Press, Ottawa

Nicol, J.I., 1970, The national parks movement in Canada. In *Canadian Parks in Perspective*, J.G. Nelson, ed., pp. 19–34, Harvest House, Montreal

Outdoor Recreation Resources Review Commission (ORRRC), 1962, *Outdoor recreation for America: A report to the President*, Washington, DC

Parks Canada, 1966, *Long term objectives and major planning assumptions*, Department of Indian and Northern Affairs, National and Historic Parks Branch, Ottawa

Parks Canada, 1971, *National park system manual*, Department of Indian and Northern Affairs, Ottawa

Parks Canada, 1979, *Parks Canada policy*, Ministry of Supply and Services Canada, Ottawa
Parks Canada, 1985, *National parks managing planning process manual*, Department of the Environment, Ottawa
Parks Canada, 1994, *Parks Canada – guiding principles and operational policies*, Ministry of Supply and Services Canada, Ottawa
Shephard, P., 1967, *Man in the landscape*, Ballantine, New York
Zinser, C.I., 1995, *Outdoor recreation: United States national parks, forests and public lands*, John Wiley, New York

3 Tourism and the establishment of national parks in Australia

C. MICHAEL HALL

Introduction

National parks are a vital element of Australia's international tourism promotion. The official promotions of the Australian Tourist Commission and the various state and territory tourism commissions frequently use images of national parks. For example, the Australian Tourist Commission regularly uses such natural icons as the Great Barrier Reef, Uluru (Ayers Rock), Kakadu National Park and rainforest images in its international promotions. Similarly, Tasmania promotes its World Heritage wilderness areas, Western Australia promotes Shark Bay and Victoria promotes its coastal and forest parks. The relationship between tourism and national parks is therefore well established in Australia. However, this relationship has changed over time and led to tensions between tourism and national park management which are particular to the Australian context.

This chapter aims to provide an overview of the development of the tourism and national park relationship in Australia and is divided into several sections which highlight the shift from a colony or state focus on national parks to a national and, more recently, international dimension. However, prior to outlining the development of the park concept it is necessary to note the legal and political context within which national parks are situated in Australia.

National parks, the Australian federation and the Australian constitution

As in other federal systems, such as Canada and the USA, there is a deliniation of powers between the Australian national government and the state governments. However, unlike Canada and the USA (see Nelson, Chapter 18), the Commonwealth of Australia was established at a time when most of the continent was already under the control of sovereign colonies, meaning that there was relatively little land available to come under federal control. Indeed, the colonies which became the states of the Commonwealth of Australia were most adamant that land was to remain under state control. Therefore, under the Australian Commonwealth Constitution Act the Commonwealth government has no direct legislative powers relating to the environment and land management. In 1900, when the Constitution was passed, environmental protection was not a legislative issue. However, some of the power that the Commonwealth does possess may be used for environmental reasons. The Commonwealth has exclusive jurisdiction in respect of the Australian Capital Territory, Australian External Territories and land owned by the Commonwealth in the states. In the Northern Territory the Commonwealth has retained ultimate authority, under the terms of the Northern Territory (Self-government) Act (1978) and regulations, through the requirement of the assent of the Governor-General before bills can become law.

Under the Constitution, the states can legislate on all matters not specifically reserved to the Commonwealth. Hence, the states have powers over such areas of environmental interest as forestry and agriculture. The major area of conflict arises from Section 109 of the Constitution, which states that when powers coincide the Commonwealth legislation shall prevail. In the early years of the Commonwealth this did not cause much concern in the states. However, as Australia has grown and technological advances have changed the face of the nation, the Commonwealth has steadily accrued more power. Nevertheless, the Constitution guarantees the existence of the states and defines the separation of Commonwealth and state powers. Therefore, the scope of powers becomes the crucial issue in any assessment of the ability of the Commonwealth to establish and protect national parks (Davis 1989a, b).

Given Australia's colonial history and its Constitution very few national parks are actually the responsibility of the national government. The majority of declared national parks are established and administered by state governments. However, since the growth of the Australian conservation movement in the late 1960s, serious tensions have emerged over the relative rights and jurisdictions of the state and federal government to conserve the environment. These tensions primarily focus on the extent to which the development of international and national concern for the environment and the creation and management of national parks should become the responsibility of the national government as opposed to the state governments. For example, Section 51 of the Constitution defines a number of Commonwealth powers that may be used to promote environmental protection: these include powers relating to trade and commerce (subsection i), taxation (iii), external affairs (xxix), corporations (xx), and 'people of any race' (xxvi). In addition, the unwritten 'nationhood' or 'implied' power may be important. As the Constitution, 'by creating the Commonwealth as a nation, must necessarily imply a grant of power to the Commonwealth to do such things and enact such legislation as is necessary for the Commonwealth to exercise its functions as a national government' (Bates, 1987, p. 38). For instance, the Commonwealth National Parks and Wildlife Act, 1975, states as one of its objects the establishment and management of national parks and reserves with regard to its 'status as a national government'.

As well as having power under these headings, the Commonwealth is entitled to act for environmental reasons alone. This is because Section 51(xxxix) of the Constitution states that the Commonwealth is empowered to take action in respect of 'matters incidental to the execution of any power vested by this constitution in the [Commonwealth] parliament'. Hence, with regarding to sandmining on Fraser Island in the 1970s, the High Court upheld the decision of the Commonwealth government to refuse export of mineral sands under the trades and commerce power, even though the decision was made on environmental and social grounds. However, the main avenue of the Commonwealth to implement international heritage agreements is the external affairs power which provides for the Commonwealth government to enact domestic legislation if the subject matter is of international concern, or if it appropriately implements the purposes of an international agreement or convention, such as the World Heritage Convention. Nevertheless, the use of Commonwealth power with respect to national parks and the environment is relatively recent, although as the following discussion will indicate, there has been a gradual shift of interest in Australia's national parks from a local to a national and international level.

The creation of Australia's first national parks

The evolution of wilderness preservation in Australia has distinct parallels with North America and New Zealand and has been particularly influenced by developments in the USA. The European settlers' encounter with the antipodean environment contained Romantic elements akin to those which operated in Canada and the USA, while the publication of Marsh's *Man and nature* and the rise of the progressive conservation movement in the USA had a major influence on Australian conservation attitudes (Powell, 1976; Hall, 1992). The themes that national parks were worthless lands and the importance of tourism, so central to the development of national parks in North America and New Zealand, are also repeated in the Australian context.

The European inhabitants of Australia were faced with a bizarre new world which was, as a contemporary commentator described, replete with 'antipodean perversities' (Finney, 1984).

> ... rare conservatory plants were commonplace; the appearance of light-green meadows lured settlers into swamps where their sheep contracted rot, trees retained their leaves and shed their bark instead, the more frequent the trees, the more sterile the soil, the birds did not sing, the swans were black, the eagles white, the bees were stingless, some mammals had pockets, others laid eggs, it was warmest on the hills and coolest in the valleys, even the blackberries [wild raspberries] were red, and to crown it all the greatest rogue may be converted into the most useful citizen: such is *Terra Australia* (J. Martin 1838, in Powell, 1976, pp. 13–14).

Similarly, the French explorer Baudin was aghast at the primitive nature of the western coast of New Holland. 'In the midst of these numerous islands there is not anything else to delight the mind ... the aspect is altogether the most whimsical and savage ... truly frightful' (in Marshall, 1968, p. 9).

Despite the adverse initial reaction to the Australian landscape, attitudes were not always unfavourable. Instead, a generally ambivalent perception of the Australian environment emerged. One of the main differences between the beginning of European settlement in Australia and in North America was the period during which initial settlement took place. The 'howling wilderness' of the New England coast and the eastern seaboard of North America was settled before the emergence of a favourable aesthetic reaction to wild places in European intellectual thought. In contrast, the first wave of European settlement in Australia occurred during a period in which favourable attitudes towards nature were developing. Therefore, by the middle of the nineteenth century a number of poets and artists were beginning to portray Australian nature in a more positive light, a situation which was to provide a favourable climate for the conservation of the landscape.

The first national parks

The first reserve in Australia which may claim some association with the national park concept was the reservation of an area of 5000 acres (2025 hectares) in the Fish River (Jenolan) Caves district in the Blue Mountains in October 1866. The caves, which had previously been a refuge for Aboriginals and bushrangers (Havard, 1934), were covered by legislation which was intended to protect 'a source of delight and instruction to succeeding generations and excite the admiration of tourists from all parts of the world' (Powell, 1976, p. 114). The protection of natural monuments with tourism potential parallels the first reservations at the Arkansas Hot Springs, Yosemite and Yellowstone. In 1870 the head of Jamieson Creek in the Blue Mountains was also reserved, while the Bungonia Lookdown was reserved in 1872. Both areas were 'beauty spots' which provided views of spectacular gorges (Prineas and Gold, 1983).

In 1879, seven years after the creation of Yellowstone, 18 000 acres (7284 hectares) of land were set aside as a national park at Port Hacking, south of Sydney. This area was increased to 14 000 hectares the following year (Black and Breckwoldt, 1977, p. 191). An exhibit organised by the Royal Society of New South Wales in 1878 contained a description of Yellowstone but it is unlikely that Yellowstone National Park provided more than an idea for a name for the new park (Slade, 1985–6). Instead, the creation of the National Park (later Royal National Park) was inspired more by a desire to ensure the health of Sydney's working population than to provide a wilderness experience. According to a member of the New South Wales Legislative Assembly, John Lucas, the park was created 'to ensure a healthy and consequently vigorous and intelligent community ... all cities, towns and villages should possess places of public recreation', while Sir Henry Parkes commented, 'The Honourable Member says it is a wilderness and that years must elapse before it can be of any use, but is it to remain a wilderness? ... certainly it ought not to remain a wilderness with no effort whatever to improve it' (1881, in Mosley, 1978, p. 27). The most likely model for the park was the large 'common' parks of urban Britain, and represented an antipodean version of the then popular views of the negative effects of the city on health and morality. The National Park was to be, 'a sanctuary for the pale-faced Sydneyites – fleeing the pollution – physical, mental and social, of the densely packed city', not an escape to wild, untamed nature (in Pettigrew and Lyons, 1979, pp. 15, 18).

The creation of the park was primarily due to the efforts of the New South Wales Zoological Society (whose aims resembled those of acclimatisation groups) and Sir John Robertson, an influential politician, former Premier, and senior member of the government. According to Pettigrew and Lyons (1979, p. 17), the area reserved, only 22 kilometres from the city centre, was available as 'a consequence of the poor quality of much of it and of the Georges River between it and the expanding Sydney'. Nevertheless, as Australian authors have proudly pointed out, New South Wales was the first colony or country to actually include the term 'national park' in legislation (Mosely, 1978).

The reasons for establishment of Australia's first national park resemble those operating in North America. First, there was no cost to the government in the reservation of land as it was already held by the Crown. Second, the land was regarded as worthless with no value for agriculture, although timber cutting and grazing were allowed to continue in the park until well into the twentieth century. Third, a railroad line enabled Sydney's inhabitants to travel to the park. However, in contrast to the American situation, the park was established to provide for mass recreation rather than the elite commercial recreation that characterised the early days of Yellowstone, although hotels were built in the park soon after it was established. In addition, the landscape value of the national park was related to the coast and rivers rather than mountain scenery or spas as in the USA, Canada and New Zealand. As in America, the area was 'improved' with suitable types of development such as military parade grounds, picnic areas, bandstands, and zoological displays. Despite these 'improvements', the park has become one of the major components of the national park system of New South Wales and has been developed to permit hiking and the protection of fauna and flora.

Factors influencing the development of the first park in New South Wales were replicated in the other colonies. For example, in 1891 the government of South Australia passed the National Park Act, which set aside the Old Government Farm at Belair, an area of 796 hectares as a reserve. The Act was designed to 'establish a national recreation and pleasure ground as a place for the amusements, recreation and convenience of the Province of South Australia'. Despite attempts by politicians and the Field Naturalists Section of the Royal Society of South Australia to allow the park to be retained in its natural state, the Playford government insisted that the park be organised along the lines of Sydney's recently established national park (Black and Breckwoldt, 1977, p. 192). 'The area was developed with tennis courts, ovals, pavilions and walking trails through the bushland. Stands of ornamental trees were planted along curving drives through the park and it became a favoured picnic area for the people of the Adelaide region' (Goldstein, 1979a, p. 215). The general perception of national parks in South Australia at that time was well summed up in a far-sighted letter that appeared in the *Register* in October, 1884:

> National parks will be useful, not only as preserves for indigenous plants and animals, but also as recreation grounds for the people. It is well to consider how comparatively few and small are the areas of this description which will be permanently available for the residents of the Adelaide Plains ... there must come at a time when these plains will be thickly populated from hills to sea, and then, if not now, the need for more breathing space will be recognised. The Mt Lofty Range is gradually passing more and more into private hands, and before many years have elapsed it will be difficult to find a place where one may enjoy the beauties of nature without fear of trespassing (in Nance, 1986, p. 215).

In 1878 Robert Collins, a pastoralist from the McPherson Ranges near the Queensland–New South Wales border, was impressed by national parks while on a trip to the USA (Goldstein, 1979b, p. 133). After his election to the Queensland parliament, Collins continually stressed the direct and indirect advantages of tourism arising from the creation of national parks (Powell, 1976, p. 115), along the lines of the advocacy of national parks in the USA and Canada. The tourism dimension further indicated in the passing of legislation 'to provide for the reservation, management and protection of ... national parks' in Queensland in 1906,

> ... areas which ... as localities are likely to become popular resorts as the population grows larger – places to which those who desire to take a holiday may like to go from time to time and know that they will get pure air, good scenery and country life (Hon. J.T. Bell, Secretary for Public Lands 1906, in Goldstein, 1979b, pp. 133–134).

The Queensland State Forests and National Parks Act of 1906 was probably the first legislation in the world concerning the procedures to be followed in establishing national parks. However, as Black and Breckwoldt (1977, p. 192) recorded, 'The Minister for Public Instruction commented that in attempting to establish a national park Queensland was following the lead given by the southern states' and the USA. The first national park created under the Act was an area of 131 hectares at Witches Falls on Tambourine Mountain. The land was judged, according to Powell (1976, p. 114), as 'unfit for any other purpose', a clear restatement of the 'worthless lands' hypothesis attached to the creation of some of the early American national parks.

Further development of the park concept

The national park concept grew slowly in the period following the federation of the Australian colonies in 1901. One of the most significant developments was the growth of bushwalking clubs following the World War I. Although such clubs were established in every state, the influence of the bushwalking clubs is most associated with New South Wales and, in particular, the efforts of Myles Dunphy. The establishment of the Sydney Bush Walkers by Myles Dunphy in 1927 served as the catalyst for the creation of several other clubs, notably the Bush Tracks Club and the Coast and Mountain Walkers. In 1932 the walking clubs combined to form the New South Wales Federation of Bushwalking Clubs. Of greater importance for the preservation of wilderness was the contribution of the bushwalkers to the establishment of the National Parks and Primitive Areas Council (NPPAC) in the same year, with Myles Dunphy as secretary.

Among the objectives of the NPPAC was the advocacy of 'the protection of existing tracks, paths and trails in use, particularly those having scenic and historical interests and values' (Dunphy, 1963, pp. 7–8 in Bardwell, 1979, p. 17). The NPPAC, along with Myles Dunphy, were strongly influenced by American conservation initiatives (Strom, 1969, p. 143). For example, in 1932 Dunphy obtained a supply of booklets on American national parks which served as propaganda for the national park idea in Australia (Thompson, 1985, p. 26), and doubtless influenced the way in which the bushwalking movement and the NPPAC approached campaigns for the preservation of natural areas in Australia.

The NPPAC's Greater Blue Mountains National Park Scheme probably represented the first major attempt of an Australian conservation group to mobilise mass support for the preservation of wilderness. On 24 August 1934, the NPPAC paid for a four-page supplement, complete with maps and photographs, to be included in the *Katoomba Daily*. The supplement was highlighted by Myles Dunphy's proposal for a Blue Mountains National Park with 'primitive areas':

> The Blue Mountains of Australia are justly famous for their grand scenery of stupendous canyons and gorges, mountain parks and plateaux up to 4,400 feet altitude, uncounted thousands of ferny, forested dells and gauzy waterfalls, diversified forest and river beauty, much aloof wilderness-and towns and tourist resorts replete with every convenience for the comfort and entertainment of both Australian and overseas visitors (National Parks and Primitive Areas Council (NPPAC) 1934, p. 1).

That the supplement attempted to link the scenic attractions of the area with tourism is hardly surprising. Australia was then in the grip of a depression, and linking preservation with positive economic benefits was logical. However, it is also interesting to note that the NPPAC (1934, p. 1) argued that the sandstone country of the Blue Mountains 'is potentially desert land', thereby reinforcing the 'worthless' lands concept of wilderness. Although the bushwalking groups and the NPPAC did much to raise awareness of national parks in the general population their overall political effect in conservation terms was rather limited and localised. Instead, it would take until the 1960s for a more effective conservation movement to emerge in Australia.

The modern conservation period

The 1960s saw the birth of environmental awareness and environmental lobby groups on the world stage. The publication of books such as *Silent spring* and the images associated with the *Torrey Canyon* oil disaster in Britain did much to raise awareness of the need for environmental protection. In addition, the European vision of the Australian landscape was gradually coming to be replaced by a more sympathetic Australian sense of place which started to value the Australian environment (Seddon and Davis, 1976). While the various Australian states had declared national parks on a piecemeal basis, it was not until the late 1960s and early 1970s that national park systems with parks under a clear single administrative authority came to be developed. Perhaps more significantly it was also at this time that parks began to be delared in areas which had significant other uses. For example, the Great Barrier Reef came to be declared a marine park due to conservation group concerns over oil drilling. Similarly, conservation groups lobbied to stop mineral sands development on Fraser Island which, like the Great Barrier Reef, is also now a World Heritage Area. In both cases arguments for the conservation of nature for its intrinsic value were entwined with economic conservationist arguments that national parks should be established because of their value for tourism (Wright, 1977; Sinclair, 1978; Hall, 1992).

Further complicating national park issues in Australia was the gradual strengthening of Commonwealth government powers with respect to the environment and national parks under the reformist Whitlam Labour Government (1972–1975). The development of Commonwealth legislation provided a mechanism by which conservation groups could seek to override state government inaction or recalcitrance in conserving natural areas through national park declarations. Indeed, Australia's signing of the World Heritage Convention in this period provided the capacity for Australia's conservation debates to become international in scope in the 1980s and 1990s. However, it should be noted that the implementation of the World Heritage Convention in Australia has more often been a debate over issues of state rights rather than the creation of an effective management regime to preserve World Heritage values (Davis, 1989a; Hall, 1992).

It has long been recognised that national parks and equivalent reserves such as wilderness areas, should be 'protected and managed by the highest competent authority of the country' (Dasmann, 1973, p. 14). While the states are the 'highest competent authority' as far as most management is concerned, this is not so with respect to protection. Dasmann (1973, p. 17) distinguishes between provincial and national parks; the former are 'more subject to local influences and changes in local policy and are therefore, in many instances, less securely protected than a national park. Furthermore, international agreements between national governments will not necessarily be binding at a provincial level'. With this in mind, as the environment has become more internationalised it is not surprising that Australian conservationists have sought ways to make international heritage agreements binding for the protection of certain parks of national and international significance that contain wilderness areas. Indeed, the significant role that the Commonwealth should play in the protection of national and internationally significant parks and reserves was observed by members of the House of Representatives (1981, p. 37):

> some areas of national and international significance should be administered by the Commonwealth as truly 'National' national parks under Commonwealth legislation ... Areas so declared would be more likely to receive more appropriate resources, and to be administered and protected in the national interest, free from purely local or state pressures. We would envisage only a small number of these parks, but that as a group they would represent outstanding areas of Australia's natural heritage.

One method that has been employed to extend protection over threatened wilderness areas of national significance has been to establish their World Heritage quality and thereby gain Commonwealth protection under the World Heritage Properties Conservation Act (1983) and other Acts and regulations that may be proclaimed to enforce Australia's obligations under the World Heritage Convention and other international heritage agreements. In this context national parks therefore find themselves as focal points for conservationist concerns over the loss of significant environmental values (for example, the current proposal for the mining of uranium in the Kakadu region in the Northern Territory). In these circumstances, tourism, although recognised as potentially having negative impacts on some park values, is still regarded as one of the great economic arguments for the establishment and maintenance of national park systems. For example, in 1997–8 Victoria's national parks received 12.6 million visitors (Department of Natural Resources and Environment 1998). National Parks are therefore an essential element in domestic and international tourism strategies the full environmental implications of which are likely yet to be realised. However, for many conservationists tourism still remains the lesser of many development evils while for governments, national parks still retain the capacity to provide economic value to otherwise worthless land and to act as a mechanism for economic development in regional Australia.

References

Bardwell, S., 1979, National parks for all – a New South Wales interlude. *Parkwatch*, **118** (September): 16–20

Bates, G., 1987, *Environmental law in Australia*, 2nd edn, Butterworth, Sydney

Black, A. and Breckwoldt, R., 1977, Evolution of systems of national park policy-making in Australia in *Leisure and Recreation in Australia*, D. Mercer ed., pp. 109–9, Sorrett Publishing, Melbourne

Dasmann, R.F., 1973, Classification and use of protected natural and cultural areas. IUCN Occasional Paper No. 4, IUCN, Morges

Davis, B.W., 1989a, Federal–State tensions in Australian environmental management: the World Heritage issue. *Environmental and Planning Law Journal*, **6**(2): 66–78

Davis, B.W., 1989b, Wilderness conservation in Australia: eight governments in search of a policy. *Natural Resources Journal*, **29**: 103–13

Department of Natural Resources and Environment, 1998, *Annual Report 1997–1998*, Department of Natural Resources and Environment, Melbourne

Finney, C.M., 1984, *To sail beyond the sunset: Natural history in Australia 1699–1829*, Rigby, Adelaide

Goldstein, W., 1979a, National parks – South Australia. *Parks and Wildlife*, **2**(3–4): April, 123–9

Goldstein, W., 1979b, National parks – Queensland. *Parks and Wildlife*, **2**(3–4): April, 130–40

Hall, C.M., 1992, *Wasteland to World Heritage: Preserving Australia's wilderness*, Melbourne University Press, Carlton

Havard, W.L., 1934, The romance of Jenolan Caves. *Royal Australian Historical Society Journal and Proceedings*, **20**(1): 18–65

House of Representatives Standing Committee on Environment and Conservation, 1981, *Second report: Environmental protection: Adequacy of legislative and administrative arrangements*, AGPS, Canberra

Marshall, A.J., 1968, *The great extermination: A guide to Anglo-Australian cupidity, wickedness and waste*, Panther Books, London

Mosley, J.G., 1978, A history of the wilderness reserve idea in Australia. In *Australia's wilderness: Conservation progress and plans, Proceedings of the First National Wilderness Conference*, J.G. Mosley, ed., pp. 27–33, Australian Academy of Science, Canberra, 21–23 October 1977 Australian Conservation Foundation, Hawthorn.

Nance, C., 1986, Perceptions of the natural environment. In *A Land Transformed: Environmental Change in South Australia*, C. Nance and D.L. Speight, eds, pp. 200–25, Longman Cheshire, Melbourne

National Parks and Primitive Areas Council, 1934, Blue Mountains National Park, Special Supplement. *Katoomba Daily*, 24 August

Pettigrew, C. and Lyons, M., 1979, Royal National Park – a history. *Parks and Wildlife*, **2**(3–4): 15–30

Powell, J.M., 1976, *Conservation and Resource Management in Australia 1788–1914, Guardians, improvers and profit: an introductory survey*, Oxford University Press, Melbourne

Prineas, P. and Gold, H., 1983, *Wild places: Wilderness in Eastern New South Wales*, Kalianna Press, Chatswood

Seddon, G. and Davis, M., eds, 1976, *Man and landscape in Australia, towards an ecological vision*, AGPS, Canberra

Sinclair, J., 1978, Conserving Australia's wilderness – progress reports: Queensland. In *Australia's Wilderness: Conservation Progress and Plans, Proceedings of the First National Wilderness Conference*, J.G. Mosley, ed., pp. 148–154, Australian Academy of Science, Canberra, 21–23 October 1977, Australian Conservation Foundation, Hawthorn

Slade, B., 1985–6, Royal National Park: the people in a people's park. *Geo: Australia's Geographical Magazine*, **7**(4): 64–77

Strom, A.A., 1969, New South Wales. In *The Last of Lands*, L.J.D. Webb, D. Whitelock
    and J. Le Gay Brereton, eds, pp. 142–150, The Jacaranda Press, Milton
Thompson, P., 1985, Dunphy and Muir – two mountain men. *Habitat*, **13**(2): 26–7
Wright, J., 1977, *The coral battleground*, Nelson, Melbourne

4 Tourism and the establishment of national parks in New Zealand

KAY L. BOOTH AND DAVID G. SIMMONS

Introduction

With the establishment of Tongariro National Park in 1894, New Zealand was among one of the first countries in the world to establish national parks. Decisions made about park establishment over the past century have shaped the parks systems that we have today, just as the actions of present-day managers will shape and constrain the options for protected natural areas in the future. For this reason, it is instructive to examine the factors which have influenced the parks system. In this chapter we give a particular focus to the relationship between tourism and park establishment.

The nature of parks and reserves in New Zealand has been influenced both by the park establishments within North America, and a British heritage. The geographic, social, cultural and economic characteristics of the 'new' countries were instrumental in the nature of the parks established, and, as noted by Sowman and Pearce in Chapter Fourteen, account for differences between the park systems established.

The European settlers, arriving from the 1840s in New Zealand, found large tracts of land untouched by the indigenous Maori people. Preservation of these wilderness areas offered the opportunity to showcase spectacular natural features, and so establish their own claim to a national identity (Runte, 1987). However, it was not for the intrinsic worth of these areas that early parks were set aside. From the outset, the recognition of the utility of 'beautiful scenery' in attracting tourists was instrumental in extending various forms of protection, as was the desire to protect resources for future use.

Today the national parks of New Zealand are major 'icons' in attracting tourists. The 'clean green' image of New Zealand is particularly dependent upon the continued integrity of these parks, an integrity that, some suggest, is being destroyed by the very tourists who flock to visit them.

In this chapter we will trace the development of national parks in New Zealand and outline the antecedent conditions and influences which have shaped their establishment. Throughout this brief historical account the role of tourism provides one of a number of salient themes in the evolution of a park system. Tourism has first been an important motive for protecting 'scenery', a tool for regional development to justify park establishment, and recently, as tourism has grown in both size and scope, it provides increasing challenges to the core preservation values of national park establishment and management.

The establishment of national parks in New Zealand

Maori views of the natural environment are currently an active area of research. While Maori are generally held to have maintained a closer spiritual relationship with the environment than have successive waves of largely European settlers, permanently protected areas did not exist although traditional practices incorporated significant local practical conservation mechanisms (*rohe*) (Matunga, 1995).

The advent of systematic European settlement in New Zealand in the 1840s slowly led to a change in the dominant environmental paradigm. While the establishment of the first national park has been linked to the 'Yellowstone' model (Devlin, 1976), as a British colony, New Zealand's establishment of the protected natural area system showed many similarities with other colonies (Hall and Schultis, 1991). Some aspects, however, were unique.

Following Roche (1981, 1984) this review of the establishment of national parks and protected natural areas in New Zealand is divided into four phases: an acquisition phase covering the period from the 1890s to the 1920s, a period of maintenance (1930s–1950s), and a management phase (1960s–late 1980s). To this can be added a business and negotiation phase from 1987 onwards.

The period of acquistion: 1890s–1920s

The American concept of protected areas, which saw the first national park established in the USA at Yellowstone in 1872, was quick to gain a foothold in New Zealand. In 1887, only 15 years after Yellowstone was set aside, the three central volcanoes of the North Island were gifted by local Maori, *Ngati Tuwharetoa*, to the people of New Zealand for the formation of a public park. This area was the genesis of the first national park in New Zealand, Tongariro.

This apparently philanthropic act came at a time of conflict for the local *Ngati Tuwharetoa* people. Other Maori, as well as the British settlers, were seeking ownership of these mountain lands (Harris, 1974). To Maori, these mountains are sacred – the places of their ancestors. Te Heu Heu Tukino, the paramount chief of the *Ngati Tuwharetoa*, was faced with the possibility that the mountains would be subdivided or lost to his tribe. Historical fact and background influences are difficult to establish, but it is likely that Te Heu Heu saw the opportunity to protect these sacred mountains from both other Maori and the increasingly powerful British by gifting them to the Crown. Devlin (1993, p. 87) suggests that, irrespective of the complex factors influencing Te Heu Heu's gift, it is clear that for Tongariro National Park 'the roots were cultural and spiritual ... a unique factor in the origins of New Zealand's protected natural areas.'

The value of the Tongariro reserve for tourism was evident in discussions about the enhancement of the park's value as a resort for those requiring a complete change and who are worn out with city life (AJHR, 1908, cited in Harris, 1974):

> I think this will be a great gift to the colony: I believe it will be a source of attraction to tourists from all parts of the world and that in time this will be one of the most famous parks in existence (NZPD, 1887, cited in Roche, 1987, p. 15).

The tourism rationale was linked to the economic imperative of the government. For example, Harry Ell, a well-known conservationist, utilised the same economic argument made in Canada (Nelson, Chapter 18) when he suggested that preservation of the native vegetation should take place alongside the main trunk railway line in order to attract tourist traffic and so provide the Railways Department with great profit (Harris, 1974).

However, Tongariro National Park was not the first protected natural area in New Zealand. In the early 1880s land surrounding Mount Egmont/Taranaki and Aoraki/Mount Cook[1] (New Zealand's highest mountain) was set aside in reserves. Indeed the basis of the later national park system is largely to be found in reserves created during this early period (Pearce and Richez, 1987).

The protection of key peaks at Aoraki/Mount Cook was linked to its tourism potential (Pearce, 1972; Thom, 1987). The influence of the European tradition of alpine tourism is apparent in the reservation of areas along the alps. Narrow reserves were also established along some routeways for scenery protection purposes for tourists (Roche, 1984), as were thermal areas, such as Rotorua, for resort development (again vey similar to early developments in the National Parks in the Canadian Rockies). Parliamentary debates of the day also make it clear that the loss of potential agricultural land was the key consideration (Devlin, 1993), with the implication that those areas without productive value were the only option for the fledging park system. Indeed the protection of Egmont National Park was primarily for water and soil conservation purposes – in order to protect the thriving pastoral farming industry developing around the mountain. In this instance the vested interest of tourism was, without doubt, overshadowed by the powerful agricultural lobby. The geographical distribution of the current protected natural area system along the upland areas and mountains of New Zealand, can be attributed to this dominant emphasis on land settlement. Where land had settlement potential, this was given preference over scenery protection (Roche, 1984; Hall and Schultis, 1991). Fortuitously, valuable scenic landscapes often occurred in areas unsuitable for settlement (Roche, 1984). It is not surprising, therefore, that 10 of New Zealand's 13 national parks fall across mountainous regions of the country – those areas for which agricultural production was not viable.

The legislation during this period reflects this sentiment. The first reference to tourism occurs in the early Scenery Preservation Act (1877) while the later Scenery Preservation Act 1903 established the importance of tourism in protecting areas – not only by the name of the Act but also by placing the Commission who

---

[1]   Mount Cook was renamed Aoraki/Mount Cook (and similarly the name of the national park changed) in 1998 whe the Ngai Tahu Claims Settlement Act 1998 was passed. The full title of Aoraki/Mount Cook is used in this chapter in recognition of the significance of this Act and its intent.

recommended reserves under the Tourist and Health Resorts Department (Hall and Higham, 1998), which coincidentally was the world's first national tourism office.

By 1920, a large proportion of today's protected natural area system was already protected, although later designation changes occurred. This time period largely determined the character of our present system of protected natural areas in terms of extent, location, size, and types of lands reserved (Roche, 1984, p. 9). Despite this early achievement, Roche (1984, p. 9) notes that protection was only in the cadastral sense. During this period the support for Arthur's Pass National Park was being established, primarily as a result of lobbying by a Canterbury botanist Leonard Cockayne. Gazetted in 1929, Arthur's Pass was the first real 'conservation' park in New Zealand, given its primary purpose of protecting native flora and fauna. Even here the argument of tourism potential was raised – although its realisation would yet depend upon enhanced transport infrastructure between Christchurch and the park (Harris, 1974).

In summary, this period was characterised by the steady reservation of lands for scenery preservation. Instrumental in this achievement were key individuals who directed and influenced the establishment of these early reserves. Also notable is the lack of clarity about the role of national parks, an issue which saw tourism and economic viewpoints gain a strong hearing alongside preservation. The cultural sanctity of parks was another primary determinant of the early parks system.

Period of maintenance: 1930s–1950s

Significant numbers of acquisitions continued to be made in this second period (Roche, 1981) but the primary developments related to the consolidation of legislation for establishing parks and reserves, in particular the Forest Act 1949 and the National Parks Act 1952. Both these Acts identified for the first time a legislative recreation mandate for the forest and national parks they established respectively, with the difference that national parks were primarily for preservation while forest parks were to be multi-use in nature. A further implication of this legislation was that individual Acts of Parliament were no longer needed to establish national parks. A rash of national park gazettals followed in the early 1950s with areas previously reserved under other mechanisms reclassified as national parks, especially the large Fiordland National Park (1952) and Aoraki/Mount Cook (1953).

The period following World War II was a time of affluence, with the growing participation in outdoor recreation in New Zealand instrumental in this increased interest in land reservation. Indeed Thomson notes that the formation of the new Federated Mountain Clubs (FMC) organisation in 1931 led to the beginning of nearly twenty years of persistent but unhurried pressure on the government over the welfare of national parks and reserves (Thomson, 1976, p. 8). The main ideas portrayed in the National Parks Act of 1952 were an expansion of a policy put forward by the FMC in the 1930s (Thomson, 1976). Both the Federated Mountain Clubs and the Tourist Hotel Corporation were represented on the National Park Authority created under the National Parks Act (1952) (Pearce and Richez, 1987). Devlin (1993) suggests a link between periods of affluence and the security of setting aside land for conservation. It is not then surprising that the 1950s and 1960s again saw large areas of land set aside for protection.

The effects of earlier acclimatisation policies, introducing exotic fish and game animals for recreational purposes, was becoming increasingly apparent during this time – native species such as the grayling fish disappeared. The heather introduced into Tongariro National Park, as habitat for the pheasant and grouse brought there for game hunting, has long outlived the birds and taken over the native tussock vegetation. One result of these ecological misadventures was the recognition, in the 1953 Reserves and Domains Act and the 1952 National Parks Act, of the need for the protection of native flora and fauna and the extermination of introduced species (Roche, 1984).

However, Roche suggests that the role of parks was still confused. On this point Thomson (1976, p. 3) notes

> it was a matter of conjecture whether some reserves really were, and whether others ought to be national parks; and although clear principles for the administration of the parks had evolved, they were nowhere plainly stated in legislation

From the gifting of Tongariro in 1887 the national park movement had, however, finally evolved to some resemblence of stability with a two-tiered administrative structure which brought together both government officers and members of public groups who had explicit interest in the parks. Among this latter group, tourism interests were often directly represented on individual park management boards as well as the national authority. Progress had been slow and painful on the conceptual side, with the early preservationist ideal always under some kind of threat; if not to make the parks 'game reserves' then to keep them purely for 'public health and enjoyment'. Preservation eventually triumphed in the 1952 National Park Act, but as Simmons (1980) reports this did not make the situation any easier – one challenge was merely replaced by another (p. 7). The challenge was that of mass recreational demand, and because public use had been as much a part of the park concept as was preservation itself, the approach here had to be one of compromise rather than conflict. Also at the end of this period, and at first almost unnoticed at the parks themselves, the arrival of scheduled commercial jet-powered aircraft in 1959 brought the beginnings of a much larger wave of international tourists.

Management period: 1960s–late 1980s

Through the 1960s, the 1970s and the 1980s there was little change in the size of the protected natural areas system as the economic boom years turned into the oil crisis, and unemployment and inflation escalated. This led to a reaction against protection of lands which signified 'locking up' of natural resources (Devlin, 1993).

However, during the first part of this period increasing income, urbanisation, mobility and infrastructure provision led to a back-country boom (Mason, 1976; Booth and Peebles, 1995). While physical and financial constraints had earlier ensured park preservation, social changes had brought about an increase in estimated visitation from 346 500 in 1962/63 to over 2 500 000 by 1977 (Lucas, 1977). Park managers responded to these pressures by requiring each park to have a 'master plan', which was to set out strategies for managing the 'preservation versus use' dilemma inherent in the legislation. Concepts and methods borrowed from other planning practices were applied to parks. Among these public participation, the use of a zoning concept (facilities, natural environment, wilderness), and regular ongoing review, were focused on the core idea that the carrying capacity of the park is not exceeded (National Park Authority, 1978, Section 3.2). Recreation and tourism were becoming major considerations in national park management.

By the 1980s, ecological principles became the driving force in selecting new areas for protection. The Protected Natural Areas Programme was launched in 1984 on these principles (Dingwall, 1984). It aimed to identify areas suitable for protection, particularly grasslands, wetlands and coastal sites which are less well represented within the existing parks and reserves network. This programme was soundly based on ecological survey, founded in scientific method (Kelly and Park, 1986). The assumption underlying this approach, then, was that the existing network of parks and reserves was not representative, indeed highly skewed towards mountain lands and forests.

Despite laudable objectives and a thorough approach, the Protected Natural Areas Programme has had little success in bringing the areas recommended for protection under a formal designation. Given that many areas recommended for protection are on private land, it brings into view a new set of issues for protecting areas – that of private gain (self-interest) versus public good (see Parker and Ravenscroft, Chapter 7). Ecological principles were not evident in early reservations, especially when reserve design is considered. Many of New Zealand's reserves are small and elongated (Roche, 1984) and thus are less ecological robust. This is especially challenging for the management of New Zealand's increasingly rare and threatened avifauna.

Thus, this period saw both a significant shift towards more 'ecological science' in questioning the current status of a system of protected areas – and growing concern about the management of recreational and touristic pressures. In New Zealand, at least, the latter pressures were only nascent at the commencement of the period, but had already grown to significant proportion by the end of the period. These pressures, coupled with significant socio-political changes, provide the theme for the current period.

Period of business and negotiation: 1987–present

Extending Roche's typology of periods of park evolution, we suggest that the late 1980s and the 1990s have shown a new approach to park establishment and management in New Zealand focused upon business-like approaches and negotiation for new protected areas. The radical change in the country's socio-economic and political regime since the mid-1980s and the restructuring of the state sector during the 1980s saw the emergence of a new institutional configuration of environmental agencies. The Department of Conservation was established in 1987 and thus, for the first time, a single agency was in control of the country's conservation estate (Booth, 1993). (See also discussion in Chapter Fourteen).

The 'business' of conservation in this current period is evident through the introduction of more business-like approaches to conservation management, increased competition for limited financial and human resources and increased commercialism (Dingwall, 1994). An example of these business approaches is the introduction of the Quality Conservation Management concept to the Department of Conservation, a variant of Total Quality Management. In part, this is in response to the recognition of a lack of departmental processes and procedures, made explicit by the Commission of Inquiry into the Cave Creek accident (Noble, 1995), in which 14 people fell to their death from a Department of Conservation platform on the West Coast. Other examples include the management of concessions, including the 500 or so tourism operations within parks, which has increasingly moved to a more business-like basis. Standard operating procedures are being introduced to obtain consistency within a department that has been criticised for its inconsistency across regions.

A major influence during this period has been the ongoing restructuring process which has seen the Department of Conservation (1996) undergo a series of major institutional rearrangements and several minor ones in its decade of existence. This has led to problems associated with the loss of staff and lack of morale within a staff unsure of their job security. Frequent changes in ministers and chief executives has further exacerbated the department's ability to get on with the job, a situation that now seems to have settled. The 'market-driven' economic policies of both major political parties have seen an increasing focus upon user-pays and revenue generation in parks in New Zealand. The Business Roundtable (Hartley, 1997) in the book *Conservation strategies for New Zealand* suggests privatising parts of the conservation estate. This would inevitably lead to charges for entry to national parks (Hall and Higham, 1998) a concept that is contrary to the current legislation and is almost sure to be strongly resisted by major recreation user groups.

The role of the tourism industry is increasingly pervasive in New Zealand society and national parks are no exception. Technological change also continues to reshape visitation (Espiner and Simmons, 1998). As Roche (1987) notes, early park advocates recognised the tourism potential of parks but today this imperative is poised to reorient the view of national parks in New Zealand. Parks have become commodities, something to attract and captivate but essentially to sell to the overseas tourist (Roche, 1987, p. 106). Roche goes on to suggest that if the revenue generation imperative of the restructured state agencies continues, then the transformation of national parks from reserves into commodities will be heightened. During this period of widespread rethinking of government's roles (including both conservation and tourism), Department of Conservation funding from government has been reduced by 20 per cent in real terms since 1987. Recently, in some key visitor destination areas (such as the newly opened Keppler Track in South Westland) funding for facilities on the Conservation Estate (including national parks) has come from tourism sources (both private and governmental).

Along with the establishment of the new government conservation agency, two new national parks were declared in 1987, Whanganui and Paparoa, the first for 23 years. About this time Kahurangi National Park was also reclassified from a forest park. In fact the new parks also provided an excellent opportunity for the Minister of Conservation to launch the new Department of Conservation. This 'marketing' approach to conservation illustrates new ways to put conservation forward in the struggle for parks in the 1990s. The political game of fighting for their share of taxpayers' dollars has not changed, but the rules of the game have.

The establishment of these three national parks follows a different pattern to earlier parks, one based on 'negotiation' and compromise. In this current era of park acquisition economic uses must be forgone, whereas previous parks had been located in areas of 'useless' land, land not suitable for agriculture and timber extraction (Rendall, 1995). Case studies of the origins of Paparoa National Park (Rendall, 1995) and Kahurangi National Park (Powrie, 1997) both illustrate the increasingly entrenched conflict of values between those who believe nature should be used to benefit humans and those who value nature for its own sake (Rendall, 1995). As a result, Paparoa National Park (see Sowman and Pearce, Chapter 14) took ten years of negotiation to come to fruition and Kahurangi, 15 years.

In his study of the establishment of Paparoa National Park, Rendall (1995) concludes that a process of negotiation and compromise led to 'deals' being struck in order to form some sort of consensus or agreement. One part of the deal finally agreed upon, was a 'sweetener' of a $600 000 seeding grant for the new park and the promise of increased tourism with national park status. Just as in the early period of park acquisition tourism was seen as an economic rationale, so too in current times it remains an incentive. Kahurangi National Park also underwent a 'negotiated' approach to establishment, but this was in the form of exclusions to the park. Areas that were seen to be 'not winnable' (lands suitable for mining, grazing and hydro-development) despite their suitability for national park designation were excluded (Powrie, 1997).

The cultural roots of the New Zealand national park system are again assuming a major influence. The increasing recognition and respect for the rights and traditions of Maori has implications for the national parks system and has given new responsibilities to both Maori and the Department of Conservation (Dingwall, 1994). The Ngai Tahu Claims Settlement Act (1998) effects significant change in the way parks are perceived and managed in the South Island, and has implications for the whole country. Cultural redress has seen the special significance of the formal change in name of the peak Mount Cook to *Ngai Tahu*, and the national park which takes it name, placing the Maori name first – Aoraki/Mount Cook. Indeed the area will be 'given back' to *Ngai Tahu* at a time yet to be confirmed and then immediately transferred to the nation. *Topuni* areas of Maori significance will be declared, laying another protection concept over top of the existing protection status, without altering tenure. Some specific conservation lands have been returned to Maori ownership, for example the Titi Islands (near Stewart Island), while Maori partnership in conservation management is to be incorporated elsewhere.

Conclusion

Now in the twenty-first century, it is clear that the protected areas system of New Zealand is still evolving. It is not well represented in certain ecosystems, reflecting the nature of the early demands upon land and water, and an early 'eye' for many areas of high scenic (and touristic) quality. Representative lowland areas, wetlands (now largely drained for agriculture) and coastal areas are missing. Acquisition may move to repositioning and reshuffling of the existing parks and reserves network rather than introducing new lands. The period of large-scale acquisition of 'wilderness' areas appears to be over. Examples of the most recent national parks illustrate that even the goal of broadening the system, to be more ecologically representative, may be problematic.

New kinds of parks have been proposed to cope better with the challenges of the 1990s and beyond. Although a limited number of marine reserves already exist, a marine park – a new concept for New Zealand – has been discussed for several years, in the Hauraki Gulf (the islands and waters surrounding Auckland, the largest city). These will undoubtedly hold strong interests for domestic and international tourists alike. Elsewhere, proposals to protect the colder, drier grasslands of the Torlesse Range and Remarkable Ranges (Dingwall, 1994), would broaden the ecological representativeness of the system. Areas like Bank Peninsula may be well suited to the protected landscapes concept utilised in Europe, which protects a living landscape. To achieve this, new legislation will be required. The proposed Kauri National Park is an example of a new concept – of non-contiguous reserve areas forming 'one park'.

Tourism interests were reported at the birth of the national park system in New Zealand at Tongariro, and have been a significant factor in the expansive era of scenery preservation. They then played a lesser role during the lean depression and inter-war years, but have constantly risen in importance as first domestic recreation, and international tourism, have become contemporary challenges. Today's park system may well be seen to face the penalty of success (Thom, 1987) as early preservation for tourism potential gives way to increasing international tourism. At various other times tourism-related issues have been both subsumed by, and over-ridden concerns about, the ecological representativeness and integrity of such as system. The present system of national parks is in many respects a reflection of these dual pressures, cast against a backdrop of shifting socio-economic values and priorities of a dominant and expansive European culture in a relatively unoccupied land. Any contemporary appraisal of resources, and what might pass as historical fact, must remain under constant review. Key challenges include establishing Maori–European partnerships to form new models of environmental management. Also important will be managing tourist and local visitation especially at key 'hot spots', and seeking appropriate rates of return from such use. These pressures are at the evolving edge of the national park systems in New Zealand: to that extent they do warrant separate analyses such as those provided by Sowman and Pearce, and Hall (this book).

References

Booth, K.L., 1993, Recreation on public lands in New Zealand – past, present and future. *GeoJournal*, **29**: 229–305

Booth, K.L and Peebles C., 1995, Patterns of use. In *Outdoor recreation in New Zealand*, P.J. Devlin, R.A. Corbett and C.J. Peebles, eds, pp, 31–62, New Zealand Department of Conservation and Lincoln University, Wellington, New Zealand

Department of Conservation, 1996, *Greenprint: conservation in New Zealand – a guide to the Department* (volume 2), Department of Conservation, Wellington

Devlin, P.J., 1976, *Summertime visitors to Tongariro National Park*, unpublished masters thesis, Department of Sociology, University of Canterbury

Devlin, P.J., 1993, Outdoor recreation and environment: towards an understanding of the use of the outdoors in New Zealand. In *Leisure, recreation and tourism*, H.C. Perkins and G. Cushman, eds, pp. 84–98, Longman Paul, Auckland

Dingwall, P. R., 1984, *People and parks: Essays in the development and use of protected natural areas*, Proceedings of Section A4e, 15th Pacific Science Congress. Department of Lands and Survey, Wellington, New Zealand

Dingwall, P.R., 1994, Antarctica/New Zealand. In *Protecting nature – regional reviews of protected areas*, J.A. McNeely, J. Harrison and P.R. Dingwall, eds, pp. 233–243, IUCN, Gland and Cambridge

Espiner, S. and Simmons, D.G., 1998, A national park revisited – assessing change in recreational use of Arthur's Pass National Park. *New Zealand Geographer*, **54**(1): 37–45

Hall, C.M. and Higham, J.E.S., 1998, Wilderness in New Zealand. In *Celebrating the parks: Proceedings of the Park Histories Conference*, E. Hamilton-Smith, ed., pp. 177–192, Mount Buffalo National Park, Victoria, Australia.

Hall, C.M. and Shultis, J., 1991, Railways, tourism and worthless lands: the establishment of national parks in Australia, Canada, New Zealand and the United States. *Australian–Canadian Studies – A Journal for the Humanities & the Social Sciences*, **8**(2): 57–74

Harris, W.W., 1974, *Three parks: An analysis of the origins and evolution of the New Zealand national park movement*, unpublished MA thesis, University of Canterbury, Christchurch

Hartley, P., 1997, *Conservation strategies for New Zealand*, (The) Business Round Table, Wellington, New Zealand

Kelly, G.C. and Park, G.N., 1986, *The New Zealand Protected Natural Areas Programme – a scientific focus*, Biological Resources Centre Department of Scientific and Industrial Research, Wellington, New Zealand

Lucas, P.H.C., 1977, *The origins and structure of national parks in New Zealand*, National Parks Series No. 7, National Parks Authority, Department of Lands and Survey, Wellington, New Zealand

Mason, G., 1976, *Back country boom*, National Parks Authority, Department of Lands and Survey, Wellington, New Zealand

Matunga, H., 1995, Maori participation. In *Outdoor Recreation in New Zealand*, P.J. Devlin, R.A. Corbett and C.J. Peebles, eds, pp. 17–30, New Zealand Department of Conservation /Lincoln University, Wellington, New Zealand

National Park Authority, 1978, *General policy statement*, Department of Lands and Survey, Wellington, New Zealand

Noble, G.S., 1995, *Commission of inquiry into the collapse of a viewing platform at Cave Creek near Punakaiki on the West Coast 1995*, Report presented to the House of Representatives by command of Her Excellency the Governor-General Department of Internal Affairs, Wellington, New Zealand

Pearce, D.G., 1972, *Tourist development at Mount Cook: patterns and processes since 1884*, unpublished MA thesis, University of Canterbury, Christchurch

Pearce, D.G., and Richez, G., 1987, Antipodean contrasts: national parks in New Zealand and Europe. *New Zealand Geographer*, **43**(2): 53–59

Powrie, S., 1997, *The environmental politics of the creation of Kahurangi National Park*, unpublished MA thesis, University of Canterbury, Christchurch

Rendall, W.B., 1995, Values and decision-making: the case of the genesis of Paparoa National Park. In *Proceedings ANZALS Conference 1995*, C. Simpson and B. Gidlow, eds, pp. 336–342, Department of Parks, Recreation and Tourism Lincoln University, Canterbury

Roche, M.M., 1981, Securing representative areas of New Zealand's environment: some historical and design perspectives. *New Zealand Geographer*, **37**(2): 73–77

Roche, M.M., 1984, Some historical influences on the establishment of protected natural areas. In *People and parks: essays in the development and use of protected natural areas*, P.R. Dingwall, ed., pp. 7–15, Proceedings of Section A4e, 15th Pacific Science Congress, Department of Lands and Survey, Wellington

Roche, M.M., 1987, A time and a place for national parks. *New Zealand Geographer*, **43**(2): 104–107

Runte, A., 1987, *National parks: the American experience*, University of Nebraska Press, Lincoln and London

Simmons, D.G., 1980, *Summertime visitors to Arthur's Pass National Park*, unpublished MA thesis, Lincoln University

Thom D., 1987, *Heritage – the parks of the people*, Lansdowne, Auckland, New Zealand

Thomson, J., 1976, *Origins of the 1952 National Parks Act*, National Park Series No. 1, Department of Lands and Survey, Wellington, New Zealand

Part Two:
Settings for Tourism

R.W. BUTLER AND S.W. BOYD

The general model introduced in the first chapter of this book was subdivided into four sections. The Historical Context has been dealt with in the previous part, and provides the background against which the first national parks were established. It is clear from the foregoing discussions that there were common elements present in the establishment of most of the early parks, and that these elements (protection of untouched landscapes and wildlife, desire to establish opportunities for tourism and associated developments, and other political and economic considerations) have continued to influence both the establishment and operation of national parks to the present. In this part a variety of settings in which national parks operate are discussed in order to illustrate the complexity of the current relationship between tourism and national parks. It is felt important to review and analyse a range of settings in which national parks exist before exploring the issues and responses which are dealt with in the chapters in Part Three.

In the first part of the book attention was paid to the basic purpose of national parks, the nature and characteristics of their first establishment, and the change in perception of the natural environments of which they were a part. This last point is a significant one, for both national parks and tourism are dynamic phenomena. While it is obvious that tourism can and does change very significantly over time, it is not always apparent or as obvious that national parks are also not static. There is little doubt that at least some of the founders of national parks envisaged that they were establishing reserves which would be preserved in the form in which they existed at the time of their establishment. Some systems strived for decades to preserve parks in this manner, but it has long become clear that establishing a park does not halt natural evolutionary processes, including vegetation succession and climax, and fluctuations in animal populations. Thus the natural settings in which parks now exist, and the environment of the parks themselves, can be very different from what they were at the time of establishment. Fires (both natural and manmade), disease among wildlife populations and vegetation, climatic change, and external influences such as pollution and exotic species introduction have all caused often significant changes in the appearance of parks and their surroundings.

Similarly, tourism has changed greatly in most park settings since the last quarter of the nineteenth century. The great changes in visitor mobility, particularly the effects of the car and the jet aircraft, the vastly increased range in the activities in which tourists engage, changes in attitudes towards activities such as hunting in

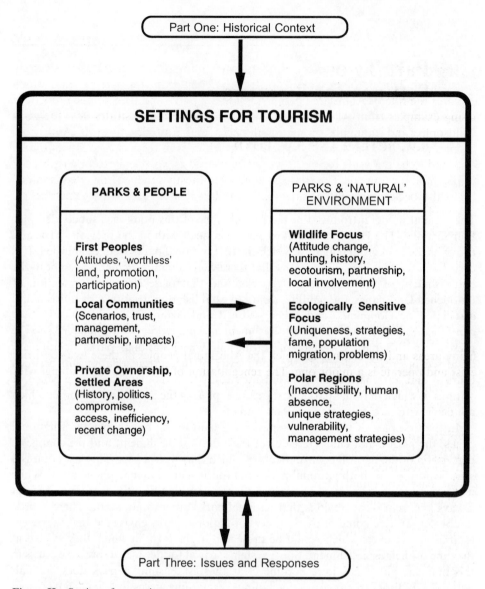

Figure II Settings for tourism

parks, and the much more varied origins and characteristics of visitors have all drastically altered the nature and scale of tourism and its relationship with national parks throughout the world. Thus both the natural and the human settings with respect to tourism in national parks have changed and continue to change greatly. A number of new settings have emerged which were not thought of when parks were first established which are illustrated in Figure II. These include aspects of the human setting such as local populations and indigenous or 'first' peoples, and parks on and including private rather than public land. On the 'natural' side, they include suitable settings for maintaining wildlife populations in contact with local and visiting populations, the maintenance of ecologically sensitive regions, and the particular and increasingly popular polar settings for tourism in national parks and similar areas.

These two broad settings, human and 'natural' are inevitably strongly interrelated. This becomes clear from the first chapter in this part by Hall, which explores the role of Aboriginal people in national parks and their tourism function. Using examples from Australia and New Zealand, he demonstrates how the early philosophy and thoughts on national parks and attitudes towards Aboriginal peoples resulted in the complex situations which exist in these two countries today. The land to be put aside for parks was often viewed as worthless except possibly for its potential for tourism. The Aboriginal peoples, mostly subdued and often landless, could also be accommodated in the parks, or already used these areas, sometimes on a nomadic basis, and presented little problem to park development. Hall shows how radically changed attitudes towards and by Aboriginal peoples have resulted in incorporation of Aboriginal views in park management and tourism development, as well as greater appreciation of the fact that the landscape contained in many parks is not untouched but represents the effects of Aboriginal use over many centuries. Using two examples, one from Australia and one from New Zealand, he explores the sensitive question of Aboriginal rights and changes in the perception of aboriginal involvement in determining the setting for tourism in national parks in specific locations. There are significant differences between Australia and New Zealand in many areas and the settings in which the Aboriginal peoples of these two countries exist and operate is a major one. The renegotiation of the Treaty of Waitangi with the Maori has resulted in a new political setting and framework for Maori involvement in national parks and, by implication, tourism. Aboriginal people in both countries have been poorly served by tourism promotion images in the past and significant differences in the portrayal of aboriginal settings have now taken place. Hall regards the examples he discusses as positive pictures of the new relationship between Aboriginal peoples and national parks, and argues that the current as well as the past Aboriginal human element should remain an important part of the national park setting.

Similar relationships are discussed by Nepal who examines the setting for tourism in parks in the high Himalayas, where local communities are present within the parks and play an active role in tourism development and the provision of tourist services. Nepal notes the rapidly increased presence of tourism in the Nepalese Himalayan parks, and the impacts which this use has brought. The environmental setting for tourism has suffered considerably through the development of trails and the use of wood for fuel to accommodate the increased numbers of tourists and those assisting them on treks and climbs. He draws clear links between the impacts on the environment and the changing role of the local population in accommodating and responding to these changes in their physical setting. Nepal illustrates how the increasing demands from tourism are affecting the human setting in terms of community life and development in the villages in and adjoining the parks. He uses three parks as examples of different approaches aimed at linking the natural and human environments in the Himalayas and the relative successes and failures of each approach. Nepal takes a consistent approach of reviewing tourism, the environment, local involvement and the relationship between these elements in assessing the overall setting for tourism in these national parks and the benefits and costs associated with it for the local communities. He concludes that tourism is welcomed and sought by the local communities but the degree of local input and control over the way in which it is achieved varies between the communities in the three areas examined. Thus the human (administrative and community) setting for tourism is of great importance in determining the degree to which tourism is felt capable of assisting the lives and economies of the communities within a difficult and sensitive physical environment.

The national parks in England and Wales are not universally recognised as national parks and do not meet the criteria of the IUCN outlined earlier. In their chapter Parker and Ravenscroft review the background to this system, explaining why the political and environmental settings were so different that they resulted in such a unique system of national parks. The late (post-World War II) establishment of this system of parks results from and reflects the long history of settlement and landscape modification in Britain, and the strongly held and widely diverse political beliefs over access to private land. Parker and Ravenscroft demonstrate clearly the compromises and modifications of positions which were made in order to establish the parks and the fact that the resulting areas are reflective of popular demand, historic imagery and economic reality, both in their location and mode of operation and management. They are critical of the result, and indicate that the pressures that have resulted on these areas from tourism and recreation have damaged the integrity of the designation and that the national parks which have resulted are not well suited for their purposes. They note the very recent (mid-1999) announcements of the current government about intended significant changes in access to the English countryside which may have major ramifications for the setting for leisure in England, particularly for recreation rather than tourism. Despite the limitations and problems resulting from the specific administrative and political setting of the national parks in England and Wales, the recognition in that system of the need to deal with problems such as major population centres within parks and the integration of other resource uses with tourism and recreation means that there are valuable lessons to be learned from establishing and operating national parks within a highly modified and long-settled landscape.

Following the theme of the interaction between the human and natural settings is the chapter by Weaver, which examines the situation of tourism and parks in ecologically sensitive areas. After a brief review of the specific problems created by the development of tourism in areas particularly vulnerable to human pressures, he reviews the setting of the Galapagos Islands off the Pacific coast of Ecuador. The isolation of the islands and the unique species which have evolved there have, of course, been made world-famous by the writings of Charles Darwin. The wildlife of the islands represent a common but very problematical paradox between tourism and national parks. It is the combined character of the uniqueness and fame of the wildlife makes it the attraction of the Galapagos National Park. Unique wildlife on its own does not attract the number of tourists which an area as relatively inaccessible as the Galapagos does, and while famous wildlife areas are clearly attractive to tourists, again, it is only the more accessible ones which attract large numbers of international tourists. However, the uniqueness of the wildlife is what makes it vulnerable to the problems which Weaver outlines, and its formerly remote setting is increasingly ineffective in providing the isolation and protection the islands once enjoyed. Weaver shows clearly the effect of increased tourism into this setting, the subsequent environmental effects and the change in the human setting through increased population migration in search of employment and income from international tourism. He reviews the actions taken to preserve the wildlife resource and the key elements of the natural setting, and their relative effectiveness and weaknesses. Weaver proposes a model which illustrates the changes in the human and natural settings of the Galapagos Islands, in the context of the impacts of tourism on the area and comments on strategies that could be introduced to mitigate the undesirable changes in this particularly vulnerable setting for tourism, a setting which is not only a national park, but also a Biosphere Reserve, Marine Resource Reserve and World Heritage Site.

The penultimate chapter in this part moves to areas of the world in which there is little or no permanent human settlement, and where the focus is clearly upon the natural setting. The polar regions of the world, discussed by Marsh, represent the ultimate areas of the world in terms of inaccessibility and hostile environment for humankind, and yet, as he demonstrates, even in these regions, tourism is having an increasing presence. While national parks exist in the Arctic regions of the world, particularly in North America, no national or international parks exist in Antarctica. The unique institutional arrangements on this continent would appear to preclude the establishment of conventional national parks as defined in the introductory chapter to this book, but Marsh discusses the nearest equivalent in that area, the Antarctic Specially Protected Areas. He proceeds by reviewing the development of tourism to the polar regions and the different approaches to dealing with this latest intrusion into a non-human setting. Marsh then discusses the emergence of parks in polar regions and the particular issues they face, reflecting the harsh physical environment, the slow reproductive rate of most species and the vulnerability of many species to impacts from humans. As with so many other parts of the world, the absence of major human settlement has not excluded the establishment of parks and reserves from political influence, and this factor is particularly important in the case of Antarctica. Marsh continues by reviewing the benefits which can accrue from tourism in polar regions, and concludes with some principles for the guidance of tourism in polar regions, which he sees continuing to grow, albeit in small overall numbers.

Emphasis shifts in the final chapter, by Lilieholm and Romney, from the human setting to that of wildlife. They note the changing ways in which wildlife have been viewed and managed in national parks, using parks in Africa as the setting. Wildlife represent a major tourist attraction in and for national parks in Africa and elsewhere, and their role has been consistent since the establishment of the African 'game parks', although the way they have been exploited has changed. Once a major attraction for hunting, especially by affluent foreigners, the wildlife is now protected from tourist hunting and has become the focus of tourist viewing. The authors note that this shift and the fact that wildlife protection is the major focus of the parks has had specific impacts on both the natural and human settings of the parks. Crucial to the management of wildlife in these parks are the concepts of equity and balance in terms of costs and benefits, particularly for the local communities. Thus although the focus of the chapter is on wildlife, the links between this element and the human setting, in and adjacent to the parks are crucial to successful park management in both human and ecological terms. Lilieholm and Romney review the nature of the relationship between tourism and wildlife and the impacts of the former on the latter, both direct and indirect, before going on to discuss the benefits and costs of wildlife conservation to the natural and human settings of the parks. They also address the important issues of mitigating the costs of protecting the natural environment that fall on local communities and reducing the impacts of the human element upon the wildlife and its habitat. They conclude the chapter with a discussion of the factors preventing the attainment of a state of sustainable tourism development in the context of wildlife-based tourism in national parks and some attempts to overcome these difficulties.

While not purporting to cover all the settings in which tourism is found in national parks, the chapters in this part range from a park system in one of the most densely populated and developed countries in the world (the UK) to the polar regions, most of which have no human inhabitants at all. They also review high mountain and oceanic island locations, along with parks in continental interior plains. The interaction between the human elements, including aboriginal peoples, economic migrants and animal husbanders, and the natural environment, including ice, water, mountains and deserts, provides the varied range of settings in which tourism is increasingly being introduced. The existence of national parks serves both to provide an added attraction to tourism through serving as a marker, and probably the most effective means of protecting these areas from tourism and other pressures. The issues raised by tourism in national parks and the responses of various systems, some of which are introduced in this part, comprise the focus of the third part of this book.

5 Tourism, national parks and Aboriginal peoples

C. MICHAEL HALL

Introduction

National parks are a Western concept and have their origins in the New World's desire to conserve nature and appropriately aesthetic landscapes for economic development through tourism. Until recently, the creation of national parks was marked by the exclusion of Aboriginal populations as undesirable elements in the 'natural' landscape. The drawing of boundaries between the natural parks and the rural human landscape available for agriculture, forestry, mining and/or grazing reflects the Cartesian divide of Western society which has long sought to separate civilisation and wilderness. However, over the past three decades the separation between natural and cultural heritage has come to be seen as increasingly artificial. In part, this has been due to the renaissance of Aboriginal and indigenous cultures in the New Worlds of North America and Australasia as well as greater assertion of native cultural values in post-colonial societies in Africa. Such developments have had enormous influence not only on the ways in which parks are managed but also in which they are established and recreated for tourist consumption.

This chapter examines the emergence of Aboriginal influences and concerns with respect to park management and its relationship to tourism in particular. It first discusses the relationship between indigenous people and the development of the park concept. It then looks at the way in which Aboriginal concerns are being incorporated into park management and tourism strategies in Australia and New Zealand. Finally, the chapter concludes by noting the development of cooperative park management strategies with respect to tourism, national parks and Aboriginal peoples and argues that such strategies will likely be increasingly utilised in park management as Aboriginal peoples assert their rights.

Early attitudes towards Aboriginal peoples and the development of the park concept

The first national parks were established as a result of a compromise between two great traditions in nineteenth-century Western thought – the Romantic and the Utilitarian (see Nelson, this volume). In Europe the Romantics provided a positive image for areas of Scotland, Switzerland and Wales which had previously been undesirable destinations and enabled them to suddenly transform themselves into popular tourist destinations. The European Romantic's perception of nature and of the New World was exported to America where it became adopted by the intelligentsia of the eastern seaboard. However, it was a perception held by those who already lived a comfortable, urban existence, rather than the pioneer. To the Romantics the New World was perceived as a new Eden in which humankind could draw close to wild nature. A cult of the primitive developed in which native peoples and the frontiersman, untouched by the civilising hand of Europeans, became archetypal Romantic heroes. Contact with wilderness was believed to give people great strength and hardiness and an innate moral superiority over their more civilised counterparts (Honour, 1975), with native peoples being represented as the noble savage of Rousseau (1978), unaffected by the 'degrading' effects of civilisation. Moreover, the Wild Man's erotic prowess allegedly made civilised man's pale in comparison (Nash, 1967). Given the significance of the Romantics to creating a positive perception of the American wilderness it should come as no surprise that the first callings for a national park to preservation both nature and native peoples should come from an artist.

In May 1832, George Catlin, a student and painter of the American Indian, arrived at Fort Pierre in what is now South Dakota. Catlin wanted to capture " 'the grace and beauty of Nature" before it was obliterated by the advance of civilization' (Nash, 1970, p. 728). However, at Fort Pierre he was shocked to discover that only a few days before his arrival a large party of Sioux Indians had traded 1400 fresh buffalo tongues for a few gallons of whisky. 'Many are the rudenesses and wilds in nature's works', Catlin reflected, 'are destined to fall before the deadly axe and desolating hands of cultivating man ...'. Yet Catlin was convinced that 'even in the overwhelming march of civilised improvements and refinements do we love to cherish their existence, and laud our efforts to preserve them in their primitive rudeness' (1968, p. 7). The Romantic influences on Catlin's thought are revealed when he noted:

> Such of nature's works are always worthy of our preservation and protection; and the further we become separated ... from that pristine wildness and beauty, the more pleasure does the mind of enlightened man feel in recurring to these scenes, when he can have them preserved for his eyes and his mind to dwell upon (Catlin, 1968, p. 7).

Catlin found the waste of animals and humankind to be a 'melancholy contemplation', but he found it 'splendid' when he imagined that there might be in the future '[by some great protecting policy of government] ... a magnificent park', which preserved the animal and the North American Indian 'in their pristine beauty and wildness'. Catlin's seminal call for 'a nation's park' highlighted the new mood in America towards wilderness. Almost exactly 40 years after Catlin's journal entry, President Ulysses S. Grant signed an Act establishing Yellowstone Park, creating the institution of which Catlin desired 'the reputation of having been the founder' (Catlin, 1968, p. 8, 9).

It is significant that Catlin perceived that such parks should contain both nature and the North American Indian. The European advance across North America meant that either through disease, war or treaty, native peoples were pushed to the periphery of land which was regarded as useful for economic development. Similarly, the first national parks were established in areas which were otherwise regarded as 'worthless' for economic development. 'In the nineteenth century a sceptical Congress had to be assured that proposed parks contained nothing of exploitable value' (Hampton, 1981, p. 45). As Runte (1973, p. 5) argued:

> An abundance of public land that seemed worthless – not environmental concern or aesthetic appreciation – made possible the establishment of most national parks in the United States. Nothing else can explain how aesthetic conservationsts, who in the past have represented only a small minority of Americans, were able to achieve some success in a nation dominated by a firm commitment to industrial achievement and the exploitation of resources. A surplus of marginal public land enabled the United States to 'afford' aesthetic conservation; national parks protected only such areas as were considered valueless for profitable lumbering, mining, grazing, or agriculture. Indeed, throughout the history of the national parks, the concept of 'useless' scenery has virtually determined which areas the nation would protect and how it would protect them.

Runte's 'worthless lands' argument arose from the very first speech in Congress which contained the elements of the national park idea. Senator John Conness of California, on introducing a bill to cede Yosemite to the State of California as a park, noted, somewhat paradoxically, that these parts of the Sierra Nevada mountains were 'for all public purposes *worthless*, but which constitute, perhaps, some of the greatest wonders in the world' (Runte, 1979, pp. 48–49). The speech reflected the dominant utilitarian attitude of the time. 'The wording reassured Conness' colleagues that no universally recognised alternative to preservation had been detected in the Yosemites' and, hence, they 'certainly could afford to recognise the valley for its substantial "intrinsic" worth' (Runte, 1983, p. 135). The creation of national parks because they were, in one sense, worthless, is a critical point to appreciate because in exactly the same way, native peoples were also expelled or forced to live on land that was otherwise worthless. The dominant utilitarian understanding of nature in the nineteenth century placed both wilderness and native peoples at the economic and cultural periphery. The Romantic perception saw the American Indian as a part of the wilderness parks. However, the utilitarian reality meant that native peoples were banished from the early parks so as not to disturb the tourists, with images of native Indians and the frontier life, usually being provided by white actors as part of the entertainment for visitors.

The location of the first national parks on the utilitarian frontier occurred throughout the New Worlds of North America and Australasia. For example, the first parks and reserves established in New Zealand were often on Maori land. The nucleus of present-day Tongariro National Park was gifted to the New Zealand government in 1887 (see Booth and Simmons, this book), with the park finally legally designated in 1894. The considerable delay between the deeding of the land by the Maori Chief Te Heuheu Tukino to the Crown and the actual establishment of the park reflected the government's concern that only 'worthless' land would be incorporated into the park. 'There had to be absolute certainty that land being added to the park had no economic value' (Harris, 1974). In speaking to Parliament on the proposed park, the Honourable John Ballance (New Zealand, 1887, p. 399) stated: 'I may say that this land is particularly suited for a national park. It has all the appearance of a park in itself, and many persons, looking at it, would imagine it had been laid out artificially, and created at enormous expense for the purpose of a park.' Ballance's comments bare witness to the aesthetic sensibilities of the colonial 'aristocracy'. The desire for parkland replete with British fauna and flora was a testament to the recreational sentiments of Victorian New Zealand and dominated the calls for the preservation of 'untouched' wild nature.

The 'worthless lands' view of national parks, so characteristic of early attitudes towards parks in Australia, Canada and the United States, was also dominant in New Zealand. In discussing Tongariro National Park the Honourable John McKenzie, Minister for Lands, told Parliament that, 'anyone who had seen the portion of the country... which he might say was almost useless so far as grazing was concerned, would admit that it should be set apart as a national park for New Zealand' (New Zealand, 1894, p. 579). In a similar fashion to the governments of Australia, Canada and the United States, the New Zealand government saw national parks as a means to develop areas through tourism, the aesthetic values of regions being the attraction to the tourist. To quote Ballance again on his proposal for a Tongariro National Park: 'I think that this will be a great gift to the colony: I believe it will be a source of attraction to tourists from all parts of the world and that in time this will be one of the most famous parks in existence' (New Zealand, 1887, p. 399).

John Matson (1892) compared the efforts made in New Zealand to protect wildlife with the absence of such attempts in the Australian colonies and appealed for the creation of 'indigenous parks' in order to preserve the animal and bird life of Australasia. Significantly, Matson quoted a New Zealand 'poet', George Phipps Williams, to conclude his case for the preservation of wildlife and their habitat, in a manner which is reminiscent of Catlin:

> Out in the wilderness is there no desolate space,
> Which you may spare to the brutes of indigenous race?
> Grant us the shelter we need from the pitiless chase.
> Gone are the stateliest forms of the apteryx kind,
> Short is the space that the kiwi is lagging behind;
> Soon you shall painfully seek what you never shall find.
> (George Phipps Williams, *A Plea of Despair*, in Matson 1892, p. 359).

Williams' comments, along with those of Catlin, may seem ill at ease with political and cultural sensibilities at the beginning of the twenty-first century. However, in the late nineteenth century such sentiments were commonplace. Maori, along with other Aboriginal peoples, were seen as the remnant of a dying race and placing them in parks and reserves, so long as the land was not required for other economic purposes, was often seen as the most appropriate course of action. Despite the initial Romantic sentiments which helped create the momentum for the establishment of parks, humans, including the Aboriginal peoples who had often created the park landscapes through their hunting and food-gathering practices, were excluded from the parks through loss of ownership and access rights, management and regulatory actions and policing strategies. Such measures were the result of ecological and cultural blindness at best, and outright racism and cultural imperialism at worse, with park boundaries serving as the demarcation between the natural and the cultural in European eyes.

Although the political status of Aboriginal peoples is still a highly contested issue in many societies, substantial shifts have occurred in management practices with respect to Aboriginal peoples and their role in national parks over the past 100 years. A number of broad social and political factors in relation to the overall rights of aboriginal peoples have contributed to these changes, including:

- A renaissance of Aboriginal culture in a number of Western countries which has led to renewed pride in traditional cultural practices
- The withdrawal of colonial powers in African and Asian states and the development of new modes of administration and management
- The assertion of ownership of and/or access to natural resources through treaty settlements and other legal channels
- Changed government policies with respect to native peoples which has led to greater economic and political self-determination and
- Greater political influence of Aboriginal peoples.

It is beyond the scope of this chapter to detail these broad changes to the position of aboriginal peoples in many countries. Instead it will focus on changes at the micro-level which have paralleled the shifts which have occurred at the macro-political level. Several factors may be identified:

- A recognition that many supposedly 'natural' landscapes are the product of a long period of Aboriginal occupancy which has created a series of ecological conditions and relationships which are dependent on certain types of human behaviours. This means that the traditional knowledge of native peoples becomes a vital ingredient in effective ecosystem management
- Growth of the tourist appeal of some indigenous cultural attractions
- Greater emphasis by park management authorities on the role of various stakeholder groups, including native peoples, in park management and the development of appropriate cooperative management strategies and
- Changed park management practices and strategies which are aimed at specifically satisfying the concerns and needs of native peoples including, in some cases, the management of national park lands owned by native peoples which are then leased to park management agencies.

The next section will examine the implications of these shifts at the micro-level with respect to the Australian and New Zealand cases.

Australia

The Australian situation provides an interesting challenge for national park management. Under the Australian constitution legal responsibility for land management is primarily a state responsibility. This has meant that the vast majority of Australian national parks are actually managed by state agencies. Nevertheless, the national government does exert a degree of influence over national park management particularly in World Heritage Sites as well as being responsible for the management of some national parks which are or were on Commonwealth territories, including such tourism icons as the Great Barrier Reef Marine Park (co-managed with Queensland), Kakadu National Park and Uluru National Park.

Overlaying the management of national parks in Australia is a highly influential environmental and conservation lobby which affected the outcome of several federal elections in the 1980s and issues surrounding Aboriginal and Islander involvement in park management.

Aboriginal rights are a highly controversial political topic in Australia. A number of High Court decisions have led to the overturning of the previous legal doctrine of *terra nullius* – the notion that Australia was unoccupied when the British claimed the continent – and has upheld Aboriginal claims to ownership of public land to which they have demonstrated ongoing traditional relationships. The declaration of *terra nullius* is clearly ridiculous as Australia had been occupied for at least 40 000 years by Aboriginal peoples and possibly even 60 000 years prior to the arrival of the First Fleet. However, moral sensibilities and political and legal structures do not necessarily coincide. The doctrine of *terra nullius* provided a basis by which the British settlers could come to own land that was obviously already occupied, although Australian Aboriginals rarely counted as people under the early laws of Australia. Indeed, it should be noted that it was not until 1966 that Aboriginals were granted full citizenship rights, including the right to vote, in Australia.

The historically weak legal position of Aboriginals was also reflected in the social position of Aborigines in Australian society. The egalitarian Australian ethic of 'mateship' did not generally extend to Aborigines, while the White Australia policy applied as much to Aboriginals as it did to migrants. Aboriginals have historically suffered from high rates of imprisonment, poor health problems, high unemployment and formal and informal segregation. Furthermore, rural Aborigines were heavily exploited by the pastoral industry in which many Aborigines worked as stockmen, 'traditionally, it also meant sexual exploitation of Aboriginal women' (Encel, 1970, p. 137). It is therefore somewhat ironic that the pastoral industry is currently one of the greatest opponents to Aboriginal land rights.

Given the often marginal position of Aborigines in Australian society it is perhaps not surprising that increased attention is being given to the possible use of tourism as a means of economic development, particularly in the more remote, economically peripheral regions, such as the Kimberleys in Western Australia and the Northern Territory where large areas of land are also set aside as national parks (Palmer, 1985; Altman, 1987a,b, 1988, 1989; Kesteven, 1987; Gillespie, 1988; Finlayson, 1991; Altman and Finlayson, 1993; Aboriginal and Torres Strait Islander Commission (ATSIC) and the Office of National Tourism, 1997). Despite concerns over undesired social impacts, Australian governments have long held out hope for tourism as a mechanism for both economic development of Aboriginal communities, particularly with respect to reducing Aboriginal unemployment rates, as well as using Aboriginal culture as a mechanism to help attract tourists. For example, in 1975 the federal Department of Tourism and Recreation argued:

> The development of tourism can provide an opportunity for many Aboriginal Australians to engage in worthwhile economic activities and increase their self-reliance. There are many areas in the States and the Northern Territory where Aboriginal participation would, in fact, enhance the appeal of a particular tourist attraction. The Department ... would seek to encourage appropriate training programs and employment opportunities so that Aborigines could gain maximum benefits from participation in tourism projects (1975, p. 7).

while 22 years later the Office of National Tourism (1997) stated:

> ... the international tourism market's increasing sophistication, with more visitors now seeking experiences which match their own particular interests in preference to 'mass tourism' experiences, involves visitors who tend to spend more than tourists on packaged tours, making them important contributors to Australia's export earnings.
>
> For these reasons, we need to build on and extend international interest in Australia beyond the traditional attractions of sun, surf and wide open spaces. We need to make potential visitors aware that Australia is also a culturally distinctive and fascinating destination with a rich indigenous cultural heritage.
>
> ... For many Aboriginal and Torres Strait Islander communities, tourism has the potential to provide a means to economic independence and a stimulus to preserving and reinvigorating their cultures.

The Royal Commission into Aboriginal Deaths in Custody (Commonwealth of Australia 1991) identified five principal areas in which Aboriginal people could participate in the tourism industry: employment, investment, the arts and crafts industry, cultural tourism, and joint ventures. However, as Altman and Finlayson (1993, p. 39) rightly observed, 'none of the five areas ... are unproblematic for Aboriginal participants. Employment in tourism-related industries requires a high level of literacy and communication skills and the adoption of cultural styles which are foreign and daunting'. Indeed, studies of Aboriginal involvement in tourism developments do not provide universal support for the notion that tourism provides direct economic benefit to Aboriginal peoples either through employment or increased income. Research in the Northern Territory and north-west Australia by Altman (1987a, 1988, 1989) and Dillon (1987), and Victoria by Finlayson (1991) and Finlayson and Madden (1994) indicate that 'commercial opportunities are likely to be limited by a cultural priority for social outcomes that may be incompatible with commercial development ... Even with a number of structural advantages, economic benefits may not accrue to Aboriginal interests, and if they do, they may be offset by related social and cultural costs' (Altman and Finlayson, 1993, p. 41). For example, there is a fear from many Aboriginal groups that contact with tourists may devalue Aboriginal culture and lead to further social breakdown in some communities. Mr S. Brennan from the Bureau of the Northern Land Council commented that the Gagudju people in the Kakadu National Park region 'do not like the idea of being a bit like a zoo, feeling that they are on display for tourists to come and see what an Aboriginal person looks like in his environment, to see whether he still walks around with a spear. They certainly do not like that concept of tourism' (in Senate Standing Committee on Environment, Recreation and the Arts, 1988, pp. 28–29).

In order to overcome the potential negative effects of tourism identified above, indigenous control of images, promotion and the product itself are regarded as extremely important as they affect not only economic development but also control of identity and heritage. A number of national parks in Australia have Aboriginal input into visitor management. However, the reality is that these parks, though often high profile, e.g. Coburg National Park and Kakadu National Park in the Northern Territory, are in the minority. The majority of national parks in Australia, though on former Aboriginal land or even land which is presently under Aboriginal claim, have little or no Aboriginal involvement in park management. Nevertheless, the

Northern Territory government, by virtue in part of the large Aboriginal population in the Territory, and the federal government, because of a series of reformist Labour Party governments, in the early 1970s and throughout most of the 1980s and 1990s, has led the way on Aboriginal land rights issues including Aboriginal ownership of national parks and Aboriginal involvement in park management, which may serve as potential models for indigenous involvement in park management not only in Australia but throughout the world.

One of the most prominent examples of Aboriginal involvement in park management in Australia is Uluru National Park, which covers approximately 1325 km^2 of arid country in central Australia (Australian National Parks and Wildlife Service, 1986). Uluru is one of Australia's most important destinations for overseas visitors and also for an increasing number of domestic tourists. It is the only national park in central Australia which is proclaimed under federal legislation. In 1987 Uluru National Park was inscribed on the World Heritage List established by the convention concerning the Protection of the World Cultural and Natural Heritage (Hall, 1992). The park has consistently attracted more visitors than any other park in the Northern Territory. In 1992 the number of visitors was estimated to be about 250 000, an increase since 1985 of 80 000 visitors per annum. Altman (1987b) noted that although the Uluru-Katatjuta Land Trust received the most comprehensive park rental payments ever received by Aboriginal interests in Australia (although minimal in comparison to mining royalties) before Aboriginal land rights were proclaimed under federal legislation in September 1985, Aboriginal interests had little control over the number of tourists who entered the park.

The Australian federal government administers the park through a leasing arrangement from the original owners, the Uluru-Katatjuta Aboriginal Land Trust. The park's management situation is compounded by the presence of the Yulara Tourist Village, a A$200 million development with two hotels, a motel, lodge, camping grounds and shopping centre, which was established prior declaration of Aboriginal ownership. The village has the capacity to accommodate over 5000 tourists. Under the terms of development, the Northern Territory Government subsidises any shortfall in the occupancy rate of the principal hotel (Wells, 1996).

The primary tourist motivation for visiting Uluru National Park is over-whelmingly to see the spectacular insulbergs Uluru (Ayers Rock) and Kata Tjuta (Mount Olga), arguably the most distinctive landscape symbols of Australia and ubiquitously used in international promotional campaigns (Altman, 1987b; Hall and McArthur, 1998). The next highest-ranking reason for visiting Uluru is to climb Uluru, while in third place is to visit the Kata Tjuta, the Olgas. Experiencing the Outback ranks fourth, while seeing the wildlife ranks ahead of learning about Aboriginal culture in the area. In contrast, the traditional Anangu owners hold different perceptions of tourism. Although three-quarters of the Anangu thought tourism was good, only one-sixth believed that tourists were motivated by an interest in some aspect of Aboriginal culture and over two-thirds thought they should learn about Anangu (Wells, 1996). Indeed, Altman (1987b) regarded tourism pressure as being too high, with 70 per cent of Anangu interviewed feeling that there were too many tourists.

Uluru National Park is administered by a board of management which comprises six members nominated by the traditional Aboriginal owners the Anangu, one member nominated by the Federal Minister responsible for tourism, one member nominated by the Federal Minister for the environment, one scientist, and the Director of the Australian National Parks and Wildlife Service (ANPWS) (now Australian National Conservation Agency). The functions of the board allow for the preparation of plans of management in respect to the park and for public comment during the preparation of the plan which is once every five years. The board is empowered to make decisions that are consistent with the plan of management and monitor the management of that park in conjunction with the Director. The board of management also gives advice to the Director and the relevant minister on all aspects of the future development of the park. The plan of management identifies four sets of values which are accorded protection and management, the most significant being the protection of the cultural and religious significance of the park to the Aboriginal people (Wells, 1996).

Anangu want to control tourist numbers and product development, and encourage tourists to learn about their culture (Institute for Aboriginal Development, 1991). Moreover, the Anangu have consciously set out to deliberately dissuade visitors from climbing the rock (Uluru), the primary reason for many people to visit Uluru (Altman, 1987b; Wells, 1996). Climbing the rock is regarded as being inappropriate and unlawful behaviour and is increasingly recognised in this way by visitors to the park (Wells, 1996). In order to do this interpretive services have been widened with the direct involvement of the traditional owners and information services to tour operators improved. In addition to including the development of a number of guided and self-guided walks and the intensive education of tour operators about indigenous heritage, the development of the Uluru-Kata Tjuta Cultural Centre is seen as symbolic of visitation to the Park increasingly on Anangu terms (Wells, 1996). According to the *Uluru–Kata Tjuta National Park tour operator workbook* produced by the Australian National Conservation Agency (ANCA) (1992) it is important that there be accurate information provided on the park particularly with respect to the promotion of Uluru as an Aboriginal national park. According to ANCA (1992) the key objectives with regard to the park's cultural resources are to:

- Utilise Anangu scientific knowledge and land management practices in the park
- Continue research into Anangu scientific knowledge and interpret this material for visitors
- Expand and develop the park's interpretation programme of Anangu explanations of the landscape
- Ensure that Anangu knowledge is seen as the primary interpretation of the park
- Ensure that non- Anangu interpretations complement Anangu interpretation
- Support and enforce existing policies and regulations regarding visitor management based on Anangu perceptions of appropriate visitor behaviour, including developing new regulations for managing visitor behaviour
- Work with Anangu to identify and conserve rock art and other archeological resources of the park and
- Record and interpret Anangu oral history to visitors.

As Wells (1996) recognised, the shift in Anungu marketing may be interpreted by some as anticipation of a wider interest in indigenous tourism product. However, more correctly it should be regarded as Anungu desire to protect their culture and landscape. Nevertheless, while Anungu can control the on-site marketing and promotion of Uluru they have little influence over the wider use of images of Uluru by tourism organisations, such as the Australian Tourist Commission and the Northern Territory Tourist Commission, nor by the tourism industry. Therefore, leading to the likelihood of inappropriate imaging of the park, particularly when the traditional concerns of national tourism organisations has been to increase visitor numbers overall rather than just select specific markets.

New Zealand

The New Zealand experience bears much similarity to the Australian situation. As discussed earlier in the chapter, several of the early parks and reserves in New Zealand were established on Maori land. However, also as in Australia, Maori had until recently little direct involvement in park management and management practices were generally unsympathetic to Maori modes of decision making (James, 1991; Keelan, 1996). For example, a *Kai Tahu* member observed of his *iwi's* (tribe's) denial of *rangitiratanga* (custodianship and responsibility for their land):

> Successive mono-cultural, imposed legislation has denied Kai Tahu the use of their traditional resources, removed their authority to regulate those resources and their own tribal members, and outlawed parts of their customary lifestyle. The current decision-making process also ignores the traditional Maori method of discussing important issues ... This sense of alienation is accentuated by the array of procedural requirements, timeframes, and operating boundaries which appear to be different for each institution ... The frustration caused by lack of consultation and exclusion from administrative functions must be seen against the Crown protection and partnership principles which Kai Tahu believed they were securing through signing the Treaty of Waitangi (Maori Tourism Task Force, 1986, p. 52).

Unlike the Australian Aborigines, the Maori had signed a treaty with the British Crown which assigned certain rights to Maori, particularly in relation to access to natural resources. Although the Crown abrogated much of its responsibilities for partnership with Maori under the Treaty of Waitangi for much of the last 150 years, the establishment of a Tribunal and a resurgence in Maori cultural and political life has seen the Crown settle claims under the Treaty which are often directly related to ownership and management of national parks and reserves which are part of the New Zealand Conservation Estate (Hall, 1996).

National parks are an essential element of New Zealand's promotion as a 'clean and green' destination overseas with over 60 per cent of international tourists visiting a part of the Conservation Estate. In addition, New Zealand has a long history of featuring Maori in its tourism promotion activities with Maori cultural activities attracting over 36 per cent of all international visitors (New Zealand Tourism Board, 1997). Unfortunately, as Barber (1992, p. 19) commented:

> Pakeha [non-Maori] New Zealanders have never been slow to exploit this indigenous culture in promotion and advertising – often in ways that drew Maori

disapproval. There was a time when foreigners could have been excused for thinking, by the posters and videos they saw, that New Zealand existed solely of flax-skirted Maori jumping in and out of steaming pools.

As Maori seek greater economic and cultural independence they are increasingly involved in developing Maori tourism products which are often owned and managed by *iwi* (Hall *et al.*, 1993; Hall, 1996; Walsh, 1996). In this climate, the communication of Maori heritage values associated with natural areas has recently become a priority for some *iwi* who seek a stronger 'presence' as *tangata whenua* (local people) in relation to landscape and natural resource management. Mountains, lakes, rivers and forest areas are considered to be *taonga* (treasure) by Maori with many *waahi tapu* (sacred places) of cultural or spiritual significance being located within the boundaries of national parks. The Maori relationship with the land also has a psychological significance known as *turangawaewae* which is the right of a person to be counted as a member of an *iwi* and thus establishes a person's 'sense of place' in relation to the land and people that occupy the land. Nevertheless, despite these significant relationships

> International and domestic visitors to natural areas, usually within national parks, are often unaware of the special Maori values of those areas and therefore lack the necessary guidance to ensure their behaviour is appropriate whilst visiting. The result is that Maori values may be offended when such natural areas are the site of inappropriate activity. (Carr, 1999)

Although the institutional arrangements for New Zealand national parks have historically excluded Maori from decision making and management processes (e.g., James, 1991), several factors, including

- The extension of Maori rights and ownership to Crown lands, including national parks, as part of Treaty settlements
- Changed legislative requirements, particularly the Resource Management Act 1991 and the Conservation Act 1987 and
- A realisation by the park agency, the Department of Conservation (DoC), that it has significant Treaty obligations and responsibilities for partnership

has meant that there have been major adjustments to management policies in the last decade. For example, the appointment of *Kaupapa Atawhai* (Maori heritage) managers within DoC and *iwi* representatives on conservation boards have provided official channels through which *iwi* could be consulted and present their 'voice' thus enabling them to exercise *tino rangatiratanga* ('full chieftainship' or 'tribal control') or *kaitiakitanga* (custodianship). Decision-making structures are also being modified to allow for Maori consensus-based decision making, while Maori values are increasingly being incorporated into conservation practice through the use of traditional ecological knowledge (Carr, 1999).

As in the case of Uluru, one area in which change is occurring is in the interpretation of Maori heritage. The content of many national park visitor centre displays traditionally explores the natural heritage of the parks from a Western scientific perspective or presents the European history of the area (Carr, 1999). However, accurate representation of Maori cultural heritage and values at visitor interpretation facilities is one means by which *iwi* may affirm their presence and strengthen their traditional relationship with the land, preferably through their active participation in all stages of the interpretation process from initial planning to the actual delivery of the information (Keelan, 1996; Carr, 1999). For example, *Ngai Tahu* have as part of their cultural development policy a desire to present a Maori perspective of natural heritage thus establishing a stronger Maori presence at natural areas throughout *Te Waipounamu* (South Island of New Zealand). By actively involving themselves in the joint management with DoC of park areas which are utilised for tourism purposes, *iwi* are able to take a positive role in protecting the *mana* (status) and integrity of the heritage located within these areas (Carr, 1999).

Under Treaty settlements Aoraki/Mount Cook has been officially recognised as a *taonga* of exceptional traditional and spiritual significance for *Ngai Tahu* (Hall, 1996). A *Topuni* (statutory cloak) of *iwi* values and associations has been placed on the mountain to enhance the *mana* of the *iwi* and ensure their authority to participate in management decisions. Under the Aoraki/Mount Cook National Park Management Plan, interpretive measures such as visitor centre displays, an audiovisual show, brochures, and, during summer holiday programmes *Ngai Tahu* interpreters, present a Maori perspective to the park visitor. It is the goal of DoC and *Ngai Tahu* that such interpretation be an effective management tool not only to educate and entertain visitors but also to increase visitor awareness and lessen visitor impacts on resources of cultural significance to Maori. For example, *Ngai Tahu* are producing a brochure about the *Topuni* or statutory cloak on Aoraki, in collaboration with DoC which will convey to concessionaires and visitors the special values of Aoraki/Mount Cook to *Ngai Tahu* and could possibly influence whether climbers do climb the mountain or, at least, result in respectful behaviour by those climbing Aoraki (Carr, 1999). Nevertheless, it should be noted that, as at Uluru, while local interpretation and promotion is aiming to communicate appropriate indigenous messages, other tour operators and tourism organisations do not necessarily have such goals.

Conclusions

The two case studies have provided two positive pictures of the relationship between tourism and Aboriginal peoples in national parks. Aboriginal peoples regard the land not only as a source of physical sustenance but also as their spiritual home. The imposition of traditional Western notions of wilderness conservation may be regarded as a form of cultural domination (Robertson *et al.*, 1992). In the case of the Uluru National Park the involvement of Aborigines in park management has been judged as extremely successful. However,

> One wonders why, when the 'Uluru experiment' has provided such a responsible and workable prototype, there remains reluctance to reproduce a range of similar contracts which should amount to an accord between the original owners of this country and those responsible for the stewardship of our national parks and protected areas (Toyne and Johnston, 1991, p. 8).

The answer to this lies in the years of racism and cultural superiority which has marked attitudes towards Aboriginal peoples by many Westerners, including conservationists, park managers, tourism operators and scientists, who have until recently failed to appreciate the deep ecological knowledge that traditional Aboriginal people have of their land (Freeman, 1979). Nevertheless, as native people's rights and political strength grows changes are occurring. Co-management strategies that involve partnership in decision making and the delegation of management responsibility, as in the case of Uluru, are being developed in natural and political environments as diverse as northern Canada (Berkes and Fast, 1996) and South Africa. For example, for a number of years, the Natal Parks Board has actively sought to develop a dynamic neighbour relation's policy, with the objective of transforming previously neutral or even negative attitudes into healthy, mutually beneficial relationships. This policy has progressed far beyond the Board's former, more traditional approach of providing neighbours on an *ad hoc* basis with natural resources, such as wood and thatch, harvested in protected areas. Today the Natal Parks Board's Neighbour Relations Policy aims to develop joint participation in conservation programmes and appropriate shared responsibilities between the Board itself and the communities who live adjacent to protected areas (Hall and McArthur, 1998). According to the Natal National Parks Board (nd), to encourage participation in protected area management and planning, a network of Neighbour Liaison Forums has been set up to:

- Resolve problem animal issues
- Provide controlled free access to protected areas and
- Formalise and honour mutual commitments.

These forums comprise leaders and members of local communities, as well as Natal Parks Board field staff at various Board stations. The Board's participation is generally to facilitate in achieving objectives arrived at through discussion, with the accent on empowerment of community members themselves.

The social changes which have taken place in South Africa demonstrate the ability for changes to occur in the interpretation and communication of heritage and to re-evaluate the way in which Aboriginal peoples are seen as a dynamic contribution to the management of national parks. Yet such a perspective is not a modern-day Romantic reinterpretation of the observations of a Catlin or a Matson. Rather it is recognition that national parks are a cultural landscape and in order for the environmental processes which create that landscape to be effectively maintained, it is vital that the cultural component through the contribution of Aboriginal peoples become a living element of contemporary park management.

References

Aboriginal and Torres Strait Islander Commission (ATSIC) and the Office of National Tourism, 1997, *National Aboriginal and Torres Strait Islander tourism industry strategy*, ATSIC and the Office of National Tourism Canberra

Altman, J.C., 1987a, The economic impact of tourism on the Warmun (Turkey Creek) Community. East Kimberley Working Paper No.19, Centre for Resource and Environmental Studies, Australian National University, Canberra

Altman, J.C., 1987b, *The Economic impact of tourism on the Mutitjulu Community, Uluru (Ayers Rock–Mount Olga National Park)*, Research School of Pacific Studies, Australian National University, Canberra

Altman, J.C., 1988, *Aborigines, tourism and development: The Northern Territory experience*, North Australia Research Unit, Darwin.

Altman, J.C., 1989, Tourism dilemmas for Aboriginal Australians. *Annals of Tourism Research*, **16**(4): 456–476

Altman, J. and Finlayson, J., 1993, Aborigines, tourism and sustainable development. *Journal of Tourism Studies*, **4**(1): 38–50

Australian National Conservation Agency, 1992, *UluruKata Tjuta National Park tour operator workbook*, Australian National Conservation Agency and Mutitjulu Community Inc., Yulara

Australian National Parks and Wildlife Service, 1986, *Nomination of Uluru (Ayers Rock – Mount Olga) National Park for inclusion on the World Heritage List*, Australian National Parks and Wildlife Service, Canberra

Barber, D., 1992, Of tourism and tradition. *Pacific Islands Monthly*, August: 19

Berkes, F. and Fast, H., 1996, Aboriginal peoples: The basis for policy-making toward sustainable development. In *Achieving sustainable development*, A. Dale and J.B. Robinson, eds, pp. 204–264, UBC Press, Vancouver

Carr, A., 1999, Interpreting Maori cultural and environmental values: a means of managing tourists and recreationists with diverse cultural values in Te Waipounamu. Unpublished seminar paper, Centre for Tourism, University of Otago, Dunedin

Catlin, G., 1968, An artist proposes a National Park. In *The American Environment: Readings in the History of Conservation*, R. Nash, ed., pp. 5–9, Addison-Wesley, Reading, MA

Commonwealth of Australia, 1991, *The Royal Commission into Aboriginal deaths in custody* (5 vols), Australian Government Publishing Service, Canberra

Department of Tourism and Recreation, 1975, *Development of tourism in Australia*, Australian Government Publishing Service, Canberra

Dillon, M.C., 1987, *Aborigines and tourism in North Australia: some suggested research approaches*. East Kimberley Working Paper No.14, Centre for Resource and Environmental Studies, Australian National University, Canberra

Encel, S., 1970, *Equality and authority: A study of class, status and power in Australia*, Cheshire, Melbourne

Finlayson, J., 1991, Australian Aborigines and cultural tourism: case studies of Aboriginal involvement in the tourist industry. Working Papers on Multiculturalism No.15, Centre for Multicultural Studies, University of Wollongong, Wollongong

Finlayson, J. and Madden, R., 1994, Regional tourism case studies: indigenous participation in tourism in Victoria. In *National Tourism Research Conference Proceedings*, Bureau of Tourism Research, Canberra

Freeman, M.M.R., 1979, Traditional landusers as a legitimate source of environmental expertise. In *The Canadian National Parks: Today and tomorrow*, J.G. Nelson and R.C. Scace, eds, pp. 345–369, University of Waterloo, Waterloo

Gillespie, D., 1988, Tourism in Kakadu National Park. In *Contemporary Issues in Development, Northern Australia: Progress and Prospects*, Vol. 1, D. Wade-Marshall and P. Loveday, eds, pp. 224–250, North Australian Research Unit, Darwin

Hall, C.M., 1992, *Wasteland to World Heritage: Preserving Australia's wilderness*, Melbourne University Press, Carlton

Hall, C.M., 1996, Tourism and the Maori of Aotearoa (New Zealand). In *Tourism and indigenous peoples*, R.W. Butler and T. Hinch, eds, pp. 155–170, International Thompson Press, London

Hall, C.M., Keelan, N. and Mitchell, I., 1993, The implications of Maori perspectives on the interpretation, management and promotion of tourism in New Zealand. *Geojournal* **29**(3): 315–322

Hall, C.M. and McArthur, S., 1998, *Integrated heritage management*, Stationery Office, London

Hampton, H.D., 1981, Opposition to national parks. *Journal of Forest History*, **25**(1): 44–46

Harris, W.W., 1974, *Three parks: An analysis of the origins and evolution of the national parks movement*, unpublished MA thesis, Department of Geography, University of Canterbury, Christchurch

Honour, H., 1975, *The new Golden Land: European images of America from the discoverers to the present times*, Pantheon Books, New York

Institute for Aboriginal Development, 1991, *Sharing the park: Anangu initiatives at Ayers Rock*, Australian National Parks and Wildlife Service, Canberra

James, B., 1991, Public participation in Department of Conservation management planning. *New Zealand Geographer*, **47**(2): 51–59

Keelan, N., 1996, Maori heritage: visitor management and interpretation. In *Heritage Management in Australia and New Zealand: The human dimension*, C.M. Hall and S. McArthur, eds, pp. 195–201, Oxford University Press, Melbourne

Kesteven, S., 1987, Aborigines in the Tourist Industry. East Kimberley Working Paper No.14, Centre for Resource and Environmental Studies, Australian National University, Canberra

Maori Tourism Task Force, 1986, *Maori tourism task force report*, Government Printing Office, Wellington

Matson, J., 1892, The Australasian indigenous park. *New Zealand Country Journal*, **16**(4): 356–360

Nash, R., 1967, *Wilderness and the American mind*, Yale University Press, New Haven, CT

Nash, R., 1970, The American invention of national parks. *American Quarterly*, **22**(3): 726–735

Natal Parks Board, undated, *Natal Parks Board neighbour relations policy* (brochure), KwaZulu-Natal Nature Conservation Service (formerly the Natal Parks Board and the Department of Nature Conservation), Natal

New Zealand, 1887, *Parliamentary Debates*, **57**: 399

New Zealand, 1894, *Parliamentary Debates*, **86**: 579

New Zealand Tourism Board, 1997, *1996 International Visitor Survey*, New Zealand Tourism Board, Wellington

Office of National Tourism, 1997, *Aboriginal and Torres Strait Islander tourism*, Tourism Facts No. 11 May (http://www.tourism.gov.au/new/cfa/cfa_fs11.html (accessed 31/12/97))

Palmer, K., 1985, *Aborigines and tourism: A study of the impact of tourism on Aborigines in the Kakadu Region, Northern Territory*, Northern Land Council, Darwin

Robertson, M., Vang, K. and Brown, A.J., 1992, Wilderness in Australia: issues and options. A Discussion Paper prepared under the auspices of the National Wilderness Inventory Steering Committee for the Minister for the Arts, Sport, the Environment and Territories Australian Heritage Commission, Canberra

Rousseau, J., 1978, *The social contract and discourses*, trans. G. D. H. Cole, rev. J. H. Brumfitt and J. C. Hall, Everyman's Library, Dent & Dutton, London and New York

Runte, A., 1973, 'Worthless' lands – our national parks: the enigmatic past and uncertain future of America's scenic wonderlands. *American West*, 10 (May): 4–11

Runte, A., 1979, *National parks: The American experience*, University of Nebraska Press, Lincoln, NB

Runte, A., 1979, *Congressional Globe*, 38th Congress, 1st session, 17 May 1864: 300, pp. 48–49.

Runte, A., 1983, Reply to Sellars. *Journal of Forest History*, **27**(3): 135–141

Senate Standing Committee on Environment, Recreation and the Arts, 1988, *The Potential of the Kakadu National Park Region*, Senate Standing Committee on Environment, Recreation and the Arts, The Parliament of the Commonwealth of Australia AGPS, Canberra

Toyne, P. and Johnston, R., 1991, Reconciliation, or the new dispossession? Aboriginal land rights and nature conservation. *Habitat*, **19**(3): 8

Walsh, B., 1996, Authenticity and representation: a case study of Maori tourism operators. In *Heritage Management in Australia and New Zealand: The human dimension*, C.M. Hall and S. McArthur, eds, pp. 202–207, Oxford University Press, Melbourne

Wells, J., 1996, Marketing indigenous heritage: a case study of Uluru National Park. In *Heritage Management in Australia and New Zealand: The human dimension*, C.M. Hall and S. McArthur, eds, pp. 222–230, Oxford University Press, Melbourne

6 Tourism, national parks and local communities

SANJAY K. NEPAL

Introduction

Since the 1982 Third World Congress on National Parks and Protected Areas, held in Bali, several influential conservation-related documents including the Second World Conservation Strategy, *Caring for the earth: a strategy for sustainable living*, *Global biodiversity strategy*, and *Caring for the earth: a strategy for survival*, have emphasised the need for people-oriented approaches to biodiversity conservation (IUCN, 1991; IUCN/UNED/WWF, 1993; WRI/UCN/UNEP, 1992). There are global case studies (Ghimire and Pimbert, 1997; Wells *et al.*, 1992; West and Brechin, 1991), comparative studies focussed on a certain geographical region (Hannah, 1992), and detailed examination of individual national parks (Nepal and Weber, 1993), all of which reiterate the need for a people-centred approach. The underlying message is that if parks and protected areas are to remain viable in future, local communities must be given a greater role in park management, and livelihood issues must be adequately addressed in park policies.

These studies consider tourism as one of the significant ways to enhance positive relationship between parks and local people. Indeed, there are several studies indicating that programmes are based on revenue generated by or through parks-based tourism have had positive impacts on local people, which not only offer employment opportunities but also develop in them positive feelings towards protected areas. The Communal Areas Management Programme for Indigenous Resources (CAMPFIRE), in Zimbabwe, and the Annapurna Conservation Area Project (ACAP) in Nepal are, arguably, the most widely cited examples of community-based protected areas management, which have successfully incorporated tourism as a major force for changing local attitudes in favour of protected areas (Nepal, 1997a).

This chapter examines the relationship between parks and protected areas, tourism, and local communities in the Nepalese Himalayas. Three popular mountain destinations, which have experienced different intensity of tourism development, have been considered to explore how tourism may, or may not, be a significant factor in improving a local people–park relationship. Moreover, it also examines how different institutional set-ups and policies affect this relationship.

This chapter is divided into three parts: the first part sets the conceptual framework for the discussion, the second concentrates on the three case studies and, finally, the third part highlights the similarities and differences of the case studies, with several policy implications. Field data and relevant information were collected during 1998 using various quantitative and qualitative methods.

Issues and concepts

Although the concept of integrating parks and protected areas with local community development and providing economic opportunities from tourism is becoming a standard policy prescription, there is a significant gap between rhetoric and reality (Nepal and Weber, 1995a). Even where limited success has been achieved, new problems have surfaced such as gender discrimination, and social inequity and injustice (Mehta and Kellert, 1998). Nevertheless, tourism is considered a resource, which is capable of expanding a partnership between local people and national parks (McNeely, 1995). In the discussions related to a local people–park relationship, tourism often plays the role of a mediator: it strengthens the conservation capacity of the park authority and, at the same time, influences local attitudes towards conservation, as it provides opportunities for local communities to benefit from conservation efforts.

The most desirable state of park-based tourism is the one, which envisages a symbiotic relationship between tourism, parks and local communities. Such a relationship guarantees satisfactory benefits for all three components. Moreover, the symbiosis is such that some forms of give and take are accepted. It is acknowledged that tourism without some negative impacts can hardly be the reality. Acknowledging this basic tenet of tourism and, making efforts to minimise the harmful effects of tourism sounds more practical than envisaging a state of tourism which does not compromise with any forms of negative impacts.

In the nexus formed by tourism, parks, and local communities, at least, seven different processes and interactions can be identified, which decide the overall fate of each of the three actors (Figure 6.1). The processes are largely dictated by the inputs, which include institutional frameworks, planning mechanisms, human and financial resources, and technological interventions. Among the inputs, the institutional framework is the most important, because it defines the framework conditions within which the three actors interact (items within the frame in Figure 6.1). The outputs from the interactions include the diversity of activities (each having its own range and scale of impacts), benefits, involvement, and stakes and interests of the three major actors. Tourism is one of the three main actors (1), which deals primarily with the development processes within the tourism sector. Its four most important components include visitors, tourism services and facilities, investors and entrepreneurs, and institutions and policies, which together shape the state of tourism development in any destination. The second main actor is the park and its various resources, which drive the demand for tourism and recreation (2). In other words, tourism development in a park context depends significantly on what it has to offer for tourists and tourism operators. The third component includes local communities and organisations, which play a crucial role in matters related to tourism development and conservation (3). Their knowledge, skills, priorities, and attitudes

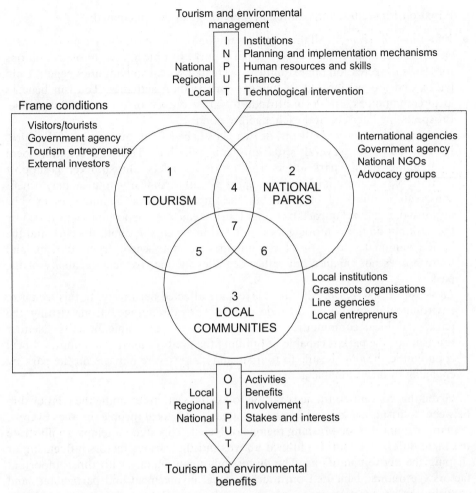

Figure 6.1. Interactions between tourism, national parks, and local communities

greatly influence the overall tourism and conservation strategy in a given destination. The interactions between the three actors result in four different outcomes, which may be positive, negative or neutral: (4) interactions between tourism, and parks (park resources being developed for tourism) result in human-influenced changes in landscapes; (5) interactions between tourism and local communities mainly relate to local involvement, benefits and multipliers; (6) interactions between parks and local communities relate to the partnership in conservation, and influence in policy and decision making, actions resulting in modified landscapes (may be an additional asset or a challenge for park management); and, (7) interaction between tourism, parks and local communities relating to the various forms of development, stakes and interests, and benefits. It is expected that a balanced interactions between the three actors will provide mutual benefits for all. It must be stressed that the interactions and outcomes are framed by the institutional environment within which they operate (see Hall, this book).

Based on Figure 6.1, three different scenarios can be anticipated:

- *Win–win–win scenario*: All three players mutually benefit. In this scenario, tourism enhances the management capability of a park. In return, favourable conditions for tourism/ recreation opportunities are created. Local communities benefit from parks, and are encouraged to support conservation activities. Tourism benefits local communities, and local attitude towards tourism or tourists is favourable. Prospects for inter-cultural exchange are good.
- *Win–win–lose scenario*: Only one or two players benefit at the expense of the third. In this scenario, several situations are possible. Tourism benefits local communities but the park suffers from tourism impacts; tourism receives support from the park without it having to support the latter. Similarly, tourism may benefit conservation efforts of the park but the impact on local communities may be negative (i.e. cultural impacts); visitors/tourism enjoy the opportunities provided by the park but do not contribute locally. Tourism benefits but both the park and the local communities lose. Local communities do not benefit from tourism, and tourism does not enhance but rather degrades the management capability of the park.
- *Lose–lose–lose scenario*: All three players are affected negatively. In this scenario, environmental conditions degrade, tourists are discouraged from visiting the park, and local communities do not receive any economic benefits. Neither tourism nor the park is capable of fulfilling the needs of local communities. Local communities become hostile to tourists and cause severe impacts on the park by engaging in unsustainable activities.

Given this conceptual framework, the following sections examine the relationship between tourism, parks and protected areas, and local people in the Everest, Annapurna, and Upper Mustang regions of Nepal. This study attempts to illustrate the three different scenarios outlined above, and the various factors influencing or shaping the above conditions. The discussions relate mainly with three important factors – economic benefits from tourism, local involvement and partnership, and contribution to conservation – which may be crucial for achieving a symbiotic relationship between tourism, parks, and local communities.

Some of the most popular tourism destinations in Nepal are located in the Annapurna, Everest, and Upper Mustang regions, which are also protected areas (Figure 6.2). While the Annapurna and Everest regions are best known for trekking and mountaineering, Upper Mustang is a special-interest tourism destination. It is particularly attractive for those who are fascinated by Tibetan Buddhism and culture, and are willing to pay a rather expensive permit fee. Some background information on environmental and socio-economic conditions, tourism development, and institutional arrangements in the three areas is provided in Table 6.1.

Table 6.1 Some aspects of environment, socio-economics, tourism and institutions in the study areas

Aspects	Everest	Annapurna (southern region only)	Upper Mustang
ENVIRONMENT			
Land area	Approximately 1150 km²	5300 km²	Approximately 2300 km²
Topography	High mountain (above 3000 m)	Middle and high mountain (>1000 m)	Arid canyons and plateaus (>2800 m)
Drainage	Dudh Koshi, Bhote Koshi, Imja Khola — several glaciers and glaciated lake	Marsyangdi, Modi, Madi, Kaligandaki — several glaciers and glaciated lakes	Kaligandaki and snow-fed local streams
Main vegetation	Alpine and sub-alpine (pine, juniper, fir, rhododendron, alpine scrub)	Alpine, Sub-alpine, Subtropical (pine, fir, Rhododendron, oak, bamboo, sal)	Alpine scrub — some dwarf trees (juniper, *Betula utilis, Caragana, Populus ciliata* spp.,)
Wildlife	Musk, deer, mountain goats, birds and pheasants	Langur, musk deer, snow leopard, different bird species	Snow leopard, lynx, black bear etc., different bird species
Uniqueness in Topography	Highest mountain in the world	Deepest gorge in the world	Arid landscape with deep canyons
SOCIO-ECONOMICS			
Total population	A little over 3000	Approximately 118 000	6700
Major ethnic groups	*Sherpa* (majority), *Rai* and *Tamang*	*Gurung, Magar, Thakali, Bhotia, Brahmin/Chetri*	*Loba (Bhotia)*
Religion	Buddhist	Mixed Hindu/Buddhists	Buddhist
Main economic base	Tourism, agriculture, pastoralism	Tourism, agriculture, remittances	Subsistence agriculture, pastoralism
Cultivated land	Less than 3%	212 km²	1422 hectares
Other economic activites	Some trading	Horticulture, trading	Trading (seasonal)
Uniqueness	Highly acclaimed high-altitude porters and guides	*Gurung* as fearsome fighters (Gurkha Army)	Uniquely Tibetan in character
TOURISM			
Type	Mountaineering/trekking	Mountaineering/trekking	Special Interest/cultural tourism (high budget only)
Tourism history	Approximately 35 years	Approximately 20 years	6½ years
Main tourist attraction	High mountains, wildlife, *Sherpa* culture	High mountains, wildlife, local culture, pilgrimage sites	Landscape, culture (walled city, ancient monastries and caves)
Visitation regulation	Access unlimited	Access unlimited	Controlled (maximum 1000 visitors/year)

Table 6.1 *(cont)*

Aspects	Everest	Annapurna *(southern region only)*	Upper Mustang
TOURISM *(cont)*			
No. of annual visitors	Approximately 17 000	Approximately 55 000	Less than 900
Total no. of lodges	224 (including lodges along Lukla-Jorsalle)	476	19 (mostly local inns)
Revenue from tourism (entry fee only)	Approximately US$ 200 000	Over US$ 800 000	Between US$ 600 000 and 700 000
Approximate direct employment	16 000 people	50 000 people	Between 1500 and 2000 people
INSTITUIONAL SETUP			
Protected Area designation	National park	Conservation Area	Conservation Area (ACAP expansion)
Date established	1976 (a World Heritage Site)	1986	1992 (World Heritage Site proposed)
Agency-in-charge	SNP, undertaking of the DNPWC	ACAP, undertaking of KMTNC	UMCDP, undertaking of KMTNC
Main partner agencies	SPCC	Several funding agencies- AHF, WWF-US	Ministry of Tourism, several donors showing interest
Others	WWF-US, Ministry of Tourism	Local government agencies	CARE, local government agencies
Degree of local involvement	Very little	Significant	None

Note:
ACAP   Annapurna Conservation Area Project
AHF   American Himalayan Foundation
DNPWC   Department of National Parks and Wildlife Conservation
KMTNC   King Mahendra Trust for Nature Conservation
SNP   Sagarmatha National Park
SPCC   Sagarmatha Pollution Control Committee
UMCDP   Upper Mustang Conservation & Development Project

The Sagarmatha (Mount Everest) National Park

Tourism

In the early 1950s, soon after Nepal opened its borders to the outside world, mountaineers started rushing into the hitherto unfamiliar Khumbu region, which was known to the outside world only because it was the location of the highest mountain in the world. Successful ascent of Mount Everest by Tenzing Norgay and Edmund Hillary in 1953 attracted numerous mountaineers from around the world. Later, trekkers started exploring the Everest region, who were mystified by the very existence of Mount Everest, the legends of *yeti* and the Sherpa people. Almost without any preparation or planning, trekking tourism, from a mere 20 trekkers in 1964, Everest is now visited by more than 17 000 trekkers every year. During peak tourist months, visitors (guides and porters included) exceed the local population by a factor of five. Similarly, the number of lodges increased from seven in 1973 to 17 in 1980, 74 in 1990, and 224 by the end of 1997 (Mattle, 1999). These lodges have an accommodation capacity of 4000 beds per night. Lodging provides direct employment to some 757 persons. During peak seasons, more than 8000 porters may be employed in trekking tourism over a period of three months. The density of trekking traffic varies between 1.4 and 27. 4 persons per kilometre per day, indicating a high visitor concentration on certain locations. If porters and guides are combined, this figure varies between 2.8 and 63.7 persons per kilometre per day. There has been remarkable progress in the services and facilities available to trekkers and mountaineers. Indeed, those who have closely followed the development of tourism in the Everest region assert that nowhere in the Himalayas is there a tourist centre as sophisticated as Namche Bazar, the heartland of tourism in the region. The trends in tourism development there and the attention Mount Everest has received in the international media, for example the recent filming of Everest in IMAX format (Breashears, 1997), suggest that the number of visitors is likely to increase.

Environment

Declaration of the Everest region as a national park in 1976 and a World Heritage Site in 1980 may have saved this region from further environmental degradation, as compared to other parts of the country. However, the rapid development of tourism has transformed the region's economy, environment and culture in an unprecedented way. As a result of tourism-related problems, Everest has been labelled 'the world's highest junkyard', and the trail to its base camp 'the garbage trail'. Namche Bazar is called a 'lodge city' where Sherpa life revolves around tourists and a small-scale, locally controlled form of capitalism (Wells, 1994). The availability of electricity in some tourist villages such as Namche, and the adoption of various alternative energy sources and energy-saving devices by the lodges, have not reduced the demand for firewood and timber. Even today, firewood constitutes a major source of energy for the majority of the lodges, while timber is naturally the main construction material. It is reasonable to assume that energy demands in the region have gone up significantly, as both the numbers of visitors and the lodges have increased dramatically. During the peak tourist seasons, lodges consume over 9 metric tons of firewood per day. Since cutting trees inside the National Park is prohibited, forested areas outside the park boundary are increasingly under stress to meet the growing demands for firewood and timber. Several villages outside the park have emerged as centres for marketing firewood and timber (Nepal, 1997b).

Garbage produced by trekking and mountaineering poses a significant environmental problem. As the visitor numbers increase every year, so does the accumulation of garbage. During the fiscal year 1993/4, 126 metric tons of garbage was collected by the Sagarmatha Pollution Control Committee (SPCC), a local NGO supported by the Nepalese government and World Wildlife Fund, USA. This increased to 243 metric tons during 1996/7, of which 60 per cent were collected from Namche Bazar only (SPCC, 1997). Overall, it is estimated that there are 17 metric tons of garbage per kilometre of a tourist trail. Owing to the heavy visitor traffic, trail conditions are rapidly deteriorating. Many trail segments exhibit signs of soil erosion, deep incision, excessive width, trail displacement, and root exposure. A recent trail assessment survey, conducted by this author, indicated that over 12 per cent of the park trails may be severely degraded and in need of immediate restoration and maintenance.

Local involvement

Local involvement in tourism-related activities has been very significant. From the very beginning, the local Sherpas had been able to benefit from tourism, mainly because they had the advantage over outsiders for being able to adjust to the region's marginal environment. Sherpas have come a long way from becoming high-altitude porters and guides to influential owners of trekking agencies based in Kathmandu. According to Fisher (1990), until 1978 Sherpas had a majority financial interest only in four trekking agencies as compared to 1985 when 30 per cent of all trekking companies were owned by the Sherpas. Similarly, it was estimated that by 1985, almost 65 per cent of all Khumbu families had income from trekking. Currently, Sherpas are mostly engaged as trekking organisers, sirdars, and guides, while the majority of porters are non-Sherpas originating from 17 different districts in the eastern, central and western hilly regions of Nepal.

Historically, Sherpas have developed a strong sense of community stewardship. Not a single individual but the whole community took responsibility for protecting common properties such as forests and grasslands. Sherpas developed their own indigenous forest and grazing land management systems, which collapsed after the government's decision to nationalise all forests and grazing land in 1957. The administering and policing protected forests prior to 1957 was based on the *shingii nawa* system, a village-level institution, composed of a powerful group of local people who annually selected villagers to act as forest guardians (Stevens, 1993). Local interests and involvement in such a system ensured sustainable use of forest resources. The nationalisation of forests and the rapid growth of tourism have had negative impacts on community stewardship and responsibility. Previously friendly neighbours have suddenly become envious and hostile competitors. Stiff competition, physical and mental stress, and the challenge of running a lodge have taken a heavy toll on Sherpa community life, resulting in a somewhat fragmented society. Erstwhile active members of the community now find very little time for communal activities. The present-day Sherpa life revolves around the tourists, in contrast to the pre-tourism and pre-forest nationalisation period when community and religion were the most important aspects of Sherpa culture (Fürer-Haimendorf, 1964).

Relationship

An examination of the relationship between tourism, national park, and local community in the Everest context reveals that there is a strong bond between Sherpas and tourism, to the extent that they are increasingly dependent on tourism as their main source of livelihood. Tourism is said to have negative effects on agriculture and has failed to induce any other economic activity in the region. It has revived, in a small scale though, the old trade between Khumbu and Tibet, but the traders are mainly Tibetans and not local Sherpas (Bichsel, 1999). Tourism has greatly benefited local Sherpas who are more than eager to associate with foreigners than other Nepalis. Tourism has benefited from the Park establishment. There is partnership between local people and tourism but the Park has been excluded from this partnership (see Goodwin, Chapter 15). While the National Park Authority has failed to make any substantial efforts to involve local communities in its conservation efforts, local Sherpas lack the initiative or motivation to engage with the Park. Even the appointment of local Sherpas as park wardens has not helped; it may have even created some confusion for the Sherpa wardens, as they are expected to maintain a softer attitude towards Sherpas and, at the same time, be obliged to the government agency. Revenues from entrance fee are hardly enough to cover the Park's regular expenditures, which greatly hinders its ability to reach out to the public with community-oriented development programmes.

Thus the Park is strictly limited to administrative and regulatory functions. Perhaps, due to the lack of government support, local Sherpas are indifferent to government-sponsored conservation activities. Local officials complain that Sherpas are more interested in profits from tourism than protecting the Park environment. Examples elsewhere in Nepal suggest also that local people are more favourable to tourism-led development than community development activities directly introduced by a project or a development agency (Mehta and Kellert, 1998). Theoretically, one would expect the local Sherpas to have strong interests in protecting the Park since the majority of them earn their livelihood from Park-based tourism. However, local communities have not been able to realise this apparent linkage between tourism, conservation and economic benefits.

The Annapurna Conservation Area

The Annapurna region is one of the most popular trekking destinations in Nepal. Designated as a Conservation Area in 1986, it is inhabited by about 118 000 ethnically diverse people. In response to the growing environmental crisis in the

Annapurna region, His Majesty's Government of Nepal (HMG) decided that designation of a national park would save the region's unique biological diversity. However, after some studies and a sort of social impact assessment had been conducted in the area by the King Mahendra Trust for Nature (KMTNC), a national non-governmental organisation established in 1984, designation of a conservation area was felt more appropriate (Hough and Sherpa, 1989, cited in Nepal and Weber, 1995b). Local people were considered custodians of their natural and cultural heritage and were assisted by the Project, the management of which was entrusted by the government to the KMTNC, a unique arrangement that did not exist anywhere else at that time.

Tourism

As is the case in Everest, tourism in Annapurna started also with mountaineering expeditions in the early 1950s. In 1950, Mount Annapurna was successfully climbed by Maurice Herjog, a Frenchman. This was the first time that a peak over 8000 metres had been climbed successfully. Several other expeditions followed suit, including the one and only expedition to the Fish Tail Mountain in 1957 led by Jimmy Roberts. It remains one of the few peaks in Nepal never to have been conquered for spiritual and aesthetic reasons. It was not until the early 1970s, when some basic infrastructures were put in place, that trekking intensified. Its proximity to Pokhara (a regional hub), good access, and high ecological and cultural diversity made Annapurna the most visited mountain destination in Nepal. The first lodge in Ghandruk, the village where ACAP started its pilot project, was opened in 1976. In 1977, Manang and Mustang (southern part) were opened for tourism, paving the way for the Annapurna Circuit Trek. In the same year, for the first time, the number of visitors to Jomsom (a village in southern Mustang) and Muktinath (a pilgrimage site located on the Manang/Mustang border) exceeded that to the Everest region. There was a dramatic increase in the number of foreign visitors, which rose from 14 332 in 1980 to 33 620 in 1986 and over 49 000 in 1996 (HMG, 1996). Similarly, there was almost a tenfold increase in the number of lodges between 1979 and 1996. There were 53 lodges until 1979, which increased to 176 in 1989, and 476 in 1996 (information based on Poudel, 1996; ACAP lodge data, 1996; and field verification by the author in 1998). During the last seven years, 300 new lodges have been established with an accommodation capacity of over 6 000 beds per night. Tourism has become a major economic activity in the region, which may have provided local employment to over 50 000 persons annually, in addition to the labour engaged in lodging.

Environment

With the proliferation of tourism, over the past two decades the Annapurna region has faced various environmental and economic problems. Localised deforestation caused by heavy demand for firewood and for timber for the construction of over 500 lodges and teashops has altered wildlife habitats. More recently, haphazard tree cutting was observed along the east–west Marsyangdi valley, particularly between Bagarchap and Pisang. A study conducted in Manang showed that the average daily household firewood consumption was 7.8 kg compared to 42.5 kg consumed by a lodge (Gurung, 1995). ACAP has made considerable progress in introducing alternative energy sources. Higher income from tourism has made it possible for the local community to afford new energy-efficient technologies, but the majority of the lodges continue to use firewood as their main energy sources (Banskota and Sharma, 1997). The seasonality and concentration of trekkers in three main areas – the Annapurna Sanctuary, the base of the Thorong Pass, and Ghorepani village (a major trail intersection) – continues to be a problem, both environmentally and socially, as visitors often complain about overcrowding in these areas. Inadequate sanitation practices and extensive non-biodegradable litter, such as plastics, tins and bottles used mainly by tourists, are primarily responsible for polluting the villages and local streams (Gurung and de Coursey, 1994). Sowernine and Shrestha, (1994) estimated that trekking tourism produces approximately 9300 *doko* (locally made bamboo basket) of waste, most of which is disposed into local streams and rivers. This is a very modest estimate considering the number of lodges at that time (roughly 400) and the carrying capacity of a *doko*, which is usually less than 20 litres.

Tourism has flourished at the expense of agriculture and livestock herding. One can observe extensive fallow land in and around the main tourist villages. Many villagers are no longer interested in agriculture since it demands more time and hard labour. Kraijo (1997) reported that many villagers either leave their land fallow or convert it into tree-plantation areas. Livestock herding, which used to be common in villages such as Ghandruk, is no longer practised.

Local involvement

Three basic principles guide the Annapurna Project: sustainability, people's participation and the *Lami* (catalyst) approach (ACAP, 1996). ACAP has been authorised by special legislation both to charge fees to visitors (currently, Nepali Rupees 1,000 per person per visit, roughly equivalent to US$15) and to retain the revenues to finance its projects related to health and sanitation, education, environmental protection, and tourism. Local contribution to such activities is increasing; for example, villagers provided 46 per cent in cash and labour for a 50 kW electricity plant installed in Ghandruk. Various management committees have been established to engage local people in conservation and community development. These committees include 37 Conservation and Development Committees, 19 Lodge Management Committees, 15 Kerosene Depot Management Committees, 21 Electricity Management Committees, two Health Centre Management Committees and a Drinking Water Management Committee. There are 288 mothers' groups throughout the region, and members of such a group actively engage in various income- and awareness-generating activities including fund-raising, trail repairs, clean-up campaigns, and observation tours. Members of these various committees are nominated or elected by the local people themselves. Thus, ACAP has encouraged local participation in resource management and helped villagers to maintain control over their resources and identify their immediate needs and priorities. This is very different from other protected areas in Nepal where resource management and protection is carried directly by the government with almost no local involvement.

Relationships

The relationships between the conservation area, tourism and local communities have been favourable. Tourism has benefited not only the local communities and conservation authority but also tourists and tourism operators. The next important step, however, is to achieve some degree of equity among the diverse communities who are scattered around the region – benefits must reach the less fortunate, non-tourist villages. The partnership between the three sectors is good, but linkages with other important economic sectors are very poor. Tourism is highly externally driven, almost all supplies come from outside including basic commodities like rice and eggs. A recent survey indicated that only about 10 per cent of the economically active household members employed in the agricultural sector stated that their occupational linkage with tourism was high (Banskota and Sharma, 1997). Thus, if tourism is not planned in an integrated way and is allowed to dominate the local economy with adverse impacts on agriculture, local communities will be increasingly vulnerable to fluctuations in tourism. ACAP's conservation activities have been successful, but too much conservation-focused tourism strategy may not help in the future. Therefore, ACAP should develop programmes which strongly link tourism with other economic sectors such as agriculture and increase the overall economic capability of the region.

The Upper Mustang region

The success of Annapurna Conservation Area Project resulted in its expansion towards the northern frontiers covering the Upper Mustang region (hereafter referred to as Mustang). With the inclusion of the Mustang and Manang regions, ACAP had control over 7629 km^2. In 1992, the Upper Mustang Conservation and Development Project (UMCDP) was launched and for the first time, the formerly restricted area of Mustang was opened up for tourism.

Tourism

Mustang, or more precisely, the area north of Kagbeni and beyond, remained in obscurity for a long time even after Nepal had opened its borders to the outside world (see Figure 6.2). For outsiders, it is an inhospitable, cold, dry, and desert country where sand and stones are the only objects ubiquitously found. Some early foreign visitors included Hari Ram, of the Survey of India who visited Lo Manthang in 1873 (Mathiessen and Laird, 1995) and Ekai Kawaguchi, a Japanese monk who in 1893 tried secretly to enter Tibet via Mustang but did not reach Lo Manthang (Peissel, 1967). The first European to set foot in Lo Manthang was the Swiss

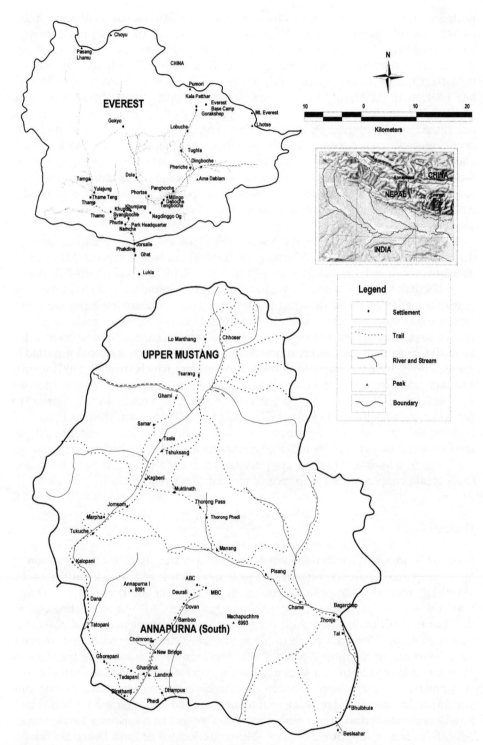

Figure 6.2.   Location map of the study areas

geologist, Toni Hagen in 1952, followed by three Tibetan scholars, Guiseppe Tucci in 1952, David Snellgrove in 1956 (he was not allowed to travel beyond Tsarang), and Michel Peissel in 1964 (Tucci, 1977; Snellgrove, 1989; Peissel, 1967). Travel was discouraged after that, as Khampa guerrillas were using Mustang as their base to fight the Chinese occupation of Tibet. Lo remained entirely closed to visitors until late 1991, when the Nepalese government decided to open it for controlled tourism. Mustang's main attractions include the walled city of Lo Manthang, which was established in the fourteenth century. Throughout the Mustang region there are several medieval monasteries and cave dwellings, which indicate its rich architectural and cultural heritage. Today, Mustang lies in the backwaters of Nepal, where economic development and environmental conditions are in the extremes. It is not surprising that, when the region was opened for tourism, local people welcomed it with a great relief, looking forward to prospects similar to those enjoyed by their southern neighbours.

Though ACAP was given the responsibility to undertake conservation and development programmes in Mustang, tourism is controlled by the Ministry of Tourism, which restricts the number of visitors to 1000 per year. A 10-day permit costs US$700; each additional day costs US$70. It is mandatory for visitors to be part of a registered agency-handled group tour. Tour groups must bring their own supplies, stay in tented camps, and dispose waste properly or carry it back. To ensure that these regulations are strictly observed, a Nepalese liaison officer, appointed for the duration of the trip, accompanies each tour group. Visitors to Mustang started in August 1992; by December there were 400 visitors. By the end of 1997, Upper Mustang had seen a total of 4334 visitors, and generated more than US$3 million for the Ministry of Tourism. Over 55 per cent of the total visitations are during the period between August and October. Since tourism is highly controlled, its impact on both the environment and the local economy is minimal. It has not encouraged any services and facilities such as lodge development and catering business. Except for the few local inns, where tour groups pitch their tents and buy occasional drinks and food, local people have failed to receive any benefits from tourism.

Environment

Mustang is not an officially designated conservation area itself but an expansion of the Annapurna Conservation Area, which has established a field office in Lo Manthang and two visitor information centres in Kagbeni and Lo Manthang. Thus, UMCDP is a semi-autonomous project managed by ACAP. As mentioned earlier, the area is a mountain desert with occasional stands of trees and small parcels of cultivated fields. There is a patch of highly degraded forest around Samar, roughly 24 kilometres, or 10 hours' walk from Jomsom, the district headquarters of Mustang. It is speculated that Mustang once may have had a very good forest cover, as manifested by the large wooden structures in several monasteries. A long settlement history, an increasing population caused by migration from Tibet, flourishing trade and war, were perhaps responsible for the demise of whatever forest did exist in the region. Some pristine forests are located around Damodar lake (a pilgrimage site for the Hindus), which is believed to have many rare and endangered mammal and bird species (Banskota and Sharma, 1998). Due to the lack of good trails and accommodation facilities, visitors normally do not venture into this area. Thus, trekking is mostly confined to the Kali Gandaki corridor, the main trail leading to Lo Manthang. Due to the low volume and short duration of tourism, environmental impacts are not noticeable, except for some litter in places such as Lo Manthang, Tsarang, Ghami, and graffiti along the trail between Kagbeni and Tshuksang. Some camping groups erect their toilet tents too close to streams and irrigation channels. Toilet holes are usually shallow, less than 12 inches deep. Trekking-related trash is not disposed of properly as evidenced by the large piles of trash in some villages. Waste is also disposed of into local streams; a pile of garbage has been seen on the Kali Gandaki riverbed, right in front of the visitor centre in Kagbeni. Some dumping pits, notably in Lo Manthang, were overfilled to capacity, mostly with household trash. Regular clean-up is necessary in Lo Manthang where local people have yet to develop the habit of proper disposal of household trash and burying dead animals, whose partially decomposed carcasses can be seen lying outside the city. These are serious health hazards, both for visitors and local people. It is likely that such low sanitation standards will create a negative impression upon visitors who come to Lo Manthang with great expectations, after paying large amounts of money and enduring the strenuous trek up and down the canyons for several days. The direct impact of tourism on architectural heritage is not obvious, but throughout Mustang, it is sad to see the decaying state of what were once splendid castles and monasteries. It is difficult to say how long the present structures will survive, but the process of decaying will surely be accelerated by increased visitation if renovation is not carried out very soon. Indeed, timely restoration of historic buildings, good information and interpretation, and improvements in some basic services and facilities will ensure a sustained visitor flow to Mustang.

Local involvement

Based on its experience in the Annapurna region, ACAP introduced its programmes in Mustang in at least, four broad areas: environmental conservation, community development, tourism management, and institutional development. Initially, it was agreed that the Ministry of Tourism returned 60 per cent of tourism revenues collected from Mustang by providing support to ACAP's various development activities there. However, only about 27 per cent was provided to UMCDP (Shackley, 1996), which was reduced recently to less than 10 per cent. Programmes implemented by UMCDP were based on a reconnaissance study conducted by ACAP in 1992 through participatory discussions with local people and various institutions in the region (ACAP, 1992). Local people had been aware of ACAP's activities in the Annapurna region, therefore they welcomed this and were enthusiastic about its programmes. They viewed tourism as one of the main opportunities to improve their livelihood conditions.

Their first disappointment came in the form of the government's tourism policy prohibiting local people from direct involvement in opening lodges and teashops, which was unlike what they had seen in the Annapurna region. The restoration of democracy in 1990 changed the political environment in Mustang. Prior to the change, the local *Raja* (king) held enormous power and was the primary decision maker regarding land and water conflicts, and other petty quarrels. With the democratic movement, many local people who had not fared well in Mustang's political and economic balance started openly to express their dissatisfaction. Local people eagerly associated themselves with various political organisations, which further created an atmosphere of rivalry and competition. As strengthening traditional institutions is one of ACAP's main objectives, this new power structure created a practical problem for ACAP. It could neither ignore the *Raja* and the local elite nor could it be indifferent to local people's needs and priorities, since ACAP was always seen as a people-oriented institution. Somehow, ACAP failed to convince local people of its neutral position. The local community felt that they had been betrayed, first by the government and now by ACAP, which failed to deliver what it had promised, or at least, what people had expected from it. Moreover, local people had expected ACAP to act promptly on some of the most important issues, such as restoration of monasteries, improved irrigation and access, and direct tourism benefits. Instead, ACAP focused on environmental issues such as plantation, energy, biodiversity and diversifying agriculture. Local people have responded to these programmes with some apprehension and indifference, holding the opinion that they had been planting trees before ACAP launched its activities there. Energy issues, particularly micro-hydro projects, have run into controversy over water for irrigation or electricity. Programmes focused on biodiversity raise villagers' suspicions as to the exact motive of ACAP, especially when it involves endangered species such as the snow leopard. When a snow leopard kills a villager's goat not only does he lose his livelihood source but also his faith in ACAP, unless he is adequately compensated. This author witnessed one such case in Dri where a shepherd showed him a dead goat, which he believed was killed by a snow leopard. Even projects related to diversifying agriculture may not be in the best interests of local people who have very limited cultivable land for such purpose. Vegetables and fruit may add to their diet but do not fill their empty stomachs. In other words, local people preferred projects that would have immediate effects on their livelihoods. ACAP had a more long-term strategy with environmental conservation as its basic mandate.

As in the Annapurna region, UMCDP has formed various committees, such as Conservation and Development Committees, Lodge/Campsite Management Committees, Kerosene Depot Committees, Electricity Management Committees, *Gomba* (monastery) Management Committees, and Mother's Groups. However, their relevance, commitment and efficiency remain much to be seen. It is reasonable to assume that without direct tourism benefits or programmes based on tourism revenues, local people's involvement in such committees will be strictly limited to formal participation only, without any practical follow-up activities.

Relationships

The above discussion indicates that relations between tourism, protected areas and local community in the Mustang context are disappointingly unfavourable. This is largely due to the exclusion of local people from tourism. While tourism has greatly benefited the government, neither the protected area agency nor the local community have received any benefits. ACAP is concerned that, without substantial outside support, it can hardly run its programmes and maintain its field base and staff in Lo Manthang. Local people are totally frustrated with the government and disappointed with ACAP because of its inability to persuade the government for a people-centred approach. Indeed, both ACAP and local communities do not have the political power to influence the government. The weak linkage between tourism, protected area and local communities can be strengthened only if the government, ACAP and local people work in partnership. Any future tourism management plans for Mustang will not succeed without this basic realisation. Limited conservation activities have been accomplished, but it is still too early to assess the success of such activities.

Summary and conclusions

Three different models can be deduced from the above discussions, with respect to relations between tourism, parks and protected areas, and local communities (Figure 6.3). In the Everest model, the overall relationship is weak. There is very little interaction between local people and the national park. Tourism has a one-way linkage with the Park; tourism relies on the Park's natural resources but the Park has to bear the environmental burden caused by tourism. In contrast, local people and tourism have forged a strong relationship. The Annapurna model suggests a relatively strong park–tourism–community relationship. There is a two-way linkage between the three components. This has been possible mainly due to ACAP's participatory approach. However, ACAP has failed to introduce programmes which link tourism with the local economy. ACAP's conservation-focused strategy has overlooked the fact that without a solid economic base, an externally driven tourism development may overall underrate the development capacity of a region, and jeopardise its long-term economic sustainability. The Mustang model indicates a very weak relationship between tourism, protected area, and local communities. Tourism has favoured the state at the expense of local communities. There, tourism and conservation constitute loose threads of development for a resource-dependent, marginal community, which does not have sufficient collective bargaining power to claim its rights for improved livelihood conditions.

The above three examples are similar in some respects and different in others. While the Everest region is home to a national park controlled by a government agency, Annapurna and Upper Mustang regions are controlled by ACAP, which is an undertaking of KMTNC. The basic mandate of a national park is to ensure adequate wildlife conservation, but recently a people-centred approach has been encouraged. ACAP's mandate centres on a people-oriented conservation strategy. Having said that, it must also be clarified that these agencies do not assume control over visitor numbers or tourism management in their areas. Since the national park is under government control, its activities are largely dictated by a rigid set of rules and regulations. The national park does not have the autonomy to freely seek cooperation from other agencies, unlike ACAP, which solicits external support through KMTNC's several overseas chapters. Thus an institutional set-up is a very

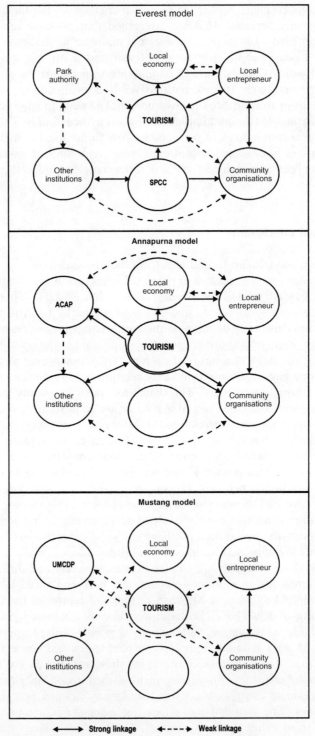

Figure 6.3. Tourism and linkages in the study areas

crucial component of a successful strategy for achieving conservation and tourism goals.

Tourism-led development is highly favoured by local communities in all the three destinations. It constitutes a vital component of rural livelihoods in the Everest and Annapurna regions, while future prospects in Mustang look very good, provided that there is a change in tourism policy. The degree of dependency on tourism is strongest for local communities in Everest, it is moderately strong in Annapurna, and weak in Upper Mustang. Tourism has been a good source of revenue for all three destinations but revenues have not remained in the hands of the protected area agency, except in Annapurna. In Everest, a significant proportion of tourism revenues comes from climbing royalty and trekking permits, which is collected by the central government authority. Entrance fees collected by the Park are not sufficient to cover its expenditure. This is true for ACAP also, but its funds are supplemented by external support and collaborations. In Mustang, tourism revenue goes to the Ministry of Tourism and to the central treasury. The idea of channelling a significant proportion of tourism revenue to finance local development projects has not materialised as envisioned. In Annapurna, the local community was consulted in all aspects of development programmes; in Everest, there was no such consultation, which was one of the reasons for local people's indifference attitude towards government-sponsored conservation activities. Indeed, the Park's conservation efforts were more wildlife-centred than human, and almost all activities were carried out without local involvement. In Mustang, ACAP wanted to employ the same principles as it did in the southern regions. However, due to the changing political situation and lack of skilful negotiation, ACAP was not able to win people's trust. Many local people thought that ACAP was receiving 60 per cent of the tourism revenue from the government as initially agreed, while in reality it was receiving less than 25 per cent. Similarly, local people were suspicious of ACAP, as it showed a tendency to form an alliance with the local elite, although this may not have been ACAP's motive.

Reflecting on the three scenarios mentioned earlier, it is clear that ACAP's activities in the southern Annapurna region exemplify the *win–win–win* situation, while the Everest example is close to the *win–win–lose* situation, where tourism and local communities benefit but the protected area loses. Similarly, the Upper Mustang case is representative of the *win–lose–lose* scenario, where tourism benefits at the expense of the protected area and local communities. It also indicates that if the government does not pay urgent attention to the problems, Upper Mustang may soon be facing the *lose–lose–lose* situation. Tourism, which strives for quality but is controlled by the government, and does not enjoy popular support from local community, cannot be a long-term viable option. In the event of a strong local opposition, which is not unlikely given the current political climate in Nepal, it will be the government suffering and not the local people, who have nothing to lose.

Needless to say, ACAP's community approach is the preferred model. However, some refinement in the approach is required, especially with regard to its focus on other economic sectors. Also, whether there has been a true local empowerment in Nepal's conservation areas including Annapurna, has been questioned recently (Heinen and Mehta, 1999). Tourism should either induce other economic activities and increase the economic sustainability of a destination or it should be planned in a way that other economic activities are developed to support it and increase its profitability. This lesson from the Annapurna experience should be considered when developing other tourism destinations elsewhere in Nepal. The discussion also suggests that the Everest National Park should make a radical departure from its current policy and management, if meaningful conservation is to be achieved. It is in the long-term interests of parks and protected areas, tourism, and local communities that a balanced approach to conservation and development should be the goal. Without such a balance benefits will be always skewed, resulting in conflicts over natural resources, and ultimately, degradation of those resources.

Acknowledgements

The author wishes to acknowledge the generous funding support provided by the Swiss Foundation for Alpine Research for this research. Comments from Professor Hans Hurni of the Centre for Development and Environment (CDE), Geographisches Institut, Universitt Bern, Switzerland, and the editors of this volume are greatly appreciated.

References

Annapurna Conservation Area Project (ACAP). 1992, *Work plan 1992–93*, The King Mahendra Trust for Nature Conservation (KMTNC), Kathmandu

ACAP, 1996, *A new approach in protected area management*, ACAP, Pokhara

Banskota, K. and Sharma, B., 1997, *Case studies from Ghandruk*, International Center for Integrated Mountain Development (ICIMOD), Kathmandu

Banskota, K. and Sharma, B., 1998, *Mountain tourism for local community development in Nepal – a case study of Upper Mustang*, ICIMOD, Kathmandu

Bichsel, C., 1999, *Dynamic der Handelsbeziehungen und ihre Bedeutung für den sozio-ökonomishen Wandel in der Region Khumbu, Nepal*, Diplomarbeit, Philosophisch-naturwissenschaftlichen Fakultät, Universität Bern, Bern, Switzerland

Breashears, D.F., 1997, The siren song of Everest. *National Geographic*, **192**: 124–135.

Fisher, J.F., 1990, *Sherpas – reflections on change in the Himalayan Nepal*, Oxford University Press, New Delhi

Furer-Haimendorf, C. von, 1964, *The Sherpas of Nepal – Buddhist highlanders*, Oxford Book Co., New Delhi

Ghimire, K. and Pimbert, M. eds, 1997, *Social change and conservation*, Earthscan, London

Gurung, C.P. and de Coursey, M., 1994, The Annapurna Conservation Area Project: a pioneering example of sustainable tourism? In *Ecotourism: a sustainable option?* E. Cater and G. Lowman, eds, pp. 177–194, John Wiley, London

Gurung, G., 1995, *Fuelwood consumption survey in Manang and Tanki Villages*, Manang District, Nepal

Hannah, L., 1992, *African people, African parks: an evaluation of development initiatives as a means of improving protected area conservation in Africa*, Conservation International, Washington, DC

Heinen, J.T. and Mehta, J.N., 1999, Conceptual and legal issues in the designation and management of conservation areas in Nepal. *Environmental Conservation*, **26**: 21–29.

His Majesty's Government of Nepal (HMG), Ministry of Tourism, 1996, *Nepal tourism statistics*, Modern Printing, Kathmandu

HMG, 1997, Solu-Khumbu District, Topographical Map, 1:50 000 scale. Map sheets No. 2786 03 and 04, and 2886 15 and 16, Survey Department, Nepal

Hough, J.L. and Sherpa, M.N., 1989, Bottom up vs. basic needs: integrating conservation and development in the Annapurna and Michiru Mountain conservation areas of Nepal and Malawi. *Ambio*, **18**: 434–441

IUCN, 1991, *Caring for the earth: a strategy for sustainable living*, IUCN/UNEP/WWF, Gland

IUCN/UNEP/WWF, 1993, *Caring for the earth: a strategy for survival*, Reed International, London

Kraijo, A., 1997, *Agriculture or forestry: a case study in Ghandruk, Nepal of the motivation of villagers to give up agricultural production and to plant trees*, thesis submitted to the Faculty of Public Administration and Public Policy, University of Twente, The Netherlands

Mathiessen, P. and Laird, T., 1995, *East of Lo Monthang – in the land of Mustang*, Timeless Books, New Delhi

Mattle, B., 1999, *Räumliche und zeitliche Entwicklung der touristischen Infrastruktur in Khumbu, Nepal*, Diplomarbeit Philosphisch-naturwissenschaftliche Fakultät, Universität Bern

Mehta, J. and Kellert, S., 1998, Local attitudes toward community-based conservation policy and programmes in Nepal: a case study in the Makalu-Barun Conservation Area. *Environmental Conservation*, **25**: 320–333

McNeely, J.A. (ed.), 1995, *Expanding partnerships in conservation*, Island Press, Washington, DC

Nepal, S., 1997a, Sustainable tourism, protected areas, and livelihood needs of local communities in developing countries. *The International Journal of Sustainable Development and World Ecology*, **4**: 123–135

Nepal, S., 1997b, *Tourism induced environmental changes in the Everest region: some recent evidence*, Centre for Development and Environment Institute of Geography, University of Bern, Switzerland, unpublished research report

Nepal, S.K. and Weber, K.E., 1993, *Struggle for existence, park–people conflict in the Royal Chitwan National Park, Nepal*, Asian Institute of Technology, Bangkok

Nepal, S.K. and Weber K.E., 1995a, *Managing protected areas under conditions of conflict*, unpublished research report, Asian Institute of Technology, Bangkok

Nepal, S.K. and Weber, K.E., 1995b, Managing resources and resolving conflicts: national parks and local people. *The International Journal of Sustainable Development and World Ecology*, **2**: 11–25

Peissel, M., 1967, *Mustang, a lost Tibetan kingdom*. Book Faith, New Delhi (reprint)

Poudel, P.C., 1996, *Tourist resources and environmental appraisal in Pokhara Region, Nepal: a geographical analysis*, PhD thesis Department of Geography, Banaras Hindu University, India

Sagarmatha Pollution Control Committee (SPCC), 1997, *Annual report for the fiscal year 1996–1997*

Shackley, M., 1996, Too much room at the inn? *Annals of Tourism Research*, **23**: 449–462

Snellgrove, D., 1989, *Himalayan pilgrimage: a study of Tibetan religion by a traveller through western Nepal*, Shambhala Publications Inc., Boston

Sowernine, J. and Shrestha, A., 1994, *Recommendations for waste management/recycling plan for ACAP and ecotourism development project in the Ghalekharka–Sikles region*, unpublished report

Stevens, S.F., 1993, *Claiming the high ground. Sherpas, subsistence, and environmental change in the highest Himalaya*, University of California Press, Berkeley, CA

Tucci, G., 1977, *Journey to Mustang 1952*, Ratna Pustak Bhandar, Kathmandu (reprint)

Wells, M.P., 1994, Parks tourism in Nepal: reconciling the social and economic opportunities with the ecological and cultural threats. In *Protected area economics and policy. Linking conservation and sustainable development*, M. Munasinghe and J. McNeely, eds, pp. 319–331, IBRD, Washington DC

Wells, M., Brown, K. and Hannnah, L., 1992, *People and parks, linking protected areas with local communities*, The World Bank/WWF/USAID, Washington, DC

West, P.C. and Brechin, S.R. eds, 1991, *Resident peoples and national parks: social dilemmas and strategies in international conservation*, University of Arizona Press, Tucson, AZ

WRI/IUCN/UNEP, 1992, *Global biodiversity strategy*, WRI/IUCN/UNEP

7 Tourism, 'national parks' and private lands

GAVIN PARKER AND NEIL RAVENSCROFT

Introduction

In its recent policy statement on the future development of tourism in Britain, the government asserts that national park authorities have a 'key role to play in tourism' (Department for Culture, Media and Sport, 1999, p. 34). In particular, they are seen to promote recreation opportunities, to provide information and interpretation to visitors, and to protect the 'special qualities' of their parks. Rather than act as the principal providers of recreation and tourism opportunities, therefore, the authorities are seen predominantly to act as catalysts, bringing together local, regional and national agencies, interests and businesses, to plan, develop and manage recreation and tourism within national parks.

In contrast to the common model of national parks as predominantly owned and managed by the nation, this chapter considers an alternative scenario, which is characterised by a plurality of ownership and management interests. Rather than unified public ownership, the model of national parks that has developed in England and Wales (the only countries in the UK to have developed a system of national parks) consists of a rich variety of owners, managers and land uses. While the public and former public sector (the utility owners privatised under the Conservative governments of the 1980s) remain the dominant landowners (owning approximately one-quarter of all the land), the majority of individual land owners continue to be working farmers (MacEwen and MacEwen, 1982; Rural Development Commission, 1998). This is very much as John Dower, the architect of the system, intended, in his influential report to government in 1945, where he described his vision of national parks as:

> an extensive area of beautiful and relatively wild country in which, for the nation's benefit ... characteristic landscape beauty is strictly preserved ... while established farming use is effectively maintained (Dower, 1945, para. 4).

This definition was later embellished, primarily to reveal the full extent of the aims of national parks:

> A national park is an area of natural and usually unenclosed country, which has been protected by law against spoilation, and in which facilities have been provided for its enjoyment by the public (Chessell, 1946, p. 16).

Rather than the conservation of nature *per se*, therefore, the purpose of national parks in England and Wales has been specifically related to the dual aims of landscape protection and informal outdoor recreation (which includes tourism). That has been within a privately owned framework dominated by the primary sector interests of agriculture, forestry and, to a lesser extent, mining. While seemingly constraining tourism development, given that very little land in any of the parks is dedicated solely to recreation (MacEwen and MacEwen, 1987), it is equally argued by some that the myriad of small-scale entrepreneurs operating within the fabric of a privatised economy may create greater opportunities than would otherwise exist (Byrne and Ravenscroft, 1989; Ravenscroft, 1990; Butler, 1998; Department for Culture, Media and Sport, 1999). The UK national parks now attract upwards of 76 million visitors (Countryside Commission, 1996) but it should be borne in mind, however, that large-scale UK and international tourism was not envisaged for the parks (contra to the US, Canadian and New Zealand systems anotated in Nelson and Booth and Simmons, this volume) at the time of the 1949 Act. This burgeoning scale of amenity use poses a dilemma for national parks, and wider countryside, planning and policy.

However, as we argue, issues about the nature and development of recreation and tourism, as expressions of one of the original purposes of the parks, have largely been down-played in a wider – and deeper – debate about the relationship between private property and public policy. We note the often-conflicting roles of local government and administration which, while being charged with fulfilling nationally derived public policy, are also answerable to a local electorate which has other values and agendas. At the top of these agendas is, invariably, the maintenance of private property rights and the exercise of the exclusivity which these rights provide (Ravenscroft, 1992, 1995; Parker, 1996a,b).

Rather than the implementation of what is essentially a managerialist rhetoric of conservation and recreation in national parks, government has thus been forced to focus public policy on the ways in which farmers and landowners can be 'persuaded' to modify – or compromise – their values. This has involved an enduring commitment to a corporatist basis upon which to promulgate public policy. Farmers and landowners have agreed, voluntarily, to provide certain public goods, such as conservation and recreation, in return for a commitment by government not to compromise their libertarian freedom, particularly with respect to the ownership, management and exclusivity of their land (Winter, 1991).

While ten areas of England and Wales have been designated as national parks, and more than 40 million people visit them annually, the chapter concludes that neither of the original policy aims has been achieved fully. Allowing farmers and landowners their freedom may have led to some recreational access, while conservation payments may have saved some individual sites, but in overall terms, farming has led to severe landscape changes, as agriculture and forestry practices have become increasingly mechanised and intensified (National Parks Review Panel, 1991; Curry, 1994). In return, government has received, at best, an uneven flow of recreation opportunities. At one end of the scale, most landowners have remained reluctant to allow informal access to their land (Peak District National Park Planning Board, 1998), while at the other, some major tourist developments have been undertaken which are of such a scale that their very presence in national parks is open to question (Council for National Parks, 1990; Council for the Protection of Rural England, 1990; Davies et al, 1991a).

Countryside access and the evolution of national parks

Although England and Wales possess a comprehensive rights of way network which has traditionally facilitated access to the countryside, the issue of gaining greater freedom, particularly to walk at will across open land, has long driven countryside access policy. Indeed, it was this debate which led to the first enquiry into the designation of national parks, conducted by the Addison Committee (1931). In suggesting a hierarchy of designated areas, in which nature conservation objectives would be catered for separately from recreational ones, the Addison Committee established the idea of 'reserves', upon which national park designation was eventually, if not explicitly, based. However, rather than Addison, it is widely recognised that the 'mass trespasses' of the 1930s were the turning point in the pre-World War II campaign to open up new areas of the countryside for public use (Hill, 1980; Rothman, 1982; Stephenson, 1989). As such, national parks became strongly identified by policy makers as a potential remedy for the 'access issue', particularly as it related to unencumbered access to the uplands of the Peak District.

Following the formation of the Ramblers' Association in 1935, Arthur Creech-Jones tabled the Access to Mountains Bill in 1936. Although Parliament initially opposed the Bill, as it had all preceding access bills, this particular proposal did proceed to the statute book in 1939. However it did so in an 'emasculated' form (Shoard, 1987). Its opponents had made numerous amendments, the principal modification being to make open access subject to voluntary and negotiated agreement, with unauthorised access amounting to criminal trespass (Cherry, 1975; Holt, 1998). Although later repealed, the Access to Mountains Act (1939) was at the time a stark indication of the power and attitude of the land lobby towards extending access rights. It illustrated the way that they had effectively dismantled a pro-access Bill. The measures in the Act left the access situation in a worse position than previously (Cherry, 1975), while also inevitably compromising the introduction of new legislation a decade later (Holt, 1998).

Events during the World War II did suggest that a change of attitude was occurring, and that the 'battle' to secure national parks effectively had been won (Chessell, 1946; Holt, 1998). The Scott Report (1942) provided strong support for the government, which believed that it could simultaneously promote both the protection of the countryside and its use for recreation. Notwithstanding the agricultural primacy of the Scott Report (1942), with its wartime exhortation that 'every acre counts' (Curry, 1994; Winter, 1996), public opinion was increasingly in favour of extending access (Cherry, 1975), particularly during the 1940s when the new national parks were being mooted. This opinion was reflected in several official reports of the time, particularly the Hobhouse Report (1947) which favoured both the introduction of national parks, as well as the extension of a right to roam over all open land. Referring to the 'right to roam', the Hobhouse Report concluded with considerable foresight that it would be a significant national investment, in terms of both health and developing new country pursuits and interests.

While it cannot be doubted that the post-war Labour government had a commitment to access, it is equally certain that it recognised that the international political economy of the late 1940s dictated the utmost priority for agriculture (Marsden et al., 1993). This priority was primarily stressed through structural reform and support of farming (Gibbard and Ravenscroft, 1997; Gibbard *et al.*, 1999). Further protection of agriculture was provided through the new statutory planning system introduced in the Town and Country Planning Act (1947). It was therefore of little surprise that national park designation, in the National Parks and Access to the Countryside Act (1949) came at the end of the government's legislative programme. By the time of enactment, national parks effectively had to fit into a rural economy already dominated by commercial agriculture and regulated by a land use system dominated by urbanised forms of control (Marsden *et al.*, 1993).

Even within this context, the passage of the bill was stormy, with the government's commitment to open access progressively weakened and finally extinguished as a promised £50 million land fund failed to materialise (Cherry, 1975; Blunden and Curry, 1990). The Act was eventually forged as a political compromise with no 'right to roam' included. It contained little in the way of new rights of access, instead building upon the initial voluntary, piecemeal approach prepared by the 1939 Act, with a voluntary system of access agreements backed up with limited powers to compulsorily purchase land for access (termed access orders). Instead of rejecting the voluntarism of the 1939 Act, therefore, the 1949 Act actually enshrined it, and in the process subjugated recreational access to both farming and nature conservation interests.

National park designation and management structure

Although there was little doubt that the 1949 Act would contain legislation to establish national parks, debate raged about which areas should be designated, and what designation should actually entail. In the event, ten national parks were identified, seven in England and three in Wales, with all of them being designated within the first six years of the Act. However, none conformed to the definition of a national park as later laid down by the International Union for the Conservation of Nature and Natural Resources (IUCN). Rather, designation under the 1949 Act was essentially related to land use planning: all land and buildings within national park boundaries were to be subject to strict development control. While permitted agriculture and forestry operations were to continue, designation was intended to prevent other forms of development, particularly related to the spread of urban areas.

In recognition of the dual conservation/recreation orientation of national parks, the 1949 Act introduced a number of other designations to meet specific aims. These included:

- *Areas of Outstanding Natural Beauty* (AONBs) – smaller areas and closer to large conurbations than national parks, and without the overt recreation and tourism remit
- *National Nature and Marine Reserves* (NNRs and NMRs) – areas of significance for nature conservation, to be either owned or managed by the state, with access strictly controlled
- *Sites of Special Scientific Interest* (SSSIs) – areas of scientific significance, in which owners would only be allowed to undertake potentially damaging

operations once they had notified the government conservation agency (notification in practice leading to the negotiation of a management agreement, through which the landowner was paid not to damage the site) and

- *Access Agreements*, a formal mechanism through which a local authority could negotiate public access to private land, in return for compensation.

Given the eventual land-use planning orientation of the parks, their administration required little more than, in most cases, the formation of a special committee of the relevant local authorities. In addition to local authority nominees to these committees, central government could appoint a number of representatives. Where national parks straddled local administrative boundaries, as they did in the Lake District and Peak District National Parks, joint planning boards were established, again combining local and national representatives. In each case, the chair of the committee or board was designated as National Park Officer. While the committees remained fully part of local government structure, with no budgetary or policy independence, the Planning Boards did gain a certain level of autonomy, particularly once they had drawn up an approved park plan (Williams, 1985).

It was certainly the intention of the 1949 Act that all the national parks should be overseen by planning boards. However, this aim was frustrated by county councils unwilling to forgo some of their power, particularly if this might have frustrated their wider aims and responsibilities within the parks (MacEwen and MacEwen, 1982). This has undoubtedly led to each of the national parks developing in its own way, with little common voice between them, no common representation in either promulgating or challenging public policy, and little attention given to issues such as the dissemination of good practice (Simmons, 1974; National Parks Review Panel, 1991).

It was not until the Environment Act (1995) that this situation was challenged formally, when the Secretary of State for the Environment was given the power to establish National Park Authorities in all new and existing national parks. While these authorities will take over all planning functions, as well as the responsibility for all staffing and management issues within the parks, Hughes (1996) cautions that their power will be constrained by the commitments which they have inherited from their predecessor committees and planning boards.

Although no new national parks have been created since the original ten (and none have thus far been created in Scotland at all), two new areas (the New Forest and the Norfolk Broads) have gained equivalent status. Indeed, despite not being referred to as national parks, the latest two are in some respects closer to the IUCN definition than the original ten. This is particularly the case for the New Forest, which has the defined boundaries characteristic of a park, while being predominantly in public ownership (the Forestry Commission) and used extensively for open access and informal recreation.

Informal recreation in national parks

Although the 1949 Act was hailed as a 'walkers' charter' (Blunden and Curry, 1990), there was no formal right to roam, as had been envisaged originally, since the government preferred to let the 'sleeping dogs of access by custom lie' (Marsden *et al.*, 1993). Rather than the right to roam, the principal mechanism for improving public access was the access agreement, with its adherence to the voluntary principal. In their review on the fortieth anniversary of the Act, Blunden and Curry (1990) argue that Lewis Silkin (then Minister for Town and Country Planning) had envisaged that local authorities would negotiate agreements over the best walking country in each national park. As they readily point out, ' ... this fine aim has not been realised' (Blunden and Curry, 1990, p. 136).

Access agreements place voluntarism at the core of the Act. The inference is that by 1949, landowners were ready and waiting to 'grant' access and that there was no need to legislate (further) to achieve this; all that was needed was an access structure to be provided. Access agreements, and the powers to make compulsory Access Orders, are the mechanisms through which national parks were envisaged to become 'national' in the access sense. Since their inception access agreements and orders have not been taken up widely by local authorities and landowners. Land under access agreement/order now totals about 35 000 hectares (less than 2.5 per cent of land within the national parks), and has changed little in the last decade (Shoard, 1987; Curry, 1994; Parker, 1996a; Meacher, 1998). Over half of the access agreements (totalling 20 120 hectares as at October 1998) have been made in the Peak District (Peak District National Park Planning Board, 1998). However, even in this case the Authority has not been able to achieve its full objectives, as it stated in a recent submission on access to open country:

> We have worked closely with landowners and land management interests for almost 50 years. We are proud of what we have achieved together through voluntary access agreements given the constraints on our resources. However, our experience in the past has been one of a lack of willingness by owners to agree new access areas. There are still 80 square miles of moorland ... in the National Park with little or no public access (Peak District National Park Planning Board, 1998, p. 1)

There is certainly an argument that more might have been achieved, in terms of volume, quality and location, without access agreements. As Blunden and Curry (1990) argue with respect to the 1949 Act, the very lack of any commitment to, or mechanism for achieving, freedom to roam cast a die on future policy development. Ultimately, they conclude, access agreements did not amount to a '... ramblers' charter to roam at will' (Blunden and Curry, 1990, p. 130); this was, and remains, one of the great failings in national parks, particularly when assessed against the criteria of the recreationists who pressured for countryside access reform in the inter-war period.

It has been widely argued that landowner responses to increasing public access have been promulgated against a background of unrelenting visitor pressure (Sidaway, 1998). This has been particularly apparent in national parks situated in popular tourist and day visitor destinations, such as the Lake District, the Peak District and Dartmoor National Parks. In each of these cases there are countless references to visitor impacts, with Dartmoor apparently no longer even experiencing a decline in pressure outside the traditional holiday season (Dartmoor National Park Planning Committee, 1995).

However, it is far from clear what this increasing level of pressure represents, given that the overall number of recreation and tourism trips in England and Wales has not grown as rapidly as past predictions have indicated (House of Commons Environment Committee, 1995). Indeed, Coalter (1996) suggests that there has not been any appreciable increase in the volume of visitors over the past ten years. What has occurred, however, is a shift in participation, particularly towards greater activity and diversity in patterns of demand (Butler, 1998). This, argues Sidaway (1998), has led to a shift in impacts, away from pressure on key sites, and towards a greater number of more isolated impacts, relating to particular types of activity.

While landowners and national park authorities continue to use the rhetoric of 'unrelenting' pressure, the House of Commons Environment Committee (1995) has postulated that the impacts are becoming more cultural than physical. This has had the effect of shifting the emphasis of concern from sites which are managed specifically for recreation and tourism, to the wider countryside in the parks, which has traditionally experienced very little pressure (Sidaway, 1998). When allied to the Labour government's commitment to extend a public 'right to roam' over such country (Department of the Environment, Transport and the Regions, 1998, 1999), new patterns of recreation in national parks will present major challenges for landowners and planners.

Such new patterns and practices of leisure in the countryside have also added to mounting pressure on landowners and managers to open up more access land. The response from the Country Landowners' Association (CLA) has largely taken the form of increased support for the voluntary approach. In successive policy documents (CLA, 1991, 1996, 1998a,b) the efficacy and benefits of an improved system of voluntary cooperation have been exhorted. In legitimising this stance, the CLA has made full use of a 'discourse of stewardship' that portrays private landowners as responsible, competent, productive and best equipped to provide recreational opportunities on a voluntary basis in rural areas (Parker, 1996a).

Planning for recreation and tourism

Apart from informal recreation, national parks are also favoured locations for a number of large-scale tourist developments and development proposals, often related to accommodation and associated 'entertainment'. Examples within national parks include the Langdale timeshare development in the Lake District, the visitor facilities and farm shop complex at Chatsworth House in the Peak District and the National Motor Museum at Beaulieu in the New Forest, with rejected proposals including a heritage gold mine at Clogau in Snowdonia and a holiday village at White Cross Bay in the Lake District. There are also examples of developments near national parks which, while outside the boundaries, have a direct impact on tourism within the parks. Examples of these include Alton Towers theme park near the Peak District, Summerwest World holiday park near Exmoor and a Lakewoods holiday village at Market Weighton near the North York Moors.

There is much concern about the impact of these types of developments, in terms of their visual intrusion, traffic generation and provision for activities which are inconsistent with national park designation (Council of National Parks, 1990). However, as developers are eager to assert, they do provide local employment and a focus for economic development in areas which are badly affected by the decline of primary industries such as agriculture and forestry (Davies *et al.*, 1991b; Elson *et al.*, 1998). This was recognised formally in the Environment Act (1995), which placed a statutory duty on national park authorities to seek to foster the economic and social well-being of their local communities.

Clearly, different types of development present different types of issues and problems. Research by Davies *et al.* (1991a) indicates that, in general, holiday village developments have been welcomed, on the basis that their positive economic benefits outweigh their limited environmental and social impacts. Theme parks and other such recreational attractions, on the other hand, are seen to be problematic, with major visual and environmental intrusions compounded by the generation of a high volume of traffic over a very limited period of time. In all cases, the research found that where proposals for public enjoyment have conflicted with the preservation and enhancement of natural beauty, government guidance (Department of the Environment, 1976) has prevailed, to the extent that the development proposals have been dismissed (Davies *et al.*, 1991b). This is supported by more recent research (Elson *et al.*, 1998), which found little evidence of active attempts by the national park authorities to foster the economic and social well-being of their communities through support for such development proposals.

Notwithstanding apparent adherence to national guidelines, much concern remains about the extent to which large scale development is permitted, even when there is little apparent relationship between the theme of the development and the qualities of the national park (MacEwen and MacEwen, 1987; Council for the Protection of Rural England, 1990; Curry, 1994). This is especially acute in relation to road building, quarrying and the location of power stations. In addition, Hughes (1996) argues that there is little evidence of the preservation of local building styles and materials in the developments which are allowed, while Williams (1985, p. 365) suggests that, rather than promoting small-scale local developments, it is precisely these which have been 'rigidly excluded' from national parks.

Discussion

Since national parks were first designated there has been intensive socio-economic and cultural change in the UK. Many of those changes were not, and could not, have been foreseen or planned for, and the way that such developments have affected the parks have been diverse. There has been increased visitor pressure, new roads, large-scale mining demand, more general pressure for building development (especially for second homes, timeshares and holiday villages) and an underlying decline of farm incomes. In the face of these changes, Hughes (1996) argues that there is very little to distinguish the activities of national park authorities from those of similar authorities operating outside the park boundaries. Indeed it is arguable that, in singling out particular areas to be known as national parks, the resulting recreation and tourist pressure has effectively destroyed the integrity of the original designation (Shoard, 1980; MacEwen and MacEwen, 1982).

On the face of it, therefore, the 1949 Act has produced a style of national park wholly unsuited to the purposes for which it was designed, access arrangements which, since the early 1950s, have been little used outside the Peak District National Park and a system of development planning and control which is largely ineffective in the face of major development proposals. From this reading, it would certainly appear that national parks are very much creatures of their time, born of a post-war optimism that farmers and landowners would make appropriate custodians of a 'national' countryside, and that local political structures would use the designation creatively, to adhere to the responsibilities that the 1949 Act had placed upon them.

The Act was thus clearly constructed, by the government, on the basis that opportunities for recreation could be created through voluntary agreement with the new breed of responsible farmers and rural custodians. Such was the apparent faith in this mechanism that, in contrast to nature conservation interests, no executive agency for recreation and tourism was deemed necessary. Rather, the National Parks Commission operated in an advisory capacity for national parks planning until 1968, whereupon it was replaced by the Countryside Commission, with its advisory remit extending to all rural areas.

In effect, therefore, the success of the 1949 Act was predicated overwhelmingly on a benign view of landowning and farming, which itself had just undergone major restructuring. Although there were many who supported this view, Holt (1998) and Stephenson (1989) both suggest that it was not ubiquitous, even within the Ministry of Agriculture. Equally, while there was little indication of the pressures which would subsequently face agriculture, the divergence between the message of custodianship and the reality of exclusion was already there to be seen: both by the reaction to the 'mass trespasses' of the 1930s, and by the content of a dissenting minority report appending the Scott Report in 1942 (see Cullingworth, 1975; Curry, 1993). Notwithstanding the benign view of agriculture, the failure to give the National Parks Commission the same status as the Nature Conservancy was a sign of poor commitment, even in 1949. That executive status should take a further 30 years to achieve, by the Countryside Commission in 1981, merely compounds this apparent lack of commitment.

Rather than the rhetoric of a 'ramblers' charter', therefore, the 1949 Act was much more aligned with a gift relationship between landowner and non-landowner (see Mauss, 1990). Averring to the popular conception that landowners had long given access voluntarily (cf. Mais, 1948), Stephenson (1989) comments that few officials in the Ministry of Town and Country Planning believed that they could achieve more than to 'regularise' this relationship through negotiated access agreements. Hay (1975) comments that the alternate side of the gift is the threat: that any compulsion to provide access would lead to a swift withdrawal of existing voluntary access. Not surprisingly, the Country Landowners' Association is currently employing a similar rhetoric when faced with renewed pressure for free access to open country (Country Landowners' Association, 1998a).

In offering some apology for the lack of vision towards recreation in the Act, it has been suggested (Blunden and Curry, 1990) that a number of issues need to be taken into account. These issues relate to either demand or finance, with a growth in demand for an increasing range of recreational opportunities coinciding with a lack of local authority finance to secure access. It is certainly the case that some activities that are popular today did not exist in 1949 (see Butler, 1998, for a list of such activities). However, to suggest that shortcomings can be explained by the range of possibilities increasing faster than the mechanism for dealing with them (including finance) is to miss the central point that the mechanisms were never adequately developed in the first place.

Conclusion

Whatever their actual status in terms of the IUCN definition, national parks in England and Wales have retained a popular image as the pinnacle of land use planning. This standing is based outwardly on the high ideals of an integrated countryside driven by farming, informed by good conservation science and open to public access and enjoyment. The actuality is somewhat different, however. The prevailing view of agriculture has never been seen to converge with those of either conservation or recreation. The designation of national park status has acted as a magnet for attracting visitors, leaving some parks suffering high degrees of congestion, erosion and pollution, as well as 'cultural conflict'; the demand for access to open country has largely gone unheeded; and national park committees and boards have been largely powerless to prevent the development of new roads, water schemes, mine workings and visitor attractions within park boundaries (MacEwen and MacEwen, 1982; Williams, 1985; Hughes, 1996). This is the result, argues Cherry (1975), of a long-term commitment to multiple objectives.

Hence the story of national parks in England and Wales is scarred with compromise and its resulting effects. Pressures on national parks and land within these areas have been played down or ignored by central government, which has instead concentrated on a range of other measures and mechanisms, such as rights of way improvements, country parks and agri-environment schemes that provide monetised access opportunities. This context has meant that national parks have in effect lived a lie, both as to their eponymity, as well as to their actual ability to provide what tourists, visitors or local people want.

References

Addison, C., 1931, *Report of the National Park Committee*, Cmnd 3851, HMSO, London
Blunden, J. and Curry, N., 1990, *A people's charter?* HMSO, London
Butler, R.W., 1998, Rural recreation and tourism In *The geography of rural change*, B. Ilbery, ed., pp. 211–232, Addison-Wesley Longman, Harlow
Byrne, P and Ravenscroft, N., 1989, *Diversification and alternative land use for the landowner and farmer*, Humberts, Chartered Surveyors, London
Cherry, G., 1975, *Environmental planning Vol II. National parks and recreation in the countryside*, HMSO, London
Chessell, H., 1946, *National parks for Britain*, Cornish Brothers Ltd, Birmingham
Coalter, F., 1996, Leisure studies, leisure policy and social citizenship: the limits of welfare or a failure of welfare institutions? Paper presented at the joint LSA/VVS conference *Leisure, time and space in a transitory society*, 12–14 September 1996, Wageningen, The Netherlands
Council of National Parks, 1990, *A vision for national parks*, Evidence to the National Park Review Panel (the Sandford Committee), Council for National Parks, London

Council for the Protection of Rural England, 1990, *Our finest landscapes*. Evidence to the National Park Review Panel (the Sandford Committee), Council for the Protection of Rural England, London

Country Landowners' Association, 1991, *Recreation and access in the countryside: a better way forward*, Country Landowners' Association, London

Country Landowners Association, 1996, *Access 2000*, Country Landowners' Association, London

Country Landowners' Association, 1998a, *Access to the countryside, Volume 1: the CLA proposal*, A response to the government's consultation paper June 1998, Country Landowners' Association, London

Country Landowners Association, 1998b, *Access to the countryside, Volume II: the CLA proposal – supporting papers*, Country Landowners' Association, London

Countryside Commission, 1996, *Visits to national parks. Summary of the 1994 findings*, Countryside Commission, Cheltenham

Cullingworth, J., 1975, *The history of environmental planning 1939–69 Vol 1*, HMSO, London

Curry, N., 1993, Countryside planning: look back in anguish. Inaugural Professorial Lecture, 28 April 1993, Cheltenham & Gloucester College of Higher Education, Mimeo

Curry, N.R., 1994, *Countryside recreation, access and land use planning*, E. & F.N. Spon, London

Dartmoor National Park Planning Committee, 1995, Written evidence in *The environmental impact of leisure activities, Vol II, minutes of evidence*, House of Commons Environment Committee session 1994–5, Fourth Report, HMSO, London

Davies, H.W.E., Ravenscroft, N., Bishop, K. and Gosling, J.A., 1991a, *The planning system and large-scale tourism and leisure developments*, National Economic Development Office, London

Davies, H.W.E., Ravenscroft, N., Bishop, K. and Gosling, J.A., 1991b, *The planning system and large-scale tourism and leisure developments: case studies*, National Economic Development Office, London

Department for Culture, Media and Sport, 1999, *Tomorrow's tourism: a growth industry for the Millennium*, Department of Culture, Media and Sport, London

Department of the Environment, 1976, *Report of the National Parks Policies Review Committee*, Circular 4/76, HMSO, London

Department of the Environment, Transport and the Regions, 1998, *Access to the open countryside in England and Wales*, Consultation Paper, Department of the Environment, Transport and the Regions, London

Department of the Environment, Transport and the Regions, 1999, *Access to the open countryside in England and Wales: the government's framework for action*, Department of the Environment, Transport and the Regions, London

Dower, J., 1945, *National parks in England and Wales* Cmnd. 6628, HMSO, London

Elson, M., Steenberg, C. and Downing, L., 1998, *Rural development and land use planning policies*, Rural Research Report No. 38, Rural Development Commission, Salisbury, UK

Gibbard, R. and Ravenscroft, N., 1997, The reform of agricultural holdings law. In *The reform of property law*, P. Jackson and D.C. Wilde eds, pp. 111–126, Dartmouth Publishing Co., Aldershot

Gibbard, R., Ravenscroft, N. and Reeves, J., 1999, The popular culture of agricultural law reform. *Journal of Rural Studies* (forthcoming)

Hay, D., 1975, Property, authority and the criminal law. In *Albion's fatal tree: crime and society in eighteenth century England*, D. Hay, P. Linebaugh, J.G. Rule, E.P. Thompson and C. Winslow, eds, pp. 17–63, Allen Lane, London

Hill, H., 1980, *Freedom to roam. The struggle for access to Britain's moors and mountains*, Moorland Publishing, Ashbourne

Hobhouse, A., 1947, *Report of the National Park Committee (England and Wales)*, Cmnd 6628, HMSO, London

Holt, A., 1998, *Winning the right to roam*, Ramblers' Association, London

House of Commons Environment Committee, 1995, *The environmental impact of leisure activities, Vol I*, Session 1994–5, Fourth Report, HMSO, London

Hughes, D., 1996, *Environmental law*, 3rd edn, Butterworths, London

MacEwen, A. and MacEwen, M., 1982, *Conservation or cosmetics? The story of Britain's National Parks*, Allen & Unwin, London

MacEwen, A. and MacEwen, M., 1987, *Greenprints for the countryside? The story of Britain's national parks*, Allen & Unwin, London

Mais, S., 1948, *The countryside and how to enjoy it*, Odhams Press, London

Marsden, T., Murdoch, J., Lowe, P., Munton, R. and Flynn, A., 1993, *Constructing the countryside*, UCL Press, London

Mauss, M., 1990, *The gift. The form and reason for exchange in archaic societies* (trans. W. Halls), Routledge, London

Meacher, M., 1998, Labour Party Conference Speech, quoted in Ramblers Association web pages October 1998. At http://ww.ramblers.org.uk/accnews.html

National Parks Review Panel, 1991, *Fit for the future*, Publication CCP 334, Countryside Commission, Cheltenham

Parker, G., 1996a, ELMs disease? Citizenship, stewardship and corporatism in the English countryside. *Journal of Rural Studies*, **12**: 399–412

Parker, G., 1996b, *Citizens rights and private property rights in the English countryside*, unpublished PhD thesis, University of Bristol

Peak District National Park Planning Board, 1998, *Annual Report 1997–8*, Peak District National Park Planning Board, Bakewell

Ravenscroft, N., 1990, The nature and extent of diversification on rural estates in Britain. *Land Development Studies*, **7**: 83–95

Ravenscroft, N., 1992, *Recreation planning and development*, Macmillan, Basingstoke

Ravenscroft, N., 1995, Recreational access to the countryside of England and Wales: popular leisure as the legitimation of private property. *Journal of Property Research*, **12**: 63–74

Rural Development Commission, 1998, Green audit kit helps towards sustainable rural tourism. *Rural Focus*, Autumn, 18–19

Rothman, B., 1982, *The 1932 Kinder trespass*, Willow Press, Altringham

Scott, M.J., 1942, *Report of the committee on land utilisation in rural areas*, Cmnd 6378, HMSO, London

Shoard, M., 1980, *The theft of the countryside*, Maurice Temple Smith, London

Shoard, M., 1987, *This land is our land. The struggle for Britain's countryside*, Paladin Grafton Books, London

Sidaway, R., 1998, Recreation pressures on the countryside: real concern or crises of the imagination? In *Leisure management: issues and applications*, M.F. Collins and I.S. Cooper, eds, pp. 85–95, CAB International, Wallingford

Simmons, I.G., 1974, National parks in developed countries. In *Conservation in practice*, A. Warren and F.B. Goldsmith, eds, pp. 393–408, John Wiley, London

Stephenson, T., 1989, *This forbidden land*, Morland Press, Ashbourne

Williams, M.V., 1985, National parks policy 1942–1984. *Journal of Planning and Environment Law*, June 359–377

Winter, M., 1991, Agriculture and environment: the integration of policy? *Journal of Law and Society*, **18**(1): 48–63

Winter, M., 1996, *Rural politics*, Routledge, London

8 Tourism and national parks in ecologically vulnerable areas

DAVID WEAVER

Introduction

The purpose of this chapter is to consider issues associated with the status of tourism in ecologically vulnerable protected areas, using the Galapagos Islands as a case study. General issues associated with tourism activity in protected areas are first outlined. After establishing the ecological significance of the archipelago and outlining its development as a multi-designated protected area, the evolution of the Galapagos tourism sector is then briefly described. The chapter goes on to outline the various initiatives that have been implemented by park authorities to manage the tourism sector, and considers the various problems that are associated both with tourism and other activities. Finally, the discussion section presents an impact model for the Galapagos Islands, considers other issues associated with tourism, and discusses the extent to which the Galapagos case study can be extrapolated to other ecologically sensitive protected areas.

Tourism in ecologically vulnerable protected areas

The relationship between tourism and protected areas is an ambivalent one (see Chapter One and Boyd, Chapter 11). Tourism provides an increasingly important incentive to retain such areas in a relatively natural state in the face of heightened pressure from stakeholders in the agricultural, logging and mining sectors. However, this incentive value is only apparent when visitation levels are high enough to generate substantial revenue flows. At such levels, the consequences of tourism may be just as detrimental in the long term as those caused by agriculture, logging or mining.

The situation is compounded in ecologically vulnerable protected areas. It has long been recognised that these settings by their inherent nature are more severely impacted by human activity. Yet, in many cases they are more attractive to tourists, and thus more susceptible to related stresses, by merit of their outstanding natural qualities (Cohen, 1978). This vulnerability can be illustrated in a revised destination life cycle model that repositions the critical capacity threshold to the point of a much lower visitor intake (depending on the degree of vulnerability). The critical stresses in

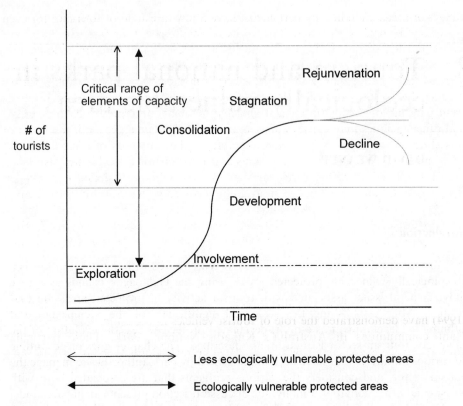

Figure 8.1. Destination life cycle in ecologically vulnerable protected areas. (Source: Weaver, 1998)

this context are more likely to occur in the 'involvement' or early 'development' stage rather than in the later 'development' stage (Figure 8.1). Hence, the management challenges posed by ecologically vulnerable parks, once the tourism sector is acknowledged as a legitimate stakeholder, are formidable.

The specific stresses potentially associated with tourism in ecologically vulnerable protected areas are diverse, and can be considered once the meaning of 'ecologically vulnerable' is clarified. This term has several dimensions. Harrison and Price (1996) refer first to ecosystems or elements of ecosystems that are inherently fragile due to their reliance upon a narrow range of environmental conditions (e.g. estuaries, other wetlands, sand dunes, coral reefs, small islands with high levels of locally adapted endemic species). They next refer to ecosystems or their constituent elements that have low resilience in relation to human activity due to extremities of topography, temperature and/or precipitation (e.g. steep mountain valleys, subarctic tundra, icecaps, high alpine meadows, deserts). To these could be added ecosystems that do not necessarily meet either of these two criteria, but which are made rare or vulnerable because of their destruction or degeneration by past human activity. These, for example, include remnants of long grass prairie in North America, and boreal or deciduous forest that remains in an essentially pristine state.

With regard to the former categories, steep mountain slopes and high alpine valleys or areas underlain by permafrost have a low threshold of tolerance for even ostensibly benign tourist activities such as small-scale tramping and primitive camping, since the associated environments are exceptionally vulnerable to erosion and other forms of disruption. In such cold climate environments, tourist-related detritus such as toilet paper and food scraps, if not removed, may remain intact for decades due to low rates of biological deterioration. Similarly, the waste residuals from parking lots, ships (in coastal and marine areas), interpretive centres, toilets and other facilities may cause extensive and lingering damage, even if the levels of waste generation and 'escape' seem tolerable by the standards of a more resilient environment. The short growing seasons and thin soils of these biomes also mean that a small tree or shrub carelessly damaged by a hiker or deliberately cut for firewood could take a century or more to be replaced by natural processes. Tourist activity, for example, has contributed significantly to the depletion of high altitude junipers in Nepal's Sagarmatha National Park (Nepal, Chapter 6; Stevens, 1993).

Parks that are ecologically vulnerable due to the presence of rare ecosystems and species, or pristine ecosystems, are also more likely to be negatively impacted by the introduction of exotic species that can opportunistically displace or disrupt the native flora and fauna. While not always the most important agent of such spread, tourism can contribute to this diffusion in a number of ways. Lonsdale and Lane (1994) have demonstrated the role of tourist vehicles in the establishment of exotic plant communities in Australia's Kakadu National Park. These particular infestations were associated with car-related infrastructure such as parking lots, but a more widespread dispersal is possible also through hikers, who may carry exotic seeds in their clothing, food supplies, or on the soles of their footwear. Compounding the management challenges is the fact that such introductions are usually inadvertent, with even the most conscientious tourists or managers therefore contributing to the problem. Other tourist activities that are especially stressful in the circumstances described above include deliberate actions such as the collection of plant or other matter (e.g. coral, fossils, fruit and berries) and the lighting of fires. Noise also can be problematic. Low overflights by tourist-carrying aircraft in high-latitude environments, introduced ironically to minimise the impacts of direct terrestrial contact, can lead to panic and disruption among fauna deep inside park areas, while at the same time causing the widespread deposition of hydrocarbon residues (Hall and Johnston, 1995). These issues are discussed below in the context of the Galapagos Islands.

The Galapagos Islands as a protected area

Setting and significance

The Galapagos archipelago consists of 13 major islands, six minor islands and 42 islets and rocks that occupy 8000 km^2 of total land area within an interior sea of 45 000 km^2 (Figure 8.2). Ecuador, which holds sovereignty over the archipelago, is located 960 kilometres to the east. The Galapagos Islands are very well known in the public consciousness as a 'living laboratory' of evolution, and this cliché is not

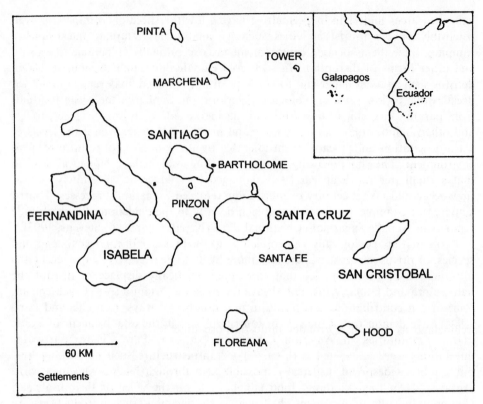

Figure 8.2. The Galapagos Islands

without justification. Among its ecological superlatives are 14 distinct types of giant tortoise and 13 varieties of finch (the so-called 'Darwin's finches' which provided the primary evidence for the theory of natural selection), all endemic to the archipelago. Other unique wildlife includes a flightless cormorant, several species of boobie, and the only species of penguin native to the northern hemisphere (GCT, 1998). With about 60 per cent of its organisms found only in the archipelago, the Galapagos has one of the world's highest rates of endemism (de Groot, 1983). It is this characteristic, conforming to Price's first category of fragile environment, that makes the area especially vulnerable to human-induced forces such as tourism. For example, a narrowly distributed, sensitive and unique species of iguana that becomes extinct in the Galapagos cannot be compensated for by the persistence of natural populations in any other location. Of particular relevance to the present topic is the tendency of some Galapagos wildlife to show little fear of humans, a trait that is due to the absence of large mammalian predators and the relative recentness of human intrusions (see Lilieholm and Romney, Chapter 10).

The ecological uniqueness and vulnerability of the Galapagos have long been recognised in attempts to formally protect the area. Several wildlife sanctuaries were established in 1934, and national park status was conferred on most of the land area in 1959 (though an actual park service was not operationalised until the late 1960s). Subsequently, the area was made a World Heritage Site in 1978, a Biosphere Reserve in 1984, and a Marine Resource Reserve in 1986. This process of multiple and overlapping designations not only recognises the unique status of the archipelago, but also serves to better ensure, at least in theory, the presence of a regulatory environment that will protect its natural qualities. At present, only about 4 per cent of the land area of the archipelago is privately owned and thus external to any formal protected area category.

Tourism in the Galapagos Islands

The period prior to 1970 was an era of incidental but uncontrolled tourism in the Galapagos islands (de Groot, 1983), suggesting that this activity may have had negative effects upon certain parts of the archipelago despite the small absolute number of visitors. Organised commercial tourism commenced in 1969 with the arrival of the first tourist vessel, which carried 76 passengers (Dex, 1998). Subsequent visitation levels to the Galapagos Islands National Park (GNP) have steadily increased, with visitor numbers approaching 70 000 per year by the late 1990s (Table 8.1). The Galapagos Islands have been described as a prestige destination on the international tourism circuit, with most of the visitors apparently meeting the criteria associated with 'soft' or passive ecotourism. That is, they tend to visit the archipelago as part of a broader multi-purpose itinerary that also includes non-ecotourism activities such as sunbathing and shopping (Nolan and Nolan, 1997). In terms of structure, tourism opportunities in the GNP are available in two modes. Cruise vessels provide on-board overnight accommodation for a period ranging from three days to two weeks, while day-trip vessels cater to tourists whose overnight accommodation is provided by local hotels. An entry fee of US$100 is obtained from every international tourist who visits the National Park. The Galapagos Islands have traditionally accounted for the majority of Ecuador's tourism revenues, though this has changed in recent years because of the development of the mainland tourism sector (Dex, 1998).

Table 8.1   Tourist arrivals to the Galapagos Islands

Year	Number	% increase	Year	Number	% increase
1970	4 500		1986	26 023	46
1974	7 500		1987	32 595	25
1975	7 000	-7	1988		
1976	6 300	-10	1989		
1977	7 788	24	1990	41 000	
1978	12 299	58	1991		
1979	11 765	-4	1992		
1980	17 445	48	1993		
1981	16 265	-7	1994	> 50 000	
1982	17 123	5	1995	55 782	
1983	17 656	3	1996	60 000	
1984	18 858	7	1997	63 000	
1985	17 840	-5	1998	65 000	

Sources: Boo (1990) and Nolan and Nolan (1997)

The inauguration of commercial tourism required the newly created park authority (the Galapagos National Park Service, or GNPS) to take tourism into consideration when planning and managing the areas under its jurisdiction. Over the next ten to fifteen years, various tourism-related management practices were adopted which have been widely described as among the most stringent in the world, at least on paper, and a model for the appropriate management of ecologically sensitive protected areas. These initiatives have come into effect in the Galapagos Islands as a result of negotiation between the park authorities, the Ecuadorian government, foreign and domestic environmental NGOs (e.g. the Charles Darwin Foundation), and environmentally progressive components of the foreign and domestic tourism sector. They are discussed individually below.

Zonation

In theory, a strategy of zonation recognises that parks must attempt to fulfil various and often incompatible objectives, and that this can be achieved by restricting the associated land uses and activities to the areas within the park that are best suited to their accommodation (Dearden and Rollins, 1993). The Galapagos Islands National Park is divided into five zones, with non-scientific tourists being allowed only in the Intensive and Extensive Visitor Zones. The former designation allows for no more than 90 visitors on shore during any given interval, while the latter zones accommodate no more than 12 visitors at a time. Initially, some 15 Visitor Zones were established, but this has since been increased to about 60 through a selective process of incremental access. As part of this strategy, tourists are prohibited from visiting islands that accommodate no exotic species (Wallace, 1993), while it is the relatively more impacted sites that are designated as Visitor Zones.

Visitation ceilings

Since the early 1970s, tourism in the Galapagos protected area has been subject to the application of visitation ceilings, not just on individual Visitor Zones but also on the protected area as a whole. A cap of 12 000 visitors was established in the 1973 Master Plan, which was raised to 25 000 in 1981 as a result of a Presidential Commission (Wallace, 1993). In the early 1990s, a new limit of 50 000 was imposed. A similar principle has been applied to the ships that provide cruises and day trips for visitors. Controlled by a system of licensing, this number has increased from about 20 vessels in the early 1970s to about 90 in the mid-1990s. As of January 1997 there were 84 cruise vessels of various capacities and standards operating in the Galapagos Islands (Dex, 1998). In effect, visitor and ship ceilings are intended to avoid the sort of *laissez-faire* and ultimately unsustainable progression of tourism development stages that is depicted in the resort cycle model (Figure 8.1).

Guide training

Because tour guides mediate the experience of contact between tourist and site, their role in the mitigation of tourism impacts in ecologically vulnerable areas is especially important. Knowledgeable and highly trained guides also minimise the need for on-site service or interpretive infrastructure, a consideration that is especially germane in those same locations. The system for providing guides in the Galapagos Islands is widely regarded as innovative and rigorous. The formal guide training programme was introduced in 1975, and makes a distinction between Naturalist guides and auxiliaries. Naturalist guides require three years of university training in the natural sciences or its equivalent, and must be fluent in English (Boo, 1990). Furthermore, they must attend an intensive one-month training course offered by the Charles Darwin Foundation, and must pass an examination to receive their license from the GNPS. Every cruise excursion and day trip must be accompanied by a licensed guide (CDRS, 1998).

On-site behaviour

No tourist can go ashore anywhere within the GNP without an accompanying licensed guide (CDRS, 1998). The normal ratio is one guide for every 16 tourists, though this may be raised to one for every 20 in the larger cruise ships (Nolan and Nolan, 1997). Aside from interpreting site attractions, the major role of the guides is to ensure adherence to an extremely rigorous protocol of tourist behaviour appropriate to such a sensitive environment. This protocol includes the restriction of hiking activity to a network of short trails about 1 ½ metres in width, limits on the amount of time spent at any one spot, a requirement that tourists must remain within a specified distance of the guide, and restrictions on noise. Also, tourists are all subjected to the fundamental rule that absolutely nothing must be removed from the environment, and nothing at all can be left behind. This includes the tourists themselves, who are not allowed to stay overnight on any of the non-settlement islands.

Tourism problems

Despite these impressive regulatory efforts, the tourism sector in the Galapagos Islands has in practice been associated with a variety of negative environmental impacts. Discussed below are the issues of on-site impacts, tourism as an agent of organism diffusion, the confinement of tourist activity to only a few sites, the relaxation of regulations, chronic underfunding and revenue uncertainties, product diversification and the impact of tourism on non-park lands.

On-site impacts

Even when followed, the innovative and comprehensive measures adopted by the GNPS have not eliminated tourism-related problems. Despite the tendency of some wildlife not to fear humans, the presence of people has caused stress among certain species. For example, as many as 95 per cent of boobies flew away from their nests when hikers approached within 2 metres, a situation that occurred frequently because of the selection of nesting sites near certain hiking trails (Burger and Gochfield, 1993). This reflects an inherent dilemma in the establishment of trails and other infrastructure, wherein the environmental circumstances that influenced their original siting may change after the trail has been constructed, as for example by the arrival of nesting birds adjacent to paths. In some cases, the site-selection process itself has proven faulty. One of the most frequently used trails, on the islet of Bartholomé, is located on sandy soils. Because of this fragile base, and because tourists are often forced to stray onto adjacent patches of vegetation in order to obtain a good foothold, the trail has degenerated into a highly visible erosional scar. Ironically, the problem could have been avoided had the trail been originally established on nearby lava beds that are largely impervious to short-term erosional effects (Wallace, 1993). The above evidence demonstrates that walking and viewing activity in the Galapagos Islands National Park, no matter how conscientiously managed, can create or exacerbate stress due to the inherent fragility of the environment.

Tourism as an agent of organism diffusion

Not all problems are so obvious or immediate in their cause-and-effect relationships. In the late 1970s, tourism vessels, no matter how high their environmental standards, were identified as a major agent for the inadvertent dissemination of insect species from island to island. Specifically, ship lights (a necessity at night for safety and navigational reasons) were found to attract many different species of butterflies and other insects, which then easily flew to land when the ships docked offshore during tourist excursions. This artificial diffusion has meant that the distribution and development of insect species can no longer be interpreted by scientists as an outcome of natural selection processes (Silberglied, 1978). The problem may be exacerbated by the presence of private yachts. These are allowed to dock off Puerto Ayora for a limited period to take on supplies, but are occasionally given permission to cruise the islands at a cost of US$200 per person per day, and then only if accompanied by a licensed guide (Nolan and Nolan, 1997).

Despite attempts to ensure that the tourists themselves do not harbour organisms that are not native to particular islands or to the Galapagos in general, it is probable that some diffusion, and thus a bridgehead effect, is also occurring as a result of on-site tourist visits. As visitation levels increase, the probability of such impacts increases in tandem. The zoning structure is intended to restrict tourism to the more resilient sites, but the tourism-induced diffusion of organisms can obviously have negative implications for areas far removed from the visitation zones or ship anchorages, suggesting that zone boundaries play only a limited role in the containment of certain impacts.

Confinement of visitation

The policy of restricting visitors to just a few of the more ecologically resilient zones may appear on the surface to be a rational way of managing tourism in ecologically vulnerable parks. However, aside from the diffusion issue raised above, tourist-confinement strategies may also potentially lead to unsustainable levels of stress within those areas where tourists are allowed to concentrate. This is simply because the space occupied by the latter areas, even with their expansion, is extremely limited in relation to the entire GNP area, thereby giving rise to high tourist densities. However, even this figure is also not entirely indicative of density levels, because of various factors that serve to further confine tourist activities within the Visitor Zones:

- Not all of the 60 sites are open at any given time, due to the periodic withdrawal of sites to allow for environmental recovery
- Many of the trails and sites are accessible only to tourists in good physical condition, thereby resulting in the overconcentration of tourists at some sites within less physically challenging locations
- Only about one-third of sites are judged to have a high level of tourist interest because of the presence of interesting and diverse wildlife populations; visitation thus tends to concentrate in these particular locations
- Temporal concentrations in certain months arise because of seasonality effects; international visitation, for example, tends to reach its highest levels in August and January.

Visitation ceiling increases

Ideally, visitor ceilings for the GPS as a whole are established taking into consideration the number and capacity of the spaces made available for tourism in the Visitor Zones. Hence, the dramatic increases in those ceilings should simply reflect comparable increases in the number of authorised visitation sites. However, this greater availability of space does not account entirely for the pattern of upward ceiling adjustments. These have also resulted from factors not directly related to ecological carrying capacity, such as political pressure exerted by various components of the tourism industry, who often argue that the advocates of lower ceilings have failed to demonstrate a solid scientific case for those restrictions. From the perspective of the GNPS, the prospect of substantial revenue increases is also an important factor (see below). A major danger inherent in this pattern is that further increases in the ceiling are likely to occur, thereby increasing the probability of a 'crash' in the local ecosystem once the critical thresholds depicted in Figure 8.1 are exceeded.

Regulation breaches

The stringent management criteria described above, including the visitation ceilings, have sometimes been relaxed in response to political, economic and other considerations. There is, for example, considerable variability in the quality and standards of the tourism ships, and those with a day trip orientation in particular. One major reason for the relaxation of these standards is the enforcement of the relevant specifications by the Navy and the Ecuadorian Tourism Commission, rather than the GNPS (Wallace, 1993). An additional consequence of this problem is the resentment that is created among those operators who adhere to high standards. Wallace (1993) also refers to the disparities in standard between the Naturalist Guides and the auxiliaries, with many of the latter being lower-paid locals appointed for political reasons rather than for their qualifications as ecotourism guides. Where the guides are ill-trained, poorly motivated or careless, the probability of inappropriate behaviour by tourists is increased. Even in the less intensive years of the early 1980s, after stringent regulations were already introduced, de Groot (1983) observed numerous violations of the rules, including littering, straying off the paths, touching or harassing animals, and excessive numbers of visitors at specific sites.

Chronic underfunding and revenue uncertainties

Many of the tourism-related problems are associated with chronic under-funding and uncertainty as to the source of operating revenues. While benefiting to a significant extent from the intervention of various NGOs (e.g. the Charles Darwin Foundation, Galapagos Conservation Trust, Conservation International, World-wide Fund for Nature), the GNP has relied heavily on entry fees as a means of facilitating the management of the Galapagos environment. Until 1995, the GNPS had direct access to all fees, but these were diverted to the federal government in 1996. As a result, the GNPS had to compete with all the other interest groups that were also lobbying for state funds. The Special Law of 1998 has partially reinstated the former funding situation (see below), though past history suggests that this concession may not continue for long, as there has always been an element of uncertainty regarding funding disbursements. Meanwhile, the GNPS depends on a patrol boat donated by a wealthy Japanese businessman, and relies on foreign NGOs to supplement feral eradication programmes and other conservation initiatives, few of which are related directly to tourism (Nolan and Nolan, 1997).

Product diversification

The tourism sector of the Galapagos Islands has traditionally emphasised 'ecotourism', though recent diversification initiatives raise further questions about the long-term sustainability of tourism. Specifically, the legalisation of sport fishing in 1995 represented a fundamental departure from the principle of non-consumptive tourism that had been implicit in the management philosophy of the islands to that point (Galapagos Coalition, 1995). More recently, large cruise ships have been allowed access to the interior sea. These concessions to 'mass' tourism, and the concurrent tendency toward the softer varieties of ecotourism, are consistent with the early 'development' stage of the destination life cycle that seems to currently characterise the Galapagos Islands.

Impacts of tourism on non-park lands

A final tourism-related problem is the effect of this sector upon the 4 per cent of the archipelago that is not included within the GNP. In conformity to park regulations, tourism ships return all their solid wastes to the town of Santa Cruz for disposal. However, the landfill in which this material is deposited is little more than an open garbage dump which fosters the multiplication of exotic vermin and contributes to ground contamination (Galapagos Coalition, 1995). In addition, some of the accelerated urban development that is occurring in the archipelago is associated with tourism. The construction of hotels and other tourism infrastructure is a direct manifestation of the latter, while the construction of housing for those migrants who arrive to seek tourism employment is an induced effect. Clearly, tourism is also a contributor to the rapid rate of population growth in the Galapagos (see below).

Non-tourism problems

Any discussion of tourism impacts in ecologically vulnerable parks must take into account the influence of the so-called 'external environment', which broadly includes other economic activities (e.g. agriculture, mining, forestry, fisheries, manufacturing), biophysical systems (e.g. climate, geophysical systems), and political and social systems, (Weaver, 1998). Yet many tourism investigations regard these external environments as tangential or ignore them altogether. This myopic approach ignores the reality that any notion of 'sustainable tourism' is meaningless if the external environment is not itself sustainable. Regarding the Galapagos Island, UNESCO in 1996 warned that the major risks to the archipelago were large-scale fishing, high levels of migration from the mainland (some of which is associated with tourism) and the introduction of non-endemic species of plants and animals. UNESCO further indicated that the World Heritage Site would be declared threatened if measures were not adopted to reverse the trend toward increased environmental degradation (Gonzalez, 1998). Interestingly, tourism was not cited as a threat, despite at least some evidence of actual or potential negative impact, as discussed above.

Introduction of non-endemic species

The Charles Darwin Research Station has identified the introduction of exotic species as the single most serious threat to the Galapagos Islands. While some of this introduction can be attributed to tourism, non-tourism sources have apparently been far more significant (CDRS, 1998). Early visits by European sailors resulted in the establishment of feral goat, pig, dog and cat populations, as well as black and brown rat populations, which have threatened the integrity of endemic species in some areas. One area alone on Isabela Island hosts a population of 80 000 feral goats, and the killing of 4900 goats on just one day in October 1998 has done little to rectify the problem in this area (GCT, 1998). Presently, an ongoing problem is posed by the escape of house pets and other domesticated animals from the small area of land that is not occupied by the National Park.

Migration

Given the archipelago's status as a province of Ecuador, the national government has long supported a policy of unrestricted migration from the mainland. The impetus for the legacy of high migration rates derives from a combination of both push and pull factors. The deep poverty and high unemployment of the Ecuadorian working class has provided an incentive for out-migration, while the Galapagos Islands have been widely perceived by mainland Ecuadorians as a promising frontier land where jobs are readily available in the fishing and service industries. Some of this migration is also associated with the prospect of tourism-related employment. Consequently, the resident population has increased from 3500 in 1974 to 10 000 in 1990 and 14 000 in 1998.

While this increase may not appear significant in comparison with the formal trans-migration programs of Brazil or Indonesia, it must be remembered that this population is confined to the 320 km^2 that are not incorporated into the National Park. Furthermore, if calculated in terms of 'resident-days' (or the number of residents multiplied by the average number of days per year that they are present in the islands), the resident presence would be much higher than the comparable figure of 'visitor days'. At any given time, there are perhaps 13 000 residents present in the archipelago, compared with about 1000 tourists. Periodically, some groups within the resident population have lobbied vocally for more land to be removed from the park for settlement purposes, or alternatively, for locals to be given more access to park authority lands for agricultural and other purposes.

Fishing

Three aspects of the fishing industry pose a threat to the environmental integrity of the Galapagos Islands. First, international factory ships carry out industrial fishing in the pelagic zone. Often intruding into the boundaries of the Galapagos Marine Resource Reserve, this exploitation is responsible for declining fish stocks, which in turn affects higher components in the regional food chain. Second, this depletion is exacerbated by the activities of smaller ships based on Ecuador's mainland. Third, the local 'traditional' fishing sector, though permitted for subsistence and small-scale marketing purposes, has been linked with the illegal commercial harvest of sea cucumbers and other marine resources that are destined for export to lucrative Asian markets. It is widely believed that this activity is being aided and abetted by Ecuadorian and international interests (Galapagos Coalition, 1995).

The power and activism of fishing interests in the Galapagos have been demonstrated on numerous occasions. From 3–15 September 1995, a group supporting the expansion of the fishing industry engaged in aggressive tactics to prevent the government from initiating controls that were to be implemented in order to protect depleted stocks. Their actions included damaging government property, occupying the National Park headquarters, blocking access to the Charles Darwin Research Station, and making threats of violence and hostage-taking against tourists and park staff (Galapagos Coalition, 1995). In the previous year, the carcasses of 39 slaughtered giant tortoises were discovered on Isabela Island, and it was widely believed that they were killed in retaliation for the government crackdown on illegal fishing (Honey, 1994). More recently, a large counter-demonstration was organised by local environmentalists and tourism operators to protest against the government's approval of large-scale fishing to within five kilometres from coast around most of the archipelago (Gonzalez, 1998).

Natural processes

A major problem for protected area managers is deciding how to react when a natural process negatively affects an ecologically sensitive resource, since such events are, by definition, a natural occurrence. Furthermore, some species of plant or animal may be vulnerable because of their inability to compete with more aggressive non-human life forms that have not been introduced by humans. Hence, the eventual extinction of such species can be seen as a normal part of evolutionary selection that does not warrant any human intervention. From a tourism perspective, however, natural disasters and other processes that lead to depletions and extinctions can have a negative impact on visitation levels. When combined with the natural tendency of the general public and many environmental managers to want to preserve threatened species, it is likely that some kind of intervention will be attempted in response to the 'disaster'. A case in point is eruption of the Cerro Azul volcano on Isabela Island on 15 September 1998, which posed a temporary threat to the local giant tortoise population (GCT, 1998).

The issue of interference becomes less problematic if the underlying causes of a 'natural disaster' have some association with human activity. The halving of the Galapagos penguin population in recent years has been attributed to the El Niño and La Niña effects (Boersma, 1998), which in turn may be influenced by global warming patterns accelerated by the release of greenhouse gases. Since this is not a 'natural' process, the case for intervention is stronger. Again, the stress is not related to tourism, but the impacts on tourism could be significant.

The Special Galapagos Law of 1998

The Special Galapagos Law, passed by the Ecuadorian government in 1998, has been greeted cautiously as a generally positive development for the environment of the archipelago. Under this legislation, an organisational structure has been established to coordinate policies and planning throughout the area. One significant implication is the transfer of additional powers to local authorities. The law also places restrictions on migration from the mainland, though various loopholes remain that could be exploited by mainlanders wishing to move to the islands. With regard to the protected area designations, the Marine Resource Reserve has been expanded to embrace a 40-mile limit around all islands, wherein only tourism and local fisheries will be allowed. Entry fee disbursements have also been re-allocated so that the GNPS and local authorities will each receive 40 per cent of the total, while the Marine Resource Reserve and quarantine authorities will each receive 5 per cent. Little mention is made specifically about tourism, despite its growth and increasing diffusion in the area (CDRS, 1998).

Discussion

As outlined in the early part of this chapter, the inherent nature of an ecologically sensitive protected area provides managers with extra challenges as they attempt to maintain both the integrity of such environments and accommodate the presence of tourists. While measures such as the Special Galapagos Law are therefore warranted, their implementation should not lead to complacency, since any legislation can be rescinded or altered by less sympathetic decision-makers. Furthermore, such laws cannot guarantee the elimination of abuses or prevent 'natural' disasters. Nor can they ensure that compliant tourist and resident behaviour are free from negative effects. Figure 8.3 summarises the impacts of tourism and other activities in the GNP. At the outset, the absence of tourist activity from the vast majority of the protected area's terrestrial component should be noted, as this would seem to indicate the retention of a mainly undisturbed environment within the park. However, the following potentially destructive influences need to be reiterated (numbers refer to numbers in Figure 8.3).

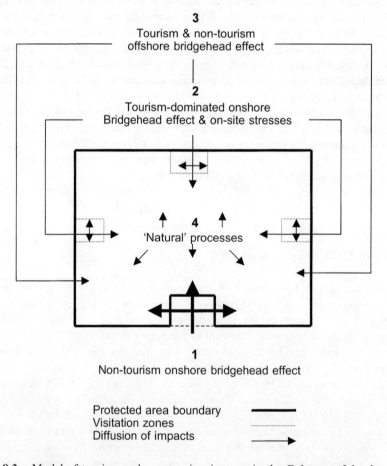

Figure 8.3.   Model of tourism and non-tourism impacts in the Galapagos Islands

1. Non-tourism onshore bridgehead effect: privately owned enclaves that comprise about 4 per cent of the archipelagic land mass continue to serve as a bridgehead for the diffusion of exotic species, especially as population pressures within these areas continue to increase. Also, these areas harbour residents who may be exploiting park resources illegally or lobbying for greater access to park lands. Thus, the influence of these enclaves is out of proportion to the amount of land that they occupy. Tourism influence is relatively minor compared to other forces in this context, but appears to be growing in conjunction with the increasing importance of tourism.

2. Tourism-dominated onshore bridgehead effect and on-site stresses: despite stringent management practices, periodically high tourist densities and on-site stresses are apparent within the Visitor Zones, while a certain amount of bridgehead effect (as tourists inadvertently contribute to the dispersal of non-native organisms) is also evident. Tourism influences are overwhelmingly dominant.

3. Tourism and non-tourism offshore bridgehead effect: an offshore effect is created by the role of tourist ships in the dispersal of organisms, as well as in the discharge of oil and other wastes and the disturbance of wildlife. A non-tourism offshore effect also exists through fishing activity, which sometimes involves the illegal use of the GNP for landing catches. In sum, there is considerable activity, both tourism and non-tourism, and both legal and illegal that occurs within the marine portion of the protected area. Tourism influences are significant in this context.

4. 'Natural' processes: the human influence in the so-called 'natural' processes can range from non-existent to significant, and can impact some or all parts of the park. These range from site factors such as volcanic eruptions and brushfires, to macro-scale processes such as global warming. Tourism influences are negligible.

Given the focus of this book, it is necessary to make additional comments about the status of tourism in the Galapagos Islands and other ecologically vulnerable protected areas. Almost inevitably, the relationship between the tourism sector and the managers of the protected area is an ambivalent one, as stated earlier. Only in rare instances has tourism been incorporated into the foundation parameters that are defined when a protected area is established. Hence, managers have not generally been accustomed to including or addressing tourism in the spectrum of relevant management issues. Also, managers are aware that tourism can and does have negative impacts upon the natural environment, and thus have tended to perceive the activity as more of an adversary than an ally, despite the trend toward sustainability (see Boyd, Chapter 11). This suspicion is likely to be even more evident in areas that have high levels of ecological sensitivity, and hence, lower carrying capacities for tourist visitation. Managers of ecologically sensitive protected areas often perceive tourism as an unwanted, additional layer of complexity that requires specific and costly management interventions, perhaps at the expense of perceived core activities.

On the other hand, whether they like it or not, park managers are becoming increasingly dependent upon revenues derived from entry fees and other tourism-related expenditures. This leads to the aforementioned paradox where increased tourism visitation is both a positive and a negative development from an environmental management perspective. This paradox can be addressed by increasing entry fees to a level where similar or greater revenues are gained from a smaller and presumably more ecologically sustainable pool of visitors. This may be effected in conjunction with a politically sensible two-tier fee structure that compels foreign visitors to pay a higher fee than domestic tourists. In the Galapagos case, foreign entry fees were doubled from US$40 to US$80 in the early 1990s, and again to US$100 in the late 1990s. Evidence from similar high demand parks suggests that this amount could probably be doubled again without seriously affecting visitor demand (see Nepal, Chapter 6e). Research from the Parc National des Volcans in Rwanda, for example, showed that non-nationals paid a daily entry fee of US$170, yet demand remained robust (Lindberg, 1991). If visitor numbers remain too high in the opinion of park managers, then increases in the entry fee can continue until the demand curve returns to a sustainable level.

Another strategy (which could be carried out concurrently) involves the introduction of site-hardening measures to gradually increase the capacity of the Visitor Zones to accommodate additional visitation, and thus generate even higher gross revenues. There is an informal consensus among Galapagos tourism operators and park managers that the park can accommodate around 70 000 visitors per year in a sustainable way under the current system (Nolan and Nolan, 1997). This may account for current levels which are in excess of the 50 000 ceiling imposed in the early 1990s. However, this could be even higher if more sites are opened, site hardening measures implemented, or the average length of stay is lowered. Wallace (1993) argues for a shift in emphasis away from wildlife-rich sites to the numerous sites that are judged to be less ecologically sensitive, but interesting from a historical or geophysical perspective. The challenge for park managers and tour guides, then, would be to successfully 'sell' these aspects of the park through effective and appropriate interpretation. What must be avoided in ecologically sensitive parks such as the GNP, as entry fees continue to escalate, is the temptation to support increased visitation purely on the grounds that the resultant revenues will somehow be sufficient to address the environmental problems created by that very influx.

The final issue is the extent to which Figure 8.3, and the issues associated with the Galapagos, are relevant to other ecologically sensitive protected areas. Many of the latter lack the spatial isolation of the GNP and the small resident population that lives in the small area of private land in its immediate proximity. Poaching and other illegal intrusions do occur, but these seem to be more limited in comparison to those that occur in ecologically sensitive parks surrounded by high-density human populations, such as Royal Chitwan National Park in Nepal and Parc National des Volcans in Rwanda. Accordingly, the same level of resource commitment required to intercept such land-based intrusions is probably not warranted in the Galapagos, although increased surveillance of the surrounding ocean may become necessary as boating activity in the region becomes more intensive. Otherwise, there are only a handful of easily monitored air gateways through which access to the archipelago can be gained.

Conclusions

Protected area designations are more frequently being used in the attempt to safeguard exceptionally fragile environments from destructive human intervention. However, the very same qualities that merit this status may tend to make such areas highly attractive to tourists, and hence vulnerable to levels of visitation that may rapidly exceed their low carrying capacities. In recognition of its unique ecological sensitivity, most of the Galapagos Islands and associated waters have been multi-designated under several protected area categories. Concurrently, a rigorous and highly regarded regulatory environment has been established to ensure that the negative impacts of the gradually increasing tourism sector are minimised. Despite these regulations, and despite the fact that tourism is excluded altogether from most of the archipelago, some negative effects have been noted in association with on-site impacts in the relatively crowded on- and off-shore zones where tourism is allowed. A more subtle impact is the role of these areas as bridgeheads for the diffusion of non-native organisms. It is reasonable to conclude on this basis that ecologically sensitive areas will inevitably experience some negative consequences as a result of tourism, no matter how ostensibly 'sustainable' the latter. For this reason, and because of the increasing reliance upon entry fee revenues, the managers of ecologically vulnerable parks such as the GNP are particularly justified in maintaining an ambivalent attitude toward tourism. They welcome the increase revenue associated with increased visitation, but must be aware of the management implications and lobbying pressures that accompany this trend. In the Galapagos, this ambivalence is reinforced by regular increases in visitation ceilings and numbers, and by recent trends toward larger cruise ships and sport fishing, which could indicate a fundamental departure from the core small-scale ecotourism principles that have hitherto characterised tourism in the park. However, even if some semblance of 'sustainable tourism' can be maintained under such circumstances, this will be rendered meaningless if the external environment that effects the archipelago is not itself sustainable. In the case of the Galapagos Islands National Park, threatening external factors include the continued expansion of feral animal populations, over-fishing, excessive migration (some of which is associated with tourism) and certain 'natural' processes that may be exacerbated by local-scale or global human actions.

References

Boersma, P., 1998, Population trends of the Galapagos penguin: impacts of El Niño and La Niña. *The Condor*, **100**: 245–253

Boo, E., 1990, *Ecotourism: the potentials and pitfalls*, Volume 2, World Wildlife Fund, Washington, DC

Burger, J. and Gochfield, M., 1993, Tourism and short-term behavioural responses of nesting masked, red-footed, and blue-footed, boobies in the Galapagos. *Environmental Conservation*, **20**: 255–259

Cohen, E., 1978, The impact of tourism on the physical environment. *Annals of Tourism Research*, **5**: 215–237

CDRS, 1998, Charles Darwin Research Station [URL document] http://polaris.net/~jpinson/welcome.html (accessed 15 February 1999)

Dearden, P. and Rollins, R. eds, 1993, *Parks and protected areas in Canada: Planning and management*, Oxford University Press, Toronto

de Groot, R., 1983, Tourism and conservation in the Galapagos Islands. *Biological Conservation*, **26**: 291–300

Dex, R., 1998, Ecuador. *International Tourism Reports*, No.3: 3–20

Galapagos Coalition, 1995, Developments in the Galapagos [URL document]   http://www.law.emory.edu/PI/GALAPAGOS/ (accessed 15 February 1999)

GCT, 1998, Galapagos Conservation Trust [URL document] http://www.gct.org/index.html (accessed 15 February 1999)

Gonzalez, M., 1998, Environment – Ecuador: A day of mourning for Galapagos Islands [URL document] http://www.oneworld.org/ips2/mar98/ecuador_env.html. (accessed 15 February 1999)

Hall, C.M. and Johnston, M.E., 1995, Introduction: Pole to pole: tourism issues, impacts and the search for a management regime in polar regions. In *Polar tourism: Tourism in the Arctic and Antarctic regions, C.M. Hall and M.E. Johnston, eds, pp. 1–26, John Wiley, Chichester*

Harrison, D. and Price, M., 1996, Fragile environments, fragile communities? An Introduction. In *People and Tourism in Fragile Environments*, M. Price, ed., pp. 1–18, John Wiley, Chichester

Honey, M., 1994, Paying the price of ecotourism. *Americas*, **46** (6): 40–47

Lindberg, K., 1991, *Policies for maximizing nature tourism's ecological and economic benefits*, World Resources Institute, Washington, DC

Lonsdale, W. and Lane, A., 1994, Tourist vehicles as vectors of weed seeds in Kakadu National Park, Northern Australia. *Biological Conservation*, **69**: 277–283

Nolan, M. and Nolan, S., 1997, Limits to ecotourism growth and sustainability: The Galapagos example. In *Pacific Rim Tourism*, M. Oppermann, ed., pp. 144–155, CAB International, Wallingford

Silberglied, R., 1978, Inter-island transport of insects aboard ships in the Galapagos Islands. *Biological Conservation*, **13**: 273–278

Stevens, S., 1993, Tourism, change, and continuity in the Mount Everest region, Nepal. *Geographical Review*, **83**: 410–427

Wallace, G.N., 1993, Visitor management: lessons from Galapagos National Park. In *Ecotourism: A guide for planners and managers*, K. Lindberg and D. Hawkins, eds, pp. 55–81, The Ecotourism Society, North Bennington, VT

Weaver, D.B., 1998, *Ecotourism in the less developed world*, CAB International, Wallingford

9 Tourism and national parks in polar regions

JOHN MARSH

Introduction

This chapter will explore the evolution and characteristics of tourism and parks in polar regions, and discuss the positive as well as problematic relationship between tourism and parks in these regions. The future of this relationship is considered, and means suggested to ensure tourism and protected areas are sustainable and mutually supportive. Polar regions are taken here to include the Yukon, Northwest Territories and Nunavut in Canada, Alaska, Greenland, Svalbard, northern Scandinavia, northern Russia, and Antarctica. Parks are taken to include all protected areas where the primary mandate is to conserve nature (reflecting the unique arrangements in Antarctica).

Tourism in polar regions

Compared with many other parts of the world, the polar regions have attracted tourists only in relatively recent times and small numbers. However, it might be argued that some explorers, scientists, gold seekers, writers and artists who ventured to polar regions around the beginnings of this century had many of the attributes of tourists, certainly helped draw public attention to these regions, and created images of them that continue to lure or repel tourists (Manweiler, 1999).

In 1827, polar tourism received a boost when Robert Everest, Himalayan explorer, visited North Cape, a northerly point on the mainland of Norway. 'During the nineteenth century, travel to Svalbard was a prestigious preserve of the wealthy. The trip was always something of an expedition, and travellers undertook it for adventure. The first organised and commercial tour to Svalbard took place in 1871' (Viken, 1995). In 1907, the artist and naturalist Ernest Thompson Seton made a 5000 kilometre canoe journey through northern Canada (Seton, 1911). In 1909, Agnes Dean Cameron, a retired school teacher from Chicago made a trip through 'the new north' of Canada, with the help of the Hudson's Bay Company which she dubbed 'the Cook's Tourist Company of the North' (Cameron, 1912). In 1912, the missionary Wilfrid Grenfell, working on the coast of Labrador, observed at least six yachts there and noted that 'among other ways to help Labrador, we had always tried to induce tourists and yachtsmen to come and visit us' (Grenfell, 1920).

In the 1920s and 1930s, the number of visitors gradually increased, penetrating further north to places such as Alaska, Canada and Scandinavia. On the 1937 voyage to the Canadian Arctic of 'SS Nascopie', the Hudson's Bay Company supply ship, 22 of 150 passengers were classified as 'official tourists.' In the 1930s, Thomas Cook and Sons advertised that they could arrange pleasure cruises to Spitzbergen, Iceland or North Cape. Between 1935 and 1939, the tourist destination of Abisko, Sweden on the Lulea to Narvik Railway attracted an average of 10–15 000 visitors.

The Second World War drew attention to several northern regions, and led to the building of the Alaska Highway that subsequently provided tourists with easier access to Alaska and the Yukon. Gradual improvements in all forms of access to the north encouraged expansion of tourism in polar regions from the 1950s. More recently, the provision of additional facilities and services for travellers, government and private promotion of tourism, and growing interest in ecotourism have led to the more rapid growth of tourism in polar regions. Concurrently, the number of parks in the north has increased, with many of them attracting tourists.

Hall and Johnston (1995, p. 11) note, 'for numerous reasons, it is impossible to estimate world-wide numbers of visitors in the Arctic and sub-Arctic. The boundaries of areas for which statistics are collected, often in different ways, do not coincide with most definitions of Arctic or sub-Arctic'. However, the World Wide Fund for Nature (1998) has provided tourist numbers for selected areas of the Arctic in the early 1990's (see Table 9.1). This indicates that Northern Scandinavia attracted more tourists by far than any of the other regions identified, followed by the northern territories of Canada, with Greenland attracting the least.

Various tourism data sets are available for particular polar regions. It was estimated (Hinch, 1995, p. 116) that the NWT of Canada received only 600 tourists in 1959, but 56 000 in 1992. Eighty-five per cent of these came in summer, a pattern typical of polar regions. The North Cape had 140 000 visitors in 1988 and 224 000 in 1993. Alaska cruise tourism began in 1957 with 2,500 tourists, but by 1994 there were about 250 000 such tourists. In explaining the spatial pattern of northern tourism, Hall and Johnston (1995, p. 13) state that 'northern destinations with greater road access have correspondingly higher tourist numbers.' This partly accounts for the 500,000 visitors to Arctic Norway, and the greater popularity of the Yukon (accessible from the Alaska Highway) compared with the NWT of Canada.

In Antarctica, tourism had its beginnings in the 19th century. Before the late 1960s numbers were only a few hundred per year, rising to around a thousand a year

Table 9.1. Tourist numbers for selected areas in the Arctic, early 1990s

Area	Tourist Numbers
Arctic Alaska	25 000
Yukon, Canada	177 000
Northwest Territories, Canada	48 000
Greenland	6 000
Svalbard	35 000
Northern Scandinavia	500 000
Russia (no data available, estimate)	few 10 000s

Source: World Wide Fund for Nature (1998) Hall and Johnston (1995)

Table 9.2.   Tourists in Antarctica

Year	Seaborne	Airborne	Total
1980–1	855	n/a	855
1981–2	1441	n/a	1441
1982–3	719	2	721
1983–4	834	265	1099
1984–5	544	92	636
1985–6	631	151	782
1986–7	1797	30	1827
1987–8	2782	244	3026
1988–9	3146	370	3516
1989–90	2460	121	2581
1990–1	4698	144	4842
1991–2	6317	178	6495
1992–3	7037	185	7222
1993–4	7957	59	8016
1994–5	8090	120	8210
1995–6	9212	155	9367
1996–7	7322	91	7413
1997–8	9473	131	9604
1998–9	10013	n/a	n/a

(Source: Enzenbacher, 1992, 1993, 1994; www.iaato.org. 1999)

Table 9.3.   Most Visited Landing Sites of Cruises to Antarctica, 1997–8

Landing Site	Visitors
Port Lockroy, Wiencke Island	6429
Whalers Bay, Deception Island	5344
Moon Bay, Half Moon Island	4382
Cuverville Island	4143
Almirante Brown Station	3991
Petermann Islands	3866
Pendulum Cove, Deception Island	3426
Hannah Point, Livingstone Island	3399
Gonz. Videla, Waterboat Point	2998
Aitcho Islands	2499

(All other sites had under 1750 visitors)

(Source: www.iaato.org. 1999)

until the late 1980s (Reich 1980). Since then visitor numbers have grown fairly steadily (Table 9.2). The sites in Antarctica visited most by cruises are indicated in Table 9.3. In 1997–8, Port Lockroy had the most visitors (6429) and over 70 other sites were visited. Most of the sites visited are around the Antarctic Peninsula and adjacent islands. However, some visits were also made to continental sites, the three most popular in 1997–8 being Cape Evans, Cape Royds and Terra Nova Bay Station. Some cruises also take in the Falkland Islands and South Georgia.

There have also been tourist flights from South America to King George Island, as well as expeditions inland, but relatively few tourists visit Antarctica this way, 131 in 1997–8, and 79 in 1998–9 (Table 9.2). Such trips offer visitors the chance to stay longer in one place or travel inland, usually for mountaineering and skiing, in areas such as the Patriot Hills. Overflights of parts of coastal Antarctica from Australia were initiated in 1976 but terminated in 1979, after one plane crashed on Mt.Erebus, killing 257 people. Such flights resumed in 1994/95, when they carried 2134 tourists, the number rising to 2958 in 1995/96, and 3301 in 1996/97 (Bauer, 1997, p. 99).

Parks in polar regions

Parks and other types of protected areas were first established in polar regions in the early decades of this century. As elsewhere, their establishment reflected growing concern about declining wildlife populations, especially migratory and rare species and those important for native subsistence or commercial purposes.

Karpowicz and Harrison (1987, p. 182) have summarised the early development of protected areas in the north. 'The first protected areas north of 60 degrees were established in 1909, when four national parks were gazetted in Sweden. During the following 40 or so years only 16 additional sites were designated before Finland declared 12 further protected areas in 1956. Expansion was again rather unremarkable in the 1960s with only a further 9 areas recognised. The situation has improved significantly since then with 81 major sites declared during the 1970s ... (and) ... five sites on Svalbard in 1973, and the Greenland National Park in 1974.'

More recently, parks have been established to protect unique scenic features and representative landscapes. Parks have been seen increasingly as a means to attract tourists, especially to areas where traditional native lifestyles have been threatened, or where other economic activities, such as mining, have proved unstable.

In 1985, it was estimated (Karpowicz and Harrison, 1987) that north of 60°, there were 175 protected areas (areas fully protected by the 'highest competent authority' that are established primarily for nature conservation reasons, and that are over 1000 hectares, or over 100 hectares if islands). Karpowicz and Harrison also noted that the two largest countries in the region, Canada and the USSR, had fewer protected areas than the smaller Nordic countries, and the size of protected areas varied enormously, from Greenland National Park with 70 million hectares to 15 tiny bird sanctuaries on Svalbard accounting for barely 19,000 hectares in total.

In 1998, it was calculated (Synge, 1998) that Norway had 21 IUCN Category 2 National Parks, Sweden had 25, Finland 32 and Russia 23. The Circumarctic Tundra Region is represented by only 2 large category 2 parks in Svalbard, there being none in Russia as yet. However, the Circumboreal Coniferous Forest Region has 61 such parks, 6 of which are the largest national parks in Europe, comprising 5.3 million hectares.

In Canada, the earliest national parks were developed in scenic places, accessible by rail, with tourism as a major motivation and therefore, were mainly in the south and west of the country. Later national parks were developed to protect endangered species, (e.g. Wood Buffalo, NWT. 1922), serve provincial recreation demand (e.g. in the Prairies), and aid in local economic development (e.g. in the Maritimes). Only when the emphasis shifted in the 1970s to designating parks to protect natural areas representative of the country's ecoregions, or in response to the spatial expansion of extractive industries, were many national parks created in the North. Three parks were created in 1972 (Auyuittuq, Kluane, and Nahanni) and five more have been established since then (Ivavik, Ellesmere Island, Vuntut, Aulavik and Tuktut Nogait) (Marsh, 1998).

Concerns about preserving the environment for traditional native uses, the resolution of land claims and the recognition that the northern wilderness could attract tourists, thus contributing to economic development, have further encouraged park creation in the north, by both national and later territorial governments. Bregha (1989, p. 224) notes that 'the importance of the land-claim process to the establishment of protected areas was first demonstrated in 1984 when the Northern Yukon National Park and the Herschel Island Territorial Park were established as part of the Inuvialuit settlement. The pattern of protected area designation through claim settlements is likely to be repeated.' However, in some areas of the north, e.g. Great Slave Lake, Bathurst Inlet and the Torngat Mountains, parks have been opposed, or delayed pending the resolution of native land claims.

In Alaska, the first 'major tract of ground set aside purposely to preserve an area for its outstanding wildlife, scenic and other natural values' was Mt. McKinley (now Denali) National Park, established in 1917 (Stenmark, 1987, p. 513). A year later Katmai National Monument was established and in 1925, Glacier Bay National Monument. The Alaska National Interest Lands Conservation Act of 1980 greatly expanded the system of parks and protected areas in that state, so that today over one third of Alaska is in national conservation system units, over half of which are in the Arctic.

The Antarctic Treaty adopted in 1959, in Article 1X, called on the contracting parties to develop measures for 'the preservation and conservation of living resources in Antarctica' (Holdgate, 1998, p. 9). Accordingly, the Working Group on Biology recommended that: 'All areas of land and freshwater, including fast ice and ice shelves, and all coastal waters south of 60 degrees South, should be recognised internationally as a nature reserve' (Holdgate, 1998, p. 9). The Group further recommended that: 'species or habitats which are especially valuable or vulnerable should be further protected by the designation of selected areas as sanctuaries within which no form of disturbance should be permitted' (Holdgate, 1998, p. 9). It was subsequently agreed that Specially Protected Areas (SPAs) should be identified to protect significant ecological features, with entry prohibited unless there were compelling scientific reasons which could not be served elsewhere. Next, to safeguard sites for scientific research, Sites of Special Scientific Interest (SSSIs) were identified. In 1989, it was agreed that two more types of protected area might be designated. Specially Reserved Areas (SRAs) were intended to extend the provisions of SPAs and SSSIs to take in geological, geomorphological, glaciological, aesthetic, scenic and wilderness features. Multiple Use Planning Areas (MUPAs) were intended to be areas with co-ordinated management to minimise environmental impacts and conflicts from a variety of activities, such as scientific research, transport, and possibly tourism. By 1996, there were 20 SPAs and 35 SSSIs, totalling 2,868 km^2 (Table 9.4). In addition there were 3 Seal Reserves covering marine areas of 215,217 km^2, as well as 72 historic sites and monuments.

Despite the designation of these protected areas, there has been increasing concern about degradation of the Antarctic environment from scientific activity,

Table 9.4. Protected areas in Antarctica, 1996

Type	Number	km^2
Specially Protected Areas	20	184
Sites of Special Scientific Interest	35	655
Seal Reserve	3	215 217
Ecosystem Monitoring Sites	4	4
Total	62	218 089
Historic sites and monuments	72	

Source: Holdgate (1998, p. 5)

tourism, harvesting of marine species, and air pollution (Brown, 1991; Marsh, 1996, Stonehouse and Crosbie, 1995). This has led to an international protocol to protect the environment, especially by prohibiting mining, and also by regulating tourism. The Protocol on Environmental Protection recognizes Antarctica as a natural reserve and commits contracting parties to protect the environment and its ecosystems. Furthermore, it consolidates SPAs, SSSIs and SRAs into Antarctic Specially Protected Areas (ASPAs), and Antarctic Specially Managed Areas (ASMAs).

It has been argued (May, 1988) that all of Antarctica should be recognised as a 'World Park', while others have advocated that, as on other continents, only areas of special scientific interest or fragility should be designated for special protection. Most recently, many people have advocated a major expansion of the number and size of Antarctic Specially Protected Areas (Lewis Smith et al, 1994; Holdgate, 1998; Marsh and Luxmore, 1998). While some of these would be established to protect representative ecosystems, or specific features of scientific interest, others would be intended to preserve scenic and wilderness areas that would appeal to visitors.

Tourism in parks in polar regions

In general parks in polar regions offer tourists unspoiled scenery, wildlife, opportunities for physically challenging and uncrowded recreation, historical features, and, adjacent to some of them, interesting communities, especially those of native peoples. They also offer less tangible possibilities for learning, spiritual rejuvenation, accomplishing something for the first time, such as the first ascent of a mountain, socialising with like-minded travellers and status, as noted below.

Denali National Park in Alaska features North America's highest mountain, Mt. McKinley, many large glaciers, and wildlife including grizzly bears, wolves, Dall sheep and moose and is well suited for wildlife viewing, mountaineering and backpacking. Katannilik Territorial Park in the NWT of Canada has been described as a place where 'adventurers may play and tourists find solitude' (Moss, 1994, p. 11).

In considering the appeal of a proposed national park in the Kiruna Mountains north of the Arctic Circle in Sweden, Sandell (1995, p. 131) notes: 'compared with the rest of Europe, its northern part is the most manifest example of this opportunity. The interior north includes extensive areas of a truly wilderness character, sometimes described as the last remaining wilderness areas in Western Europe.' Similarly,

Northwest Russia has been described as 'a new arena for people's special interests, not least for people attracted by wilderness.' (Viken *et al* 1995, p. 110).

In general, it can be said that parks in polar regions, compared with those in other parts of the world, attract relatively few tourists (Eagles, 1999). This is exemplified in the case of tourism in national parks in northern Canada. The most popular national park in this region, Kluane National Park reserve, attracts on average only 70 000 tourists annually, while the least popular park, Aulavik, recently has had under 50 visitors annually. During the last decade, total attendance at the seven parks has remained around 80 000 visitors annually (www.cpaws.org 1999).

Visitation levels in U.S. National Park Units in Alaska are generally higher than those in Canada but similarly varied. Glacier Bay National Park in southern Alaska received some 405 246 in 1998 (of whom 339 406 were on cruise ships), Katmai National Park had 45 000 visitors, Wrangell-St. Elias National Park received 25 000 visitors, while many other units were visited by far fewer tourists, for example, Gates of the Arctic National Park with only 4000 (www.nps.gov/parklists.ak 1999).

If one considers, on the basis of Antarctic Treaty regulations and the Environmental Protocol, all of Antarctica as a protected area, or 'world park', then all tourism there depends on, takes place in, and has impacts upon this continental protected area. However, if one considers only the areas within Antarctica that are individually designated as Antarctic Specially Protected Areas, then tourism is not dependent on them. Indeed the purpose of these ASPAs, as noted above, is to protect areas of scientific interest by restricting access to them. Accordingly, only rarely are any of these areas visited by tourists. Antarctic Specially Managed Areas, while intended to conserve the environment through restriction and co-ordination of activities, can be entered without a permit, so are more likely to be visited by tourists. For example, it has been estimated (Fanta, 1997) that the Admiralty Bay ASMA on King George Island is visited on average by 1500 cruise tourists each summer. It should also be noted that some of the designated historic sites and their surroundings are visited by tourists.

Benefits of park tourism

Park tourism has often been encouraged and supported by park proponents and managers as well as tourism agencies and local communities on the basis of assisting conservation and providing economic benefits to local communities. It has been argued that public use and appreciation of parks will engender public and political support for them. Sandell (1995, p. 137) notes that in justifying a proposed park in northern Sweden it was stated that 'it is good for nature conservancy if much larger groups of people than at present can be given the possibility of genuine and first-rate experiences of nature.'

One of the objectives of the International Association of Antarctic Tour Operators is 'to create a corps of ambassadors for the continued protection of Antarctica by offering the opportunity to experience the continent first hand' (www.iaato.org 1999). An Antarctic cruise leader (German, 1999) said some tourists 'come as 'continent baggers', trying to get their last continent and leave as ambassadors to the preservation of Antarctica.' However, Bauer (1997, p. 183), on the basis of his visitor surveys in Antarctica, contends that 'tourists themselves do not see themselves as ambassadors, but that other groups, in particular tour operators, like to attach this label to them, perhaps to justify their own actions.'

Park tourism can be economically lucrative, offering private profit and financial support for parks. McNamee (1989, p. 90) has noted that 'parks are already under heavy pressure to serve economic goals,' and that '70 per cent of Canada's national parks are located in economically depressed regions ... (and) ... Most major park developments, such as roads, accommodation and recreational facilities are meant to increase tourism revenues and economic gains to local communities.' It has been suggested (IUCN, 1994, p. 36) that 'if planned and managed for sustainability, tourism can be a very positive force, bringing benefits to protected areas and local communities alike.' With respect to the proposed Torngat Mountains National Park in Labrador, 'Tourism, for example, would provide the community with jobs such as guiding, chartering boats, providing accommodations and food as well as selling their exquisite crafts to park visitors.' (www.cpaws 1999).

Regarding the economic returns from tourism in Antarctica, Bauer (1997, p. 89) has pointed out that 'although visitor numbers are small, during the 1996/97 season Antarctic tourism was nevertheless a A$50 million plus industry. On a per passenger basis this gross revenue generated during a four-month season from mid-November to early March is one of the highest in the world ...'

Problems with Park Tourism

Tourism has long caused impacts in many parks that are sometimes problematic and contentious, requiring management solutions (Marsh, 1983). Some of the main types of impacts and management responses to them are given below, along with examples from protected areas in polar regions.

The soils, especially permafrost soils, and vegetation of most polar regions are particularly vulnerable to human impacts, especially by motor vehicles, but even by pedestrians. Means to reduce them include prohibiting access to especially vulnerable areas, closing areas when they are especially sensitive, restricting certain recreation activities, hardening surfaces, and educating visitors.

As wildlife in parks in polar regions may be endangered and sensitive to humans, but often a prime attraction for tourists, and numerous efforts are being made to ensure such impacts are minimised. An important attraction in some parks in polar regions, is the opportunity for sport fishing. However, polar waters tend to have very limited productivity, so management of fishing is required to ensure the maintenance of fish stocks. In Katmai National Park, Alaska, a state fishing license is required, catch and release is encouraged and there are bag limits for specific sites. Bears are also a major attraction in Katmai National Park but for safety reasons and to ensure bears are not displaced this wildlife tourism is carefully managed (see Vaske, Donnelly and Whittaker, Chapter 13).

As increasing numbers of tourists visit polar regions, whether parks or elsewhere, more attention has to be given to waste management (Marsh and Elliot, 1994; Johnston and Madunic, 1995). The disposal of sewage is especially problematic as the cold climate and frozen soils inhibit decomposition, and the use of conventional disposal and treatment methods. However, while these and other concerns have been expressed about the environmental impacts of tourism in Antarctica, Bauer (1997, p. 11) concluded that: 'at present levels of visitation, type of tourists and forms of tourism, there appears little cause for major concern with regard to environmental degradation'.

While polar regions are often thought of as uninhabited wilderness, there are numerous archaeological and historical remains, which are vulnerable to unintentional and occasionally intentional damage or removal. Parks in Arctic regions contain archaeological sites of scientific and spiritual significance, and historic sites associated with exploration, whaling, the fur trade, and World War 2. Antarctica has historical sites associated in particular with exploration, whaling and scientific research (Hughes and Davis, 1995). Most park agencies have policies, regulations and management strategies for protecting such sites, while, where appropriate, making them accessible to tourists and providing interpretation.

There have long been arguments over the appropriate means of travel within these parks (Marsh, 1987), and in particular, disagreement on appropriate levels of air and motor boat access. While most parks in polar regions do not have communities within them, there are communities, often primarily indigenous, adjacent to some of them, and such communities may use the parks for traditional purposes, such as wildlife harvesting. Although it is recognised that tourism can benefit communities and parks economically, concern has been expressed globally about negative impacts of tourism on communities, especially indigenous communities. While some parks may produce economic benefits, it should be emphasised that others have few facilities, services or products to offer the tourist, and tourists that are attracted may be very self-sufficient.

There has been a long history of bringing polar regions to public attention, in recent decades as tourist destinations (Alaska, 1999; Tourism Yukon, 1999). In the last decade scholars have analysed the images presented of some polar regions, such as the Canadian Arctic, especially in tourism advertising, and questioned their representativeness (Manweiler, 1999; Milne *et al* 1998). Not only have there been calls for more representative and accurate advertising of the north and its tourism opportunities, but also for more involvement of local communities and indigenous peoples in providing educational and interpretation information and services in parks and elsewhere for tourists. This has been achieved, for example, at Twin Falls Park, near Hay River, NWT, where the Dene Cultural Institute, five Dene communities and their Elders co-operated to develop an interpretive tour of the community, where visitors 'actually get to participate directly in dance, music, the ceremonies, or producing arts or traditional crafts.' (Lawrence, 1999, p. 2).

Concern has long been expressed about the hiring of non-local people by park agencies and tourism companies in northern regions. An example of a response to this concern is afforded by the Government of the Northwest Territories which introduced a programme of training and certification for northerners, especially native people, to learn about guiding and interpretation so they could take advantage of the increasing ecotourism in this region.

Conclusion and Recommendations

While tourists made forays into some polar regions in the late 19th century, tourism has only been of consequence in these regions since the 1950s. Even now, compared with other parts of the world, the volume of tourism in polar regions is very limited. However, tourism is increasing in many polar regions and is also increasingly diverse in terms of the clientele, their activities, and impacts.

The economic, social and environmental impacts of this tourism are also increasing in many parks. Some of these impacts have been positive, helping to justify parks and providing economic opportunities, but some have been negative, causing environmental damage and resentment in some communities. Thus, there have been increasing demands to control tourism so as to minimise undesirable social and environmental impacts. Experience is being gained, especially by tour operators, park managers and native communities, that can help to ensure that tourism and parks become more sustainable in polar regions.

Some specific recommendations relating tourism in polar parks are proposed. First, the levels and types of tourism in protected areas must be monitored (Eagles, 1999) along with the impacts of tourism on park environments and local communities. Second, levels of acceptable change to park environments, the tourist experience and local communities must be determined. Following these steps, policies, plans, and management strategies at regional, park and community levels should be adopted to ensure levels of acceptable change are not exceeded, and programmes should be implemented to educate tour operators, tourists and local communities so as to minimise the negative impacts of tourism. Tourism should be planned in order to provide direct economic benefits to parks and local communities.

Finally, tourism in parks in polar regions should be guided by the 'Ten Principles for Arctic Tourism' advocated by the World Wide Fund for Nature (1998). These include making tourism and conservation compatible, supporting the preservation of wilderness and biodiversity, using natural resources in sustainable ways and minimising consumption, waste and pollution. On the human side they involve respecting local cultures, historic and scientific sites, ensuring communities benefit from tourism, having trained staff to ensure responsible tourism, making tourism educational and requiring safety rules to be followed.

It can be expected that there will be continued growth of tourism in polar regions, and to a growing array of parks and other locations in these regions. However, as in the past, factors such as cost, climate, accessibility, safety and environmental concern, will limit this growth of tourism. Accordingly, the polar regions will remain much less important tourist destinations than other parts of the world. There will be continuing expressions of concern about the impacts of tourism on the environment communities and native people of polar regions, but it seems likely that management of such impacts will be innovative and effective, and of relevance to other parts of the world.

Bauer (1997, p. 11), on the basis of a Delphi exercise with experts on Antarctica, concluded with respect to tourism that 'future activities would most likely continue to be ship-based and would mostly take place in the Antarctic Peninsula region. Panel consensus also identified an increase in adventure tourism activities as a possibility but only as a small proportion of total tourism. Large scale, land-based tourism facilities were not seen as likely developments in the medium to long term future.'

These comments are probably equally applicable to most polar regions.

Dedication

This chapter is dedicated to Ron Seale who, until his untimely death in Iqaluit in February 1999, had an abiding interest in the North, worked to create parks there, while respecting native interests, and was an avid traveller in this region.

References

Alaska, State of., 1999, *Alaska: Official State Guide and Vacation Planner*. Department of Commerce and Economic Development: Fairbanks

Bauer, T., 1997, *Commercial Tourism in the Antarctic: Trends, Opportunities, Constraints and Regulation*. Ph.D. thesis. Monash University, Melbourne

Bregha, F., 1989, Conservation in the Yukon and Northwest Territories. In E.Hummel, ed., pp. 211–225, *Endangered Spaces: The future for Canada's Wilderness*. Key Porter, Toronto

Brown, P., 1991, *The Last Wilderness: Eighty Days in Antarctica*. Hutchinson, London

Cameron, A.D., 1912, *The New North: Being Some Account of a Woman's Journey through Canada to the Arctic*. Appleton, New York

Eagles, P.F.J., 1999, International Trends in Park Tourism. Unpublished paper. University of Waterloo, Waterloo

Enzenbacher, D., 1992, Tourists in Antarctica: Numbers and Trends. *Polar Record*, 28 (164), 17-22

Enzenbacher, D., 1993, Tourists in Antarctica: Numbers and Trends. *Tourism Management*, April, 142–146

Enzenbacher, D., 1994, Antarctic Tourism: An Overview of 1992/93 Season Activity, Recent Developments and Emerging Issues. *Polar Record*, 30 (173), 105–116

Fanta, E., 1997, Antarctic Specially Managed Areas (ASMAS) as a Useful Method for Avoidance and Minimisation of Cumulative Impacts: the Admiralty Bay Example. In: De Poorter, M. and Dalziell, J.C. eds. pp. 125–132, *Cumulative Environmental Impacts in Antarctica: Minimisation and Management*. IUCN, Gland, Switzerland

German, D., 1999, Personal interview

Grenfell, W.T., 1920, *A Labrador Doctor*. Hodder and Stoughton, London

Hall, C.M. and Johnston, M.E. eds, 1995, *Polar Tourism: Tourism in the Arctic and Antarctic Regions*. Wiley, Toronto

Hinch, T.D., 1995, Aboriginal People in the Tourism Economy of Canada's Northwest Territories. In: Hall, C.M. and Johnston, M.E. eds, pp. 115–130, *Polar Tourism: Tourism in the Arctic and Antarctic Regions*. Wiley, Toronto

Holdgate, M., 1998, The Antarctic Protected Areas System in the New Millenium. In: Njastad, B. ed., pp. 8–19, *Antarctic Protected Areas Workshop: Workshop Report*. Norsk Polarinstitutt, Tromso

Hughes, J. and Davis, B., 1995, The Management of Tourism at Historic Sites and Monuments. In: Hall, C.M. and Johnston, M.E. eds, pp. 235–255, *Polar Tourism: Tourism in the Arctic and Antarctic Regions*. Wiley, Toronto

IUCN. 1994. *Parks for Life: Action for Protected Areas in Europe*. The World Conservation Union, IUCN, Gland, Switzerland

Johnston, M.E. and Madunic, D., 1995, Waste Disposal and the Wilderness in the Yukon Territory, Canada. In: Hall, C.M. and Johnston, M.E. eds, pp. 85–100, *Polar Tourism: Tourism in the Arctic and Antarctic Regions*. Wiley, Toronto

Karpowicz, J. and Harrison, J., 1987, Tourism and Conservation: Case Studies in the Canadian North. In: Nelson, J.G., Needham, R., Norton, L. eds, pp. 179–218, *Arctic Heritage: Proceedings of a Symposium*. Association of Canadian Universities for Northern Studies, Ottawa

Lawrence, R., 1999, The Dene Cultural Institute Helps Turn Park in the Right Direction. *Transition*. June–July, 1–2

Lewis Smith, R.I., Walton, D.W.H., and Dingwall, P.R. eds, 1994, *Developing the Antarctic Protected Area System.* IUCN, Gland, Switzerland

Manweiler, J. 1999 *Seeing is Believing? The History of the Pictured Landscape and Tourism in the High Eastern Arctic.* MA thesis. Trent University, Peterborough, Canada

Marsh, J.S., 1983, Canada's Parks and Tourism: A Problematic Relationship. In: Murphy, P.E. ed., pp. 271–307, *Tourism in Canada: Selected Issues and Options.* University of Victoria, Victoria

Marsh, J.S., 1987, Tourism and Conservation: Case Studies in the Canadian North. In: Nelson, J.G., Needham, R., Norton, L. eds, pp. 298–322, *Arctic Heritage: Proceedings of a Symposium.* Association of Canadian Universities for Northern Studies, Ottawa

Marsh, J.S., 1996, The Impacts of Tourism in Antarctica. In: Ceballos-Lascurain, H. ed., pp. 76-77, *Tourism, Ecotourism and Protected Areas.* IUCN, Gland, Switzerland

Marsh, J.S., 1998, Some Words about National Parks, Past, Present and Future. In: Needham, R.D. ed., pp. 37–58, *Coping with the World Around Us: Changing Approaches to Land Use, Resources and the Environment.* University of Waterloo, Waterloo

Marsh, J. and Elliot, N., 1994, *Arctic Waste Management: Development of Appropriate Strategies for Northern National Parks and other Federal Facilities.* Trent University, Peterborough

Marsh, J.S. and Luxmore, R., 1998, Identification of New Antarctic Specially Protected Areas. In: Njastad, B. ed., pp.70–71 *Antarctic Protected Areas Workshop: Workshop Report.* Norsk Polarinstitutt, Tromso

May, J., 1988, *The Greenpeace Book of Antarctica: A View of the 7th Continent.* Macmillan, Toronto

McNamee, K.A., 1989, Fighting for the Wild in Wilderness. In: Hummel, E. ed., pp.63–82, *Endangered Spaces: The Future for Canada's Wilderness.* Key Porter, Toronto

Milne, S., Grekin, J., and Woodley, S., 1998, Tourism and the Construction of Place in Canada's Eastern Arctic. In: Ringer, G. ed. Pp.110–120, *Destinations: Cultural Landscapes of Tourism.* Routledge, London

Moss, J., 1994, Engineering Wilderness. *Arctic Circle.* Spring, 10–27

Reich, R., 1980, The Development of Antarctic Tourism. *Polar Record,* 20 (126), 203–214

Sandell, K., 1995, Access to the 'North' – But to What and for Whom? Public Access in the Swedish Countryside and the Case of a Proposed National Park in the Kiruna Mountains. In: Hall, C.M. and Johnston, M.E. eds, pp. 131–145, *Polar Tourism: Tourism in the Arctic and Antarctic Regions.* Wiley, Toronto

Seton, E.T., 1911, *The Arctic Prairies.* Scribners, New York

Stenmark, R.J., 1987, National Parks and Protected Areas in the Arctic: Alaska. In: Nelson, J.G., Needham, R. and Norton, L. eds, pp. 514–528, *Arctic Heritage: Proceedings of a Symposium.* Association of Canadian Universities for Northern Studies, Ottawa

Stonehouse, B. and Crosbie, K., 1995, Tourists Impacts and Management in the Antarctic Peninsula. In: Hall, C.M. and Johnston, M.E. eds, pp. 217–233, *Polar Tourism: Tourism in the Arctic and Antarctic Regions.* Wiley, Toronto

Synge, H. ed., 1998, *Parks for Life: Proceedings of the IUCN/WCPA European Regional Working Session on Protecting Europe's Natural Heritage.* The World Conservation Union, IUCN, Gland, Switzerland

Tourism Yukon. 1999. *Canada's Yukon: 1999 Vacation Guide.* Whitehorse: Tourism Yukon.

Viken, A., 1995, Tourism Experiences in the Arctic – the Svalbard Case. In: Hall, C.M. and Johnston, M.E. eds, pp. 73–84, *Polar Tourism: Tourism in the Arctic and Antarctic Regions.* Wiley, Toronto

Viken, A., Vostryakov, L. and Davydov, A., 1995, Tourism in Northwest Russia. In Hall, C.M. and Johnston, M. eds, pp. 101–114, *Polar Tourism: Tourism in the Arctic and Antarctic Regions.* Wiley, Toronto

World Wide Fund for Nature, 1998, *Linking Tourism and Conservation in the Arctic.* WWF, Norway, Oslo

www.cpaws.org/parksolutions/torngats.html. 1999.

www.iatto.org. 1999

www.nps.Gov/parklists/ak.html. 1999

10 Tourism, national parks and wildlife

ROBERT J. LILIEHOLM AND LISA R. ROMNEY

Introduction

Tourism based on wildlife and nature has been widely promoted for its potential to sustainably finance both conservation and economic development (Boo, 1990; Card and Vogelsong, 1995). In addition, tourism can promote environmental awareness both locally and abroad, and generate significant foreign exchange earnings (Whelan, 1991; Eagles, 1997). In poor developing countries, tourism can provide economic support to communities that have lost access to natural resources as a consequence of national park creation. Indeed, in cooperation with rapidly growing cultural tourism, well-planned wildlife tourism development may be a remote region's best option for economic development (Wild, 1994; Budowski, 1976).

However, the industry's rapid expansion in recent years has led to many of the same problems of conventional tourism like visitor crowding, dispossession of Aboriginal populations, habitat loss, and stress and behaviour modification of wildlife (Romeril, 1989, Farrel and Runyun, 1991). Critics point to minibuses jammed with camera-clicking tourists harassing wildlife and degrading ecosystems. Even the oft-cited benefit that tourism can change wildlife from a liability to an asset for communities is questioned. Indeed, while tourism has grown rapidly throughout Africa over the last few decades, many important wildlife species like elephants, rhinoceros, and large carnivores have continued to suffer significant declines from poaching.

The debate over the impacts of tourism resembles in many ways the ancient Roman personification of Africa itself – a woman holding a cornucopia in one hand and a scorpion in the other. Yet despite this duality, one must recognise that tourism is a rapidly growing industry that will continue to expand. Moreover, the economic returns from tourism are increasingly essential to the maintenance of many national parks. As a result, understanding and mitigating tourism's adverse impacts is critical if it is to play a positive role in conservation and development.

For African national parks, understanding the impacts of tourism on wildlife is particularly important. Wildlife, especially big game, was an important motivator in the creation of reserves in colonial Africa, and written accounts of hunting safaris in the late nineteenth and early twentieth centuries fuelled the imagination of millions (Roosevelt, 1910). With time, tourism replaced hunting as a non-consumptive and more sustainable use of wildlife (Shaw and Williams, 1992). Not surprisingly, many African national parks have been developed and managed for wildlife-based tourism, and have as their primary goal the protection and maintenance of wildlife populations.

This chapter discusses the impacts of tourism on wildlife in the national parks of sub-Saharan Africa, including island archipelagos. Also described are strategies that can reduce adverse impacts in order to maintain the integrity of parks and their attractiveness for tourism, on which their future largely depends. Central to the discussion is the concept that tourism should more equitably balance the costs and benefits of conservation, which are often disproportionately shared by local communities. This balance can be achieved through the creation of mutually beneficial, self-sustaining mechanisms that support tourism, wildlife, institutions, and communities.

Conservation and visitation trends in African national parks

Other chapters in this book describe the rapid world-wide growth of tourism. In response to this growth, and in recognition of increased global interest in nature conservation, a significant system of nature reserves has emerged in Africa. For example, roughly 10 per cent of Kenya has been reserved for nature conservation. Other countries with significant areas devoted to conservation include Tanzania (11.5 per cent), Botswana (18.2 per cent), Zimbabwe (11.3 per cent), Senegal (10.8 per cent), and Zambia (29.1 per cent) (Akama, 1996; Eagles, 1997).

The economic importance of these areas is growing as well. For example, South Africa's 18 national parks receive 2 million visitors each year (personal communication, R. Willys, Director, South African National Parks, March 1999). The beaches and wildlife of parks in Seychelles attract 150 000 visitors each year (personal communication, J. Nevill, Director, Seychelles Conservation Section, May 1999). Increasingly, African national parks are being used by residents. Sixty per cent of visitors to South Africa's national parks are residents, with 20 per cent coming from other African countries, 10 per cent from Europe, and 5 per cent from North America (personal communication, R. Willys, Director, South African National Parks, March 1999). Forty per cent of the visitors to Mauritius' national parks are residents (personal communication, Y. Mungroo, Director, Mauritius National Parks and Conservation Service, April 1999), as are 80 per cent of those visiting Nigerian parks (personal communication, L.B. Margura, Director, Nigerian National Park Service, May 1999).

Impacts of tourism on wildlife

Tourists engage in many types of activities while visiting national parks, including hiking, biking, nature observation, photography, picnicking, and educational study. Related commercial activities include the filming of popular nature documentaries. These activities rely on a variety of transport modes, including travel by foot, bicycle, automobile, bus, fixed-wing aircraft, helicopter, and motorised and non-motorised watercraft. All these activities and modes of travel can impact wildlife and the broader park ecosystem.

The magnitude and types of activities undertaken in parks is dependent on many factors, including the services and infrastructure available, visitor needs and desires, and the resource of interest (Shackley, 1996). For example, most ecotourism literature promoting African national parks features abundant images of Range Rover journeys across grassy savannas heavily populated with wildlife (Adams and McShane, 1992). Indeed, foot travel may be prohibited in savanna parks due to the high risk of animal attack.

While the wide vistas and abundant wildlife of savanna ecosystems offer ideal viewing conditions, many other environments have been preserved as parks and offer tourism opportunities. Marine parks provide opportunities for whale watching and viewing marine avifauna. River and lake boating trips offer tourists the advantage of covering large areas with ease. Moreover, boat travel is often less intrusive on wildlife, allowing visitors closer experiences. Island, desert, and coastal parks each have their own unique advantages and disadvantages, and may include both terrestrial and aquatic tourism opportunities. Finally, the dense forests of many West and Central African nations may teem with wildlife, but limited visibility can disappoint visitors (Sournia, 1996). Instead, forested parks offer unique experiences like the sights, sounds and smells of dense tropical forest, and abundant insect and birdlife. To increase the chance of viewing forest wildlife, fauna may be habituated to human observation, as is common with gorillas and chimpanzees in the forested parks of Uganda, Rwanda, and Tanzania.

Direct impacts of tourism on wildlife

Within each of these different ecological settings, visitors can impact park wildlife through a variety of means. The most direct impact tourists have on wildlife is death resulting from vehicle accidents. For example, in Nigerian national parks, managers are concerned over vehicle injury or death to all kinds of wildlife (personal communication, L.B. Margura, Director, Nigerian National Park Service, May 1999). In Yankari and Kainji Lake National Parks, bushbuck, roan antelope and hartebeest are common roadway fatalities. Stricter enforcement of speed limits and visitor-education programmes are being used to reduce losses. While comparable data are not available for African parks, research in Yellowstone National Park suggests that 1–2 per cent of the Park's elk and mule deer and wolves are killed by motorists each year (personal communication, M. Biel, Biologist, Yellowstone National Park, June 1999). There, areas with poor road conditions had fewer fatalities due to reduced vehicle speeds. Ironically, this suggests that efforts to promote tourism through facility development may increase wildlife loss if developments include improved road construction and maintenance.

Tourism can seriously threaten the health of anthropoid primates since they have little resistance to human diseases. This is a particularly significant issue for mountain gorillas, since only about 650 individuals remain in remote areas of Uganda, Rwanda, and the Democratic Republic of Congo (formerly Zaire). In western Uganda's Bwindi Impenetrable Forest and Mahinga National Parks, strict visitor guidelines minimise the risk of disease transfer to gorillas. Restrictions limit party size and visit duration, and require that tourists keep at least 5 metres from the apes (Bourne, 1998). In addition, visitors must be over age 15 (to minimise exposure to childhood diseases), and tourists with colds or other obvious illnesses are prohibited.

Tourism can also impact wildlife through stress and behavioural modification due to proximity, feeding, accidental fires, noise, traffic, and harassment. Munyi (1992) has described scenes in Kenya where as many as 30 minibuses surrounded lions, cheetahs and leopards to allow tourists close-up photo opportunities. The impacts of visitor viewing can be highly species-dependent. For example, Weaver (1998) reports that 41 per cent of all viewing time in Kenya's Amboseli National Park is spent watching lions and cheetahs, despite their low numbers. Such pressure may cause sensitive species like cheetah to fail at hunting, or discontinue the use of habitat heavily visited by tourists. Other sensitive species may forgo the use of critical habitat for nesting or foraging, resulting in increased mortality and reduced health, fecundity, and population levels. Fleeing wildlife may injure themselves or others, and the young may become orphaned and killed. Displacement can also lead to increased competition for resources in less-visited areas. In the Seychelles Islands, beach visitors have disrupted nesting sites for many shorebirds, including the greater frigate bird (personal communication, J. Nevill, Director, Seychelles Conservation Section, May 1999). Fishing and power-boating can adversely affect both terrestrial and aquatic species in rivers, lakes, and coastal parks (Knight and Gutzwiller, 1995; Shackley, 1996).

Poor waste management, food refuse, and feeding of animals by tourists can cause some wildlife populations to proliferate beyond desirable levels, creating an imbalance in the park ecosystem, as well as safety threats to tourists. For example, in Ethiopia's Awash National Park, wildlife feeding on visitor trash is a growing problem (personal communication, T. Hundessa, Ethiopian Wildlife Conservation Organization, May 1999). Also at the Park, hand feeding of baboons and other monkeys in campgrounds is creating management concerns over altered animal behaviour and visitor safety. In Nigeria's Yankari National Park, feeding of baboons is a problem, with recent laws passed to prohibit the practice (personal communication, L.B. Margura, Director, Nigerian National Park Service, May 1999).

Tourist contact can lead to a loss of fear of humans, resulting in more frequent and serious encounters between tourists and wildlife. For far-ranging or migratory animals that travel beyond park borders, a lower fear of humans can lead to increased crop-raiding and encounters with villagers, as well as a greater susceptibility of wildlife to poaching. These wildlife-villager encounters can lead to increased hostility between local residents and park management.

Indirect impacts of tourism on wildlife

Although much of Africa has been impacted by humans through fire, livestock grazing, hunting, agriculture, fencing and water development (Adams and McShane, 1992), habitat modification from tourism activities is increasingly affecting wildlife.

For example, heavy vehicle traffic can damage vegetation, leading to lower forage quality. Munyi (1992) reports that minibuses filled with tourists travel haphazardly across open grasslands, degrading the very resource that sustains Kenya's large wildlife populations. Soil erosion, especially in riparian and coastal dune zones, can adversely affect water quality and aquatic life (Shackley, 1996). Increased human presence can lead to more frequent fires, as well as the introduction of exotic flora and fauna, leading to a wide range of potential impacts on habitat and wildlife (Lonsdale and Lane, 1994). In the Seychelles, frequent boat anchoring associated with snorkelling and scuba diving is destroying both soft and hard coral reefs, and in turn adversely impacting fish populations (personal communication, J. Nevill, Director, Seychelles Conservation Section, May 1999).

The construction and operation of tourist facilities and associated infrastructure like roads and water systems can also alter the habitat upon which wildlife depends. In Ethiopia's Awash National Park, such developments are adversely affecting oryx, greater and lesser kudu, and gazelle (personal communication, T. Hundessa, Ethiopian Wildlife Conservation Organization, May 1999). Similar problems are reported in the country's Simien Mountains National Park, with affected species being walia ibex and gelada baboons. Sewage, pesticides, photopollution from artificial lighting, and air pollution from minibuses can have both subtle and significant impacts, depending on the degree of activity and the species involved.

The economic importance of wildlife may lead to park policies that allow animal populations to reach unsustainably high levels in order to enhance visitor-viewing opportunities and avoid unpopular culling programmes (Stoddard, 1999). In Yellowstone National Park, some ecologists charge that the National Park Service has allowed elk and bison herds to expand to the point where grazing pressure has virtually eliminated willow and aspen regeneration (Chase, 1986). The loss of these tree species has led to a decline in once-abundant beaver. A similar cycle may be occurring in some African parks, where elephant populations may grow beyond sustainable levels and uproot trees in search of forage.

It is important to recognise, however, that not all tourism impacts on wildlife are negative. For example, increased tourism in Mauritius has resulted in greater recognition of the importance of wildlife and the recent creation of the National Parks and Conservation Service (NPCS) (personal communication, Y. Mungroo, Director, NPCS, April 1999). These developments have led to several new conservation projects that benefit endemic birds like the kestrel, pink pigeon, and echo parakeet in Black River Gorges National Park. On a broader scale, tourism can lead to increased recognition and support for conservation programmes. This is particularly true since tourists tend to be relatively wealthy, highly educated, and influential both at home and abroad (Eagles, 1992; Navrud and Mungatana, 1994). Indeed, tourists returning from exotic national parks often become lifelong advocates for parks, wildlife, and conservation programmes. Moreover, the economic importance of wildlife and tourism has supplied the revenues and incentives for better management, and in the case of the mountain gorilla, increased ranger contact has meant that populations are well monitored and better protected from poaching (Davey, 1996).

Benefits and costs of wildlife conservation

National parks create a wide range of benefits to society, ranging from the protection of environmental quality and services, to various recreational benefits and revenues realised through ecotourism. Developing countries have increasingly recognised the economic importance of wildlife and national parks, and have responded by setting aside significant areas for conservation. Yet despite general recognition of the benefits of parks and wildlife, measuring these benefits is difficult because they tend to be non-marketed and hence not easily quantified. Quantifying both the benefits and costs of wildlife conservation is important, however, especially when conservation is an option that competes against alternatives including the extraction of market-valued resources (Dixon and Sherman, 1990; Lindberg, 1991).

A significant body of literature describes the revenues generated by tourism in African national parks (see International Resources Group, 1992; Langholz, 1996; Bourne, 1998). But tourism receipts comprise only a small portion of the total economic value generated by wildlife and national parks (Fausold and Lilieholm, 1999). An early study by Brown and Henry (1989) estimated an average recreational value of US$727 per visit to Kenya to view elephants. Munyi (1992) cites that each elephant in Kenya generates US$14 375 in tourism revenues, totalling US$200 million each year. A later study by Navrud and Mungatana (1994) estimated the annual economic value of viewing flamingos in Kenya's Lake Nakuru National Park to be US$7.5–15 million. Flamingo viewing, the Park's most popular attraction, accounted for over one-third of the Park's total wildlife value.

While national parks create many benefits, they can also incur considerable economic and social costs. Economic costs include park establishment and management expenses, along with opportunity costs resulting from forgone options for extractive uses as resource-rich lands are placed under strict environmental protection. Social costs can be enormous. For example, many African national parks were created through the forced resettlement of established communities. The creation of the 170-square-mile Ranamafano National Park in Madagascar in 1991 resulted in the displacement of 72 000 people from areas in and around the Park (Durbin and Ratrimoarisaona, 1996). The designation of parks is often accompanied by the loss of traditional use rights by local communities. In Kenya, many communal lands were placed under state control, creating significant resentment in dispossessed communities (Akama et al., 1995). Loss of access to local resources may require travelling farther to gather medicinal plants, wild foods, and fuelwood. More restrictive hunting and trapping laws can destroy the traditional lifestyles of subsistence peoples and overnight turn hunters into poachers. In some instances, entire communities have been imprisoned for poaching-related offences (Akama, 1996).

Finally, protected wildlife populations can prosper to the point where animals with less fear of humans increasingly impact local communities through confrontations and crop-raiding. Oftentimes, marauding wildlife use parks as sanctuaries from which to raid the fields of surrounding villagers. Moreover, local villagers are regularly killed by lions, buffalos and elephants near protected areas (Munyi, 1992). In addition to these direct risks from wildlife are the risks to patrolling park rangers from heavily armed poachers.

Mitigating the costs of environmental protection to local communities

Nature conservation can create an allocation imbalance between the costs and benefits of protection, where protected area benefits accrue to broad, global constituencies and future generations, while costs are assumed by rural residents who are least able to afford them. These locally borne costs, unless offset by gains from ecotourism, can undermine local park support and threaten the viability of both communities and protected areas (Place, 1991; Ashton, 1991; Young, 1992; Boonzaier, 1996; Wells, 1996). This is particularly true in sub-Saharan Africa, where 29 of the world's 36 poorest nations are located. Amid this backdrop of hunger, preventable poverty-related disease, and high infant mortality rates, it can be difficult to justify setting aside productive lands for wealthy foreigners to observe wildlife.

When human and wildlife interests collide, wildlife invariable suffers unless it can be transformed from a liability into an asset (Child, 1995). In East and Southern Africa, this has been achieved through various revenue-sharing programmes between parks and local communities. Under Zimbabwe's successful CAMPFIRE (Communal Area Management Programme for Indigenous Resources) programme local communities gain an economic interest in wildlife via hunting revenues generated through culling of surplus wildlife (Potts *et al.*, 1996).

To be sustainable, economic linkages between parks, communities, and other partners should be mutually-reinforcing and market-based, leading to systems that respond to local values and distribute benefits and costs equitably and with flexibility and transparency (Whitesell *et al.* 1997). Moreover, linking park activities with cultural tourism, service sector development, and the sale of crafts can further enhance employment. These developments may have positive gender impacts as well since women are the primary producers of handicrafts. Unfortunately, revenue-sharing programmes can only work where tourist demand is of sufficient scale to generate adequate support revenues. This may not be possible in countries where poor infrastructure limits visitation (Durbin and Ratrimoarisaona, 1996).

Efforts to develop tourism should consider economic multipliers, and the leakage of currency from local economies. For example, poorly developed tourist areas may contribute relatively little to local economies since many goods and services must be supplied from outside the region. Local control and public participation in tourism development can ensure that traditional lifestyles and community values are respected (Aussie-Stone, 1992; Lillywhite, 1992), minimising adverse impacts on communities and gaining public support to ensure tourism's long-term viability (Drake, 1991; International Resources Group, 1992). A variety of sources can aid communities in tourism development (Victurine, 1999). Historically, NGOs have been active in promoting ecotourism and, as a result, may have great influence on national conservation and tourism policies (Wild, 1994). More recently, large development assistance organisations like the World Bank and the US Agency for International Development have been active in ecotourism projects.

Strategies for mitigating adverse tourist impacts on wildlife

Tourism can play a positive role in conservation and development. To ensure this end, however, ecotourism's positive and negative impacts must be carefully considered within a comprehensive park management plan. Once specific management objectives are developed, a wide variety of mitigation strategies can be used to ensure that tourism's impacts are compatible with conservation goals.

Alleviating crowding in national parks

Crowding resulting from overuse and uneven use can adversely affect both parks and wildlife (Butler, 1991). For example, in Kenya's Amboseli National Park, 90 per cent of visitors used 10 per cent of the Park area, and 50 per cent of use occurred between 3:30 and 4:30 pm (Shackley, 1996). Similarly, Weaver (1998) reports that 62 per cent of Kenya's visitors in 1994 visited only six of the country's 57 national parks and nature reserves. A variety of methods to alter visitation and use patterns are described below.

Limiting visitation through higher fees, quotas and lotteries

Restricting the number of visitors to popular sites can benefit both wildlife and visitors. A variety of methods are available, including: (1) rationing permits; (2) allowing entry on a first-come, first-served basis; (3) setting quotas; (4) implementing lotteries; and (5) setting higher fees. Many parks have recently increased their fees in an effort to reduce visitation and/or increase revenues. Since many non-resident tourists are price inelastic (i.e. relatively unresponsive to changes in price), significantly higher fees may be required to reduce demand (Navrud and Mungatana, 1994). Two-tiered pricing schemes can then ensure that price-conscious residents are not excluded. In some situations, requiring certain qualifications (e.g. visitors must be researchers engaged in scientific studies, or certified divers) can reduce visitation to desirable levels.

Controlling visitor use and access within national parks

Controlling visitor flow, temporal and spatial dispersion, and modes of travel can also reduce the adverse impacts of tourism on wildlife. Strategies can increase visitation across broader areas, or concentrate visitors to areas more conducive to tourism. Zoning can be used to protect sensitive resources from visitor impacts, or to spatially separate incompatible uses (Eagles, 1997). Often, zoning creates core protection areas of limited use, surrounded by buffers where a wider range of activities can be accommodated (Lilieholm and Romm, 1992; Kelson and Lilieholm, 1997, 1999). Core protection areas may include sensitive breeding grounds, migratory routes, or habitat for species with minimal tolerance for human contact. In the Seychelles, zoning areas of high biodiversity for low tourism use has been effective in protecting sensitive resources (personal communication, J. Nevill, Director, Seychelles Conservation Section, May 1999). In Kenya's Amboseli National Park, annual tourist carrying capacities were increased from 80 000 to 120 000 with less environmental impact through spatial and temporal dispersion (Weaver, 1998). Fences can also be used to control visitor movement (Shackley, 1996). Encouraging tourists to visit underutilised areas of parks can reduce crowding. For example, in Uganda's Bwindi Impenetrable Forest National Park, gorilla trekkers may have to wait two weeks before viewing gorillas. To generate additional revenue for local communities and occupy tourists while they wait to see gorillas, the International Gorilla Conservation Programme has sponsored jungle walks and climbs to a nearby dormant volcano. Expanded use may be inappropriate, however, if it opens up *de-facto* refuges to undesirable human impact.

Promoting tourism at alternative public and private reserves

Alleviating overcrowding in national parks can also be achieved by promoting alternative sites like underutilised parks, wildlife reserves, and private or community reserves. In Zimbabwe, private black rhinoceros reserves are providing both habitat and tourism opportunities. The role that private reserves can play in conservation is just beginning to be realised in much of Africa. Indeed, the majority of the 133 rhinoceros auctioned in South Africa in 1995 were sold to private reserves (Anon., 1996). Like their public counterparts, private reserves face a host of challenges, including poaching, limited budgets, political unrest, and community opposition (Langholz, 1996). To foster the development of private and community reserves, Munyi (1992) suggests that operators be granted expanded rights to wildlife, including entrance and hunting fees, and revenues from the sale of animal products like hides, claws, teeth, and tusks.

Creating new national parks

The creation of new parks and reserves can relieve visitation pressure on existing facilities. Nigeria currently plans seven new parks over the next five years (personal communication, L.B. Margusa, Director, Nigerian National Park Service, May 1999). In Mauritius, three new national parks are being considered (personal communication, Y. Mungroo, Director, Mauritius National Parks and Conservation Service, April 1999). In the Seychelles, two to three new parks are likely, along with at least one park expansion (personal communication, J. Naill, Director, Seychelles Conservation Section, May 1999). Ethiopia is currently planning up to six new parks in anticipation of increased visitation and population growth (personal communication, T. Handessa, Ethiopian Wildlife Conservation Organization, May 1999).

Improved design of park facilities

Improved park facilities can enhance visitor satisfaction and protect environmental quality. For example, existing facilities can be retrofitted to reduce energy needs for lighting, heating, and cooling. Water conservation measures can be particularly beneficial in arid environments, along with environmentally sound waste treatment. The layout and design of new facilities can incorporate these measures as well, while being more compact and located in less sensitive areas.

Popular sites can be 'hardened' through paved trails or the construction of walkways to allow for increased use and reduced impact (Shackley, 1996). For example, Muthee (1992) found that off-road driving by vehicles created the most negative impacts from tourism in Kenya's Maasai Mara Reserve, and recommended an expanded road network with a strict ban on off-road driving.

In addition, new facilities can be used to allow access to new areas or attractions, thereby reducing crowding at more heavily used sites. For example, in Uganda's Kibale National Park, local communities have constructed a boardwalk trail to allow visitors to explore a wetland ecosystem that was previously inaccessible (personal observation by the first author). A small access fee and guiding service allows locals to generate direct economic benefits from tourists.

Improved habitat and wildlife protection

Improving habitat and protecting wildlife are two important ways to enhance both wildlife and tourism. Many parks have increased patrols in an effort to control poaching, thereby reducing wildlife losses. More frequent patrolling can also be incorporated into monitoring programmes to continuously evaluate the status of wildlife and other park resources. Habitat improvements can also enhance wildlife populations, and can serve to concentrate animals for more effective viewing. For example, in Hwange National Park, artificial watering holes have supported increased numbers of wildlife while providing locations for the construction of viewing platforms (Potts *et al.*, 1996). Although controversial, the use of electric fences to control wildlife movement can lead to enhanced viewing opportunities and reduced crop-raiding and contact with local villagers (Munyi, 1992).

Animal habituation

Animal habituation to human observation is used to improve the likelihood that tourists encounter difficulty in locating forest-dwelling wildlife like primates. The mode of habituation is important, however, since observational habituation is generally considered to be less detrimental to animal behaviour than conditioning through feeding. In Uganda's Bwindi Impenetrable National Park, increasing tourist demands before the 1999 killings led to discussion of habituating three more gorilla troops. The proposal created some concerns, however, since it was feared that habituated gorillas are more susceptible to poaching, and that crop-raiding and confrontations with local villagers would increase (Bourne, 1998).

Educational programmes for visitors, guides, and tour operators

A variety of educational programmes can be used to enhance visitor satisfaction while minimising tourism's impacts. Visitor education is important in reducing negative impacts like littering and the feeding and harassment of wildlife. Publications, ranger talks, individual contacts, signs, and interpretive displays can inform visitors of park regulations and their importance. These methods have been effective in reducing animal feeding and littering problems in Ethiopia's Awash National Park (personal communication, T. Hundessa, Ethiopian Wildlife Conservation Organization, May 1999). Training for park rangers, guides and tour operators can lead to improved visitor satisfaction and reduced impact by channelling visitors to areas where viewing can be best accommodated. Training can also focus on controlling visitor behaviour.

Educational tourism and specialised tours

Another area of opportunity is educational programmes offered through field schools or university study abroad. In programmes offering university credit, students may be able to spend a semester abroad at less cost than remaining on campus (Lilieholm *et al.*, 1998). Specialized tours can also be used to relieve overcrowding in popular areas, generate additional income, and take advantage of currently underutilised park attractions. For example, many tourists have interests in birds, insects, geology, archaeology, culture, and history. One particularly promising area of ecotourism is avitourism for birdwatchers.

Attracting sensitive tourists and volunteers

Finally, specifically targeting tourists that are sympathetic to conservation issues can be an effective way to reduce the adverse impacts of tourism on wildlife. Such tourists may be more accepting of primitive, more ecologically friendly facilities. For example, many South Africans travel to Zimbabwe's Hwange National Park because they feel it is less-developed than their own Kruger National Park (Potts *et al.*, 1996). Some tourists may even donate time to assist with park projects. Organisations like Earthwatch solicit volunteers to travel to parks and other natural areas to work on research projects. These research/education links are particularly beneficial since they can lead to the creation of knowledge useful for management. Moreover, research projects can often lead to long-term collaborative partnerships between national parks and universities from around the world (Lilieholm *et al.*, 1997).

Ensuring sustainability through adaptive resource management

Mitigation strategies should be implemented within an 'adaptive management' framework where management is viewed as an on-going experiment that is monitored and evaluated over time with respect to pre-established criteria based on management goals (Walters, 1986). In national parks, obvious criteria include population levels of key fauna, habitat quality and quantity indicators, and visitation. Visitor surveys are important as well since they can indicate tourist perceptions of crowding (Shackley, 1996), assess knowledge of low-impact behaviour and park regulations, and determine which aspects of the park are important. This last item is useful since services or facilities that cause adverse impacts to wildlife may not be valued by visitors, and can hence be eliminated.

In order to recognise the broader context within which most parks exist, monitoring programmes should consider trends beyond protected area boundaries. Population, jobs and income can indicate human pressure on the environment. Moreover, visitor-related gambling, racism, prostitution, and drug and alcohol abuse can undermine local support for tourism and conservation (Card and Vogelsong, 1995). To ensure the long-term viability of the park and surrounding communities, monitoring methodologies should be well defined, consistent, ongoing, rapid, and inexpensive.

Barriers to reaching sustainable tourism development and wildlife protection

Many barriers can limit the ability of parks to alleviate the adverse effects of tourism on wildlife. At the agency level, insufficient and unstable funding, poor communications, inadequate equipment, and personnel shortages, and staff turnover are all commonplace. Knowledge is also lacking about the effectiveness of alternative mitigation strategies. On the local level, disparities between community costs and benefits associated with wildlife protection and tourism is an ever-present issue. In promoting policies, it is important to avoid overestimating the likely benefits of ecotourism since unrealistically high expectations can quickly turn to disillusionment.

At broader national and international levels, developing strong tourism policies can promote development and ensure that tourism provides net benefits for wildlife, parks, and communities. Indeed, Sournia (1996) cites the lack of national tourism policies as one reason why west and central African nations lag behind other regions of Africa. Effectively implementing policies requires communication and cooperation at multiple levels of government (Wild, 1994). In some cases, the boundary-crossing nature of ecosystems may necessitate international cooperation, as with the Mara–Serengeti ecosystem corridor between Amboseli (Kenya) and Mount Kilimanjaro National Parks (Tanzania).

Corruption can hamper effective management (Eagles, 1997). For example, tourists may bribe park officials to gain access to restricted areas. What appears to be a small bribe by a tourist may equal several months' pay to a park ranger. Moreover, tour operators may place profits ahead of environmental protection (Wild, 1994). Fortunately, many visitors appear to be sensitive to these issues, and are increasingly interested in the environmental and cultural impacts of tourism (Rymer, 1992; Wild, 1994). Corruption can have a positive side, too. For example, in Mobutu's Zaire, it was reputed that the dictator himself was pocketing revenues from gorilla ecotourism. As a result, the country's gorillas were placed under constant military protection (Davey, 1996).

Political instability can seriously threaten tourism (Eagles, 1997). The 1994 genocide in Rwanda, coupled with revolution in the former Zaire and tourist killings in Uganda, have severely reduced mountain gorilla tourism. Such incidents, while often of isolated occurrence, are widely publicised by the international media (Eagles, 1997; Langholz, 1996), and can lead to travel advisories, voided travel insurance, and reduced visitation. Instability can directly affect wildlife populations as well, as when four mountain gorillas were inadvertently killed in crossfire between Rwandan troops and Interhamwe rebels.

Finally, in countries with limited tourism, promoting the industry may offer the best prospects of enhancing wildlife. Underutilised tourist destinations may result from negative market images, lack of foreign exchange for capital development, lack of trained personnel, weak institutional frameworks for planning and management, and political instability (Ankomah and Crompton, 1990). These constraints are present in much of West and Central Africa, as well as some countries within heavily visited East and Southern Africa (e.g. Uganda and Madagascar, respectively). In such cases, tourists may be lured by abundant wildlife, lower prices, and fewer crowds.

Conclusion

Tourism has great promise to finance sustainably both conservation and development. While the industry's rapid growth in recent decades has brought with it problems traditionally associated with more conventional forms of tourism, nature-based tourism may represent the only viable form of economic development in many poor, remote regions of the globe (see Weaver, Chapter 8).

Tourism can have both direct and indirect impacts on wildlife. These range from auto/wildlife accidents to disease transfer and behaviour modification. Not all these impacts are negative, however, since ecotourism in particular has successfully turned wildlife and conservation into marketable commodities in many parts of the world. Ensuring the long-term success of nature-based tourism largely depends on creating local incentives to conserve and protect environmental amenities. To do this, tourism must equitably balance the costs and benefits of conservation, which are often disproportionately shared by local communities. This balance can be achieved through the creation of mutually beneficial, self-sustaining mechanisms that support tourism, wildlife, institutions and communities. In areas with limited tourism, policies that attract and support environmentally and culturally sensitive tourism can increase local economic opportunity, as well as local support for conservation programmes.

References

Adams, J.S. and McShane, T.O., 1992, *The myth of Wild Africa: conservation without illusion*, University of California Press, Berkeley, CA

Akama, J S., 1996, Western environmental values and nature-based tourism in Kenya. *Tourism Management*, **17**(8): 567–574

Akama, J.S., Lant, C.L. and Burnett, G.W., 1995, Conflicting attitudes toward state wildlife conservation programs in Kenya. *Society and Natural Resources*, **8**: 133–144

Ankomah, P.K. and Crompton, J.L., 1990, Unrealized tourism potential: The case of sub-Saharan Africa. *Tourism Management*, **11**(3): 11–27

Anon., 1996, Good and bad at game. *The Economist*, (340): 69–71

Ashton, R E., 1991, The financing of conservation: The concept of self supporting eco-preserves. In *Ecotourism and resource conservation: a collection of papers*, J.J.A. Kuster, ed., Ecotourism and Resource Conservation Project, Omni Press, Madison, WI

Aussie-Stone, M., 1992, Planning a culture hotel for an indigenous community. In *World Congress on Adventure Travel and Ecotourism*, Adventure Travel Society, Englewood, CO

Boo, E., 1990, *Ecotourism: the potentials and pitfalls*, Wickersham Printing Co. Inc., Lancaster, PA

Boonzaier, E.A., 1996, Local responses to conservation in the Richtersveld National Park, South Africa. *Biodiversity and Conservation*, 5: 307–314

Bourne, J., 1998, Gorillas in our midst: deep in Uganda's impenetrable forest you can watch mountain gorillas at play in the wild. *Audubon*, 100(5): 70–73

Brown, G. Jr and Henry, W., 1989, *The economic value of elephants*. Paper 89-12, The London Environmental Economics Centre, London

Budowski, G., 1976, Tourism and environmental conservation: conflict, coexistence or symbiosis. *Environmental Conservation*, 3(1): 27–31

Butler, R.W., 1991, Tourism, environment, and sustainable development. *Environmental Conservation* 18(3): 201–209

Card, J.A. and Vogelsong, M.J., 1995, Ecotourism as a mechanism for economic enhancement in developing countries. In *Linking tourism, the environment, and sustainability*, S.F. McCool and A.E. Watson, eds, pp. 57–60, USDA Forest Service General Technical Report INT-GTR-323

Chase, A., 1986, *Playing God in Yellowstone*, Atlantic Monthly Press, Boston, MA

Child, G., 1995, *Wildlife and People: The Zimbabwean Success*, Wisdom Foundation, New York

Davey, S., 1996, Under African skies. *TNT Magazine*, London

Dixon, J.A. and Sherman, P.B., 1990, *Economics of protected areas: a new look at benefits and costs*, Island Press, Washington, DC

Drake, S., 1991, Development of a local participation plan for ecotourist projects. In *Ecotourism and resource conservation: a collection of papers*, J.J.A. Kusler, ed., pp. 68–81, Ecotourism and Resource Conservation Project, Omni Press, Madison, WI

Durbin, J.C. and Ratrimoarisaona, S., 1996, Can tourism make a major contribution to the conservation of protected areas in Madagascar? *Biodiversity and Conservation*, 5: 345–353

Eagles, P.F., 1992, The travel motivations of Canadian ecotourists. *Journal of Travel Research*, 21(2): 3–7

Eagles, P.F., 1997, International ecotourism management: using Australia and Africa as case studies. IUCN World Commission on Protected Areas, Conference on Protected Areas in the 21st Century: From Islands to Networks, 23–29 November, Albany, Australia

Farrel, B.H. and Runyan, D., 1991, Ecology and tourism. *Annals of Tourism Research*, 18(1): 26–40

Fausold, C.F. and Lilieholm, R.J., 1999, The economic value of open space: A review and synthesis. *Environmental Management*, 23(3): 307–320

International Resources Group, 1992, *Ecotourism: A viable alternative for sustainable management of natural resources in Africa*, US Agency for International Development. Washington, DC

Kelson, A.R. and Lilieholm, R.J., 1997, The influence of adjacent land activities on wilderness resources. *International Journal of Wilderness*, 3(1): 25–28

Kelson, A.R. and Lilieholm, R.J., 1999, Transboundary issues in wilderness management. *Environmental Management*, 23(3): 297–305

Knight, R.L. and Gutzwiller, K.J., 1995, *Wildlife and recreationists: coexistence through management and research*, Island Press, Washington, DC

Langholz, J., 1996, Economics, objectives, and success of private nature reserves in sub-Saharan Africa and Latin America. *Conservation Biology*, 10(1): 271–280

Lilieholm, R.J., Paul, K.B., Sharik, T.L. and Loether, R., 1998, Education's role in sustainable development: Uganda's Kibale National Park. *Natural Resources and Environmental Issues*, 7(1): 123–129

Lilieholm, R.J., Kasenene, J., Isabirye-Basuta, G., Sharik, T.L. and Paul, K.B., 1997, Research and training opportunities at Makerere University Biological Field Station, Kibale National Park. *Uganda Bulletin of the Ecological Society of America*, **78**(1): 80–84

Lilieholm, R.J. and Romm, J.M., 1992, The Pinelands National Reserve: an intergovernmental approach to nature preservation. *Environmental Management*, **16**(3): 335–343

Lillywhite, M., 1992, Reactive or proactive: Botswana's low impact ecotourism development plans. In *World Congress on Adventure Travel and Ecotourism*, Adventure Travel Society, Englewood, CO

Lindberg, K., 1991, *Policies for maximizing nature tourism's ecological and environmental benefits*, World Resources Institute, Washington, DC

Lonsdale, W.M. and Lane, A.M., 1994, Tourist vehicles as vectors of weed seeds in Kakadu National Park, Northern Australia. *Biological Conservation*, **69**: 277–283

Munyi, S.W., 1992, Kenya ecotourism workshop. *Contours*, **5**(8): 30–32

Muthee, L.W., 1992, Ecological impacts of tourist use on the habitats and pressure-point animal species. In *Tourist Attitudes and Use Impacts in Maasai Mara National Reserve*, C.G. Gakahu, ed., pp. 18–38, Wildlife Conservation International, Nairobi, Kenya

Navrud, S. and Mungatana, E.D., 1994, Environmental valuation in developing countries: The recreational value of wildlife viewing. *Ecological Economics*, **11**: 135–151

Place, S.E., 1991, Nature tourism and rural development in Tortuguero. *Annals of Tourism Research*, **18**(2): 186–210

Potts, F.C., Goodwin, H. and Walpole, M.J., 1996, People, wildlife, and tourism in and around Hwange National Park, Zimbabwe In *People and tourism in fragile environments*, M.F. Price, ed., John Wiley, New York

Romeril, M., 1989, Tourism: The environmental dimension In *Progress in tourism, recreation, and hospitality management*, Vol 1, C.P. Cooper and A. Lockwood, eds, Belhaven Press, London.

Roosevelt, T., 1910, *African game trails*, Scribners, New York

Rymer, T.M., 1992, Growth of U.S. ecotourism and its future in the 1990s. *FIU Hospitality Review* **10**(1): 1–10

Shackley, M., 1996, *Wildlife tourism*, International Thomson Business Press, London

Shaw, G. and Williams, A., 1992, *Critical issues in tourism: a geographical perspective*, TJ Press, Padstow

Sournia, G., 1996, Wildlife tourism in West and Central Africa. *Ecodecision* (Spring): 52–54

Stoddard, E., 1999, Africa in quandary over elephant population. Reuters, 28 June

Victurine, R., 1999, Building tourism excellence at the community level: Capacity building for community based entrepreneurs. In *Uganda Journal of Travel Research* (in press)

Walters, C., 1986, *Adaptive management of renewable resources*, Macmillan, New York

Weaver, D., 1998, *Ecotourism in the less developed world*, CAB International, New York

Wells, M.P., 1996, The social role of protected areas in the new South Africa. *Environmental Conservation*, **23**(4): 322–331

Whelan, T., ed., 1991, *Nature tourism: managing for the environment*, Island Press, Washington, DC

Whitesell, S., Kyampaire, O. and Lilieholm, R.J., 1997, Human dimensions research needs in Uganda's Kibale National Park. *Forum*, **14**(4): 65–71

Wild, C., 1994, Issues in ecotourism. In *Progress in tourism, recreation and hospitality management*, Volume 6, C.P. Cooper and A. Lockwood, eds, pp. 12–21, John Wiley, New York

Young, M., 1992, Towards a meaningful ecotourism definition (preliminary paper). WWF, Sydney

Part Three:
Issues and Responses

S.W. BOYD AND R.W. BUTLER

The third part of the book focuses on Issues and Responses. Issues are assumed to be the product of the history within which parks have been established (Part One) as well as the specific setting, both people and nature-oriented, in which tourism exists in national parks (Part Two). For instance, the length of time that tourism has been a factor in parks may determine to a considerable extent which issues may arise, as will the length of time a particular park system has been in existence. Parks with a long history of tourism, not surprisingly, can bring with them a multiplicity of issues that require attention. Chapters within the first part of the book are a testimony to this reality. Issues can also arise from the characteristics of the settings themselves, namely the type of people that tourism has to interact with, examples here include local communities and 'First Peoples' that reside inside parks or on adjacent lands. Chapters by Hall and Nepal in Part Two clearly illustrated how tourism interaction with other peoples can result in a range of issues that require attention. Issues can also arise from tourist/visitor interaction with the physical characteristics of park environments. As noted in chapters by Marsh, Weaver and Lilieholm and Romney (Part Two) it is often the fragility and sensitivity of settings, along with their level of tolerance to human impact, that results in issues emerging with respect to tourism. Given the constraints of space, it is only possible in this part to examine what may be considered as key issues that influence tourism within national parks. While the focus in these chapters is directed at tourism, some discussion is provided on non-tourism issues, such as conflict over other park uses.

As outlined in Figure III below, key issues addressed include sustainability, resource conflicts, managing visitors, mitigating tourism impacts, partnerships, and cooperation. What is not shown in the figure are the various linkages that exist between and across issues. For example, it is possible to argue that sustainability can be linked to all other issues present. Sustainability is best achieved where conflict is absent between park uses and users, when tourists are well managed, their impacts mitigated, and where partnership and cooperation are promoted and encouraged. Equally, there are obvious links between resource conflicts and mitigating tourism impacts, and between partnerships and cooperation. The arrow at the bottom of the figure suggests that issues, and how they are addressed, have some bearing on the future context of tourism in national parks.

Before providing commentary on each chapter contained within this part, a number of general points need to be made. First, focus is not on addressing issues

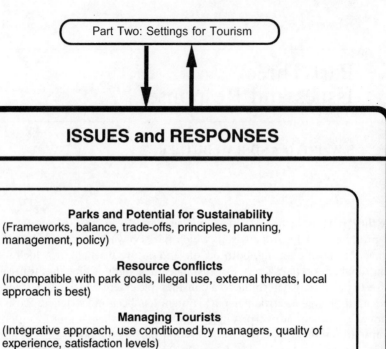

Part Two: Settings for Tourism

ISSUES and RESPONSES

Parks and Potential for Sustainability
(Frameworks, balance, trade-offs, principles, planning, management, policy)

Resource Conflicts
(Incompatible with park goals, illegal use, external threats, local approach is best)

Managing Tourists
(Integrative approach, use conditioned by managers, quality of experience, satisfaction levels)

Mitigating Tourism Impacts
(Management frameworks, normative approach, encounter levels, acceptability of impacts)

Partnerships
(Opportunities, feedback of benefits, early involvement of local population, a negotiated approach)

International Co-operation
(Cross-border parks and partnership, typology of parks, key challenges, promoting peace)

Park Creation in New Areas
(History, instability, limited institutional arrangement, ecotourism focus, better planning and management)

Part Four: Future Context

Figure III Issues and responses

alone, but also in providing some responses to them. The type of responses offered will be addressed within the individual descriptions of chapters. Second, discussion is raised beyond mere description of issues as they apply to specific case examples. Contributors have grasped the opportunity to develop and apply a range of frameworks, models, management procedures and typologies to issues, and have used this approach to offer responses to them. While the frameworks are applied within specific settings for particular parks and park systems, they are put forward as having global relevance and utility.

A plethora of research studies have focused on the concept of sustainability and Boyd offers a synthesis of key developments. The position taken in his chapter is that sustainability may be envisioned as a broad issue and an acceptable park goal, and that as a concept it should not be limited to a discussion of tourism in parks alone. Instead, the argument is put forward that parks can only be true examples of sustainable landscapes if all activities, including tourism, are placed on a sustainable path. To this end a number of frameworks are presented as a response to understanding the complexity of the concept and applying it within a parks context. One framework addresses parks in general; stating that elements of balance and the need to accept trade-offs between uses and park users based on the priority assigned to park mandates is essential if sustainability can be realised. Citing research undertaken on the Canadian parks system, Boyd proposes a sustainability framework that provides a qualitative 'measure' of how park activities are seen to be performing. In specifically addressing tourism in parks, a sustainable tourism development framework is developed around three broad elements of principles, planning and management and again applied to the Canadian parks system. A range of tourism characteristics are examined which either support sustainability or not, and which have wider application than the Canadian context alone. A secondary objective of this chapter is to examine the role of policy in advancing sustainability in parks. Sustainability was found either to have been present in some form over the history of parks systems policy development or was being used as the key principle in how parks can be planned and managed at present and in the future.

Dearden addresses the issue of resource conflicts, citing three reasons why they occur. First, tourism is not always accepted as being compatible with park goals where these aim to maintain ecological integrity. He cites Banff National Park in the Rocky Mountains of Canada as an apt example of this resource conflict, noting that park's long association with tourism and how most tourist development has occurred in the Montane zone of the park, important for its rare ecology and wildlife. The response offered to this conflict situation has been to place a moratorium on development, and to strengthen the National Parks Act (1998) which legislates how much development can take place in each of Canada's national parks. Dearden notes that another response is to push for stronger emphasis toward maintaining ecological integrity in parks rather than promoting use.

The second reason for conflict situations to arise is through illegal use of park resources by people in the surrounding environs. Dearden uses a three-dimensional model to outline the various factors that need to be taken into consideration. There is a need to understand the temporal dimensions of occurrence, the motivation behind illegal uses, and the extent of environmental damage that can result from illegal activities. Based on research on parks in Thailand, he suggests there is a need to accept a different management response to each park where illegal use is present. Dearden argues the merits of adopting an idiographic approach on the basis that parks are very much individual landscapes, suggesting that one possible solution is to put in place negotiated agreements between park authorities and local peoples.

The third reason for resource conflicts to arise is from land uses outside parks being incompatible with those inside parks. In discussing these external threats, Dearden examines work on stressors on parks, noting that in the case of Canada, many result from tourism and visitor activities. In light of these three reasons for resource conflict, Dearden suggests there is no generic solution to problems and that because problems arise locally, a localised approach to resolution is best.

Vaske, Donnelly and Whittaker address the challenge of mitigating tourist use and subsequent impacts; an issue recognised as arising out of tensions between use and protection in parks. Focus is directed at planning and management frameworks that have evolved which provide decision makers with key information about types of use and the impacts they generate. They identify a number of common elements: opportunities, indicators, standards, and collaboration. In linking actions with standards, they identify approaches that can be taken to mitigate visitor impacts, including capital development, education (including enforcing regulations) and restricting the level of use by imposing limits. Based on the management framework literature, they propose a normative approach that may be used to establish management standards, to limit levels of impact to those considered acceptable, based on the frequency of encounters.

This approach is tested within three case situations in North America (Gwaii Haanas National Park Reserve and Haida heritage site, Canada; Brooks River, Katmai National Park, Alaska; Columbia Icefield, Jasper National Park, Canada) that cover both front and backcountry settings. There is discussion on how information collected on norms, and levels of acceptable impact have been integrated with area management. In the first case study, this approach helped to determine maximum numbers of people per day, maximum numbers in a party, tolerance levels to aircraft noise and the value of running a visitor orientation programme. The latter emphasised 'leave-no-trace' camping, and raised visitor awareness of the impacts they can exert on the environment, that in turn may lead to less management intervention and less disruption to visitor experiences. At Brooks River, a premier brown bear viewing area, it was noted that bear use of the area has risen despite increased visitation, but that a fixed capacity was still needed on platforms to maintain viewing experiences. Development changes where visitor facilities were relocated away from the river to minimise bear–human interactions were also encouraged. In the third case (Columbia Icefield), increased visitor use of a frontcountry attraction and the impact this has had on visitor experiences was assessed through a number of social carrying-capacity surveys carried out from 1992 to 1997. Results showed that experiences have remained high and that crowding was only a concern in the visitor centre at the site. All three case examples help illustrate the value of applying a normative approach as a response to assigning levels of use and evaluating their impact on overall visitor experiences.

Sowman and Pearce also placed their attention on the issue of visitor management, suggesting that an appropriate response in New Zealand is to adopt an integrated approach which links use with demand, acknowledges stakeholders, and takes into account the processes through which visitor management is undertaken. To this end, a general framework of visitor management is proposed, where links are made between visitors, the resource base (the national park itself), and various contextual elements making up the specific setting in which interaction takes place. They see visitor management to be visitor use that is conditioned by managers to varying degrees, given the specifics of the setting involved. A number of aspects of visitor management are raised: the quality of visitor experience which needs to be kept in context with the area's management objectives, the level of visitor satisfaction, the extent to which conflict may be minimised, and the techniques used to manage visitors.

The integrated framework is assessed within two New Zealand parks: Westland and Paparoa. Contextual elements focus on the role that the Department of Conservation (the government conservation agency) plays in parks management, noting that provision of services and facilities in parks has not kept pace with increases in visitation, most of which is international in origin. As for characteristics, attention here is directed at the range of natural tourist attractions present, visitor profiles (in terms of party size, time spent, purpose for visiting), the tiered visitor management system in place, and the role played by private operators to provide services, mostly tours, to visitors. Limited discussion is provided on linkages, exceptions being those that exist between management and private operators in the form of concession agreements. A number of key issues are raised: access, interpretation, visitor safety, inter-group conflict and crowding. Using visitor surveys in both parks the issue of access, or the lack thereof to key natural attractions, is addressed in detail as a key factor in explaining the differences in visitor satisfaction recorded, this being a particular challenge requiring a solution. In applying an integrated approach to visitor management, Sowman and Pearce conclude that because of the complexities involved, this type of approach helps to bring all the key aspects together from which processes at work can be better examined and appropriate decisions taken on visitor management.

Based on results from a three-year comparative and collaborative research project on tourism in and around three national parks (Keoladeo in Bharatpur, India; Komodo in Indonesia; and Gonarezhou in Zimbabwe), Goodwin discusses the issue of partnership between parks and local peoples. Attention is directed at the opportunity for ecotourism within these national parks, where emphasis is placed on the need to reshape the tourist product to ensure that benefits derived feed back into park conservation, and that they also reach local communities. One way to increase this benefit is to have a differential fee structure in place, where international tourists are charged more than domestic ones and where governments are not subsidising for affluent foreign tourists. This issue is examined by surveys of visitor willingness to pay, the results of which confirmed that in all three parks there was opportunity to raise entrance charges for international visitors. Caution, however, needs to be exercised here, as a two-, three- or fourfold increase in charges may reduce numbers visiting and therefore result in less visitor spending in the local area. Goodwin also assesses the extent to which opportunities exist for local communities to provide essential park services, noting that these can be dramatically influenced by local circumstances. One area, which appears fruitful, is the interest by international tourists in experiencing local culture (music and dancing, village tours, having a meal cooked by local people), all of which have local community support. In terms of developing partnerships, Goodwin stresses the importance of having the direct involvement of local communities in both the planning and implementation of tourism development, commenting on the acceptance of this by tour operators operating to these destinations. At the core of partnerships are the benefits to be enjoyed, which, according to Goodwin, need to be based on having negotiated a clear and shared set of partnership objectives to minimise conflicts that can arise as tourism develops.

Evidence from the case studies is presented to illustrate that while benefits can accrue to conservation and local communities, a vast amount of revenue is lost through leakage. This can be reduced by the tourism industry developing linkages with the local communities as the source for goods and services. Another response is the development of leasehold agreements as are in place in the southeast lowveld in Zimbabwe. Goodwin concludes by stressing the need to create and strengthen those institutions that exist at the local level that are based on partnership to channel tourism potential into local economic gain.

In the next chapter, Timothy discusses international parks (those that straddle and cross political lines), examining the challenges they face, both in their designation and management. Key issues emerge including the need for cross-border partnership to protect park resources, to reduce over-exploitation on all sides, to avoid unnecessary costs in provision of facilities and services, to combine marketing and promotion of the area, and to minimise conflicts that can occur over the use of internationally shared resources. A brief review is provided of locations where international parks have been created and where opportunity exists to create them in the future. Timothy develops a typology of international parks, with three distinctive types: those that are found directly on both sides of a border and which function as one entity; those that are found only on one side but where management is joint with an adjoining country; and those where two contiguous protected areas are found adjacent to each other but which are separately managed. Timothy found that the level of cooperation in each type of park varied but it was greatest in parks in the first type.

The role of international parks as tourist attractions is explored through a number of North American case studies: Waterton-Glacier International Peace Park, The International Peace Garden and Roosevelt Campobello International Park. Key challenges emerging for international parks in general discussed by Timothy include bridging the cultural and political gap that can often exist, accommodating sovereignty and territoriality issues, operating around border formalities, coping with fortifications that exist, marginality, and managing parks where different levels of development exist. Timothy accepts that while these challenges prevent total integration occurring, cross-border partnership is key if these park landscapes are to be truly sustainable. Some concluding comments are made on the role of these parks in promoting peace and harmony between nations. It is suggested that tourism, linked with resource conservation in these settings, has a very important role to play in building understanding between different peoples and different cultures.

The last chapter in this part addresses the issue of establishing parks and park systems in countries that are in the early stages of developing their tourism potential and which are emerging from years of political and socio-economic instability.

Cresswell and Maclaren provide discussion on the growth of tourism, and the establishment of national parks and their tourism potential within Cambodia and Vietnam. With respect to Cambodia, Cresswell and Maclaren note that while recent legislative agreements are in place to help establish a system of protected areas and offer early steps toward park management, problems remain in how parks are protected and managed. These include no clear mandates for parks, no cooperation across ministries involved in park management (parks are illegally forested and used by local people as a source for fuel), a limited budget, park personnel that lack training in park management techniques, and no overall effective strategy in place to manage the system of national parks. In terms of tourism development within Cambodia's national parks, emphasis is being directed at ecotourism with little foresight given to how sites within parks are planned and managed. In their examination of national parks in Vietnam, Cresswell and Maclaren comment that national parks were established against a history of biodiversity loss. This has continued despite legislation to protect areas. As a result, integrated conservation development projects are viewed as offering a solution, and comments on one project are offered. As for tourism development within parks, again emphasis is focused on the potential of ecotourism, with discussion on a number of parks and where a stakeholder approach is used to involve local communities in the development of ecotourism. Cresswell and Maclaren conclude the chapter by carrying out a SWOT analysis to assess ecotourism in national parks. They argue that ecotourism development must be supportive of rural development as well as the area's conservation objectives.

As commented earlier, the chapters comprising this part should not be viewed as addressing all issues that arise within parks. While the focus has been on tourism, elements within chapters by Boyd, Dearden and Timothy have alluded to non-tourism issues such as the wider challenges of achieving sustainability, addressing illegal uses in parks and encouraging cross-border partnership in general park management. Overall responses to issues are shown as varied, illustrating that solutions will be tied very much to the specifics of each setting and the context in which issues have arisen. The development of innovative approaches to issues presented within the chapters offers new thinking and ideas as to how national parks may be planned and managed.

11 Tourism, national parks and sustainability

STEPHEN W. BOYD

Introduction

Ever since the Brundtland Commission (WCED, 1987) adopted the sustainable development concept, it has received phenomenal attention, with interest quickly spreading throughout academic, corporate, business and political circles. The degree of permanence which it appears to have achieved in a relatively short time span may be viewed, however, as positive. A key factor in the extent of its popularity is that implicit within the concept has been a powerful recognition for the need for change to occur, within both our societies and economies and the relationships that exist between economic growth and environment (however the latter is defined). However, amid the euphoria, the level of acceptance surrounding it needs to be balanced against the reality that even a decade on from the report there remains a lack of consensus over what is meant by it, what elements can and should be linked to it, and whether or not the ideals behind it can be translated into reality. Part of the problem rests with the fact that it has been adopted as a 'panacea' for many problems and issues without any clear understanding that the solution(s) needed may vary given the nature of the problem, the scale and time frame involved, and the goals and objectives set out to be achieved. As a result, what has emerged has been many different 'pictures' of sustainable development, all of which may be relevant in certain contexts and for particular issues.

Tourism has long been recognised to fit well with the ideals of sustainable development as it is an activity and industry which relies on the maintenance of a robust and healthy environment for its long-term well-being in many areas. It is not surprising that sustainable development has gained the attention of tourism researchers (e.g. France, 1997; Stabler, 1997; Wahab and Pigram, 1997; Hall and Lew, 1998; Middleton and Hawkins, 1998; Mowforth and Munt, 1998) because as a concept it addresses concerns over the abuse and over-use of resources, embraces principles of sensible and common sense environmental management and recognises the need for change, all key elements that are important where tourism planning, development and management are concerned (Nelson *et al.*, 1993; Butler and Pearce, 1996; Wall, 1997; Butler, 1999).

National parks, often the most recognisable form of protected environments, have a well-established connection with tourism. From early days, tourism has been encouraged in park systems worldwide as it helped to fulfil the 'enjoyment' mandate of many national parks agencies (see Nelson, Hall, Booth and Simmons, this book). This being the case, an ironic situation is now developing in national parks in association with tourism. While tourism is indeed promoted, the focus of priority is shifting towards the 'protection' mandate as opposed to use (where tourism is included as a recognised type of use). Yet, given the rising pressures of financing many park systems, increasingly more tourism is being targeted as the preferred solution. Conflict over park mandates is avoided on the basis that the type of tourism being encouraged is that classed under the broad labels of 'sustainable', 'responsible' and 'environmentally conscious'. In the unlikely event that tourist interest in visiting national parks (where the visit is an integral part of their overall holiday experience) will diminish in the near future (see concluding chapter by Butler), attention must shift towards how tourism, in line with sustainability principles, is planned, developed and managed to suit national park environments.

The primary focus of this chapter is to direct the sustainability debate to the context of national parks, on the basis that as a concept it offers great utility in how parks may be planned and managed for tourism. Following a brief review of sustainability and tourism, a number of frameworks are offered to the reader which incorporate sustainability with respect to national parks, and around which further debate is invited. First a general sustainability framework is advanced in which the argument is made that tourism must be viewed as only one sector of use among an array of other sectors present in parks, and that key issues of balance and an acceptance for the need for trade-offs are essential for effective planning and management to take place (Boyd, 1995). A second framework is presented that focuses specifically on sustainable tourism development alone for national parks (Boyd and Butler, 1997). Both frameworks are based on research undertaken specifically within the context of the Canadian national parks system, but some discussion is provided to extrapolate findings, where appropriate, to national parks in general. A secondary objective within the chapter is to examine the extent to which sustainability has emerged as an integral part of National Park policy. Discourse here is offered on park policy for Canada's national park system, with limited attention given to policy as it applies to national parks in England and Wales (see also Ravenscroft and Parker, Chapter 7). The overall purpose behind these two objectives is to establish sustainability as a key **response** both as a management tool as well as offering directives as to how parks can fulfill their mandates with respect to protecting their natural resource base at the same time as providing and managing for tourism opportunities.

Tourism and sustainability

A copious literature exists on sustainability and tourism, often focusing on the relationship between the environment in general and tourism in particular (e.g. Budowski, 1976; Wall and Wright, 1977; Mathieson and Wall, 1982; Inskeep, 1987; Romeril, 1989; Butler, 1991; Farrell and Runyan, 1991; May, 1991; McKercher, 1993; Butler, 1993; Wahab and Pigram, 1997; Hall and Lew, 1998). Despite the level of attention the concept has received by tourism researchers, there remains a general unwillingness to be critical with the term. However, a number of writers have called for caution, stating that the term is still relatively new and that enthusiasm for linking sustainable development with tourism may need to be tempered by the reality that there is still a lot that is not known about tourism and its relationship with the environment (Wheeller, 1993; Wall, 1997; Butler, 1999). In addition, much of what has been published on the topic has been aspirational in nature and it is still plausible to argue that there remains a paucity of empirical information to demonstrate clearly that tourism can be sustainable in nature (Wheeller, 1993), and probably at best will be only achieved in a few localised settings (Hall, 1998; Butler, 1998).

Although coined in the World Conservation Strategy of 1980, sustainability is not a new concept. While it may have appeared in our lexicon of new buzzwords since the 1980s, the term has a long history (Hall, 1998) with the early conservation movement in the mid-nineteenth century in North America which gave rise to the first national parks and the 'wise use' of resources as advocated by Gifford Pinchot of the US Forest Service and his followers in the 1940s acting as early antecedents to the term. It is possible to argue that in a generic sense that it is as old as time itself and that environmental thinking through time has been representative of varying levels of sustainability (see Table 11.1), where the change in the relationship between economy and environment has resulted in various stages of sustainability being realised.

For purposes of discussion here, a more current time frame is adopted. The 1960s and 1970s witnessed the development of modern mass tourism, which emerged against a backcloth of heightened concern for the environment as expressed in the concepts of Boulding ('spaceship earth', 1966) and Hardin ('tragedy of the commons', 1968). Mirroring these developments was growing support for the need for a symbiotic relationship to develop between humankind and environment, heightened by reports such as Rachel Carson's (1962) *Silent spring* and the Meadows *et al.* (1972) report for the Club of Rome. It could be argued that these paved the way for the sustainable development concept as they voiced concern over exploitation of resources and over-use of specific environments. However the paradox exists in that while tourism may have emerged in this climate, it did not respond to these concerns or echo these sentiments.

Instead emphasis was on the promotion of mass tourism, the growth of ubitiquous resort development with little concern and understanding over impacts that tourism created even in national parks and similar areas. What is interesting, however, is that if the sustainable development phenomenon of the late 1980s and 1990s is taken as a second wave of green environmental thinking, then the ideas implicit within it have now found expression in, and are mirrored by, sustainable tourism. This shift in direction is, in part, a response by the tourism industry to better align itself with environmental concerns, but also an opportunity to market itself as taking responsibility for the changes it can exert on environments, selling itself on a green programme of better accountability. What is perhaps significantly different in current thinking on sustainable development, as compared to good conservation of the past, has been the added elements of ethics and equity (Boyd and Butler, 1997; Butler, 1999) which the Brundtland Commission raised to the fore and which have direct relevance for tourism.

Table 11.1 Evolution of thought regarding sustainability over time

PHASE 1	SUSTAINABILITY
Time period	• Pre-industrial period
Reason	• People lived sustainably because they had to as over-use resulted in migration or starvation, because there were two few to matter, or because of the limited technology restricting the level of development possible (driven by the wish to survive)
Result	• Symbiosis of development with nature
PHASE 2	CONDITIONAL SUSTAINABILITY
Time period	• Industrialisation period
Reason	• Belief in the basic assumption of no limit to humanity's power over nature (economically driven)
Result	• Non-explicit emphasis for economic growth. Development promoted over the desire for conservation
PHASE 3	UNSUSTAINABILITY
Time period	• Post-Industrialisation
Reason	• Over emphasis on economic growth without considering the environmental cost
Result	• Explicit economic growth-oriented economy. Further depletion of the natural resource base needed for future generations
PHASE 4	RETURN TO SUSTAINABILITY
Time period	• The present and immediate future
Reason	• Economic and moral duty to provide for the needs of future generations, and because environmental problems are too severe to be ignored
Result	• Economic growth and development within ecological limits: complementarity of environmental protection and economic development

Source: Boyd (1995, p. 41)

It is not the purpose here to detail here all the developments that have emerged on tourism and its connection with sustainability. Instead, summation is offered to the reader on the focus research has taken. Four possible broad headings emerge here as being useful: early initiatives of the term, debate over definition, development of principles, indicators and standards, and concern over the lack of success stories in terms of actual implementation.

• *Early initiatives*: The development of an Action Strategy for Sustainable Tourism Development presented at Globe '90, represented one of the first initiatives to apply the concept of SD to tourism. Formulated by an interdisciplinary body of Canadian researchers, the Strategy was framed within a context of sustainable development, reflecting key aspects of tourism as an industry, the effects of tourism, and the planning needs of tourism, setting forth specific guidelines to be addressed by both the industry and various levels of government. An early collaborative initiative was the Bali Sustainable Development Project of which tourism was one component (Wall, 1993). With emphasis placed on culture, addressing features such as the continuity of natural resources and production, and viewing development as the process which enhances the quality of life, this research was important as it helped establish early criteria that could be viewed as useful if sustainable development was to be realised. In the context of Bali these were ecological integrity, efficiency, equity, cultural integrity, community, integration–balance–harmony and development as realisation of potential (Wall, 1993). Other early research in the early 1990s included the work of the sub-committee on tourism for the Australian National Strategy for Ecologically Sustainable Development, which outlined how tourism could move toward ecological sustainability (ESD, 1991).

- *Debate over definition*: It quickly emerged that a major difficulty in linking tourism with sustainable development stemmed in part from a lack of clear definition of the term. Butler (1993) was the first tourism researcher to provide a definition of tourism in the context of sustainable development, arguing it to be different to what has been labelled sustainable tourism. He stated the former as representative of '... tourism which is developed and maintained in an area (community, environment) in such a manner and at such a scale that it remains viable over an indefinite period and does not degrade or alter the environment (human and physical) in which it exists to such a degree that it prohibits the successful development and well-being of other activities and processes' (Butler, 1993, p. 29). In contrast, sustainable tourism can equate to any form of tourism that has been able to maintain its viability in an area for an indefinite period of time. This says nothing about impacts, the nature of change that tourism can exert and its effects, and which have little in common with the generally accepted principles of sustainable development. The issue of an appropriate definition is a problematic one as the nature of the definition may change depending on the context and nature of tourism involved. As such, it is highly unlikely as Butler (1999) notes that a universally recognised and accepted definition will be adopted. What is perhaps more important has been the development of principles against which SD in tourism can be gauged to be working.

- *Development of principles, indicators and standards*: Within the early SD literature a range of principles emerged as being linked to the concept: ethics, equity, self-empowerment, social justice, social self-determination, rights, democracy and power sharing (e.g. WCED, 1987; Pearce, 1988; Gardner and Roseland, 1989; Shearman, 1990; Robinson *et al.*, 1990). From this list, the first three have been embraced within tourism SD literature, where self-empowerment is taken to read as greater local involvement. Globe '90 Action Strategy was the first to address the need to establish principles, to be quickly followed by a number of endeavours to identify specific indicators and to determine standards. The first of these took the form of a seminar and workshop, hosted by the Heritage Resources Centres, University of Waterloo in October 1991 at the bequest of Industry, Science and Technology, and Tourism Canada to develop ideas and assemble information on monitoring and on useful indicators of sustainability. The result of the workshop was the edited text *Tourism and sustainable development: monitoring, planning, managing* (Nelson *et al.*, 1993) which, according to its editors, provided 'a useful basis for thinking about planning, management and decision-making in tourism and related activities' (p. vii). With respect to addressing appropriate indicators by which tourism could be monitored, Butler (1993) and Wall (1993) were quick to point out at that time there was a lack of acceptable indicators of the health of tourism. However, within the volume a number of ideas were put forth. Kreutzwiser (1993), for example, noted that indicators had to be sensitive to temporal change and spatial variation; have predictive or anticipatory capability; provide relative measures of conditions based on threshold values previously determined; be practical to apply; and have conceptual validity. Payne (1993) suggested indicators and monitoring techniques for sustainable tourism, while Marsh (1993) developed an index of tourism sustainability (a revised edition of this book is to be published shortly, Nelson, personal communication).

A second endeavour was the work of the World Tourism Organisation (1993) which was quick to note the concept of sustainability to be a powerful one for defining an appropriate approach to tourism development. Six broad principles were identified: more comprehensive planning; more consultative and democratic planning; the forming of new institutional relationships between government, industry, and destination communities; measuring the environmental impacts of sustainable tourism in physical, social and cultural terms; measuring the economic impact of proposed tourism development; and the calculation of carrying capacity at tourism destinations. While these were all laudable principles, the problem has been in implementing them. The development of specific indicators for sustainable tourism development should provide a useful way forward. In terms of specific indicators, the WTO suggested a range that were useful at a national scale (e.g. area protected; percentage of national territory) as well as a comprehensive list that were site-specific (e.g. site-stress index), ranges which were expanded in 1995 and 1997. Millar (forthcoming) has applied existing indicators produced by the WTO as well as the UN to determine their specific ability of demonstrating the extent of progress an individual tourism resort is making toward the goal of sustainable tourism. An expected outcome of this work is the development of indicators for sustainable tourism which are objective, quantifiable, reliable, that have wide applicability and are academically endorsed.

- *Success stories*? Alongside the debate on the relationship between sustainable development and tourism, the topic of alternative forms of tourism has emerged to provide specific examples of tourism which may support sustainability principles, but it is unclear as to whether they can be heralded as success stories. Part of the problem here was that the application of sustainable tourism was somewhat hijacked by the emergence of the debate over alternative types of tourism, and as such discussion focused on what was meant by the term 'alternative' (i.e. small-scale, developed by local people, based on local nature and culture, and paying particular attention to functioning within an area's carrying capacity (Krippendorf, 1987; Smith and Eadington, 1992)) and how it represented a departure away from mass tourism and its characteristics (e.g. large numbers, significant impacts, exploitative local interaction). Discussion has also tended to focus on a few select tourism types, namely ecotourism, nature tourism and special interest tourism (Innskeep, 1987; Boo, 1990; Fennell and Eagles, 1990;

Farrell and Runyan, 1991; Whelan, 1991; Dearden and Harron, 1992; Weiler and Hall, 1992; Smith and Eadington, 1992; Weaver, 1998) with little attention on whether alternative types are more appropriate as descriptors of what tourism ought to be emulating than as actual types of tourism (e.g. responsible, sustainable, appropriate, just and ethical). Concern has been raised that alternative types of tourism have been naively viewed as they fail to be an effective solution to mass tourism, have significant impacts themselves, are elitist and at worst may be responsible for the introduction of tourism to areas that have not yet been subjected to tourism development (Cohen, 1989; Butler, 1990; Wheeler, 1991, 1992).

It would be wrong to imply there has been no success stories of implementation towards sustainable tourism development. The fact that a number of tourism texts on the topic have devoted entire sections to experiences, and that there is now a *Journal of Sustainable Tourism* would suggest the contrary to be true. However, the absence of any extensive time period in order to gauge if tourism is sustainable, as well as the lack of effective monitoring of changes along with assessment of impacts, may mean it is still too early to determine whether tourism is indeed sustainable.

Sustainability and parks

Introduction

Given the extent of interest over sustainability, it is somewhat surprising how little of this research has been specifically focused on national parks. As of late a number of texts have been produced on parks and protected areas, but these have either focused on one particular park system (e.g. Dearden and Rollins, 1993), or addressed broad issues of planning and management (Pigram and Sundell, 1997; Nelson and Serafin, 1997). Sustainability, as a concept within parks *per se*, has received limited attention. Instead, attention has more often been directed at the role ecotourism can play within the park context (Ceballos-Lascurain, 1996) as representative of tourism which is sustainable in form. While it is accepted that ecotourism as a form of tourism is well suited to national parks and protected area context (e.g. Bottrill and Pearce, 1996) it is equally important to recognise that ecotourism can and does take place outside of national parks (e.g., Boyd and Butler, forthcoming) and should therefore not be viewed as the only form of tourism suitable or sustainable within protected areas.

There have been some exceptions to this line of thinking. Nelson (1987) notes the importance that conservation strategies, where national parks represented only one component, could play in operationalising sustainable development. Woodley (1993), in developing suitable indicators of sustainability for parks, challenges the appropriateness of using the term sustainable tourism within a park context, putting forward the argument that if there is to exist any type of sustainability, then it must be based first on ecosystem sustainability. He states that terms like sustainable tourism are more likely to be misnomers as tourism operates within actual ecosystems and therefore any impacts generated by tourism are essentially ecosystem impacts. As a result, the key must be to ensure that ecosystems, particularly in areas such as national parks, are maintained on a long-term basis through monitoring their state or condition of park ecosystems to ensure they maintain ecosystem integrity. In so doing, focus is directed away from activities like tourism to the wider challenge of protection.

Case study: Canadian national parks

Other research on tourism and sustainable development in parks started from the premise that as a setting, parks offer great potential to be examples of sustainable landscapes (Boyd, 1995). Accepting that any 'measure' of sustainability is hard to quantify, research was undertaken to obtain perceptions of experts such as policy makers, park superintendents and academics in order to develop some 'under-standing' of what is meant by sustainability when applied specifically to national parks. Results from this particular study are important as the research represented the first attempt to assess sustainability within a complete park system, and not just as it applied to certain activities. A tangible outcome was the development of a sustainability framework composed of a series of stages (see Figure 11.1). It should not be read as a step-by-step approach that individual park managers should follow, rather it should be viewed as a tool that individual managers can use that allows them to compare sustainability attributes identified for the system as a whole to conditions existing within their particular park. It should also be stressed that the attributes identified within the framework are somewhat general in nature and that the degree to which they have applicability to actual parks is subject to the characteristics of individual parks themselves. The framework was built around the extent of consensus of respondents, identifying those elements perceived to be supportive of sustainability and those where the opposite was the case.

The findings in the framework are important for a number of reasons. First, the contextual elements present within Stage 1 offer a useful base against which sustainability within a park context may be set. Of the four elements (objectives, scale, political structure and societal change), determining objectives in terms of type of sustainability desired (ecological, economic, social or mixed) was argued to be the most important. This, it may be argued, is influenced by the scale of setting involved (complete park system or zones within individual parks), the political structure in place (top-down, bottom-up or mixed) that offers and ensures change, and lastly, the need for societal change to occur (long-term perspective taken and change of thinking on specific issues) to ensure action is taken that promotes change, where concepts, ideas and relationships between issues are re-evaluated in the pursuit of sustainability itself.

Second, the general attributes that are identified within Stage 2 represent relevant criteria of sustainability that have wide applicability to national parks. The link between both stages was made on the assumption that the type of objective(s) pursued influences how sustainability is defined, and that each general attribute in

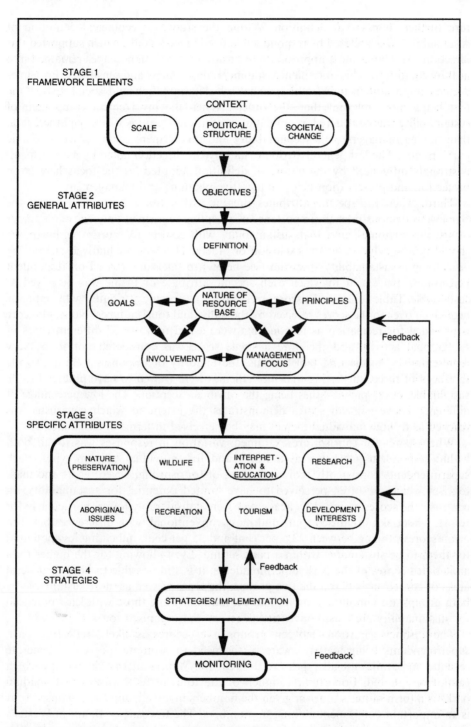

Figure 11.1. Summary diagram of the 'sustainability framework'

turn further shapes that definition. Within the study, an ecological definition of sustainability was prefered by respondents reflecting park goals, which supported this direction. Attributes most appropriate to ensure that park landscapes remained in a healthy condition included resilience, stability, adaptiveness and sensitivity. Principles deemed important included ethics, social self-determination and social justice, the first being more relevant than the others. When the involvement component of sustainability was considered, representation of interest groups was thought less vital than having managers with accountability and involvement taking place as public participation. The last general attribute, namely the direction taken by management, is strongly influenced by the nature of definition adopted, as the focus here is on protection and preservation before integrative planning and management.

Third, when the specific attributes present within Stage 3 are considered, the framework demonstrates the importance of accepting tourism as only one of a number of specific attributes, and that sustainability with respect to tourism within parks should not be achieved at the exclusion of others. This was qualitatively 'tested' by developing a sustainability spectrum (see below) to 'measure' (based on respondent perception), the extent to which each specific attribute or theme was perceived as sustainable. Table 11.2 lists the scores received for all specific attributes, with emphasis here given over to the scores received by the individual tourism types. No single score is provided for recreation as respondents were asked to score 37 different types of recreational activity and therefore a single score was considered not to be very representative. As the first table reveals, the majority of responses were above the threshold of three, suggesting that most themes were viewed to have potential to be sustainable, development issues being the obvious exception. The low percentage of difference between mean scores demonstrates the extent to which consensus was reached as to how individual themes may be perceived in terms of sustainability.

When scores for tourism are examined, variation in responses was found both within respondent groupings as a whole and for individual tourism types. Park superintendents consistently scored all types of tourism high, even resort and mass tourism which are often perceived to have limited potential for sustainability. In contrast, the scores assigned by academics were considerably lower, particularly for resort, winter/ski, organised tours and mass/conventional, with differences between mean scores ranging between 22.5 per cent and 35 per cent, indicating less potential for them to be sustainable within a park setting. Even allowing for the higher than anticipated scores of the park superintendents, it is still possible to identify general areas of consensus between the two groups; the types viewed as more sustainable by both groups are remote, mountain and ecotourism, while those with least potential for sustainability are mass/conventional, resort and organised tours.

The distinct variation between groups over scores is likely reflecting park superintendents being acutely aware of the need to promote tourism to generate revenue and while not all types are desired, they represent market sectors which cannot be ignored. For example, much of the tourism to townsites in Canadian parks is a form of mass tourism given the numbers involved, and the organised tour is an important component making up numbers. The townsite of Bannf in Western Canada is an apt example (see Dearden, this volume). In contrast, responses by academics may be more of a reflection of what types of tourism they viewed to be best suited to national park landscapes in a more abstract context.

Table 11.2 Comparison of responses to sustainability scores for themes present in national parks

Themes	Mean score (park superintendents) range 1–5	Mean score (academics) range 1–5	% of difference between mean scores[a]
Nature preservation	3.4	3.9	12.5
Wildlife	3.3	3.7	10.0
Interpretation/education	3.2	3.5	7.5
Recreation	3.0–4.2	2.1–3.4	Not calculated
Research	3.6	3.6	0.0
Aboriginal issues	3.1	2.8	7.5
Development issues	2.4	1.7	17.5

Tourism types	Mean score (park superintendents) range 1–5	Mean score (academics) range 1–5	% of difference between mean scores[a]
Remote	4.2	3.9	7.5
Mountain	4.2	3.8	10.0
Cultural	3.8	3.6	5.0
Winter/ski	3.9	2.7	30.0
Heritage	3.8	3.5	7.5
Adventure	4.2	3.5	17.5
Ecotourism	4.1	3.9	5.0
Resort	3.2	2.3	22.5
Organised tours	3.6	2.3	32.5
Mass/conventional	3.1	1.7	35.0

[a] Difference is expressed as a percentage of the maximum possible difference

Note: Key to understanding mean score values in the table:
The following spectrum addressed the *perceived* nature and level of sustainability possible for any given theme and was set up as follows with the following scores:
1 = Unsustainability (impacts and threats result in ecological damage of the various components within parks which cannot be corrected; the degree of negative impact (perceived) of development/use on the park environment is high).
2 = Intermediate stage between conditional sustainability and unsustainability (increasing stress placed on park systems; low tolerance present; impacts still perceived as positive or negative, but no ecological damage occurs).
3 = Conditional sustainability (stress placed on the park environment by activities present; high tolerance within park systems; the degree of impact is limited and can be perceived as positive or negative).
4 = Intermediate stage between sustainability and conditional sustainability (limited stress placed on park environment, very high ecological tolerance within systems, the degree of positive impact (perceived) of development/use on the environment is low).
5 = Sustainability (minimal stress placed on the environment; degree of positive impact (perceived) of development/use on the environment is high; a symbiosis of development/use with nature is present).

Source: Boyd (1995, pp. 211–212)

The presence of dual mandates within park systems, namely the protection of natural and cultural heritage and the provision for visitors of the opportunities to enjoy and benefit from the parks, is an added problem managers face in that the trade-offs made to meet both of these mandates have impacts on sustainability within parks. This was examined in the Canadian parks study by asking park superintendents and academics to place a range of park activities on a protection–use spectrum where 10 on the scale (0–10) represented total protection, with 0 representing a situation of total use. Figure 11.2 illustrates responses given by park superintendents in which a number of distinct groups are formed along the trade-off line. Only two activities (lumbering, mining) were seen as falling on the development/ use end of the spectrum. At the opposite end, five activities (wildlife protection, endangered species protection, interpretation and education, nature studies and search and rescue operations) scored highly on preservation, the last activity being included on the basis of the low level of impacts it creates. The remaining activities were found to be closely grouped, with only a 15 per cent difference over their range of scores. Table 11.3 shows how park superintendent's responses compared with those given by academics. A similar pattern emerges, with only three activities having large differences in terms of mean scores. Mechanised forms of recreation received a value which indicated limited emphasis on protection compared to use, a middle ground position was taken on search and rescue, while a stronger emphasis toward protection was noted for nature reserve maintenance.

Table 11.3 Responses to the trade-off between use and protection for park activities

Park activities	Mean score (park superintendents) range 0–10	Mean score (academics) range 0–10	% of difference between mean scores
Endangered species protection	8.2	9.3	11.0
Mining	1.3	0.3	10.0
Mechanised forms of recreation	5.8	3.1	27.0
Tourism	5.8	5.8	0.0
Eco-tourism	6.6	7.3	7.0
Research	6.3	6.9	6.0
Passive forms of recreation	6.0	7.0	10.0
Traditional activities	5.4	4.3	11.0
Lumber activity	1.1	0.8	3.0
Nature reserve maintenance	5.6	7.5	19.0
Wildlife protection	8.3	8.9	6.0
Nature studies	7.2	7.8	6.0
Interpretation & education	7.2	7.6	4.0
Search & rescue operations	7.0	5.4	16.0
Access & circulation maintenance	5.1	4.8	3.0
Infrastructure for recreation & tourism maintenance	5.4	4.8	6.0
Disposal of waste	5.5	5.7	2.0
Accomodation (front country) provision	5.2	4.8	4.0
Accommodation (back country) provision	5.6	4.9	7.0

Source: Boyd (1995. p. 217)

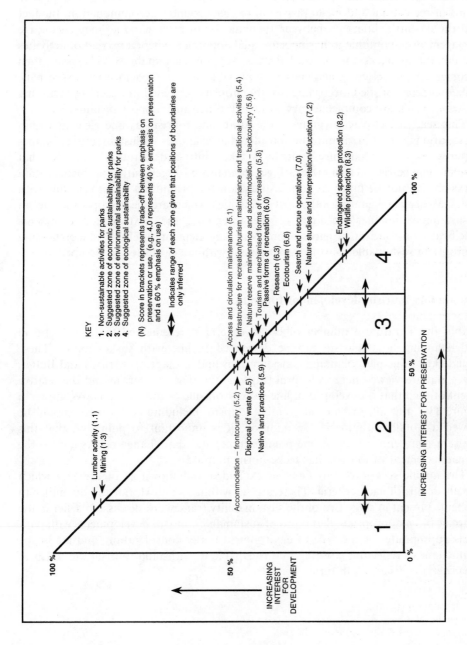

Figure 11.2 Trade-off model applied to national park activities based on responses of park superintendents

Overall, the extent to which activities were clustered around the middle of the spectrum means that implications for sustainability are unclear. For example, while the trade-off results imply that parks should encourage ecotourism and passive forms of recreation, and make provision for backcountry accommodation, the fact that there is little difference between the majority of park activities may encourage management to continue a 'business as usual approach' where a myriad of activities are present in parks that overall do not support sustainability. The issue then becomes one of selecting activities that provide the right balance to ensure park mandates are satisfied according to the priority assigned to each by selecting activities which are complementary with each other and support sustainability.

This section has placed emphasis on addressing tourism as one element within parks, arguing that for them to be considered as examples of sustainable landscapes requires that more than just tourism is taken into consideration. The fact that tourism may be viewed as a major trigger mechanism for generating problems within parks should not be taken as sole justification for promoting tourism in line with sustainability and ignoring other park activities which are clearly operating in an unsustainable manner. In light of the foregoing, the next section comments specifically on tourism in parks, identifying key elements useful in understanding appropriate sustainable tourism development within a protected landscape.

Sustainable tourism development for parks

Within the literature a number of broad criteria have emerged that are useful in understanding how tourism can be developed in line with sustainability. These include key principles, planning considerations and management (Boyd and Butler, 1997) and are viewed here as helpful to gauge the type of tourism and the relative extent of each that is developed in line with or outside of these criteria. As shown in Figure 11.3, not all forms of alternative tourism, including ecotourism, should be viewed as totally sustainable. In addition, it is important to point out that this diagram represents a view at one point in time, and that change occurs and so the dynamic element of tourism has to be borne in mind.

The middle section of this figure is expanded and shown as Figure 11.4 which reveals details of each criteria. These are set within a context, not too dissimilar to elements present in stage two of the sustainability framework discussed earlier in the chapter, of an appropriate definition of sustainable tourism development, with park goals appropriate for the type of environment under consideration, and landscape characteristics reflecting a setting that is capable to withstand tourism use. Each of the criteria is discussed in turn.

Key principles

As the framework shows, these are taken to be equity, ethics, keeping use levels relative to carrying capacity and promoting a conservation-based focus; principles noted as having relevance in the development of the general sustainability framework earlier. In the climate of SD to omit ethics and equity as key principles

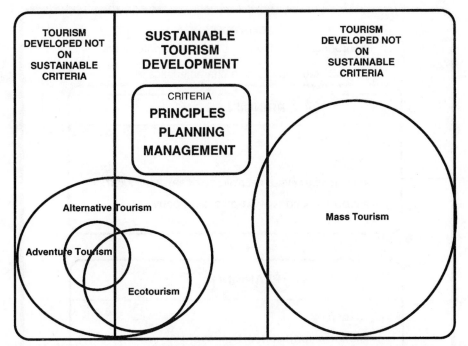

Figure 11.3. Conceptual framework illustrating types of tourism and sustainable development criteria. Source: Boyd and Butler (1997)

would be viewed as morally wrong given the industry's endeavours to promote tourism that is sustainable (Krippendorf, 1987; Prosser, 1992; D'Amore, 1993; Wight, 1994; Hultsman, 1995). Yet their implementation for tourism within a parks context is often problematic and has resulted primarily in the development of codes of ethics and conduct where adoption is often *ad hoc* in manner (Wight, 1994). Limited adoption of guidelines and codes of conduct, however, must be seen as all the more critical where tourism is promoted in protected environments and as such, compliance with guidelines and codes is vital otherwise the impacts resulting could have serious consequences for the health and long term well being of these environments. The difficulty of promoting equity in parks is often best demonstrated when issues of access are involved, as these are often constrained by the people involved, the degree of difficulty in gaining access to certain areas, and who can enjoy and participate in certain tourism-related activities. National parks should be accessible to all sectors of the population. Unfortunately nature does not serve efficiently the needs of those who are disabled or disadvantaged. Human-designed structures like boardwalks and public transport services provide some obvious assistance to the disadvantaged but for the most part access in parks will not be equitable, and such features may generate opposition from wilderness purists.

The third principle of keeping use levels below a region's carrying capacity is equally fundamental to promoting sustainable tourism development within parks. There is now agreement that no universal magic number constitutes the carrying capacity for any setting. Instead it is recognised that capacity varies according to the type of setting, the element of the capacity being measured, and visitor expectations

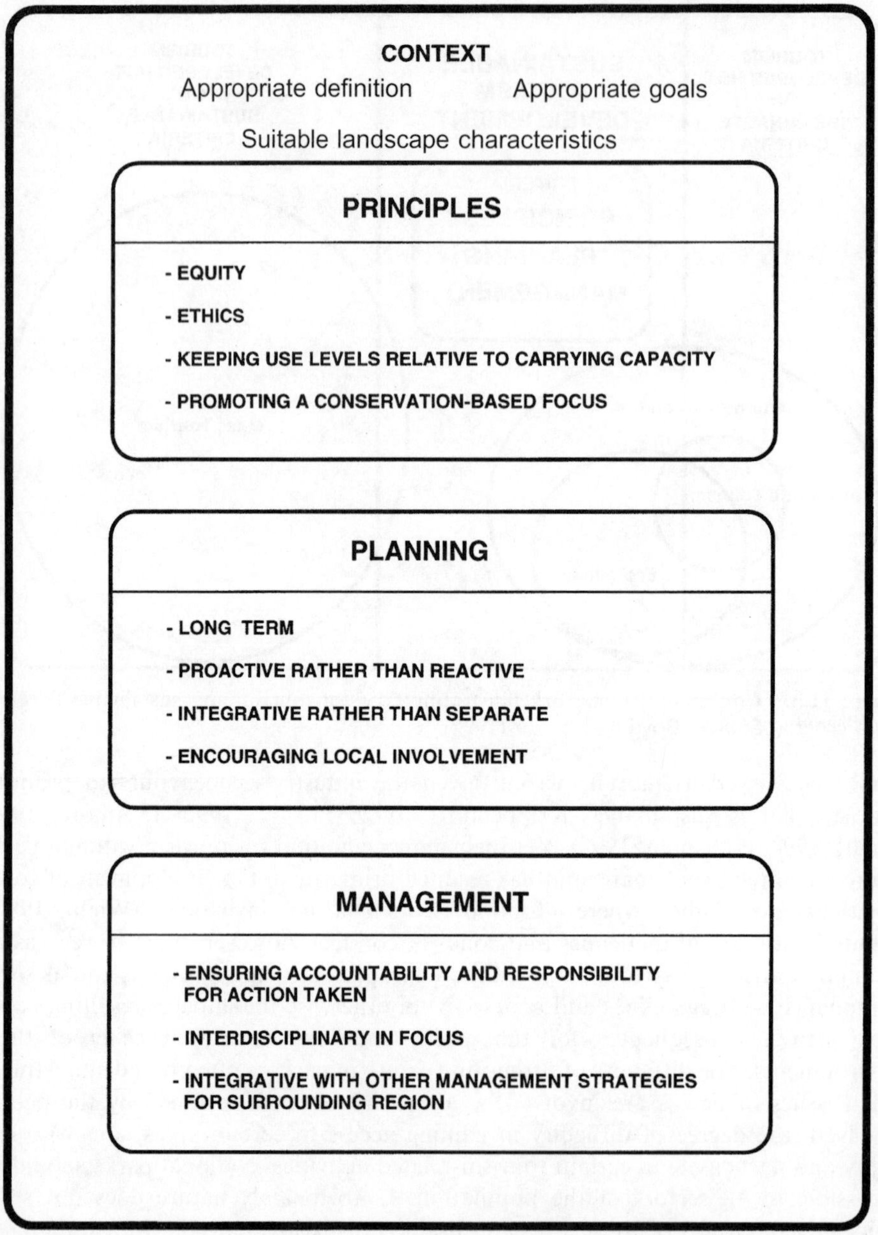

CONTEXT

Appropriate definition   Appropriate goals

Suitable landscape characteristics

PRINCIPLES

- EQUITY

- ETHICS

- KEEPING USE LEVELS RELATIVE TO CARRYING CAPACITY

- PROMOTING A CONSERVATION-BASED FOCUS

PLANNING

- LONG TERM

- PROACTIVE RATHER THAN REACTIVE

- INTEGRATIVE RATHER THAN SEPARATE

- ENCOURAGING LOCAL INVOLVEMENT

MANAGEMENT

- ENSURING ACCOUNTABILITY AND RESPONSIBILITY
  FOR ACTION TAKEN

- INTERDISCIPLINARY IN FOCUS

- INTEGRATIVE WITH OTHER MANAGEMENT STRATEGIES
  FOR SURROUNDING REGION

Figure 11.4. Sustainable tourism development criteria. Source: Boyd and Butler (1997)

and experience, and that both natural and human-induced change will occur (Stankey and McCool, 1986; Shelby and Heberlein, 1986). It is best, therefore, to view carrying capacity from the perspective of how an area can be best managed to avoid over-use.

This may involve managers limiting maximum numbers of visitors in certain areas and activities (Butler, 1996) or basing use levels on desired norms for certain activities (see Vaske, Donnelly and Whittaker, this volume) set within broader management frameworks (Clark and Stankey, 1979; Stankey *et al.*, 1985; Graham *et al.*, 1988; Butler and Waldbrook, 1991; Butler *et al.*, 1992; Loomis and Graefe, 1992; Boyd and Butler, 1996). In essence, when it comes to tourism carrying capacity in national parks it must remain low, often because of the fragile nature of these environments and also to ensure that the areas' ecological integrity is maintained. This has major implications for the types of activity that can be offered to the visitor and in turn the experiences they receive.

The last principle (conservation-based focus) requires that priority in parks is given to the maintenance of ecological integrity over other forms of use, such as tourism. One way this can be achieved is by advocating an ecosystem approach to how parks are managed (Regier, 1993; Slocombe, 1993). This should not be taken to mean that other forms of activity such as tourism are excluded. Rather it requires that tourism be monitored to ensure ecosystem integrity is maintained (Woodley, 1993). With future pressures encouraging more tourism within national parks, the challenge rests in the other two criteria of planning and management, to ensure the perpetuation of natural environments that are essentially left unaltered by human activity, but which allow for secondary mandates of public under-standing, appreciation and enjoyment of these landscapes to be met.

Planning

Focus with this criterion is not to promote a particular planning approach like normative (Timothy, 1996) or collaborative (Getz and Jamal, 1994; Dowling, 1993) but rather to note key planning attributes applicable for promoting sustainable tourism development within parks. Four are set out below.

First, tourism planning must be long term in nature; a position taken given that protected landscapes are expected to face increased pressure to offer greater opportunities for tourism. Unfortunately, many planning agencies are not allowed to act in a long-term manner as their mandates are often constrained by the short time their political masters are in office. Second, planning should be proactive as opposed to merely reacting to problems when they arise. This involves identification of suitable tourism activities, the extent of their use both spatially and temporally, and the level of use acceptable given the type of park setting concerned. In addition, it requires that clear strategies be in place to address certain types of problems, but an approach that is adaptive to changing conditions and environment as opposed to one that has developed in an *ad hoc* manner that lacks flexibility. Third, planning should be integrative as opposed to separate on the basis that tourism represents only one possible land use within national parks. The fourth element, encouraging local involvement in planning, is rather more contentious. While many approaches to tourism planning (collaborative, community, normative) advocate that local citizenry should have an effective voice in planning, caution must be exercised as it is a dangerous assumption to state that local people are always in the best position to make appropriate decisions and take effective action where planning parks is involved. An exception to this may be indigenous/traditional peoples whose 'expertise', it is often argued, stems from the fact they essentially live, and have lived, off the land itself. For parks in such areas, indigenous peoples need to have a greater input in the role they play in how parks are planned, but with an acceptance that 'undesirable' impacts may arise from many of their traditional activities. The key issue is that their level of activity is still sustainable.

Management

The third criterion within the framework is the wider issue of management. The nature of management undertaken is often conditioned by the nature of the setting in which the activity is promoted. Tourism within protected areas is fundamentally problematic and as such management must be all-encompassing. Three specific aspects of management which apply to sustainable tourism development are: (1) the degree of accountability and responsibility of managers, (2) the vision to accept other approaches and (3) the willingness to integrate tourism with other resource users and uses present.

The need to ensure accountability and be responsible for action taken is not a new idea. Butler (1991) noted this factor as one of the fundamental problems for areas where use levels exceed capacity limits. Hardin (1968) essentially alluded to this in his early discourse on over-use of our common resources. The term 'responsible' has almost become synomnous with 'sustainable' in that any attempt to attain sustainability requires that action be taken which is responsible. A great deal of importance rests with those to whom managers are accountable and for what they are accountable. In settings such as national park systems or protected areas where some form of agency is effectively in charge and clear policy is in place, this issue is less of a concern than in other tourism areas. Second, management needs to be interdisciplinary in its focus, and open to ideas from outside 'normal' management philosophy. Given the diversity of activities present within parks and to a lesser extent other protected areas, a perspective that is open to many viewpoints may be of benefit for managers. As managers try to satisfy mandates that stress protection as opposed to mandates which encourage the parks to be used and enjoyed, a goal of promoting sustainability in general may be more appealing. This would allow managers to address the social, economic, and environmental issues as opposed to a more restrictive ecological focus on maintaining an area's natural integrity. Third, management must be integrative with strategies for activities surrounding parks and protected areas. This is essential as external influences on protected landscapes can only be effectively addressed through greater cooperation with neighbouring jurisdictions, particularly for those threats that managers of protected areas have no control over (Nelson, 1987, 1993, 1994).

Application

In the sustainability study undertaken on the parks system in Canada by this author, all three of the above criteria were found to be present, but to varying degrees. It is not the intention here to comment on the application of each criterion to this particular example as this is present elsewhere (Boyd and Butler, 1997). Instead, attention is directed at the consensus reached as to what constituted specific characteristics of sustainable tourism development appropriate for parks. Park Superindents were asked to score fifteen possible characteristics on a scale of $+2$ (strongly agree) to -2 (strongly disagree). The five most favoured characteristics by park superintendents, in order of strength of agreement were controlling tourists in fragile and unique areas; preventing the expansion of activities and facilities which are viewed as undesirable; tourism which does not degrade the environment that it is dependent on; tourism development which maintains the ecological integrity of the landscape and; development which is low in impact. Characteristics found not to be in support of sustainable tourism development were tourism which alters the environment but at the same time maintains its ecological integrity; tourism which places an emphasis on economic benefits alone; development similar to what is present in parks and; encouraging the development of small-scale accommodation inside parks (Boyd, 1995, p. 153). When their responses were compared to those given by academics, little variation was found to be present. Table 11.4 shows that for the majority of characteristics there was general agreement with the issues stated, two saw varied responses with both groups voicing disagreement to three of the characteristics. Using the mean scores each characteristic received, issues which elicited strongest agreement included controlling tourists in fragile and unique areas, preventing the expansion of activities viewed as undesirable, development which is low in impact, tourism development which maintains ecological integrity of the landscape and tourism which does not degrade the environment it is dependent on. There was agreement as to what characteristics were not acceptable, namely, tourism that places emphasis on economic benefits only (mean scores of 4.8 and 4.6), tourism which is seen to have a symbiotic relationship with other park activities (mean scores of 4.1 and 4.0) and development similar to what is now current within the parks. These findings are useful as they provide management with some insight into what characteristics of tourism are supportive of sustainability and which are not.

Sustainability, parks and policy

Specific policy pertaining to sustainability has somewhat lagged behind the use of the term. Where policy exists, an added problem has been that a gap exists between endorsement and implementation, often the result of ineffective institutional arrangements to create good challenges of communication among all groups involved (Pigram, 1990). Policy within some of the early park systems is well established with clear procedures and techniques in place to foster strong communication to promote implementation. These have included the use of public participation and the development of policy, which is implemented on a park-by-park basis through the development of national park plans. This section addresses the development of policy as it applies to parks in Canada and to a lesser extent for England and Wales, with the purpose of illustrating that park policy has been closely aligned to thinking that is in line with sustainability.

Canadian park policy had its first expression in the National Parks Act (1930) which stated that parks were to be left unimpaired for present and future

Table 11.4 Comparing responses to sustainable tourism characteristics for Canadian national parks

Sustainable tourism characteristics	Agree	Varied	Disagree	Mean score (parks sup.)	Mean score (acad.)	% difference[a]
Development which is low in impact	XO			1.7	1.2	12.5
Development similar to what is not current			XO	3.6	3.9	7.5
Controlling tourists in fragile and unique areas	XO			1.4	1.1	7.5
Preventing visitors from encroaching in areas that require permits for access	XO			2.0	1.1	22.5
Tourism development which maintains ecological integrity of the landscape	XO			1.7	1.3	10
Allowing only tourism types which have low environmental impact	XO			1.9	1.9	0
Preventing the expansion of activities viewed as undesirable	XO			1.4	1.2	5
Encouraging development of small-scale accommodation		XO		3.5	2.9	15
Locating all forms of accommodation outside parks		XO		2.7	3.1	10
Tourism that places an emphasis on economic benefits only			XO	4.6	4.8	5.0
Tourism types that have a positive economic, social and ecological component	XO			1.9	1.8	2.5
Tourism which remains viable over time	XO			2.6	1.6	20
Tourism which does not degrade the environment it is dependent on	XO			1.6	1.1	12.5
Tourism which alters the environment, but maintains its ecological integrity			XO	4.0	4.1	2.5
Tourism which is seen to have a symbiotic relationship with other park activities	XO			2.5	1.4	27.5

X = response of park superintendents
O = response of academics
[a] Difference is expressed as a percentage of the possible maximum difference.
Mean score: range 1–5 (1 = very appropriate, 2 = appropriate, 3 = some relevance, 4 = little relevance, 5 = inappropriate)

Source: Boyd (1995, p. 204)

generations, but that use was permitted to ensure they were enjoyed by visitors and were of benefit to present and future generations. It was, in essence, a *de facto* policy statement as it applied to all parks. The first officially recognised policy did not appear until 1964. Set against a pro growth/development climate, the 1964 policy recognised the importance of the preservation of nature but also gave emphasis to resource use in order to accommodate the demands of visitors (National and Historic Parks Branch, 1964). A new policy was framed in 1979 that took into account the rising concern and awareness towards environmental degradation of this time. Focus changed toward protection with reference to ecological integrity and the need to maintain this within parks (Parks Canada, 1979). The current policy appeared in 1994, and while it was heavily influenced by sustainability thinking, this was not taken up as the overriding objective, and greater emphasis was given to the maintenance of ecological integrity through adopting an ecosystem-based approach to management (Parks Canada, 1994). This involved

> a more holistic view of the natural environment and ensuring that land use decisions take into consideration the complex interactions and dynamic nature of park ecosystems and their finite capacity to withstand and recover from stress induced by human activities (Parks Canada, 1994, p. 33).

Human activities which threaten the integrity of park ecosystems are not permitted, to 'ensure the perpetuation of natural environments essentially unaltered by human activity' (Parks Canada, 1994, p. 34). This apparent shift in thinking has implications for tourism across this park system. While the policy states that Parks Canada has no mandate for tourism, it still recognises the role of tourism in terms of the image it has for tourism to and within Canada, as well as the economic and social benefits that result from visitation. Tourism which is viewed as sustainable is encouraged, namely those forms 'which maintain and enhance ecological and commemorative integrity, respect intrinsic values of protected heritage areas, and provide for education and recreation opportunities which help foster a sense of Canadian identity' (Parks Canada, 1994, p. 14).

While this brief preview of policy for the Canadian parks would imply that major shifts in thinking have occurred over time, it is equally possible to suggest that no real 'significant' change has occurred since the phrasing of the 1930 Act (Boyd, 1995) and that sustainability ideals have been present throughout policy development. The phrasing of the Act was very similar to the phrasing used to define sustainable development by the WCED in 1987, both addressed inter- and intra-generational equity, ethics and balance between protection and use. The Act could, therefore, be taken as an early example of sustainable development, in days prior to the coining of the term and the existence of a national policy for national parks in Canada. The wise use of park resources in the 1960s equally can be read as meaning that sustainability was being undertaken in the parks prior to the actual use of the term itself, as use of park resources was in the context of the importance placed on preserving the natural features in the parks. Likewise, the use of the concept of ecological integrity, first appearing in general terms only in the 1979 policy, but much more specific in the 1994 policy, may be viewed also as yet another expression of sustainability, but with the emphasis on the ecological dimensions of the term. In sum, one is forced to question how much change has really occurred in policy. The concepts used may have changed over time, with the impression that change in thinking has occurred, but the reality has been that parks have continued to be managed, for the most part, along the lines of sustainability, regardless what terminology has been used.

Recent policy development has emerged to support the adoption of sustainability for parks set within working landscapes as opposed to wilderness/protected landscapes. Parks in England and Wales are undergoing changes in both planning and management. Since policy was last prescribed (1988), two developments have occurred that requires re-evaluation to be made: (1) the passing of the Environment Act (1995) and its implications for overall park purpose, how they are administered and managed; and (2) an increased understanding of sustainable development. The Environment Act set out the purpose for parks to be:

- Conservation
- Education/recreation
- Fostering economic and social well-being of park communities

It also required National Park Authorities (NPAs) to produce a National Park Management Plan (NPMP) setting out policies for managing each park. Sustainable development has been taken up as the main principle underlying the policies contained within each NPMP. Furthermore, sustainability has been embraced as the concept best suited to meet park needs and appropriate to confront various issues present within parks such as the provision for housing, transport issues, mineral demands, waste generation and disposal, energy use, tourism and leisure and changes, in agriculture, fisheries and forestry as they affect park landscapes (Countryside Commission, 1997). Sustainability is present in how a vision for parks is defined and developed and is particularly explicit in the approach taken to the three main themes (the purpose of parks) contained within individual park management plans. When the purpose is to promote understanding and enjoyment of the special qualities of parks, a strategic recreational policy is in place to follow agreed principles for tourism appropriate to English and Welsh national parks as set down by the Countryside Commission in 1989. Ensuring the purpose of economic and social well-being of local communities calls for a sustainable level of local services and facilities, giving priority to national park community needs. The pursuit of achieving sustainable landscapes is further supported by the fact that a vision set out for NPMP is one which takes a long-term view, is developed and implemented through partnership with others and where a regular programme of monitoring is to be put in place to measure progress and determine if targets set are met (Countryside Commission, 1997, p. 9). In sum, the direction management planning is taking in parks for England and Wales is to embrace sustainability as a general policy directive to ensure park mandates are satisfied given the 'working landscapes' the parks are set within.

Conclusion

This chapter has addressed the concept of sustainability as it applies to tourism in national parks. The purpose was not to provide a general discussion of sustainability across a range of park systems, but rather to develop the concept as a response to issues and challenges related to tourism which park managements face. A conceptual approach was used to demonstrate the complexity of the concept itself and its applicability in providing direction to national parks across myriad park contexts. In conclusion, sustainability has wide applicability to parks and should not be limited to specific park activities such as tourism alone. Second, sustainability has potential as an overall management tool, where importance is attached to achieving an appropriate balance of activities and themes, accepting trade-offs are made to accommodate park mandates and the emphasis given to each. Third, if the focus is to assess the potential of parks as landscapes for sustainable tourism development, then this activity should not be envisaged as separate, but rather linked to other themes and issues present for parks. The sustainable tourism development framework presented in this chapter provides general direction as to how this can be pursued by parks. Fourth, national park environments have well advanced policy that supports sustainable thinking in how they are both planned and managed. The implementation gap has been bridged in national park environments by having a history of institutional arrangements, which ensures that statements of intent are translated into reality 'on the ground'.

As with all new buzzwords, there is the danger that they can become irrelevant, outdated and not all that appropriate in practice. Sustainability as a concept is not a new buzzword, although it is often characterised as such. Although emphasis has been given in this chapter to a North American context, what has been offered on parks within a working environment context would suggest the term has great scope to address issues of park planning and management. National parks represent diverse landscapes, where ensuring sustainability helps to satisfy varying mandates and as such critics should not be too quick to dismiss its applicability out of hand.

References

Boo, E., 1990, *Ecotourism: the potentials and pitfalls*, Vols. 1 and 2, World Wildlife Fund, Washington, DC

Bottrill, C.G. and Pearce, D.G., 1996, Ecotourism: towards a key elements approach to operationalizing the concept. *Journal of Sustainable Tourism*, **3**(1): 45–54

Boulding, K., 1966, The economics of the coming Spaceship Earth. *In Environmental Quality in a growing economy*, Johns Hopkins Press, Baltimore MD

Boyd, S.W., 1995, *Sustainability and Canada's national parks: suitability for policy, planning and management*, unpublished PhD thesis, Department of Geography, University of Western Ontario, Canada

Boyd, S.W. and Butler, R.W., 1996, Managing ecotourism: an opportunity spectrum approach. *Tourism Management*, **17**(8): 557–566

Boyd, S.W. and Butler, R.W., 1997, Sustainable tourism development in protected areas. In *Proceedings First International Sustainable Tourism Conference*, pp. 114–132, Hue, Vietnam

Boyd, S.W. and Butler, R.W., forthcoming, Definitely not monkeys or parrots, probably deer and possibly moose: opportunities and realities of ecotourism in Northern Ontario. *Current Issues in Tourism*

Budowski, G., 1976, Tourism and environmental conservation: Conflict, coexistence, or symbiosis? *Environmental Conservation*, **3**: 27–31

Butler, R.W., 1990, Alternative tourism: pious hope or Trojan horse? *Journal of Travel Research*, **28**(3): 40–45

Butler, R.W., 1991, Tourism, environment, and sustainable development. *Environmental Conservation*, **18**(3): 201–209

Butler, R.W., 1993, Tourism – An evolutionary perspective. In *Tourism and sustainable development: monitoring, planning, managing*, J.G. Nelson, R.W. Butler and G. Wall, eds, pp. 27–43. Department of Geography Publication Series, No.37 and Heritage Resources Centre Joint Publication No.1, University of Waterloo, Waterloo, ON

Butler, R.W., 1996, The concept of carrying capacity for tourism destinations: dead or merely buried? *Progress in Tourism and Hospitality Research*, **2**(3–4): 283–293

Butler, R.W., 1998, Sustainable tourism – looking backwards in order to progress?. In *Sustainable tourism: a geographical perspective*, C.M. Hall and A.A. Lew, eds, pp. 25–34, Addison-Wesley Longman, Harlow

Butler, R.W., 1999, Sustainable tourism: a state-of-the-art review. *Tourism Geographies*, **1**(1): 7–25

Butler, R.W. and Pearce, D.G., eds, 1995, *Change in tourism: people, places and processes*, Routledge, London

Butler, R.W., Fennell, D.A. and Boyd, S.W., 1992, *The POLAR model: a system for managing the recreational capacity of Canadian heritage rivers*, Heritage Rivers Board, Environment Canada, Ottawa

Butler, R.W. and Waldbrook, L.A., 1991, A new planning tool: the tourism opportunity spectrum. *The Journal of Tourism Studies*, **2**(1): 1–14

Carson, R.L., 1962, *Silent spring*, Houghton Mifflin Company, Boston

Cellabos-Lascurain, H., 1996, *Tourism, ecotourism and protected areas*, World Conservation Union, Gland (Switzerland)

Clark, R.N. and Stankey, G.H., 1979, *The recreation opportunity spectrum: a framework for planning, management and research*, USDA General Technical Report PNW–98, Government Printing Office, Washington, DC

Cohen, E., 1989, Alternative tourism – a critique. In *Towards appropriate tourism: the case of developing countries*, T.V. Singh, H.L. Theuns, H.L. and F.M. Go, eds, pp. 127–142, Peter Lang, Frankfurt am Main

Countryside Commission, 1997, *National park management plans guidance – advisory booklet*, Countryside Commission Postal Sales

D'Amore, L., 1993, A code of ethics and guidelines for socially and environmentally responsible tourism. *Journal of Travel Research*, **31**(3): 64–66

Dearden, P. and Harron, S., 1992, Tourism and the Hilltribes of Thailand. In *Special Interest Tourism*, B. Weiler and C.M. Hall, eds, pp. 96–104, Belhaven Press, Toronto

Dearden, P. and Rollins, R. eds, 1993, *Parks and protected areas in Canada: planning and management*, Oxford University Press, Toronto

Dowling, R., 1993, An environmentally-based planning model for regional tourism development. *Journal of Sustainable Tourism*, **1**(1): 17–37

ESD (Ecologically Sustainable Development) 1991, *Final report – tourism*, Australian Government Publishing Service, Canberra

Farrell, B.H. and Runyan, D., 1991, Ecology and Tourism. *Annals of Tourism Research*, **18**(1): 26–40

Fennell, D.A. and Eagles, P.F.J., 1990, Ecotourism in Costa Rica: a conceptual framework. *Journal of Park and Recreation Administration*, **8**(1): 23–34

France, L., ed., 1997, *The Earthscan reader in sustainable tourism*, Earthscan, London

Gardner, J.E. and Roseland, M., 1989, Acting locally: community strategies for equitable sustainable development. *Alternatives*, **16**(3): 36–48

Getz, D. and Jamal, T.B., 1994, The environment-community symbiosis: a case for collaborative tourism planning. *Journal of Sustainable Tourism*, **2**(3): 152–173

Graham, R., Nilsen, P. and Payne, R.J., 1988, Visitor management in Canadian national Parks. *Tourism Management*, **9**(1): 44–62

Hall, C.M., 1998, Historical antecedents of sustainable development and ecotourism: new labels on old bottles? In *Sustainable tourism: a geographical perspective*, C.M. Hall and A.A. Lew, eds, pp. 13–24, Addison-Wesley Longman, Harlow

Hall, C.M. and Lew, A.A., eds, 1998, *Sustainable tourism: a geographical perspective*, Addison-Wesley Longman, Harlow

Hardin, G., 1968, The tragedy of the commons. *Science*, **162**: 1243–1248

Hultsman, J., 1995, Just tourism: an ethical framework. *Annals of Tourism Research*, **16**(1): 49–59

Innskeep, E., 1987, Environmental planning for tourism. *Annals of Tourism Research*, **14**: 118–135

Kreutzwiser, R., 1993, Desirable attributes of sustainability: indicators for tourism development. In *Tourism and sustainable development: monitoring, planning, managing*, J.G. Nelson, R.W. Butler and G. Wall, eds, pp. 243–247, Department of Geography Publication Series, No. 37 and Heritage Resources Centre Joint Publication No. 1, University of Waterloo, Waterloo ON

Krippendorf, R.A., 1987, *The holiday makers: understanding the impact of leisure and travel*, Heinemann, London

Loomis, L. and Graefe, A.R., 1992, Overview of NPCA's visitor impact management process.

Paper presented at the IVth World Congress on Parks and Protected Areas, Caracas, Venezuela, 10–21 February

Marsh, J.S., 1993, An index of tourism sustainability. In *Tourism and sustainable development: monitoring, planning, managing*, J.G. Nelson, R.W. Butler and G. Wall, eds, pp. 257–258, Department of Geography Publication Series, No. 37 and Heritage Resources Centre Joint Publication No. 1, University of Waterloo, Waterloo ON

Mathieson, A. and Wall, G., 1982, *Tourism: economic, physical, and social impacts*, Addison-Wesley Longman, London

May, V., 1991, Tourism, environment and development: values, sustainability and stewardship. *Tourism Management* 12(2): 112–118.

McKercher, B., 1993, The unrecognised threat to tourism: can tourism survive sustainability? *Tourism Management* **14**(2): 131–136

Meadows, D.H., Meadows, D.L., Randers, J. and Behrens, W.W., 1972, *Limits to growth: a report for the Club of Rome's Project on the Predicament of Mankind*, Universe Books, New York

Middleton, V.T.C. and Hawkins, R., 1998, *Sustainable tourism: a marketing perspective*, Butterworth-Heinemann, Oxford

Millar, G., 1998, Ending the name game: criteria for tourism to be sustainable. Paper presented at the 7th International Symposium Society and Resource Management, University of Missouri, 27–31 May

Millar, G., forthcoming, The development of indicators for sustainable tourism

Mowforth, M. and Munt, I., 1998, *Tourism and sustainability: new tourism in the Third World*, Routledge, London

National and Historic Parks Branch, 1964, *National park policy*, Queens Printers, Ottawa

Nelson, J.G., 1987, National parks and protected areas, national conservation strategies and sustainable development. *Geoforum*, **18**(3): 291–319

Nelson, J.G., 1993, Beyond parks and protected areas: from public lands and private stewardship to landscape planning and management. In *Parks and Protected Areas in Canada: Planning and Management*, P. Dearden and R. Rollins, eds, pp. 45–56, Oxford University Press, Toronto

Nelson, J.G., 1994, The spread of ecotourism: some planning implications. *Environmental Conservation*, **21**(3): 248–255

Nelson, J.G. and Serafin, R., eds, 1997, *National parks and protected areas: keystones to conservation and sustainable Development* Springer-Verlag: Berlin/Heidelberg/New York

Nelson, J.G., Butler, R.W. and Wall, G., eds, 1993, *Tourism and sustainable development: monitoring, planning, managing*, J.G. Nelson, R.W. Butler and G. Wall, eds, Department of Geography Publication Series, No. 37 and Heritage Resources Centre Joint Publication No. 1, University of Waterloo, Waterloo, ON

Parks Canada, 1979, *Parks Canada Policy*, Ministry of Supply and Services, Ottawa

Parks Canada, 1994, *Guiding principles and operational policies*, Ministry of Supply and Services Canada, Ottawa

Payne, R., 1993, Sustainable tourism: suggested indicators and monitoring techniques. In *Tourism and sustainable development: monitoring, planning, managing*, J.G. Nelson, R.W. Butler and G. Wall, eds, pp. 249–253, Department of Geography Publication Series, No. 37 and Heritage Resources Centre Joint Publication No. 1, University of Waterloo, Waterloo, ON

Pearce, D.W., 1988, Economics, equity and sustainable development. *Futures* **20**(6): 598–605

Pigram, J.J., 1990, Sustainable tourism – policy considerations. *Journal of Tourism Studies*, **1**(2): 2–7

Pigram, J.J. and Sundell, R.C., eds, 1997, *National parks and protected areas: selection, delimitation, and management*, Centre for Policy Research, University of New England, Armidale, NSW

Prosser, R.F., 1992, The ethics of tourism. In *The environment in question: ethics and global issues*, D.E. Cooper and J.A. Palmer, eds, Routledge, London

Regier, H.A., 1993, The notion of natural and cultural integrity. In *Ecological integrity and the management of ecosystems*, S. Woodley, J. Kay and G. Francis, eds, pp. 3–18, St Lucie Press, Ottawa

Robinson, J.G., Francis, G., Legge, R. and Lerner, S., 1990, Defining a sustainable society: values, principles and definitions. *Alternatives*, **17**(2): 36–46

Romeril, M., 1989, Tourism and the environment – accord or discord? *Tourism Management*, **10**(3): 204–208

Shearman, R., 1990 The meaning and ethics of sustainability. *Environmental Management*, **14**(1): 1–8

Shelby, B and Heberlein, T.A., 1986, A conceptual framework for carrying capacity determination. *Leisure Sciences* **6**(4): 433–451

Slocombe, D.S., 1993, Implementing ecosystem-based management: development of theory, practice, and research for planning and managing a region. *BioScience*, **43**(9): 612–622

Smith, V. L. and Eadington, W.R., eds, 1992, *Tourism alternatives: potentials and problems in the development of tourism*, University of Pennsylvania Press, Philadelphia

Stabler, M.J., ed., 1997, *Tourism and sustainability: principles to practice*, CAB International, Wallingford

Stankey, G.H., Cole, D.N., Lucas, R.C., Peterson, M.E. and Frissell, S.S., 1985, *The Limits of Acceptable Change (LAC) system for wilderness planning*, USDA Forest Service General Technical Report INT–176, International Forest and Range Experiment Station, Ogden, Utah

Stankey, G.H. and McCool, S.F., 1986, Carrying capacity in recreational settings: evolution, appraisal and application. *Leisure Sciences*, **6**(4): 453–473

Timothy, D.J., 1996, *Tourism planning in a developing destination: the case of Yogyakarta, Indonesia*, unpublished PhD thesis, Department of Geography, University of Waterloo, Ontario, Canada

Wahab, S. and Pigram, J.J., eds, 1997, *Tourism, development and growth: the challenge of sustainability*, Routledge, London

Wall, G., 1993, towards a tourism typology. In *Tourism and sustainable development: monitoring, planning, managing*, L.J.G. Nelson, R.W. Butler and G. Wall, eds, pp. 45–58, Department of Geography Publication Series, No. 37 and Heritage Resources Centre Joint Publication No. 1, University of Waterloo, Waterloo ON

Wall. G., 1997, Sustainable tourism, unsustainable development. In *Tourism, development and growth: the challenge of sustainability*, S. Wahab and J.J. Pigram, eds, pp. 33–49, Routledge, London

Wall, G. and Wright, C., 1977, *The environmental impact of outdoor recreation*, Department of Geography, University of Waterloo

Weaver, D.B., 1998, *Ecotourism in the less developed world*, CAB International, Oxford

Weiler, B. and Hall, C.M., eds, 1992, *Special interest tourism*, Belhaven Press, London

Wheeller, B., 1991, Tourism's troubled times: responsible tourism is not the answer. *Tourism Management*, **12**(2): 91–96

Wheeller, B., 1992, Alternative tourism – a deceptive ploy. In *Progress in tourism, recreation and hospitality management 4*, C.P. Cooper and A. Lockwood, eds, pp. 140–145, Belhaven Press, London

Wheeller, B., 1993, Sustaining the ego. *Journal of Sustainable Tourism*, **1**(2): 121–129

Whelan, T., ed., 1991, *Nature tourism: managing for the environment*, Island Press, Washington, DC

Wight, P., 1994, Environmentally responsible marketing of tourism. In *Ecotourism: a sustainable option?* E. Cater and G. Lowman, eds, pp. 39–56, John Wiley, Chichester

Woodley, S., 1993, Tourism and sustainable development in parks and protected areas. In *Tourism and sustainable development: monitoring, planning, managing*, J.G. Nelson, R.W. Butler and G. Wall, eds, pp. 83–96, Department of Geography Publication Series, No. 37 and Heritage Resources Centre Joint Publication No. 1, University of Waterloo, Waterloo, ON

World Commission on Environment and Development (WCED), 1987, *Our common future*, Oxford University Press, New York

World Tourism Organisation (WTO), 1993, Sustainable development: an appropriate approach to tourism. *WTO News*, **5**: 3–5

12 Tourism, national parks and resource conflicts

PHILLIP DEARDEN

Introduction

Parks and other protected areas are tangible manifestations of resource use allocations of which land use is one component. The dominant way in which such use allocations are made is through the marketplace. However, the market cannot, and was not meant to, represent all values in society. Beauty, justice, integrity, love, some of the highest human values, receive short shrift in market economics. Over a hundred years ago this was recognised formally at the national level in terms of land use when the nation that most prided itself on adherence to the rights of the individual and market values, the USA, designated Yellowstone as the world's first national park in 1872. Since that time, the family of protected areas, of which national parks are just one member, has spread throughout the world.

This spread hardly bespeaks of a crisis or fundamental fault in the idea of national parks, as some authors would have us believe (e.g. Alcorn, 1993; Ghimire, 1994; Vandergeest, 1996). Rather it endorses the inter cultural nature of the values which societies receive from protecting certain areas of the landscape from the market forces that tend to destroy such values. Many authors (e.g. Sax, 1980; Lemons, 1987; Rolston, 1994; Dearden, 1995; Wright, 1996) have discussed these values in some detail, but here they can be summarised as aesthetic, historical, recreational, spiritual, tourism, educational, scientific, ecological benchmarks and the protection of ecological capital and processes. Different types of protected area place varying degrees of emphasis on the relative priorities to be accorded these different values. The World Conservation Union's (IUCN) international classification is used to categorise these different priorities, outlining six different categories of protected area. This volume is primarily concerned with category II protected areas, national parks, that are defined as 'Natural area of land/sea, designated to (a) protect the ecological integrity of one or more ecosystems for present and future generations, (b) exclude exploitation or occupation inimical to the purposes of designation of the area and (c) provide a foundation for spiritual, scientific, educational, recreational and visitor opportunities, all of which must be environmentally and culturally compatible' (IUCN, 1994).

From this internationally accepted definition it is clear that the main priority for national parks is the protection of ecological integrity and that activities that impair ecological integrity are to be excluded. The Canadian National Park Policy, for example, states unequivocally that 'Protecting ecological integrity and ensuring commemorative integrity take precedence in acquiring, managing, and administering heritage places and programs. In every application of policy, this guiding principle is paramount' (Ministry of Supply and Services, 1994, p. 16).

Resource conflicts

Conflicts over resource use in national parks occur fundamentally for three reasons. The first relates to the inherent incompatibility of some of the fundamental values that society is seeking from parks. If national parks are to protect ecological integrity for this and future generations in the strictest sense then provision of access and facilities for recreation and tourism is *ipso facto* contrary to this goal. Conflicts thus arise from tourism as a legitimate but often incompatible use of parks (e.g. see Wang, 1997). One of the best-known examples of this kind of problem is that of Banff National Park in Canada and this will be discussed in more detail in this chapter.

The second kind of resource conflicts arise from activities that occur within the national park but that are illegal. These activities may include poaching of timber and fauna and clearing of lands for agricultural purposes. Although illegal, they may be tolerated by park management in some instances as a concession to local interests. Such is the case in many lesser-developed countries where poverty in populations surrounding parks is a major problem. This kind of problem will be illustrated mainly by reference to studies undertaken by the author in Thailand over the past 15 years and a generic model is presented that helps clarify the heterogeneous nature of these activities.

The third kind of resource conflicts occur where land uses outside the administrative boundaries of the parks have a detrimental impact upon the protected area values that the park is trying to promote. These are often known as 'external threats' and have become to be one of the major management concerns in protected areas over the last decade (Machlis and Tichnell, 1985). The challenges presented by these kinds of problems will be illustrated again largely with reference to the Canadian national parks.

Legitimate resource conflicts within national parks

As explained in the introduction, there are a variety of values that society expects to realise from protecting certain areas of land from market forces. However, these uses are not always complementary and may indeed conflict with one another. The main source of conflict is usually between recreation/tourism uses and the requirement to protect ecological integrity for this and future generations. Perhaps nowhere has this conflict been more keenly honed and studied than in Banff National Park and World Heritage Site in the Rocky Mountains of Canada, and this case will be used to illustrate this particular resource conflict in more detail.

Banff National Park, Canada

Tourism was the fundamental reason why Banff was initially established as a national park, the third national park in the world in 1885 (see Nelson, this volume). At the time Canada was not short of wilderness, although it could be correctly argued that massive decimation of wildlife was already apparent as symbolised by the almost total annihilation of the bison and the beaver, that 50 years before had been both widespread and in great abundance. Canada was, however, short of money. The government in Ottawa had brought British Columbia into the federation and was building a railway that would link resource-rich western Canada with the markets of the east. As the railroad builders approached the Rocky Mountains and expenses grew, it was with some relief that the hot springs on Sulphur Mountain were discovered.

The government, however, was not alone in the enterprise. The Canadian Pacific Railway held a monopoly for development along the railway and began to build infrastructure in Banff that would propel it onto the international circuit for spa towns. The hotsprings were developed into bathing pools and a luxurious hotel created. Canadian Pacific advertised it as 'Fifty Switzerlands in One' as they tried to lure the sons and daughters of the British Empire away from their European playgrounds to this wild corner of the Empire, and they were successful. Banff became one of the most well-known of the elite tourist spots of the world (McNamee, 1993).

From these beginnings the fortunes of Banff have fluctuated over time as interests and markets have changed. However, tourism has remained as the major driving force for over 100 years (Dearden and Berg, 1993). The Canadian National Parks Act (1930), borrowing from the USA, stated that the parks were to be 'protected unimpaired for ... future generations' but they were also dedicated to the people of Canada for their 'benefit, education and enjoyment', and it was certainly the latter aspect that was given priority in the early years. Park management revolved mainly around enhancing visitor experiences, but as numbers of visitors continued to climb it became increasingly apparent that the parks were not being left 'unimpaired', and that in fact quite serious environmental degradation was taking place.

In Banff, one symbol of this is the extinction of the endemic Banff longnose dace which used to live in a marsh downstream from the hotsprings. Discovered in 1892, it was declared officially extinct in 1987 (Cosewic, 1987). It was likely a combination of factors that led to the extinction. Tropical fish were introduced into the warm waters of the marsh where they flourished and were able to out-compete the dace. The dace may also have interbred with other species of dace, and collection for scientific reasons probably also helped to reduce numbers. However, it seems that the most important factor in its extinction was the decision to allow a hotel to chlorinate hot spring water and discharge it into the marsh. The chlorine reacted to form chlorinated hydrocarbons, which are very toxic to fish, even in low concentrations. Shortly thereafter, the Banff longnose dace disappeared for ever. Hence it was pressure from tourism that led to Banff's first extinction. The significance of this is emphasised by a continent-wide study by Newmark (1986) that on the basis of minimum viable population, analyses suggested that the four mountain parks in Canada (Banff, Jasper, Yoho and Kootenay), covering some 20 000 square kilometres, are the only ones in North America that are large enough to maintain populations of all native fauna.

Banff was not alone in providing clear evidence that park environments were becoming degraded as a result of over-use from tourism. As a result the National Parks Act was amended in 1988 to explicitly state that ecological integrity, not provision of recreational opportunities, was the prime goal of the national park system. This did not, however, instantaneously reduce pressure on Banff, the main focal point of this resource conflict. Banff is a major international tourist destination, attracting over 3.5 million visitors every year worth hundreds of millions of dollars to the economy. On the other hand, clear scientific evidence indicated that populations of all major predators were falling and the grizzly bear would be extirpated from the park within the next 25 years (Banff–Bow Valley Study, 1996).

Although the amount of tourist infrastructure in Banff is greater than that in Yellowstone, Yosemite, Great Smoky Mountains and the Grand Canyon combined, it is not just the amount of development *per se*, but rather its spatial location in relationship to ecosystem characteristics that makes the resource conflict so intense (Banff–Bow Valley Study, 1996). Most of Banff National Park is rock and ice. The town site itself is located in the most productive and rarest habitat, the Montane zone, which covers between 2 per cent and 5 per cent of the park (Figure 12.1). This

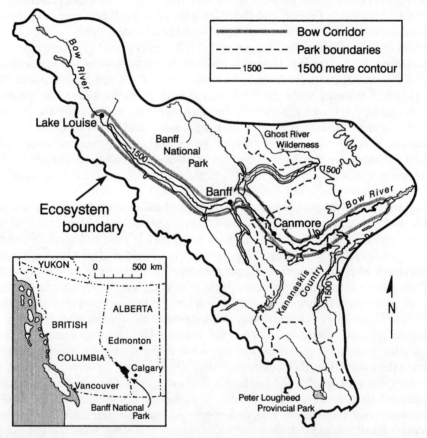

Figure 12.1. Map to show location of Banff, Banff National Park and the Bow Valley corridor

zone has frequent chinook winds, low snow accumulation, warm winter tempera-
tures, migration routes and diverse habitats. These conditions are favourable for a
dense concentration of wildlife and the zone has critical winter refuge areas. The zone
is the smallest in the province of Alberta, occupying less than 1 per cent of the land
area.

The zone is also very attractive for development purposes. Over 70 per cent of the
zone has already been occupied by highways, golf courses, towns and resorts. The
main montane area within the park is along the Bow Valley. Part of the Valley is
within the Park and administered under the National Parks Act. The rest of the
valley is outside and administered by many different federal, provincial and
municipal agencies, with very different mandates. Within the Park the 4 kilometre
wide valley contains the four-lane Trans-Canada highway, the 1A highway, a
national railway, an airstrip, a 27-hole golf course, three ski resorts, the village of
Lake Louise and the town of Banff (population 7500). Banff town site takes up more
than three-quarters of the largest block of montane habitat in the park. Between
1985 and 1992, building permits worth over $360 million were issued in Banff.
Shopping space almost doubled between 1986 and 1994. Banff has three times the
amount of shopping space per person as exists in the largest city in Canada, Toronto!
Canadian Pacific, the owner of the landmark Banff Springs Hotel, proposed adding
nine more holes of golf to the existing twenty-seven at the hotel, 200 more guest
rooms and associated staff housing. The CP-owned Chateau Lake Louise has
proposed a convention centre, new guest rooms and staff housing and development
of a health club and tennis courts.

This development within the park cannot be considered alone. Further downstream in the Bow Valley, the population of Canmore (Figure 12.1) is growing as
quickly as Banff. There are plans for four 18-hole golf courses, over 2000 new hotel
rooms and 6000 housing units by one developer and an 18-hole golf course, 1250
rooms and 1600 housing units by another developer just outside the boundary. Other
developers have tabled plans for three more 18-hole golf courses, 140 recreational
vehicle sites and 50 chalets in the area.

In the light of these extreme tourist pressures the minister established a moratorium
on all development in the Bow Valley and appointed a two-year enquiry:

> to develop a vision and goals for the Banff–Bow Valley that will integrate
> ecological, social and economic values to complete a comprehensive analysis of
> existing information, and to provide direction for future collection and analysis of
> data to achieve ongoing goals to provide direction on the management of human
> use and development in a manner that will maintain ecological values and provide
> sustainable tourism (Banff–Bow Valley Study, 1996, p. 9).

An extensive public consultation process was devised with a round-table
approach involving 14 different interest sectors. All recommendations that achieved
consensus from this group were adopted.

On the basis of this input the task force made many recommendations that are too
detailed to review here (see Banff–Bow Valley Study, 1996). The essence, however,
was clear. There is definitive scientific evidence of significant environmental
deterioration in the Banff–Bow Valley largely due to tourism growth. If this growth
is allowed to continue there will be serious and irreversible harm to ecological
integrity. There will continue to be many attractive and profitable economic

opportunities related to tourism, but this tourism needs to be more clearly linked to park values and the achievement of ecological integrity. Human use needs more effective methods of management and limitation and the Park Management Plan and Town Plan for Banff must be revised accordingly.

On the basis of the report the minister announced that there would be no new land made available for commercial development within the park, the population of the town site would be capped at 10 000 permanent residents, the airport would be closed and the management plan for the park and the town site revised. The report also led to more far-reaching changes for the national park system in Canada when in June 1998 it was announced that the National Park Act would be amended to legislate a fixed amount of development in every national park community in the country. As part of this package, the Banff town site was to be reduced in size by 85 hectares or 17.4 per cent. The total amount of new commercial space allowed in Banff would be less than half that requested by the town. Significantly, a block on the main town avenue would be cleared of commercial development to make way for an environmental education centre that will focus on the national park story, the role parks play as core areas in larger regional ecosystems like the Rocky Mountains, and how park communities can be models of sustainability.

After over a century of domination by tourism interests, it seems as if there have been some serious moves to address some of the conflicts between tourism and conservation values. Following the amendments to the National Park Act in 1988, many environmentalists assumed that park management practices would change to reflect the prime emphasis on ecological integrity. Such was not the case (e.g. see Wipond and Dearden, 1998), and it really took strong political action in Banff before a redress in values was reflected in management activities.

Illegitimate resource conflicts within national parks

The above case illustrated some of the challenges presented by resource conflicts that occur as a result of competing legitimate uses of the park environment. In many parts of the world a more serious challenge to see protection of park values is created by the illegal activities of people surrounding the park. The impacts of these activities can be extremely severe (Kramer *et al.*, 1997). In many cases lands that have been designated as parks provide the last examples remaining of the particular habitat. If the habitat suffers from further degradation as a result of illegal activities following designation then very real threats of extirpations and extinction may occur (e.g. see Fan and Soon, 1996).

It is important to recognise that a wide range of illegal activity is possible for a variety of motives. One tendency in the often quite bitter debates in the literature on this topic (e.g. see Alcorn, 1993; Redford and Stearman, 1993; Saberwal, 1997; Karanth and Madhusudan, 1997) has been a failure to recognise these differences. Hence authors, while disagreeing bitterly, may, in fact be talking about quite different aspects of illegal use. A main tenet of this chapter and works published elsewhere (e.g. see Dearden, 1998) is the need to recognise these differences, as appropriate management responses vary. A simple three-dimensional model (Figure 12.2) can be used to illustrate the main axes of variation.

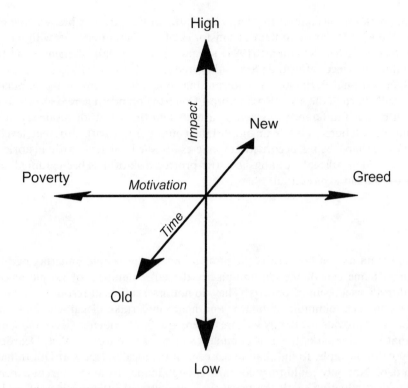

Figure 12.2.   Model of different dimensions of illegal use of park resources

Temporal dimensions

One main question relates to the length of time that an illegal activity has been undertaken. At one end of the scale are activities that have been undertaken by people indigenous to the region of a park for centuries. As our knowledge of ecosystems and ecosystem processes has increased we have become much more aware of the impacts that our forefathers have had on planetary ecosystems. In other words, often what we see and think of as a pristine habitat untouched by humans might, in fact, be the product of centuries of selective human influences. However, it is important to realise that there is a wide range of variation even in these long-term impacts. Human activities such as fire, for example, might have a significant and indeed dominant role in the ecosystem characteristics in some areas. In other areas the impacts of humans over the long term might be minimal.

In considering this length of time variable another major factor is whether the activities pre- or post-date park establishment. Again there is a tendency in the litera-ture to assume that all activities by 'local' people necessarily predate park establishment (e.g. Vandergeest, 1996). In fact in studies in several parks in Thailand it is clear that this is often not the case. Recent migrants may move to an area and start new activities within park boundaries. Others may join existing villages and add to ongoing activities. In Doi Inthanon National Park in Northern Thailand, for example, Dearden *et al.*, (1996) found that the population had tripled in the 15 years following park establishment. In Thap Lan National Park in Northeast Thailand, a park with one of the most contentious histories of conflict, interviews with villagers (Tanakanjana, 1996a; Ketanond, 1997) suggest that over half of them came from surrounding provinces after the park had been declared. In the villages surrounding Pang Sida National Park, surveys indicate that only 20 per cent of the population were actually born in the area (Royal Forest Department, nd). There is clearly a wide variation between different protected area units and the length of residency of sur-rounding populations. This is an important consideration with different levels of sympathy perhaps being accorded to long-established villages with historic use rather than villages illegally established after protected status has been granted, often related to tourism exploitation.

Motivation

A second main axis of concern is the motivations of the people undertaking illegal activities. At one end of the continuum are the large numbers of people who are acting directly as a result of poverty. They do not have sufficient resources to be able to survive to even minimum standards and hence undertake illegal activities out of desperation to provide for family welfare. There is a lot of evidence (Kerr and Currie, 1995) that in many parks this is a dominant source of resource conflict. Dearden *et al.*, (1996), for example, found that 46 per cent of the local villagers at Doi Inthanon were in debt. Not only could they not raise enough money to cover current expenses, but their debt situation, with the usual usurious rates of interest charged by local moneylenders, drove them to even greater forest exploitation. Tungittiplakorn (1997) has also found that poorer Hmong families are more likely to hunt in local protected areas than wealthier ones. These findings are echoed in the Philippines by Shively (1997). Ketanond (1997) found poverty to be a major problem in villages in the north-east of Thailand at Thap Lan National Park and surveys by Kasetsart University (1982) and PDA (1990) found a similar situation in villages surrounding Khao Yai National Park. The more geographically extensive study by Tanakanjana (1996a) in all regions of Thailand found that only 4 per cent of respondents rated their household income status as good or high and 56 per cent perceived their dependency on park resources for their livelihood as moderate to high. She concludes that 'as long as people still need to grow crops, collect plants, cut wood, fish and hunt within the parks for household uses and for income, it is almost impossible for them to think and act on protecting natural resources, especially when those behaviours limit them in fulfilling their basic needs' (Tanakanjana, 1996b, p. 17).

It should not be assumed, however, that all park resource exploitation by locals is a result of poverty, nor the result of subsistence activities. Villagers interviewed in Khao Sok National Park in southern Thailand had originated in the north-east of Thailand and had cut down the forest in the national park and were growing coffee as a commercial crop sponsored by a local influential figure. Ketanond (1997) found many such links between illegal activities, such as logging and land clearing for agriculture, villagers and sponsorship by rich and important figures. Vandergeest (1996) also reports that the local villagers' use of a wildlife sanctuary in southern Thailand was not related to poverty.

Another example of exploitation motivated more by greed than necessity occurred in the winter of 1998 in Thailand when a major corruption scandal erupted in the northwestern province of Mae Hon Song, along the border with Myanmar, where there are two protected areas, the Salween National Park and Wildlife Sanctuary. One of the few remaining blocks of protected areas in Northern Thailand to retain significant biodiversity values, such as large mammals, conservationists were angered to learn of a huge illegal logging operation in the heart of the sanctuaries that allegedly cut some 43 000 logs. Operated by Karen refugees from Myanmar who had been allowed to stay in the Park, and financed by influential Thai figures, the scandal dominated headlines in the news for weeks as a long succession of authorities became implicated in taking bribes from the operation.

Thailand also had a banner year for fires in national parks in 1998. World Heritage Site Huay Kha Khaeng suffered more extensive damage than ever before, as did World Heritage nominee, Khao Yai, and other prominent parks such as Doi Inthanon. The smoke was so thick in Northern Thailand that Thai Air suspended flights to Mae Hong Son. In all these cases, there seems to be little doubt that these fires were human caused as small fires had been started in many different locations. Essentially the reasons were the same as in previous years, local people were starting fires to clear more farmland, burning their fields adjacent to protected areas or seeking to increase the productivity of the parklands for grazing and mushroom production. Unfortunately many of the fires got severely out of hand and did extensive damage to surrounding evergreen formations that are not adapted to fire stress.

The fires also hit the headlines as various groups blamed each other for starting and/or failing to control the fires. Lowlanders and some NGOs blamed the highlanders and their slash and burn agriculture; highlanders and some NGOs blamed park officials trying to increase their budgets; park officials blamed highlanders. Whoever is right, there is no doubt that the situation is very complicated. It is not unknown, for example, for rich lowlanders to pay highlanders to start fires, so that they can later claim that the land is degraded and should be removed from the protected area system. Also, following a cabinet resolution last year, park officials were told not to enforce relocation plans for villagers that could prove occupancy. Clearing land is one good way to try to prove occupancy. Following mass encroachment in the parks this directive has now been rescinded.

Environmental impact

The third axis of concern in Figure 12.2 relates to the amount of ecological damage caused by the illegal activities. Some activities that are small scale and have been carried on for long periods in the past may have little significant ecological impact upon the park. Collection of renewable resources such as honey and fast-growing plants are typical examples. At the other end of the continuum are activities that fundamentally alter the characteristics of the environment such that ecological integrity is compromised. Extinction would be the extreme case, where an ecosystem component is completely removed for all time as a result of human activities. Species do not, however, have to be completely removed for the ecosystem to sustain considerable impacts. When species are reduced in abundance below a certain threshold they may no longer be able to fulfil their ecological role in the community. This is known as 'ecological extinction' and can have very severe consequences for future ecosystem development (Redford, 1992). As Michael Soule (1996) put it,

> Most of the surviving species of big tropical animals (larger than pigeons and rabbits) will soon disappear outside of protected areas ... These larger animals...often determine the physical structure and spatial distribution of other species in ecological communities. When the large animals disappear, the ecological changes are often swift and profound' (p. 24).

Discussion

The purpose of presenting the model discussed above was to illustrate the heterogeneous nature of illegal activities that occur on parklands. Although technically against most national park legislation and international standards, resource use that is motivated by poverty, established before the park was designated and is of marginal ecological impact surely deserves a different management response than new ecologically damaging, commercial activities funded by wealthy people. This is the pragmatic view that has been taken in most cases by the National Parks Division in Thailand where there is some informal sensitivity towards the context of the resource conflict.

One of the challenges in taking such a case-by-case approach is that often there is inadequate scientific knowledge upon which to base the decisions regarding the long-term ecological impacts of many activities. Little is known of ecosystem characteristics and processes. Furthermore, in general, scientists do not know enough about the requirements of many tropical species to be able to judge whether various activities will have a longer term detrimental impact (Heywood *et al.*, 1994). Even activities that might seem relatively benign can result in unforeseen consequences. Islam and Islam (1997) describe how the collection of immature bamboos and wild bananas in the forests between Ramu and Ukhia in Bangladesh has led elephants to increasingly forage in crop fields and come into conflict with local peoples.

One of the fundamental reasons why parks are protected from human activities is in order to establish some ecological benchmarks against which to assess change in the vast majority of the rest of the landscape outside the parks. This rationale has led some authors (e.g. Arcese and Sinclair, 1997) to suggest that some parks should be maintained solely for this benchmark function where no human use whatsoever (including tourism) is allowed. Nonetheless, the reality in many less-developed countries is that total exclusion of illegal activities is impossible. Perhaps it is better to have a negotiated agreement between park authorities and local villagers (see Goodwin, this volume) that might allow some less-damaging activities than to have a complete ban that is totally ignored. Much depends upon the local context, and an idiographic approach makes most sense.

Conflicts resulting from land uses outside parks

The final category of resource conflicts to be briefly mentioned here relates to those that may occur outside the legislated boundaries of a park but nonetheless may have a significant detrimental impact on park values. In recent years park managers and scientists have become increasingly aware of the major impacts that such external threats may pose. In one of the first global surveys Machlis and Tichnell (1985, p. 11), defined threats as '... those activities of either human or natural origin that cause significant damage to park resources, or are in serious conflict with the objectives of park administration and management'. Such threats are often generated from legitimate land uses and span a wide range from global air pollution that may occur at great distances from a park or from activities directly adjacent to a park boundary, such as forest harvesting and inappropriate tourism infrastructure.

Most work in this area has either been concerned with threat surveys over large areas, globally, nationally or regionally (e.g. Machlis and Newmann, 1987), or concentrated upon the specific aspects of one particular threat (e.g. McCrea *et al.*, 1993). Parks Canada, for example, undertook stress assessments on the national park system in 1992 and 1997. The latest survey of 36 parks (Parks Canada, 1998) identified stressors originating inside the park, within the region, or outside the park (Figure 12.3). Many stressors originate both inside and outside parks reflecting the high degree of development that now surrounds many national parks. Transportation and utility corridors had significant impacts on 25 parks and urbanisation on 24 parks. Of particular relevance to this discussion are the 26 parks that reported tourism and visitor facilities as a major cause of stress. This in turn leads to other visitor-related stressors such as introduction of exotic plant species (21 parks), pollution from sewage (14 parks) and solid waste (15 parks). Similarly, high visitor numbers lead to disturbance of wildlife such as grizzly bears (Gibeau *et al.*, 1996). The case study of Banff–Bow Valley discussed earlier illustrates some of these tourism-generated resource conflicts.

In terms of stressors originating solely outside parks, forestry affected 20 parks, agriculture 17 and mining 16. The many ways in which agriculture and forestry can affect the ecological integrity of parks is shown in Table 12.1. In addition to these ecological impacts it should also be remembered that parks are established by society to realise a whole range of values, of which ecological values are but one important component. Dearden and Doyle (1998), for example, in a threat assessment of Pacific Rim National Park in British Columbia, found that the most serious threat to park values in terms of documentation and considering spatial and temporal impacts was scenic degradation as a result of forest harvesting activities outside the park.

Conclusions

Parks have been established by governments throughout the world as a means of protecting certain areas of the earth's land and water surfaces from market and other forces. They are thus areas that belong to all the people of the particular political unit that has so designated a park for current and future generations. Resource conflicts occur when:

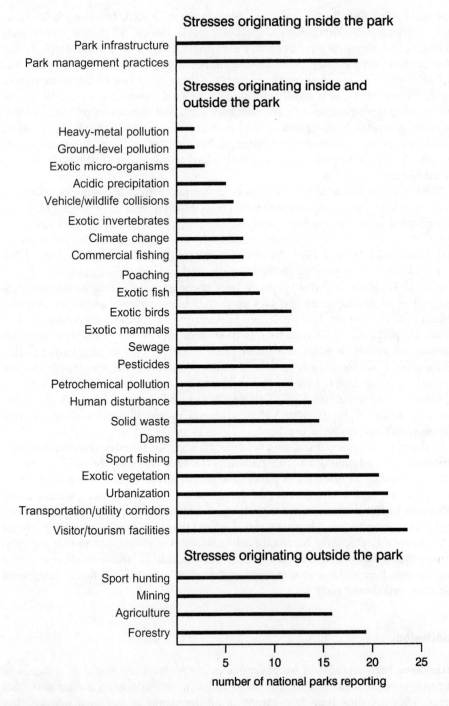

Figure 12.3. Sources of stress on parks (Note: the questionnaire was administered during 1995 in the national parks located in Ontario)

Table 12.1 Agricultual and forestry impacts on the ecological integrity of parks

Type of Impact	Agriculture	Forestry
Significant change to the genetics of a population that reduces the viability of a species	9	16
Population reduced so that its function in the ecosystem is severly reduced	11	19
Population increases so that its function in the ecosystem is drastically changed	11	17
Loss of a native species in an ecosystem	9	12
Significant change in ccommunity structure	10	23
Significant habitiat fragmentation	18	23
Significant habitat loss	17	21
Significant change in water or soil chemistry	15	10
Significant modification of the physical environment	14	12
Significant change in air quality	7	2
Significant change in water levels or regime	10	6

- The legitimate goals of the parks are found to be in conflict with each other, such as when provision of opportunities for tourism start to impinge upon the protection of ecological integrity of the park
- Certain groups of people seek access to park resources for uses that are not in keeping with the protection of park values and are against international norms and national legislation for parks and
- Developments outside parks which may be consistent with legislation have a negative impact upon the protection of park values.

There is no generic solution to these problems. Each must be understood in terms of its origin and degree of impact on park resources. If the problem is illegal extraction of park resources as a result of poverty, then provision of alternative income opportunities, preferably those that encourage conservation such as ecotourism (e.g. see Brockelman and Dearden, 1989; Dearden, 1995; Hvenegaard and Dearden, 1998), is a possible management approach. If, on the other hand, the illegal extraction is generated by excessive greed of rich people, then it is unlikely that modest rural development projects are going to work. Similarly, if the main impacts on park values originate outside parks then there is little point on management concentrating solely on within-park strategies.

Understanding of these individual challenges calls for a much more idiographic approach to park management than has been taken in the past. Localised problems often require localised solutions (see Vaske, Whittaker and Donnelly, this volume). There are limits, however, to flexibility. This is the essence of having 'national' parks that are managed to 'national' standards that reflect international norms. These international norms are informed by the knowledge that 25 per cent of mammal species are threatened with extinction, as are one third of primates (IUCN, 1996). Humans now appropriate over 40 per cent of the net primary productivity of the planet to support themselves. The most optimistic projections suggest that population will double by the end of the next century leading to an even greater proportion of the life of the planet being channelled to meet just one end – assuaging human appetites. Already, planetary ecosystems are showing severe signs of strain, climates are changing, waters are polluted, fish have disappeared and extinction levels have soared. Parks are a bulwark against the degradation of planetary ecosystems. An overview of natural resource management in Thailand in the late 1980s concluded that '... species which depend on forests for survival will soon survive only within the protected area system' (TDRI, 1987, p. 104). The same is true for many areas throughout the world (Soule, 1996). However, parks cannot solve this problem alone. They are too small, too few, too isolated and too vulnerable to the threats described in this chapter. Understanding the resource conflicts that challenge the delivery of park values is a first step to controlling or preventing their efforts.

References

Alcorn, J. B., 1993, Indigenous peoples and conservation. *Conservation Biology*, **7**: 424–426

Arcese, P., and Sinclair, A.R.E., 1997, The role of protected areas as ecological baselines. *Journal of Wildlife Management*, **61**: 587–602

Banff–Bow Valley Study, 1996, *Banff–Bow Valley: at the crossroads*, Summary Report of the Banff–Bow Valley Task Force, Auditor, General of Canada, Ottawa

Brockelman, W. and Dearden, P., 1990, The role of nature trekking in conservation: a case study in Thailand. *Environmental Conservation*, **17**(2): 141–148

CNPPA/IUCN, 1996, *1996 IUCN Red List of threatened animals*, IUCN, Gland, Switzerland

Corlett, R.T. and Turner, I.M., 1997, Long-term survival in tropical forest remnants in Singapore and Hong Kong In *Tropical forest remnants: ecology, management, and conservation of fragmented communities*, W.F. Laurance and R.O. Bieerregaard, eds, pp. 333–346, University of Chicago, Chicago

Cosewic, A., 1987, *Canadian Species at Risk 1987*, Environment Canada, Ottawa

Dearden, P., 1995, Ecotourism, parks and biocultural diversity: The context in Northern Thailand. In *Ecotourism: concept, design and strategy*, S. Hiranburana, VV. Stithyudhakarn and P. Dhamabutra, eds, pp. 15–42, Institute of Ecotourism, Srinakharinwirot University, Bangkok

Dearden, P., 1998, Protected areas in Thailand: thoughts on future direction. In *Tropical forestry in the 21st century: Volume 5 Parks and protected areas*, S. Chettamart, D Emphandu and L. Puangchit, eds, pp. 8–22, Kasetsart University, Bangkok

Dearden, P. and Berg, L., 1993, Canada's national park: a model of administrative penetration. *The Canadian Geographer*, **37**(2): 194–211

Dearden, P., Chettamart, S., Emphandu, D. and Tanakanjana, N., 1996, National parks and hilltribes in Northern Thailand: a case study of Doi Inthanon. *Society and Natural Resources*, **9**: 125–141

Dearden, P. and Doyle, S., 1998, External threats to Pacific Rim National Park Reserve. In *Themes and issues of Canadian geography II*, C. Stafel, ed., pp. 121–136, Salzburger Geograpische Arbeiten, Salzburg

Fan, Z. and Soon, Y., 1996, The wildlife conservation system and main wildlife protection programs in China. *TigerPaper*, **23**: 22–28

Giberd, M.L., Herrero, S., Kansas, I.L. and Benn, B. 1996, *Grizly bear population and habitat status in Banff National Park: a report to the Banff Bow Valley task force* prepared for the Banff Bow Valley task force, Banff, Alberta

Ghimire, K.B., 1994, Parks and people: livelihood issues in national parks mangement in Thailand and Madagascar. *Development and Change*, **25**: 195–229

Heywood, V.H., Mace, G.M., May, R.M. and Stuart, S.N., 1994, Uncertainties in extinction rates. *Nature* **368**:105

Hvenegaard, G. and Dearden, P., 1998, Linking ecotourism and biodiversity conservation: a case study of Doi Inthanon National Park, Thailand. *Journal of Tropical Geography*, **19**: 193–211

IUCN, 1994, *Guidelines for protected area management categories*, Gland, Switzerland

Islam, M.Z. and Islam, M.S., 1997, Wildlife status in the evergreen forests between Ramu and Ukhia of Cox's Bazar Forest Division. *TigerPaper* 24: 9–13

Karanth, K.U. and Madhusudan, M.D., 1997, Avoiding paper tigers and saving real tigers: response to Saberwal. *Conservation Biology*, 11: 818–220

Kerr, J.T. and Currie, D.J., 1995, Effects of human activity on global extinction risk. *Conservation Biology*, 9: 1528–1538

Ketanond, P., 1997, *People, parks and biodiversity conservation: a case study of Thap Lan National Park, Thailand*, MSc thesis, University of Victoria

Kramer, R., van Schaik, C. and Johnson, J., 1997, *Last stand: protected areas and the defense of tropical biodiversity*, Oxford University Press, Oxford

Lemons, J., 1987, United States' national park management: Values, policy, and possible hints for others. *Environmental Conservation*, 14: 329–340

Machlis, G.E. and Newmann, R.P., 1987, The state of national parks in the neotropical realm. *Parks*, 12(2): 3–8

Machlis, G.E. and Tichnell, D.L., 1985, *The state of the world's parks*, Westview Press, Boulder, CO

McCrea, R.C., Hanau, M.T. and Fischer, J.D., 1993, An assessment of the sensitivity of lakes in Pukaskwa National Park to acidification. In *Science and the management of protected areas*, J.H.M. Willison, ed., pp. 425–435 Elsevier, Amsterdam

McNamee, K., 1993, From wild spaces to endangered places: A history of Canada's National Parks. In *Parks and protected areas in Canada: planning and management*, P. Dearden and R. Collins, eds, pp. 17–44, Oxford University Press, Toronto

Newmark, W.D. 1986, Species–area relationship and its determinants for mammals in western North American national parks. *Biol. J. Linn. Soc.*, 28: 65–82

Parks Canada, 1994, *Guiding principles and operational policies*, Ministry of Supply and Services, Ottawa

Parks Canada, 1998, *State of the Parks, 1997*, Minister of Public Works and Government Services Canada, Ottawa

Redford, K.H., 1992, The empty forest. *BioScience*, 42: 412–422

Redford, K.H. and Stearman, A.M., 1993, Forest-dwelling native Amazonians and the conservation of biodiversity. *Conservation Biology*, 7: 248–255

Rolston, H., 1994, *Conserving natural value*, Columbia University Press, New York

Royal Forest Department, nd, *Management plan for Pang Sida National Park*, National Parks Division, Bangkok (in Thai)

Saberwal, V.K., 1997, Saving the tiger: more money or less power? *Conservation Biology*, 11: 815–817

Sax, J., 1980, *Mountains without handrails: reflections on the national parks*, University of Michigan Press, Ann Arbor, MI

Shively, G.E., 1997, Poverty, technology, and wildlife hunting in Palawan. *Environmental Conservation*, 24: 57–63

Soule, M., 1996, The end of evolution? *World Conservation*, 1: 24–25

Tanakanjana, N., 1996a, *Analysis of nonconforming behavior of local people in the national park system of Thailand*, Kasetsart University, Bangkok (unpublished)

Tanakanjana, N., 1996b, *Analysis of nonconforming behaviors of local people in the national park system of Thailand*, PhD dissertation, Colorado State University, Fort Collins

Thailand Development Research Institute (TDRI), 1987, *Thailand natural resources profile: is the resource base of Thailand's development sustainable?* National Environmental Board, Department of Technical and Economic Cooperation, US AID, Bangkok

Tungittiplakorn, W., 1997, Impacts of cash cropping on wildlife biodiversity in Hmong communities in Northern Thailand. Unpublished paper, University of Victoria

Vandergeest, P., 1996, Property rights in protected areas: obstacles to community involvement as a solution in Thailand *Environmental Conservation*, 23(3): 259–268

Wang, C.Y., 1997, Environmental impacts of tourism on US national parks. *Journal of Travel Research*, 35: 31–42

Wipond, K. and Dearden, P., 1998, Obstacles to maintaining ecological integrity in Pacific

Rim National Park Reserve. In *Linking protected areas with working landscapes, conserving biodiversity*, N.W.P. Munro and J.H.M. Willison, eds, pp. 901–910, Science and Management of Protected Areas Association, Wolfville

Wright, R.G., 1996, *National parks and protected areas: their role in environmental protection*, Blackwell Science, Cambridge, MA

13 Tourism, national parks and impact management

JERRY J. VASKE, MAUREEN P. DONNELLY
AND DOUG WHITTAKER

Introduction

From a campfire discussion on the banks of the Madison River on the Yellowstone Plateau the national park idea arose from concern that important natural features should be part of a public 'commons' rather than exploited by private interests (Nash, 1982). But while the preservation of natural features has always been a central principle in North American national park management, the provision of opportunities to enjoy those features has been equally important (see Nelson, Chapter 18). This dual mandate creates an inevitable tension, because any use has some impacts on natural features or tourist experiences. As more people have gained the time, financial resources, and inclination to visit parks over the past half-century, the notion that we are loving the parks to death has become a common theme in park management.

The over-use problem provides a classic illustration of Hardin's (1968) tragedy of the commons. Individual use is not the problem, but as each new person visits a park, they may incrementally and collectively degrade the resource or experience for all. In many commons situations, the general solution – constraining use through mutual coercion, mutually agreed upon – is relatively difficult to attain. In the national parks, however, there are both institutional resources and a widely agreed-upon cultural mandate to constrain those collective uses that cause unacceptable impacts. In recent years, at least at the philosophical and legal mandate level, it has become clear that protection trumps use in the national parks (Nash, 1982; Oelschlaeger, 1991; NPS, 1991).

Unfortunately, the same societal value shift that favours protection (Dunlap, 1991; Steel et al., 1994; Stern and Dietz 1994), also increases the demand for recreation in national parks, especially in frontcountry settings (Lime, 1996). At Arches National Park in Utah, for example, visitation increased nearly 170 per cent between 1980 and 1994. At Mount Rushmore National Monument in the Black Hills, the number of rockclimbers grew from less than 50 people in 1987 to approximately 4000 in 1995 (Lime et al., 1996). Addressing the tension between use and protection thus continues to be a management and research challenge.

Biologists and social scientists have explored these issues in national parks and other wildland areas for the past half-century. Biological studies have documented impacts from various forms of recreation in wildland settings (see Boyle and Samson, 1985; Hammitt and Cole, 1987; Knight and Gutzwiller, 1995; Kuss *et al.*, 1990; Liddle and Scorgie, 1980 for reviews), while social studies have demonstrated the impacts visitors have on each other's park experiences (see Kuss *et al.*, 1990; Manning, 1986; Shelby and Heberlein, 1986). This work has repeatedly suggested that human use impacts are complex, and that evaluative judgements are needed to decide if the impacts constitute damage. The devil is not inherent or inevitable, but resides in the details of the type of use, the type of impacts, and the acceptability of those impacts. The key to determining this acceptability, in turn, rests with standards that define high quality recreation experiences and ecological health. We believe that 'ecological health' is best understood and defined by humans rather than a scientific absolute to be discovered by humans. Philosophical support for this view can be found in Fleischmann's (1969) excellent short essay on 'the biological fallacy' (the idea that 'nature' does not care one way or the other about ecological change), or Steinbeck and Ricketts' (1941) argument to avoid 'teleological thinking' (the assumption that there is some master plan within nature). In a more applied sense, Kennedy and Thomas (1995) note that even so-called 'biocentric' natural resource values emanate from human social values, and suggest that resource management frameworks that acknowledge this are more likely to be successful at managing for those values than ones that assume a nature-advocacy position.

Several planning and management frameworks have evolved to help decision makers collect, organise, and consider information about use and impacts. These frameworks (e.g. Limits of Acceptable Change (LAC), Visitor Impact Management (VIM), and Visitor Experience and Resource Protection (VERP)), all feature common elements that form the basis for good management (Stankey *et al.*, 1985; Graefe, *et al.*, 1990; NPS, 1997). In this chapter, we review these common elements, and provide three national park examples to illustrate how the principles have been examined and applied in research and management.

Common elements of impact management frameworks

While the competing recreation planning frameworks (i.e. LAC, VIM, VERP) differ in their specific procedural steps, all advocate several basic elements or principles.

Define opportunities

An enduring principle of recreation management is that people desire a diversity of recreation experiences. Such experiences are created through the interaction of social and physical conditions, and the visitors' expectations and preferences for those conditions (Manfredo *et al.*, 1996). Managers do not create *experiences*, but are responsible for creating *opportunities* for experiences by manipulating social, environmental, and managerial conditions. The first step in all planning frameworks is thus explicit recognition of the type of recreation opportunity managers are trying to provide.

This step generally involves developing qualitative descriptions of opportunities. A description of a backcountry opportunity in the remote Bechler region of Yellowstone Park National Park, for example, might include low interaction levels between users, no structural development, few signs of previous use or management, and opportunities for risk-oriented recreation and self-reliance. In contrast, a description of a frontcountry opportunity in the geyser basins around Old Faithful would include high levels of interaction between visitors, opportunities for interpretation and other learning activities, high levels of facility and service development, and low potential for self-reliance challenges.

In developing these opportunity definitions, it is important to recognise that neither backcountry nor frontcountry are inherently of higher quality than the other; they are simply different. While a backpacker interested in a wilderness experience might find Old Faithful tame, urbanised, and over-managed, the family who simply wants to see and learn about geysers does not. In turn, the family may not be comfortable hiking and camping in grizzly country, or approaching thermal features without the safety of boardwalks and warning signs. In all cases, the issue is defining the conditions that contribute to quality for that type of opportunity. There are high-quality and low-quality wilderness experiences, just as there are high-quality and low-quality frontcountry experiences. The manager's task in this step is to qualitatively define which conditions are consistent with high quality.

Opportunity definitions sometimes spring from legislative mandates (e.g. the Wilderness Act's call for virtually no development, opportunities for solitude, and an 'untrammeled' environment), but more often are developed from traditional uses and experiences that evolve in certain areas at certain times. The planner's task is to explicitly recognise what currently exists and then what should exist, shifting from a reactive management mode (where opportunities are created by default) to a pro-active one.

Indicators and standards

Qualitative definitions, however, are not enough. The central principle in all the prominent planning frameworks (LAC, VIM, VERP) is the use of indicator variables and standards to *quantitatively* define appropriate conditions for each type of experience. Indicators are the biophysical, social, managerial or other conditions managers and visitors care about for a given experience. Standards are the amount of a condition that management is trying to attain (or avoid exceeding). In the Yellowstone backcountry example above, for instance, an indicator of social interaction levels may be the number of encounters with other groups per day, while the standard for high quality may be less than three. An environmental indicator might refer to the area of disturbed/compacted vegetation at campsites, with the standard for high quality being less than 500 square feet.

While there are multiple possible indicators and standards for a given experience, the goal is to select a few key indicators/standards that represent the relevant components of an experience. Indicators and standards are important because they:

- Articulate in unambiguous terms what outputs management is trying to provide
- Focus attention on specific conditions and problems
- Help establish priorities for management
- Provide a base for measuring the rate and magnitude of change
- Help the public clearly understand what management is trying to accomplish and
- Link concrete, on-the-ground conditions with more intangible, qualitative experiences.

Selecting indicators and standards is an iterative rather than linear process. There is a need to look ahead to what actions might be employed to meet standards, as well as a need to look back at the opportunity definitions management is trying to provide. Indicators and standards also need to be developed collaboratively with the public and other stakeholders to ensure that there is agreement. A number of approaches to collaborative planning (see discussion below) have been utilised, but surveys of park users or the public offer one important source of information about appropriate standards for many natural resource conditions. Recreation users are experts about what conditions they prefer in natural resource settings, and when there is agreement about standards for those conditions, managers can use that information to establish useful standards.

Linking actions with standards

Once standards have been set to define experience quality and resource health, the next steps involve brainstorming actions that will help meet those standards, and then choosing among the alternatives. Linking actions with standards is important because it lets the public understand why certain actions are being taken, and what management hopes to accomplish. While it is beyond the scope of this chapter to review the full range of actions that could be taken to provide various conditions defined by standards, it is important to recognise that different actions have different consequences in different settings. Three general approaches to minimising visitor impacts are discussed below.

One strategy employs a 'technical fix', usually through capital developments or improvements. Such technical fixes are used to: (1) minimise impacts to biophysical resources (e.g. harden a trail to prevent erosion, create pit toilets to prevent human waste impacts); (2) provide education/interpretation opportunities (e.g. development of an informational kiosk or visitor centre); or (3) accommodate the sheer volume of use (provide expected facilities such as parking or toilets).

The idea behind many of these actions is that enough money thrown at a problem can fix even the most damaging human impacts. The high costs and limited success of river restoration and endangered species recovery efforts suggest this idea has limitations, but facilities development can often diminish recreation use impacts by focusing use away from sensitive areas and onto hardened sites like trails, pull-outs, and wildlife viewing platforms. The downside to these actions is that they have the potential to dramatically affect other components of the recreation experience or environment. Hardened facilities can take some of the wildness out of a natural setting, or attract even greater use.

A second approach, education, is sometimes used to enhance opportunities by providing desired information (e.g. interpretation), or to change behaviour that may be causing social or biophysical impacts. Driven by the belief that people will stop undesirable behaviour once they are aware of the impacts it causes, education is often viewed as a panacea for addressing recreation impacts. Theory (Blamey, 1998; Schwartz, 1977) and research (Kim and Shelby, 1996; Stern et al., 1986), however, suggest that pro-environmental norms that regulate behaviour are activated only when two conditions are met. First, individuals must possess an awareness of the consequences their behaviour has on other visitors and the physical environment. Second, individuals must accept some responsibility for their actions. Information and education may make visitors aware of the consequences of their actions, but does not necessarily increase their ascription of personal responsibility. Education/ persuasion attempts are also less successful when the behaviour in question brings personal rewards. Wildlife photographers, for example, get better shots by getting closer to, or provoking reactions from, animals. This does not eliminate the continued need for resource impact education, but simply recognises that education alone may not always work.

As a back-up to education, regulations are often employed to enforce behaviour norms through fines and other formal sanctions. Regulations can be quite effective (e.g. restrictions on campfires have virtually eliminated fire-ring impacts in some national parks), but are often intrusive or change the type of experience provided. People frequently visit wildland areas to escape civilisation's rules and reminders of rules.

A final approach, use limits, restricts the number of people that can be in an area and presumably limits the level of impacts. Unfortunately, the relationships between density levels and impact variables are neither simple nor uniform (Vaske et al., 1995a). Most impacts do not exhibit a direct linear relationship with user density. In fragile alpine parks, for example, even a few visitors can have severe impacts on the vegetation and soils. Similarly, in wilderness environments, encounters with relatively few other recreationists can disrupt the desired experience opportunity. For some social impacts (most notably encounters in linear settings such as rivers), however, use levels are correlated with impacts and limiting use can pay important dividends.

Because use restrictions constrain visitor freedom and do not always achieve the desired outcome of reducing biophysical and social impacts, most planning frameworks advocate exploring all other options before implementing use limits. Waiting to implement use limits, however, can be problematic. With each year of incremental use increases, it becomes more and more difficult to turn the clock back to previous use levels.

Collaborative approach

The final common principle of the planning frameworks (LAC, VIM, VERP) is the need to involve the public and stakeholders in the decision making, regardless of whether one is defining opportunities, choosing indicators or standards, or deciding among action strategies. Collaborative planning in the natural resource arena has typically focused on including stakeholders (e.g. commercial operators, adjacent landowners, conservation interest groups) on planning teams. This has the advantage of both ensuring that their expertise and opinions are considered, and that these players buy into and take some responsibility for decisions in the plan. In many cases, it is these stakeholders that can apply the political pressure to implement plans.

Because different stakeholders are interested in different types of experiences, impact management decisions are often contentious. Moreover, there are usually trade-offs between minimising impacts and implementing regulations or other undesirable consequences. In these cases, having good information about group and public preferences for and acceptability of different experiences, standards, or actions that might be used to meet standards becomes essential. The following discusses one theoretically based approach to collecting and analysing survey data related to standards, which is at the heart of impact management frameworks.

Standards and the normative approach

The concept of norms provides a theoretical framework for collecting and organising information about users' evaluations of conditions and has proven useful in establishing management standards for how much impact is too much. While definitions of the concept vary, one research tradition suggests norms are standards that people use to evaluate behaviour or the conditions created by behaviour as acceptable or unacceptable (Vaske et al., 1986). Norms thus define what behaviour or conditions should be, and can apply to individuals, collective behaviour, or management actions designed to constrain collective behaviour (Shelby et al., 1996).

Norm methods explore individual responses to behaviour or conditions (personal norms), and then aggregate responses across groups (social norms), allowing the characteristics of norms to be explored empirically. Jackson (1965) pioneered this structural approach, although others have offered advances in question format and analysis techniques (Vaske et al., 1993). This normative approach allows researchers to define social norms, describe a range of acceptable behaviour or conditions, explore agreement about the norm, and characterise the type of norm (e.g., no tolerance, single tolerance or multiple tolerance norms; Whittaker and Shelby, 1988).

Normative concepts in natural resource settings were initially applied to encounter impacts in backcountry (encounter norms measure tolerances for the number of other contacts with other users per day). The focus on encounters in backcountry worked because encounter levels were generally low, survey respondents could count and remember them, and encounters have important effects on the quality of experiences when solitude is a feature. Most studies showed that encounter norms across these backcountry settings were stable and strongly agreed upon, usually averaging about 4 encounters per day (Vaske et al., 1986).

More recently, norm concepts and methods have been applied to a greater diversity of impacts and settings (Shelby and Vaske, 1991; Shelby et al., 1996). Encounter norm research in higher density frontcountry settings, for example, has demonstrated more variation in visitors' tolerances for others as well as lower levels of agreement (Donnelly et al., in press; Manning et al., 1996; Roggenbuck et al.,

1991; Vaske *et al.*, 1996). This led some researchers to examine norms for interaction impacts different than encounters (Martinson and Shelby, 1992; Shelby *et al.*, 1987; Whittaker and Shelby, 1993; Whittaker, 1992). Norms for angler proximity, percentage of time within sight of others, incidents of discourteous behaviour, competition for fishing areas, waiting times at rapids and boat launches, and amount of angler interference have all been examined. These alternative interaction impacts are often more salient than encounters in higher use settings, and deserve more research attention (Basman *et al.*, 1996; Whittaker and Shelby, 1996). Other researchers have explored normative evaluations of development levels (Vaske and Donnelly, 1998), biophysical impacts at campsites (fire rings and bare ground) (Shelby *et al.*, 1988), and instream flows for hiking and boating (Shelby and Whittaker, 1995, 1996).

Taken together, this work suggests that normative methods can facilitate understanding visitors' evaluations of social and environmental conditions, and has proven helpful to managers. Applying this information in real planning situations, however, is complex. The following examples illustrate how normative information was integrated into impact management efforts in North American national parks. We have chosen examples ranging from a low-density backcountry setting (Gwaii Haanas National Park Reserve/Haida Heritage Site) to a high-density frontcountry setting (Columbia Icefield in Jasper National Park) to illustrate the diversity of impact issues under which these concepts and approaches can be applied.

Three application examples from North American national parks

Gwaii Haanas National Park Reserve and Haida Heritage Site, Canada

Until recently, most national park research in North America has focused on backcountry, wilderness, or wild river settings (Lime *et al.*, 1996). Such resources have pristine natural features and are widely agreed upon as solitude-oriented places. Gwaii Haanas National Park Reserve and Haida Heritage Site in British Columbia illustrate this type of park setting.

The Gwaii Haanas Archipelago is located in the southern portion of the Queen Charlotte Islands/Haida Gwaii, approximately 640 kilometres north of Vancouver and 100 kilometres west of the British Columbia mainland. Gwaii Haanas consists of 138 islands that stretch 90 kilometres north and south. The land area within the Archipelago is 1470 km^2 with over 1600 kilometres of shoreline.

Visitors are attracted to Gwaii Haanas by its rich cultural and natural heritage and uncrowded wilderness setting. The natural features range from rugged mountains with deep fjords to coastal forests and subalpine tundra. The variety in sea life, birds and mammals provides visitors with unparalleled wildlife viewing opportunities. The islands are also rich in their cultural history. More than 500 Haida historic sites have been identified, including villages, rock shelters, and burial sites. International recognition of the area came in 1981 when UNESCO, in consultation with the Haida Nation, declared Anthony Island/SGaang Gwaii, including the village site of Nan Sdins, a World Heritage Site. Although visitors are drawn to the natural and cultural features of Gwaii Haanas, the island setting, coupled with the lack of roads and trails, makes access to the islands difficult. Travel is only by water or by air. Since infrastructure is limited, visitors must be essentially self-reliant or travel with a licensed tour operator (Gajda, 1996).

An estimated 2000 people visit Gwaii Haanas yearly (Gajda and Stronge, 1998). Due to weather constraints, most of this use is concentrated during July and August. Kayaking, powerboating, and sailing are the most popular recreation activities. Based on 1997 data, two-thirds of these visitors travelled with a commercial tour operator, while a third were independent visitors. Although these estimates vary from year to year, the overall pattern and distribution of use has remained relatively constant.

Management decisions are guided by the 1993 Gwaii Haanas Agreement between the Council of the Haida Nation and the government of Canada. The agreement relates to the region designated by the Haida Nation as a Heritage Site and by Canada as a National Park Reserve. This partnership provides for equal representation of both parties in the planning, management and operation of Gwaii Haanas, while respecting both parties' designations and interests.

The Gwaii Haanas backcountry management plan reflects the dual mission of preservation and visitor enjoyment common to many national parks (Archipelago Management Board (AMB), 1996). The goals are to provide opportunities for solitude in a setting where visitors can learn about the area's natural and cultural heritage, without negatively impacting the physical environment. Recognising the importance of stakeholder involvement in achieving these objectives, the AMB sought input for the management plan from four target audiences: (1) recent visitors to the islands, (2) commercial tour operators, (3) local residents, and (4) members of the general public who are concerned with protecting fragile ecosystems like Gwaii Haanas (Gajda, 1996).

This collaborative approach involved a series of innovative public involvement techniques. In 1995, for example, a survey was conducted with a representative sample of visitors to the islands. The survey was unique in that it included both a paper questionnaire and a VHS video portraying a series of situations that visitors were likely to have experienced during their trip (Vaske et al., 1995b). A combination of trip diaries (Gajda and Stronge, 1998) and surveys (McCarville, 1997) were also completed by visitors in 1997. In 1997, questions from the 1985 survey were included to provide a comparison with the previous research and to evaluate the effectiveness of a visitor orientation programme. Public meetings were held at several locations both on-island and in Vancouver. While these latter techniques were helpful in obtaining input from local residents and commercial tour operators, public meetings are often not representative of the range of affected publics. To compensate for this shortcoming and to enhance a stakeholder dialogue necessary for discussing management issues, an interactive website was established in 1996 (Gajda, 1996). This website (http://harbour.com/parkscan/gwaii) identified eleven major management issues and asked participants to evaluate management options for each issue. While the opinions of individuals from such electronic communication media should not, and were not at Gwaii Haanas, used as the sole source of input, the Internet does broaden the scope of interaction with stakeholders and is likely to become a more popular public involvement technique in the future (Gaede and Vaske, 1999).

Consistent with the visitor impact management frameworks, information obtained through these collaborative planning initiatives provided data on the indicators and standards of concern to the AMB. For example, results from the 1995 (Vaske et al., 1995b) and 1997 (Gajda and Stronge, 1998) surveys indicated that, given current levels of use: (1) the visitors' norms for acceptable encounters with kayakers, motorboaters and sailboaters had not been exceeded, (2) the vast majority of visitors did not feel crowded, and (3) most were satisfied with their experience. To maintain this positive visitor experience, an interim cap of 175 people (maximum) on any given day was established. This restriction represented the maximum peak use level based on records from previous years and was selected so as to not unduly restrict access (AMB, 1996). The backcountry management plan will determine a permanent capacity limit through the ongoing visitor experience monitoring programme.

The survey research (Vaske et al., 1995b) also helped clarify visitor reactions to other impact indicators (e.g. norms for group size, the presence of anchored tourist camps, noise from aircraft). On average, visitors said it was acceptable to see as many as 15 people at access areas, 10 people at an attraction site; and two other groups (group size less than seven) while camping. Based on these findings, the AMB restricted party size to 12 people including guides on shore at any one time (AMB 1996). In addition, groups must be out of sight and sound of other groups to ensure an uncrowded experience and to minimise the impact of visitor encounters.

The group size policy has been in existence for three years and is working well at the access areas and wild places. At the attraction sites, however, managing group size has proven more difficult. Due to trip-schedule constraints and variable weather conditions, multiple groups may request access at the same time, resulting in the number of people exceeding the limit of 12. Under these circumstances, visitors are asked to wait in a queue or to limit their stays to allow other groups to access the site.

The AMB also expressed concern over the presence of anchored tourist camps in Gwaii Haanas. These camps are moveable, house-like structures, built upon a floating platform. At issue was the appropriateness of such facilities in the backcountry (wild places), at attraction sites and the access areas to Gwaii Haanas. The survey data provided a clear mandate for managing this type of infrastructure (Vaske et al., 1996). Over 90 per cent of all visitors believed that such camps are unacceptable for wild places within Gwaii Haanas. Even among those who used an anchored tourist camp, 61 per cent evaluated this type of facility as unacceptable for a wild place. Three-quarters of all visitors also reacted negatively to the presence of anchored tourist camps at attraction sites. On the other hand, there was support (70 per cent) for anchored camps at access areas across kayakers, motorboaters, and sailboaters. This pattern of findings among the three visitor groups, as well as among those who actually used these facilities, strongly supported management actions that prohibit the development of anchored tourist camps in wild places or attraction sites. As a result, this type of infrastructure no longer exists within the boundaries of Gwaii Haanas (AMB, 1996).

An additional indicator of concern to the AMB was the impact of noise from aircraft. Evaluations of visitor tolerances (norms) for aircraft sounds were enhanced by the video footage in the 1995 survey (Vaske et al., 1995b). This footage offered both visual and auditory cues for respondents by showing a short video clip of a seaplane taking off from a bay, and executing a slow, banked turn up and away from the camera. A series of norm-tolerance limit questions indicated that over 40 per cent of kayakers and a quarter of the motorboaters and sailboaters were disturbed by the number of aircraft. Half of the kayakers and about a third of the motorboaters and sailboaters were disturbed by the sound of aircraft. Visitors were most tolerant of hearing aircraft in access areas and least tolerant in wild places. These findings supported the AMB's aircraft policy which encourages pilots to use routings and elevations that minimise noise disturbance to wilderness travellers and restricts operators from landing within the interior lake and alpine areas. No low overflights or passes over Haida Gwaii Watchmen base camps or the Steller sea lion rookeries are permitted (AMB, 1996).

Finally, the Gwaii Haanas visitor orientation program was started in 1996 with the objectives of increasing safety and reducing visitor related impacts (e.g. leave-no-trace camping). Results from the 1997 post-trip survey suggested that most visitors found the orientation useful and interesting (McCarville, 1997), but it was unclear if visitors were putting the orientation messages into action. Future campsite monitoring data may provide managers with an indication of how well visitors are practising leave-no-trace camping. If the orientation programme can raise visitors' awareness of the consequences of their actions on the environment as well as the experiences of others, there is less need for management intervention in the protected area – less infrastructure and less enforcement. As a result, there is minimal disruption to the visitor's Gwaii Haanas experience.

Brooks River, Katmai National Park, Alaska

National parks often feature nodal development at an attraction site, even if this is in a remote location. These areas may take some effort to access, but they feature relatively high levels of use and development. While not strictly a backcountry setting, the opportunities offered may include an interesting mix of wilderness and more developed recreation features. A fishing and brown bear viewing area at Brooks River in Alaska's Katmai National Park provides an example of this type of setting.

Brooks River is one of the premier brown bear viewing areas in the world. The river is about a mile and a half in length and connects two large lakes; it features an impressive run of sockeye salmon (over 100 000 annually), which has attracted both humans and brown bears for thousands of years. Recent human use of the area began when anglers discovered the area's sport fishing potential in the 1950s. A small lodge was developed at the river's mouth, and a campground and other small-scale facilities followed in the 1960s. Viewing platforms were also built at Brooks Falls (1983) and near the river mouth (1992).

Bears have always used Brooks River when salmon were available, although concentrations of viewable bears were largely unknown before the late 1970s, probably because hunting and poaching were common (Squibb, 1991). When expanded park boundaries led to less hunting and stronger anti-poaching enforcement, more bears began to use the river. By the early 1980s, reliable numbers (estimates range from 25 to 35) of viewable bears were congregating on the river (Squibb, 1991). The bears use of the river occurs during two distinct periods, first in July (when salmon migrate upstream and can be caught as they negotiate the falls), and then in September and October (when spawned-out and dying fish are available in the lower river). The number of bears using Brooks River has increased in recent years (currently estimated at around 35 to 40 bears), probably in response to total population increases on the Alaska Peninsula (Potts, personal communication). The current total bear population in the Katmai area is estimated at between 1500 and 2000 (Norris, 1993).

Brooks River is a remote location, accessible only by boat or floatplane. Bear viewing is the focus of most visits, especially in July and September, although people also enjoy the area's fishing, hiking, nearby geological features, and cultural heritage (Whittaker, 1997). Most bear viewing takes place from the platforms at the river mouth (a 5-minute walk from the lodge) or at the Falls (a half-hour walk). There are also viewing opportunities on the lakeside beaches and along the river, although visitors are more exposed in these locations. Bear encounters in or near the lodge or campground complexes are also common because these facilities are essentially on top of bear travel corridors.

Visitation to Brooks River has increased substantially since the early 1980s, when less than 5000 visitor-days were recorded each year, and total daily day use in July rarely exceeded 100 people per day. More recently, over 15 000 visitor-days per year are common, and peak use in July sometimes exceeds 300 people per day (Whittaker, 1997). Increased visitation to Brooks has led to increasing concern about the impacts of human activity. The National Park Service initiated an area planning effort called a Development Concept Plan (DCP) in 1989 to address impact issues and development alternatives. Although the DCP addressed a comprehensive list of concerns, the effort focused on three: (1) impacts on the area's brown bear population and their behaviour; (2) safety and liability with regard to human–bear interaction; and (3) visitor experience degradation. The two most controversial actions being considered in the plan were relocation of existing development from critical bear habitat and limits on the number of day visitors (overnight use is already limited by available facilities).

Applying visitor impact frameworks to these issues began with clear definitions of the opportunities available at Brooks. Planning suggested that there were important seasonal differences (July versus September), as well as activity differences (bear viewing versus fishing). Some of these were further confirmed by normative data (see below).

Indicators and standards were developed for biological and cultural impact issues. Some standards focused on bear–human interactions because of the location of the lodge and campground along bear travel paths. Other standards concentrated on preventing any additional impacts to cultural sites (Native Alaskans had used the area for thousands of years), and impacts on brown bear use and behaviour in the area.

Interestingly, bear use of the area has actually risen in recent years despite increasing human activity in the area. While several Brooks bears generally avoid all human activity, and specific interactions with humans can cause bears to leave an area about one fifth of the time (Olson and Gilbert, 1994), many other bears have learned habituation behaviour that allows them to ignore human activity and continue to use the area (Squibb, 1991). A committee of researchers and managers reviewing 20 years of research concluded that impacts on bears could generally be addressed through development changes (moving the lodge and campground out of the river corridor) and that the quality of the viewing experiences were resources at greatest risk from increasing use levels (Norris, 1993).

Research on viewing experiences examined capacity norms on viewing platforms (how many is too many people at one time?). Results showed there was strong agreement about capacity standards for a smaller platform at the Falls in July, and the larger platform at the river mouth in September, but there was less agreement about capacities on the larger platform during the July high use season (Whittaker, 1997). Results suggested that late-season viewers were interested in a lower density experience, and that the size and design features influence evaluations of how many is too many, but that there are limits to the strategy of building larger platforms in order to allow increased use. At some point, the number of people on a viewing platform becomes unacceptable for the Brooks River experience (about 30 to 40 people at one time in July, and 15 to 20 in September). Actions designed to help meet standards included a recommendation to move the lodge and campground about a mile away from the river in order to minimise bear–human interactions and trespasses. Similarly, platform capacity standards were used to help determine an overall area capacity, and to help suggest the sizes of any relocated lodge and campground (which essentially act as a use limit on overnight use). Although day-use limits were proposed also, political pressures have thus far prevented them from being implemented.

This latter point illustrates the advantage of collaborative planning, which was not as thoroughly integrated into this effort as possible. Concessionaires who have run the lodge as well as multiple air taxi services that benefit from high day-use levels at Brooks were not deeply involved in the effort. While survey work of users helped suggest the standards in the plan, buy-off from these other stakeholders was not a focus of the effort. Without stakeholder support, opposition to the plan has delayed actions, while incremental increases in use continue each year.

Columbia Icefield, Jasper National Park, Canada

While some national park research documents a levelling off of visitation to backcountry areas, frontcountry resources have experienced explosive growth in visitor numbers (Lime *et al.*, 1996). A variety of reasons have been suggested for this dramatic growth. First, the increasing popularity of activities such as mountain biking, rock climbing, sigthseeing, wildlife viewing, and visiting interpretive centres has stimulated visitation to frontcountry areas that are readily accessible by vehicle. Several hundred thousand visitors, for example, are now attracted each year to the Moab Slickrock Bike Trail and the nearby Arches and Canyonlands National Parks in Utah (Fix, 1996). Second, some national park attractions (e.g. Old Faithful, South Rim of Grand Canyon, Mount Rushmore) are simply must-see features that do not have substitutes. As the populations (both within the USA and internationally) continue to grow, visitation to these attractions is likely to continue. Third, given the popularity of people travelling internationally on tours and the ageing of populations, motorcoach tours to national parks have increased substantially. Between 1985 and 1994, for example, the total number of buses entering all national parks in the United States increased by 80 per cent – from 160 000 buses (1985) to 291 000 (1994). Some individual parks witnessed exponential growth patterns in the number of motorcoach tours (e.g. Bryce Canyon National Park (Utah) – 377 per cent increase; Mesa Verde National Park (Colorado) – 210 per cent increase; Yosemite National Park (California) – 235 per cent increase) during this same period (Lime *et al.*, 1996). Providing high-quality visitor experiences in these high-density frontcountry settings introduces unique management challenges. This section examines how managers at one such attraction area/park (the Columbia Icefield/ Jasper National Park) are using visitor impact principles in their planning and management.

The Columbia Icefield is the most heavily visited day-use area in Jasper National Park. More than 890 000 visitors travelled the Icefields Parkway through the park in 1990; with over 425 000 stopping at the Columbia Icefield area. Of these, over two thirds (290 000) visited the Parks Canada information centre; and 330 000 visited the adjacent Athabasca Glacier on one of the commercial snocoach tours offered by the Brewster Corporation. ('Snocoaches' are passenger-carrying vehicles equipped with tracks instead of wheels in order to traverse glaciers.) The annual compound growth rate of visitors to Brewster's facilities from 1980 to 1993 has been 6.8 per cent. Projections indicate that by the year 2000, the site could approach anywhere from 730 000 visitors (low-growth scenario) to more than one million visitors (high-growth scenario).

Parks Canada policy documents and plans describe the available visitor opportunities. For example, the Jasper National Park Management Plan (Parks Canada, 1988, p. 124) explicitly recognised that the Columbia Icefield snocoach operation provides a unique park experience. The accessibility created by the snocoach provides an exceptional opportunity for increasing visitor understanding, enjoyment, and appreciation of the glacier – an environment that is not normally accessible to the vast majority of the visitors. The plan further recognises differences in appropriate density levels by segmenting the park into a series of management zones. In Zone III, where the Columbia Icefield is located, higher concentrations of use and more infrastructure development are allowed than are found in zones with lower-numbered designations.

Consistent with the visitor-impact management frameworks, both ecological and social indicators and standards were established. From an ecological perspective, for example, an evaluation of waste water management options for the visitor centre redevelopment project was prepared by Reid Crowther and Partners Ltd (1990). A variety of design flows for water and sewage were considered for both low and high visitor growth scenarios. Strategies for reducing sewage flow such as installing low-flow fixtures and modifying the water supply system to reduce bleeding were examined. Results indicated that neither the snocoach capacity nor the highway capacity were limiting growth factors for a new visitor centre.

In 1991, the Strategic Information Section from Parks Canada summarised the existing visitor research from the Columbia Icefield. Two primary sources of information were used: (1) a 1990 Parks Canada visitor survey and (2) a visitor segmentation study (Coopers and Lybrand Consulting, 1991). In general, the visitors were characterised as older couples of foreign origin who were making their first visit to the Icefield. Visitors were also segmented on how the individual arrived at the site – a motorcoach tour (48 per cent) or their own vehicle (52 per cent).

Motorcoach visitors have increased 16 per cent per annum from 1984 to 1990, compared to a 3 per cent increase per year for individual travellers. By 2001, motorcoach travel is expected to nearly triple (from 205 000 to 601 000 visitors). The individual travel segment that stops at the Icefield is projected to increase 46 per cent by the year 2001 (from 220 000 to 322 000 visitors). Virtually all the motorcoach visitors take the Brewster snocoach tour; 55 per cent of the independent travellers took the snocoach during 1991. Because motorcoach tours tend to arrive during peak hours (11:00 am to 3:00 pm), visit the same area of the glacier, remain at the site for a fixed period of time, and have little flexibility in altering their schedules, circulation and crowding problems are more likely to be associated with this group. By way of contrast, the independent traveller has the freedom to visit less heavily used locations on the glacier or to leave the area totally when density levels become unacceptable.

In 1992, an initial social carrying-capacity study was conducted to examine the impact of current use levels on the visitors' experiences and to explore the users' evaluations/expectations for the services provided (Vaske and Donnelly, 1992). Although the findings from this pretest provided an initial examination of the area's carrying capacity, sampling constraints (e.g. the study began late in the season), small sample size, and unknown response rates limited the generalisability of the data.

In an effort to correct the deficiencies identified during the 1992 pretest, a follow-up study was conducted during the summer of 1993 (Vaske et al., 1994). The results of the 1993 investigation indicated that crowding (an impact indicator) was not a problem for the glacier experience, but was a concern in the visitor centre. Eleven per cent or fewer felt moderately or extremely crowded on the ice road, regardless of the daily density levels. Crowding at the snocoach turn around location was slightly higher, but still only about a fifth felt crowded across the three daily density levels examined (i.e. <2500, 2500 to 3000, >3000). Perceptions of crowding in the visitor centre, however, were related to daily densities. When daily use level was less than 2500, 35 per cent of the visitors were crowded. As daily use level increased to between 2500 and 3000 visitors, crowding increased to 49 per cent. On the highest density days, 69 per cent felt crowded in the facilities.

During the summer of 1996, a third social carrying-capacity study was conducted (Vaske and Donnelly, 1997). Three impact indicators (perceived crowding, visitor satisfaction, general experiential learning) were selected for inclusion in this monitoring effort. Perceived crowding was measured at four different locations: (1) at the snocoach transfer area, (2) on the glacier, (3) in the visitor centre, and 4) in the Icefield exhibit hall. Satisfaction was measured in terms of the visitor's overall evaluation of the experience, as well as the impact of the number of other visitors on the respondent's enjoyment of the experience. The third impact indicator, general experiential learning, asked survey respondents to evaluate how their visit added to their knowledge of: (1) glaciers, (2) avalanches, (3) geology, and (4) climate change. Results of the 1996 investigation indicated that, among the snocoach visitors, the existing conditions were consistent with the management standards established for the three impact indicators. For those who accessed the glacier on foot, the existing conditions were consistent with the management standards, with the following exceptions: (1) perceived crowding at the Icefield Visitor Centre, (2) overall satisfaction with the experience, and (3) learning about avalanches.

Although the 1996 study did not allow for a complete examination of why the crowding standard was exceeded for visitors who accessed the glacier on foot, the data did suggest these visitors were not explicitly avoiding the visitor centre due to concerns with crowding. Moreover, the new visitor centre appears to be alleviating some of the crowding associated impacts. In the 1993 study, for example, 79 per cent of the snocoach visitors reported some level of crowding at the Icefield Visitor Centre. With the new centre, this estimate decreased among the 1996 snocoach visitors to a level that was within the management standard goal.

In 1997, a fourth visitor impact management study was conducted focusing explicitly on the visitor centre (Vaske and Donnelly, 1998). Three impact indicators were selected for inclusion in the study: (1) experiential learning messages (e.g. knowledge obtained about glaciers, the interrelationship of glaciers with the environment, and the role of national parks), (2) perceived crowding in the Glacier Gallery and the Icefield Visitor Centre, and (3) visitor satisfaction with the gallery and the exhibits. Standards for *general* experiential learning, perceived crowding, and visitor satisfaction were based on the 1996 study (Vaske and Donnelly, 1997). Standards for the *specific* experiential learning indicators and for visitor satisfaction with the Glacier Gallery were based on past research. Results indicated that the existing conditions met or exceeded the standards for 21 of the 24 possible indicators. All 15 of the experiential learning indicators and the six indicators for satisfaction with the Glacier Gallery achieved their respective standards.

Data collected in 1996 indicated that crowding on the glacier was not an issue for either snocoach or non-snocoach visitors. In the Glacier Gallery, the crowding standard was met for snocoach visitors during both the 1996 and 1997 study years. Crowding in the gallery was not a problem for non-snocoach visitors in 1996, but was an issue during 1997. In the visitor centre, however, the crowding standard was exceeded for non-snocoach visitors in 1996 and for both groups (snocoach and non-snocoach) in 1997.

In summary, the Columbia Icefield has been, and is likely to continue to be, the most heavily visited day-use area in Jasper National Park. Such levels of visitation can be partially attributed to the unique partnership that exists between Parks Canada and the Brewster Corporation. Without the snocoach tour, the number of visits to the area would undoubtedly decline. With fewer visitors, however, the quality of the experience would not necessarily increase. The snocoach visitors across all social impact studies consistently rated the quality of their Icefield experience high, reported a positive learning environment and, with the exception of the visitor centre, have relatively low perceptions of crowding. Similarly, even though crowding in the Glacier Gallery is becoming a concern for non-snocoach visitors, the results indicate that Parks Canada is still providing a high-quality learning environment.

Conclusion

Understanding and managing for the impacts caused by human activity in North America's national parks is complex. Individuals in natural resource settings may directly or indirectly influence the recreational experience of others and may directly or indirectly negatively impact the physical environment. Tangible outcomes of increasing use (e.g. encounters between visitors, loss of ground cover) lead to a variety of perceptual (e.g. crowding, re-evaluating the normative definition of acceptable conditions) or behavioural (e.g. changes in frequency of visitation) responses by visitors. Amount of use affects the quality of the recreation experience, but only through a series of mediating variables. For example, not all individuals are equally tolerant of increasing recreational use. Summarising the tolerances of recreationists to impacts is difficult because different individuals apply different normative standards when evaluating the presence of others or the impacts visitors create. The extent to which one type of use (e.g. kayakers versus motorboaters) impacts another depends on the social and personal norms visitors use to evaluate the appropriateness of specific behaviours. Given a basic tolerance level to a particular type of recreation, the outcome of increasing use levels may still depend on the time (e.g. peak versus shoulder season) and place (e.g. backcountry versus frontcountry) of human disturbance.

Despite this complexity, progress has been made in understanding the diverse social and ecological consequences associated with recreational activity in natural resource settings. All the prominent planning frameworks (LAC, VIM, VERP) outline a sequential process of assessing and managing visitor impacts. By attending to the basic steps of:

(1) Defining appropriate experience opportunities for specific management objectives
(2) Identifying key impact indicators
(3) Setting quantitative standards for the selected impact indicators
(4) Inventorying and monitoring existing conditions against the standards and
(5) Linking management actions to standards when impacts exceed standards

natural resource managers are afforded a game plan for dealing with visitor impacts. These common elements of the planning frameworks thus provide a means to an end, not an end in themselves.

The three examples presented in this chapter covered a range of national park settings, from backcountry to frontcountry. Different issues and problem conditions were associated with each park, but all were approached in similar ways. In each case study, setting standards represented a central component. These standards were essentially expressions of value judgements about acceptable levels of impact. 'Values are inescapable elements of any rational decision-making process' (Davidoff and Reiner, 1973). Most natural resource problems do not revolve around resource questions, but rather around questions of values (Shelby and Heberlein, 1986). In many situations, time and energy is spent collecting information about the physical environment when the problem is essentially human and unlikely to be resolved by biological or physical impact data.

A major problem with the natural resource literature is that impact and evaluation are often confused (Shelby and Heberlein, 1986). The confusion can be illustrated by the term resource damage. Damage refers to both a change (an objective impact) and a value judgement that the impact exceeds some standard. While most people would agree that use should be limited when resource damage occurs, there is less consensus about what constitutes resource damage. All human use has some impact. Whether the impact is damage depends on management objectives and standards, expert judgements and broader public values. It is not necessary to abandon terms like resource damage, but it is important to break the concept into two parts – the impact component (environmental or experiential change) and the evaluative component (the acceptability of the change).

Given the need for evaluative information and the potential complexity of obtaining such data, the normative model has emerged as a useful way to conceptualise, collect and organise evaluative judgements in resource management (Vaske et al., 1986). Over the past two decades, more than 75 papers (including the case studies presented here) have been published or presented on the concept of normative applications to natural resource management (Shelby et al., 1996). Using norm theory to structure the research has allowed individual studies to build on one another and reflects the growing maturity of the field.

Overall, the planning frameworks (LAC, VIM, VERP) offer a road map for tackling natural resource problems, while norms provide a theoretical under-pinning for understanding the issues and assessing evaluative information. Although much has been learned over the past few decades, it is important to not forget the lessons learned and knowledge gaps illustrated by the three case studies presented in this chapter. First, while norms for acceptable behaviours and conditions in the backcountry are well understood, norm research in the frontcountry is still in its infancy. More research exploring the range of norms frontcountry visitors' use when making evaluative judgements is clearly needed. Second, not all stakeholders share the same norms. To be effective, managers need to adopt a collaborative planning process where all interested parties can express their views on acceptable management actions. Third, the task of managing visitor impacts is not over when a management action has been implemented. Monitoring of key impact indicators is critically important to determine whether the actions are producing the desired outcomes without altering other characteristics of the experience for the tourist.

References

Archipelago Management Board (AMB), 1996, Gwaii Haanas National Park Reserve/Hiada Heritage Site public planning program. Draft strategic management plan. Newsletter No. 3, Gwaii Haanas NPR/Haida Heritage Site, Queen Charlotte, BC

Basman, C.M., Manfredo, M.J., Barro, S. C., Vaske, J.J. and Watson, A., 1996, Norm accessibility: An exploratory study of backcountry and frontcountry recreation norms. *Leisure Sciences*, **18**: 177–191

Blamey, R., 1998, The activation of environmental norms: Extending Schwartz's model. *Environment and Behavior*, **30**: 676–708

Boyle, S.A. and Samson, F.B., 1985, Effects of non-consumptive recreation on wildlife: A review. *Wildlife Society Bulletin*, **13**: 110–116

Coopers & Lybrand Consulting, 1991, *Socio-economic analysis of the Columbia Icefield redevelopment study*, Calgary, Alberta

Davidoff, P. and Reiner, T.A., 1973, A choice theory of planning. In *A reader in planning theory*, A Faludi, ed., pp. 11–39, Pergamon Press, Oxford

Donnelly, M.P., Vaske, J.J., Whittaker, D. and Shelby, B., 2000, Toward an understanding of norm prevalence: A comparative-analysis. *Environmental Management*, **25**: 403–414

Dunlap, R.E., 1991, Trends in public opinion toward environmental issues. *Society and Natural Resources*, **4**: 285–312

Fix, P.J., 1996, *The economic benefits of mountain biking: Applying the TCM and CVM at Moab, Utah*, unpublished master's thesis, Colorado State University, Fort Collins

Fleischman, P., 1969, Conservation: the biological fallacy. *Landscape*, **2**, 23–26

Gaede, D.B. and Vaske, J.J., 1999, Using the Internet as a survey research tool: potentials and pitfalls. *International Journal of Wilderness*, **5**, 26–30

Gajda, A., 1996, Public consultation in cyberspace: A test at the Gwaii Haanas National Park Reserve and Haida Heritage Site. *International Journal of Wilderness*, **4**: 28–31

Gajda, A. and Stronge, M., 1998, *Gwaii Haanas user statistics – 1997*, Internal report, Heritage Resource Conservation Gwaii Haanas NPR/Haida Heritage Site Queen Charlotte, BC

Graefe, A.R., Kuss, F.R. and Vaske, J.J., 1990, *Visitor impact management: the planning framework*, National Parks and Conservation Association, Washington, DC

Hammitt, W.E. and Cole, D.N., 1987, *Wildland recreation: ecology and management*, John Wiley, New York

Hardin, G., 1968, The tragedy of the commons. *Science*, **78**: 20–27

Jackson, J.M., 1965, Structural characteristics of norms. In *Current studies in social psychology*, I.D. Steiner and M.F. Fishbein, eds, pp. 301–309, Holt, Rinehart, and Winston, New York

Kennedy, J.J. and Thomas, J.W., 1995, Managing natural resources as social value. In *A new century for natural resources management*, R.L. Knight and S.F. Bates, eds, pp. 311–322, Island Press, Washington, DC

Kim, S. and Shelby, B., 1996, Effects of information on user's personal norm and rule-violating behavior in a recreation setting. *Journal of Korean Forestry Society*, **85**: 251–259

Knight, R.L. and Gutzwiller, K.J. (eds), 1995, *Wildlife and recreationists: coexistence through management and research*, Island Press, Washington, DC

Kuss, F.R., Graefe, A.R. and Vaske, J.J., 1990, *Recreation impacts and carrying capacity: a review and synthesis of ecological and social research*, National Parks and Conservation Association, Washington, DC

Liddle, M.J. and Scorgie, H.R.A., 1980, The effects of recreation on freshwater plants and animals: a review. *Biological Conservation*, **17**: 183–206

Lime, D.W. (ed.), 1996, *Congestion and crowding in the national park system: guidelines for management and research*, MAES Misc. Pub. 86–1996, Department of Forest Resources and Minnesota Agricultural Experiment Station, University of Minnesota, St Paul, MN

Lime, D.W, McCool, S.F. and Galvin, D.P., 1996, Trends in congestion and crowding at recreation sites. In *Congestion and crowding in the national park system: guidelines for management and research*, D.W. Lime, ed., pp. 9–26, MAES Misc. Pub. 86–1996, Department of Forest Resources and Minnesota Agricultural Experiment Station, University of Minnesota, St Paul, MN

Manfredo, M.J., Driver, B.L. and Tarrant, M.A., 1996, Measuring leisure motivation: A meta-analysis of the recreation experience preference scales. *Journal of Leisure Research*, **28**: 188–213

Manning, R.E., 1986, *Studies in outdoor recreation*, Oregon State University Press, Corvallis, OR

Manning, R.E., Lime, D.W., Freimund, W.A. and Pitt, D.G., 1996, Crowding norms at frontcountry sites: A visual approach to setting standards of quality. *Leisure Sciences*, **18**: 39–59

Martinson, K.S. and Shelby, B., 1992, Encounter and proximity norms for salmon anglers in California and New Zealand. *North American Journal of Fisheries Management*, **12**: 559–567

McCarville, R., 1997, *Gwaii Haanas survey results*, report prepared for Canadian Heritage, Heritage Resource Conservation Gwaii Haanas NPR/Haida Heritage Site, Queen Charlotte, BC

Nash, R., 1982, *Wilderness and the American mind*, Yale University Press, New Haven CT

National Park Service, 1991, *National parks for the 21st century: the Vail agenda*. Report and recommendations to the Director of the National Park Service Steering committee of the 75th Anniversary Symposium Vail, Colorado, 26 October

National Park Service (NPS), 1997, *VERP: The visitor experience and resource protection (VERP) framework, a handbook for planners and managers*, USDI National Park Service Denver Service Centre, Denver, CO

Norris, L., 1993, *Final report of the bear research committee with recommendations to the planning team, Brooks River DCP/EIS*, USDI-NPS Denver Service Centre

Oelschlaeger, M., 1991, *The idea of wilderness: from pre-history to the age of ecology*, Yale University Press, New Haven, CT

Olson, T. and Gilbert, B., 1994, Variable impacts of people on brown bear use of an Alaskan river. *International Conference on Bear Research and Managemen*, 9(1): 97–106

Parks Canada, 1988, *Jasper National Park management plan*, Canadian Parks Service, Environment Canada

Reid Crowther and Partners Ltd, 1990, *Columbia Icefields visitor centre redevelopment: evaluation of wastewater management options*, Report Number 22938, Toronto

Roggenbuck, J.W., Williams, D.R., Bange, S.P. and Dean, D.J., 1991, River float trip encounter norms: Questioning the use of the social norms concept. *Journal of Leisure Research*, 23: 133–153

Schwartz, S.H., 1977, Normative influences on altruism. In *Advances in experimental social psychology*, L Berkowitz, ed., 10: 221–279

Shelby, B. and Heberlein, T.A., 1986, *Social carrying capacity in recreation settings*, Oregon State University Press, Corvallis OR

Shelby, B. and Vaske, J.J., 1991, Using normative data to develop evaluative standards for resource management: A comment on three recent papers. *Journal of Leisure Research*, 23: 173–187

Shelby, B., Vaske, J.J. and Donnelly, M.P., 1996, Norms, standards and natural resources. *Leisure Sciences*, 1: 103–123

Shelby, B., Vaske, J.J. and Harris, R., 1988, User standards for ecological impacts at wilderness campsites. *Journal of Leisure Research*, 20: 245–256

Shelby, B. and Whittaker, D., 1995, *Virgin River instream flow assessment: recreation and aesthetics*, Bureau of Land Management Arizona State Office, Phoenix

Shelby, B. and Whittaker, D., 1996, Flows and recreation quality on the Dolores River: Integrating overall and specific evaluations. *Rivers*, 5: 121–132

Shelby, B., Whittaker, D., Speaker, R. and Starkey, E.E., 1987, *Social and ecological impacts of recreation use on the Deschutes River Scenic Waterway*. Report to the Oregon Legislature, Oregon State University, Corvallis, OR

Squibb, R., 1991, *Bear use of Brooks River: summary of information relevant to management*, unpublished report on file at Katmai National Park and Preserve Headquarters, King Salmon, AK

Stankey, G.H., Cole, D.N., Lucas, R.C., Petersen, M.E. and Frissell, S.S., 1985, *The limits of acceptable change (LAC) system for wilderness planning* (Rep. INT–176), US Department of Agriculture Forest Service Intermountain Forest and Range Experiment Station, Ogden, UT

Steel, B.S., List, P. and Shindler, B., 1994, Conflicting values about federal forests: A comparison of national and Oregon publics. *Journal of Forestry*, July: 36–42

Steinbeck, J. and Ricketts, E.F., 1941, *Sea of Cortez: A leisurely journal of travel and research*, The Viking Press, New York

Stern, P.C. and Dietz, T., 1994, The value basis of environmental concern. *Journal of Social Issues*, 50: 65–84

Stern, P.C., Dietz, T. and Black, J.S., 1986, Support for environmental protection: The role of moral norms. *Population and Environment*, 8: 204–222

Vaske, J.J., Decker, D.J. and Manfredo, M.J., 1995a, Human dimensions of wildlife management: An integrated framework for coexistence In *Wildlife and recreationists: coexistence through management and research*, R, Knight and K. Gutzwiller, eds, pp. 33–49, Island Press, Washington, DC

Vaske, J.J. and Donnelly, M.P., 1992, *Social carrying capacity at the Columbia Icefield: Initial report*, report submitted to Parks Canada

Vaske, J.J. and Donnelly, M.P., 1997, Monitoring social carrying capacity at the Columbia Icefield. HDNRU Rep. No. 34 Colorado State University, Fort Collins, CO

Vaske, J.J. and Donnelly, M.P., 1998, *An evaluation of the Glacier Gallery in the Columbia Icefield visitor centre*, HDNRU Rep. No. 37, Colorado State University Human Dimensions in Natural Resources Unit, Fort Collins, CO

Vaske, J.J., Donnelly, M.P., Doctor, R.M. and Petruzzi, J.P., 1994, *Social carrying capacity at the Columbia Icefield: Applying the Visitor Impact Management framework*, HDNRU Rep. No. 11, Colorado State University Human Dimensions in Natural Resources Unit, Fort Collins, CO

Vaske, J.J., Donnelly, M.P., Freimund, W.A. and Miller, T., 1995b, *The 1995 Gwaii Haanas visitor survey*, HDNRU Rep. No. 24, Colorado State University, Human Dimensions in Natural Resources Unit, Fort Collins, CO

Vaske, J.J., Donnelly, M.P. and Petruzzi, J.P., 1996, Country of origin, encounter norms and crowding in a frontcountry setting. *Leisure Sciences*, **18**: 161–176

Vaske, J.J., Donnelly, M.P. and Shelby, B., 1993, Establishing management standards: Selected examples of the normative approach. *Environmental Management*, **17**: 629–643

Vaske, J.J., Shelby, B., Graefe, A.R. and Heberlein, T.A., 1986, Backcountry encounter norms: theory, method and empirical evidence, *Journal of Leisure Research*, **18**: 137–153

Whittaker, D., 1992, Selecting indicators: Which impacts matter more? In *Defining wilderness quality: the role of standards in wilderness management – a workshop proceedings*, B Shelby, G. Stankey and B. Shindler, eds, pp. 13–22, General Technical Report PNW-GTR–305, USDA Forest Service

Whittaker, D., 1997, Capacity norms on bear viewing platforms. *Human Dimensions of Wildlife*, **2**: 37–49

Whittaker, D. and Shelby, B., 1988, Types of norms for recreation impacts: Extending the social norms concept. *Journal of Leisure Research*, **20**: 261–273

Whittaker, D. and Shelby, B., 1993, *Kenai River carrying capacity study: important conclusions and implications*. Report to Alaska State Parks, National Park Service RTCA project report, Anchorage, AK

Whittaker, D. and Shelby, B., 1996, Norms in high-density settings: results from several Alaskan rivers. Paper presented at the 6th International Symposium on Society and Resource Management, The Pennsylvania State University, May

14 Tourism, national parks and visitor management

PHILIPPA SOWMAN AND DOUGLAS PEARCE

Introduction

One of the most pressing problems of national parks and protected areas today is how to cope with the burgeoning number of visitors seeking recreation in natural environments. The continuing growth in visitor demand in national parks discussed in earlier chapters has given rise to an ever-increasing need for appropriate and effective visitor management. A significant amount of research has been undertaken dealing with such aspects as visitor use and satisfaction (Kearsley, 1996; Espiner and Simmons, 1998), the varied impacts of park visitors (Buckley and Pannell, 1990; McNeeley et al., 1992) and different management techniques (Corbett, 1995; Sem et al., 1996). Much of this research has been undertaken in isolation, commonly with a particular emphasis on either demand- or supply-side matters rather than linking the two together. There is now a growing recognition of the need for a more integrated approach to visitor management in national parks which seeks to bring together resource use and visitor demand more explicitly, to acknowledge the range of stakeholders involved and to examine the processes through which visitor management occurs (Fennell and Eagles, 1990; Wilson, 1993; Gunn, 1994; Charters et al., 1996; Hall et al., 1996; McKercher, 1996). The goal of this chapter is to develop this latter approach by presenting an integrated framework for analysing visitor management and to illustrate its application with reference to two national parks in New Zealand.

An integrated framework of visitor management

Visitor management has been defined as 'the practice of ensuring visitors achieve a quality experience; it is the management of visitors in a manner which maximises the quality of the visitor experience while assisting the achievement of the area's overall management objectives' (McArthur and Hall, 1996, p. 37). Building on the earlier work of Fennell and Eagles (1990), Wilson (1993) and Carter (1996), Figure 14.1 depicts a conceptualisation of visitor management in national parks in terms of the different parties involved, the linkages between these and the resource base (the national park) and the setting (or set of contextual elements) in which this

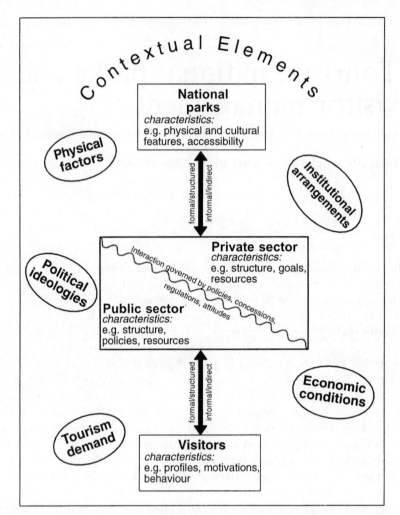

Figure 14.1. A conceptual framework for an integrated approach to visitor management in national parks

interaction occurs. In essence, in this context visitor management is seen as the process by which visitors' use of a national park is structured by an intervening group of managers who determine, influence or organise the interaction between demand (the visitors) and supply (the national park). Varying degrees of visitor management may exist, from instances where all visits are tightly controlled to others where visitation may appear to occur largely independently or in a very unstructured fashion. But even in the latter situation the mere establishment of a national park implies a minimum of management.

In applying this general framework to real-world situations the following steps are taken. First, as Figure 14.1 is depicted as an open system in which the focal elements are conditioned by key contextual factors, the latter need to be clearly established. Second, the characteristics of each of the elements must be identified: the national parks, the park visitors and the managers. The linkages or interactions between these different elements can then be established and the management issues which result from them identified and solutions to these found.

Contextual elements

As in other chapters in this volume (see Nelson, Hall, Parker and Ravenscroft) and other studies (Pearce and Richez, 1987; McNeeley *et al.*, 1992) have shown, tourism and national parks have not evolved in the same way and to the same extent in different parts of the world and at different periods. Significant differences in policies and practices, in levels of demand and resources available, occur, for example, between developed and developing countries, between Europe and New World lands such as the USA, Canada, Australia and New Zealand. These differences have their origins in broader political, economic, cultural and physical elements. Knowledge and appreciation of these is essential for fully understanding how a particular system may function and why particular issues may arise. External environments, for instance, may provide funding, establish legitimacy or determine the nature of public–private sector partnerships; they might be seen as lean or wealthy, as supportive or hostile (Pearce, 1992). The scale at which these elements need to be addressed will vary depending on whether our concern is with a country-wide system of national parks or of specific parks within that system. In the latter case the focal parks need to be set in the broader context of national policies whereas in the former the creation of these policies may be the issue. Likewise, visitor management in national parks will be influenced by broader issues of demand and the nature and structure of tourism in the area, region or country concerned.

Characteristics

In terms of the national parks, consideration must be given to identifying their distinctive physical and cultural features, how these act as attractions and condition the way in which visits and visitor activities may take place. National parks, by their very nature, contain natural or cultural features renowned for their exceptional qualities but which may also be rare, fragile and subject to damage from visitors or conflicting uses. Distinctive landscapes, for example in alpine or coastal areas, may also be the result of harsh or dynamic physical conditions and processes which in turn may have serious implications for managing visitors. Indeed, parts of many national parks are high-risk areas. While the key features of national parks are commonly discussed in terms of their attractiveness to visitors and limiting factors identified with regard to impacts and notions of carrying capacity, interpretation of the broader implications of their physical conditions for visitation is often lacking.

A considerable body of work (Sowman, 1998) has now been undertaken on the basic characteristics of park visitors. Many exhibit common socio-demographic characteristics: young, active, well-educated professionals frequently dominate park user surveys (Booth and Peebles, 1995). Other research has focused on the images, motivations, levels of satisfaction and behavioural patterns of park users and considered the management implications of these factors, for example in terms of social carrying capacity (Higham, 1996).

Other than in a very general way, comparatively little attention has been paid until recently to those charged with managing visitors to national parks. Where once park management might have been essentially, if not entirely, in the hands of a national park service, growing interest is now being given to the respective roles and responsibilities of both the public and private sectors, with private concessionaires' or operators' activities often complementing those of the park authorities (Charters et al., 1996; Eagles, 1996; Sem et al.,1996). National park authorities, especially in the less-developed countries, often lack the technical, economic, and organisational resources required to manage and develop tourism activities in their protected areas effectively (McNeely et al., 1992). Prasser (1996) argues there are many limitations and problems with the public sector monopoly approach to managing national parks. For example, the total area of reserves is growing as a result of public demand but the financial resources to manage these areas are not. Carter (1996) claims that unless greater private sector involvement occurs the natural resources will degrade, the demand for publicly funded facilities will continue to exceed capacity, and visitors to protected areas will not receive the level of experience they seek. The long-term success of park tourism, it is argued, requires the cooperation of both the public and private sectors in management (Carter, 1996; Eagles, 1996; Hundloe, 1996). For the public administrators, the private sector can be used to decrease significantly the level of financial resources needed to provide equivalent levels of service while for the private sector, public administrators should be viewed as staff responsible for the care and maintenance of the core business resource (Carter, 1996). What needs to be remembered here, however, is that visitor management may be only one component of the overall park management process – conserving the base resource is usually the prime function of the public sector. Establishing the characteristics, roles and responsibilities of all those involved in park management thus becomes an integral part of the approach outlined in Figure 14.1.

Linkages

To understand how the three sets of elements in Figure 14.1 function as a system, consideration needs to be given to the nature and extent of the linkages that exist within and between them. In some instances these linkages may be very structured and formal. Tourists visiting a national park, for example, might do so by taking a commercially guided walk or helicopter flight provided by a concessionaire operating under a formal agreement with the national park authority which specifies how many visitors may be taken, under what conditions and for what fee. In other cases, the interaction is informal and indirect: visitors may make their own way to view some scenic feature, having no direct contact with park staff but taking advantage of tracks and information provided by them and thereby being managed, consciously or not. So far very little work has been undertaken on the nature and extent of these linkages or inter-relationships (Fennell and Eagles, 1990; Wilson, 1993; McKercher, 1996). Considerable scope exists for innovative research in this area, particularly in determining the impact of different types and levels of interaction on effective visitor management.

Issues and solutions

Assessment is also needed in terms of what constitutes effective visitor management in national parks and what issues management needs to resolve. Following McArthur and Hall's (1996) definition of visitor management outlined earlier, such an assessment might focus on the quality of the visitor experience. Determining levels of visitor satisfaction with different dimensions of their visit and identifying factors which enhanced or reduced the quality of their experience would thus be one means of pursuing this question. Where levels of satisfaction are uniformly high, visitor management might be thought of as being effective. When lower levels of satisfaction are recorded, issues may be identified which require a change or improvement in management to effect a solution. Eagles (1996) states that park visitors' satisfaction is closely correlated with environmental quality, the adequacy of facilities and programmes and the accuracy of expectations.

However, care should be taken not to over-emphasise the visitor perspective for, as McArthur and Hall (1996) note, maximising visitor experience should be seen in the context of an area's overall management objectives and, as is well known in the case of national parks, the goals of preservation and use do not always coincide. Where private sector partners are also involved the situation becomes even more complex for while these operators may have a conservation ethos and goals, their basic aim is usually to make money – those that are not economically viable will eventually close down (Wilson, 1993).

Another approach is that adopted by McKercher (1996), notably the exploration of sources of inter-group conflict. Citing Jacob and Schreyer (1980), McKercher (1996, p. 99) sees conflict in outdoor recreation as 'interference with goals attributed to another's behaviour'. By means of a survey, he examined the values and views of various stakeholders in the Victorian Alps and identified both similarities and differences in the opinions they held. Unfortunately the survey was limited to opinion leaders and the views of the tourists themselves were not sought. Again, once sources of conflict have been identified solutions may be pursued, though it will often not be realistic to assume all parties' goals will be met equally.

A wide array of techniques has been developed to manage visitors in national parks and other protected areas (Corbett, 1995; Eagles, 1996; Hall and McArthur, 1996; Sem et al., 1996). These include: regulating visitor behaviour, modifying the setting, managing the visitor experience and facilitating public–private sector cooperation. It is argued here that the selection and implementation of the most appropriate mix of these techniques in any given situation will be improved by adoption of the integrated approach presented in Figure 14.1 as this will permit a better understanding of the issues which have arisen, the factors that have given rise to them and how the system functions as a whole. These matters are illustrated in more detail in the following section with regard to Westland and Paparoa National Parks.

Visitor management in Westland and Paparoa National Parks

The application of the integrated approach outlined in Figure 14.1 can be further illustrated by reference to aspects of a larger study of visitor management in two

New Zealand national parks – Westland and Paparoa – which formed the basis for the derivation of the framework discussed here (Sowman, 1998). Full details of the methodology are provided in the original study. A comparative approach involving two parks was adopted to facilitate understanding of the influence of local conditions and responses to these while keeping the study manageable. The Franz Josef Glacier valley and Dolomite Point, the two highest use sites in these parks, attracting respectively 200 000 and 300 000 visitors a year, form the focal points for this study. In each case a range of data-collection methods and analytical techniques was employed, including: structured interviews with park staff and operators, visitor surveys (125 respondents at Westland, 142 at Paparoa), analysis of policy documents and field observations. Given the broad range of information required, the use of multiple methods will be needed in any integrated analysis of visitor management.

Contextual elements

Westland and Paparoa are two of the country's thirteen national parks, the long history of which has been outlined in Booth and Simmons (this volume). In terms of more recent contextual change, the most significant impact has been the radical restructuring of the state sector since the mid-1980s (Le Heron and Pawson, 1996). One consequence of this was the creation in 1987 of a single government conservation agency, the Department of Conservation (DoC). Booth (1993, p. 301) describes the new agency as 'a product of a new set of influences, namely the government's economic paradigm of greater accountability and increased efficiency in the public sector'. The Department of Conservation became the government's sole conservation advocate and manager of national parks and other conservation areas, including managing their use for recreation and tourism (Booth, 1993). It thus has a dual (and often conflicting) task, managing for both conservation and use. The department's recreation function is described in the Conservation Act (1987) as follows:

> ... to the extent that the use of any natural or historic resource for recreation is not inconsistent with its conservation, to foster the use of natural and historic resources for recreation, and to allow their use for tourism.

But as Booth (1993) explains, neither the terms 'recreation' and 'tourism' are defined, nor are the words 'foster' and 'allow'.

The Department of Conservation has a decentralised structure, the office in Wellington being complemented by three regional offices, thirteen conservancies and various area offices. Policies and plans are prepared at different levels: a national Visitor Strategy has been developed (DoC, 1996a), each conservancy is required to prepare a Conservation Management Strategy and each national park has its own management plan. Increasing emphasis is being put on cost recovery. This is likely to see more co-funding of facilities and services and some widening of user charges beyond the current operator concessions (Kearsley, 1997). Major restructuring occurred within the department as a result of the 1995 Cave Creek tragedy in which fourteen people lost their lives as a result of a platform collapse in Paparoa National Park.

The provision of services and facilities within national parks, and on the conservation estate in general, is coming under increasing pressure as expansion of the Department of Conservation's budget has not matched the growth in international visitor numbers and continuing demand from domestic users (Pearce and Simmons, 1997). Over the decade 1988–97, annual international visitor arrivals in New Zealand increased from 864 892 to 1 497 183. Promotion of the country has been increasingly based on its 'clean and green' image, of which national parks are a significant component. Growth in the Asian markets has focused on the gateways and major resorts but more peripheral regions such as the West Coast have benefited from such longer-stay segments as the West Europeans and Australians and from a trend towards more active adventure-based travel as a complement to the more traditional sightseeing circuits of the country. Downturns in other sectors, such as mining and forestry, have also seen the region place greater emphasis on tourism as a means of economic development and job creation.

Characteristics

Westland and Paparoa National Parks are located on the West Coast of the South Island (Figure 14.2) and contain rugged, spectacular and distinctive natural landscapes for which the relatively remote and sparsely populated region is renowned. Westland National Park (117 626 hectares), stretches from the coast to the Main Divide of the Southern Alps to the coast and comprises dense forests, high mountains, spectacular glaciers and fast-flowing rivers (DoC, 1996b). The Fox and Franz Josef Glaciers are among New Zealand's foremost natural tourist attractions and are within only a few minutes of the main tourist highway.

At Paparoa National Park (30 327 hectares), the juxtaposition of the coast, the karst and the mountains has 'resulted in one of the most scenic and dramatic stretches of accessible coastline in the country, a bold sequence of sculptured headlands in limestone, sandstone and granite interspersed by wild beaches and sandy coves' (DoC, 1996b, p. 50). The park's main attraction is Dolomite Point at Punakaiki, a headland renowned for its surge-pools, geyser-like blowholes, and especially its remarkably even-layered stacks of platy limestone, aptly named the Pancake Rocks (Dennis and Potton, 1987). The Dolomite Point walk is described by the Department of Conservation (DoC 1996b) as one of the finest coastal short walks in the country providing easy access to some of the most spectacular lowland scenery (Plate 14.1). Other visitors make their way onto the Paparoa Range, explore the subterranean karst landscapes with adventure tourism operators or visit the petrel colony south of Punakaiki River.

Results from the visitor survey (Table 14.1) confirm that it is the general scenic qualities of the parks or the specific features of Franz Josef Glacier and the Pancake Rocks that visitors enjoy most, though the latter may be a function of sampling procedures. However, while being attractive to visitors, the physical environment may also be hazardous for them or vulnerable to their use, both situations having major management implications. The Franz Josef Glacier valley is a very dynamic environment, subject to extreme climatic events and geologic instability. Visitor safety and access to the valley and terminal face of the glacier is affected by a range of natural processes including: precipitation (rainfall in the glacier valley and

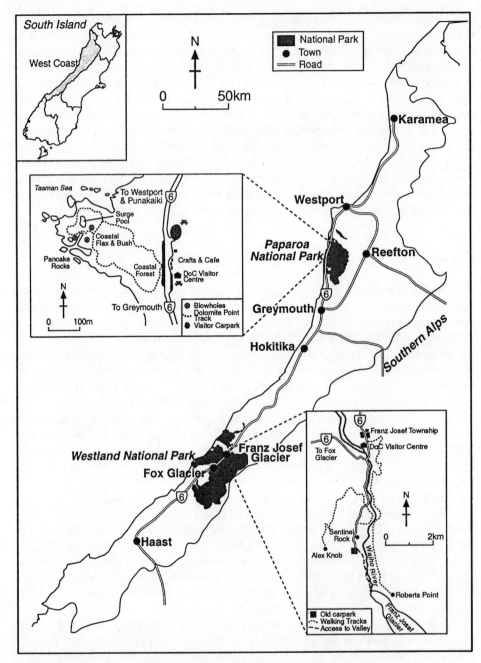

Figure 14.2. Westland and Paparoa National Parks: location and place names

Plate 14.1 The view from Dolomite Point, Paparoa Park. (Photo: D. Pearce)

snowfall in the neve), the advance and retreat of the glacier, high river flow, aggradation and degradation of the river bed and instability of valley walls leading to rock falls and erosion (Bamford *et al.*, 1995). Though more stable, Dolomite Point is also potentially dangerous due to the presence of the blowholes and steep cliffs and the coastal vegetation found there is fragile.

A full range of profile information was included in the visitor survey but only the main features are reported here. Both parks attract a mix of domestic and international visitors. Respondents tended to be elderly and retired or professional. About half were travelling with a partner, and a quarter with friends. The majority

Table 14.1 What visitors most enjoyed about their visit to Westland and Paparoa National Parks

What visitors enjoyed most about their visit	Westland National Park (%)	Paparoa National Park (%)
Scenery	70.8	50.0
Franz Josef Glacier/Pancake Rocks	10.4	30.4
Peace and quiet	3.8	5.8
How the park is maintained	5.7	2.2
Activities	8.5	4.3
Other	0.9	7.2

Source: Sowman (1998)

were first-time visitors on a longer trip (commonly of two to six weeks for Westland park visitors), making only a short visit to one or both parks. Almost half of the Paparoa visitors spent less than an hour there; about half of the Westland visitors overnighted in the area. While many were visiting the parks because of their general scenery or specific features, a sizeable proportion (27 per cent for Westland, 39 per cent for Paparoa) did so because it was 'en route', that is, they dropped in while driving past as part of a general sightseeing trip on the West Coast. The fact that the sites were in national parks was important for just over a third of the visitors; for most of the remainder it was a minor or incidental reason. About 10 per cent of the respondents were unaware either site was in a national park.

Figure 14.3 shows the conservancy structure relating to visitor management in the

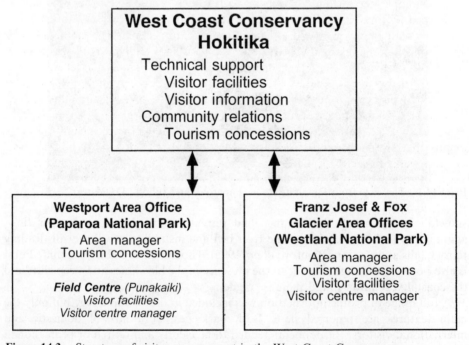

Figure 14.3. Structure of visitor management in the West Coast Conservancy

Department of Conservation consists of a two- or three-tier system. Partly due to its large size, Westland National Park is managed from two area offices, one in the Franz Josef township and one in Fox Glacier. Paparoa, however, being a smaller park, has an Area Office located in Westport and a Field Centre at Punakaiki. Field Centres provide a physical presence by the department at a site, such as a national park, remote from its Area Office. Staff at the Area Offices are mainly involved in delivering conservation outputs in the field whereas the Conservancy Office staff, based in Hokitika, are largely involved in sustaining the delivery of those outputs. Staff in Hokitika are specialists in a variety of areas and supply advice and technical expertise to the Area Offices. In terms of visitor management, the staff of the area offices or field centres are responsible for running the visitor information centres and for the day-to-day management of facilities, access and concessions within the park, with technical support (e.g. visitor information strategy) coming from the conservancy office. The West Coast Conservancy is also part of the department's Southern Region, with an office being situated in Christchurch. The role of the regional offices is to improve the management processes and systems used by the conservancies. Having a regional office located in the South Island enables the department to have a greater understanding of specific or unique issues associated with individual conservancies and areas at a broader scale. Formulation of departmental policy occurs at head office in Wellington but all areas of the department are able to comment and provide input into documents, such as the national Visitor Strategy, before they are finalised.

Some aspects of visitor management, notably guided visits and activities, are handled by private concessionaires (Table 14.2). The majority are small scale and owned and operated by family groups or partnerships. These operations were largely established by locals in the preceding ten years, often as a means of providing the operators with employment, but also as a response to demand. The unique lifestyle offered through managing a tourism operation within a national park was also an important motivation. Different operators draw on different market segments. Younger visitors tend to take part in adventure tourism activities such as those offered by Coast and Mountain Adventures and Franz Josef Glacier Guides. Kea West Coast Tours and Paparoa Nature Tours also appeal to younger groups. However, not all their activities are adventurous. Kamahi Tours mainly receives visitors that are middle-aged to elderly as the operation consists of a bus ride and leisurely walks to see the sights. European and Australian visitors appear to be the most interested in taking part in tours within the West Coast's national parks although Asian and American visitors have more recently been involved in Kamahi Tours. Paparoa Nature Tours attracted many New Zealanders.

Linkages

Linkages and contact between the three parties – park visitors, the Department of Conservation and the private sector operators – occurs in a variety of ways and at varying levels. The relationship between the Department of Conservation and tourism operators is formalised by the concession agreement. This document sets a concession fee and requires the concessionaire to 'comply with all statues,

Table 14.2 Characteristics of park concessionaires

Operation	Year established	Reason established	Concession details	Employment	Type of visitors	Annual visitors
Paparoa Nature Tours	1991	Job creation for family, educate visitors	Valid 10 years, 5% of annual earnings	Partners	Mainly under 30, 50% New Zealanders, rest European	1000 pa
Kea West Coast Tours	1990	Responding to demand, offered a unique lifestyle	Valid 10 years, 5% of annual earnings	Partners and part-time over summer	FITs Australian European	Not available
Coast and Mount Adventures	1995	Protect birdlife, create jobs, responding to demand, create a product that creates a market	Valid 10 years, % unknown	3 part-time (2 guides and one office manager	20–45 years old, German, Australian and New Zealand, mainly professionals	Not available
Franz Josef Glacier Guides	1990	Create jobs, lifestyle	Valid 7 years, 7.5% of annual earnings	20 guides	20–35-year-olds FITs, packpackers, mainly English and Australian	30 000–35 000 pa
Mount Cook Ski Plane	1997–8	Operation already existed and didn't want it abandoned	Valid 5–7 years, through parent company, different concession fees for Westland and Mount Cook	Pilot plus one part-time for flight calls	North American, Australian, German, Swiss, British, New Zealanders, varied — mainly professional	Not available
Kamahi Tours	1994	Responding to demand, creating a product lifestyle opportunity	Valid 5 years, 7.5% of annual earnings	Partners	Mainly middle-aged to elderly Asia, South Africa, Europe, Australia, America mainly retired professionals	Not available

Source: Sowman (1998)

ordinances, regulations, bylaws and other enactments affecting or relating to the site or affecting or relating to the concession activity' (DoC, 1996c, p. S5.01). This includes abiding by the Conservation Act (1987) and relevant conservation management strategies and national park management plans. Safety regulations are also stated which require the concessionaire to operate in a 'safe and reliable manner' (DoC, 1996c, p. S13.01). Individual operations may also have specific conditions imposed which must be adhered to. Concessions to tourism operators thus provide a means of managing certain aspects of visitation, generating revenue for the department and promoting conservation through the conditions imposed.

A small number of formal meetings between the department and the concessionaires are held each year while other contact may occur informally. All the operators interviewed in both parks said they had very little contact with the department, with interaction being primarily issue driven. Four of the six stated that if contacted the department's staff were generally approachable and helpful but one expressed the view that 'The Department of Conservation have no contact that I'm aware of other than to collect the bloody cheque every six months and be obstructive and bureaucratic with new proposals' (Sowman, 1998, p. 84). Operators in both parks complained that consent procedures through the department take too much time and paperwork. This process often makes interaction with the department daunting for operators. Most stated they had very little input in dealing with visitor management issues within national parks with all commenting that they would appreciate the opportunity to do so.

Direct contact between park visitors and the Department of Conservation and tourism operators appears to be rather limited (Table 14.3). Contact with the department largely takes place in the visitor centres rather than out in the parks where interaction is more indirect, as visitors make use of park facilities or respond to various management practices. The majority of visitors have no direct contact at all with the tourism operators, but the small proportion who do take part in commercially organised activities may have a short but intensive period of contact in which considerable emphasis is put on interpretation.

Table 14.3 Levels of contact between visitors, DoC staff, and tourism operators

Level of contact with DoC Staff	Westland National Park (%)	Paparoa National Park (%)
No contact at all	31.1	62.7
Have Visited visitor centre	59.7	16.9
Have spoken to DoC staff	0	11.3
Have seen DoC staff	9.2	9.2
Level of contact with tourism operators		
No contact at all	60.2	93.7
Have seen a tour guide	11.0	2.1
Have spoken to a tour guide	14.4	3.5
Have taken part in tour	14.4	0.7

Source: Sowman (1998)

Issues and solutions

A number of visitor management issues have already been recognised by the Department of Conservation at the intense interest sites ('frontcountry sites where very high visitor use occurs within a relatively confined area') at Dolomite Point and Franz Josef Glacier in the West Coast Conservation Management Strategy (WCCMS) (DoC, 1996b, p. S7.2.6) and the park management plans (DoC, 1989, 1992). For Franz Josef these include: acknowledging the dependence of the local tourist industry on the availability of access to the major glaciers, recognising the importance of interpretation of the features and ecology of the area by staff to visitors, inter-group conflict resulting from aircraft noise, guiding concessions and visitor safety and natural hazards. Paparoa's management issues are not as complex due to the smaller scale of the park and the physical nature of the environment but increased visitation is likely to lead to an increase in associated impacts on the environment, especially the coastal fringe, karst, caves and cave entrances. Other issues there include: overcrowding, protection of iwi values, problems with traffic and parking (the highway bisects the site), adequacy of interpretation and location and adequacy of associated visitor services.

Such issues can be explored further from a visitor perspective through information generated in the visitor survey relating to satisfaction with a number of dimensions of visitation and management. Figure 14.4 reveals different levels of satisfaction between visitors to the two parks. With the exception of the range of activities available, mean satisfaction levels at Paparoa are relatively high, particularly with regard to the interrelated aspects of closeness to the attractions, accessibility and safety. In contrast, lower levels of satisfaction are recorded by Westland visitors, especially in terms of accessibility and the cost of activities. Closer examination of accessibility, the dimension on which the greatest difference occurs, provides insights into the impact of differences in the resource base and management constraints and responses relating to these.

Paparoa and Westland vary significantly in terms of ease of access to their main attractions. At Paparoa, the Dolomite Point track enables visitors to get extremely close to both the Pancake Rocks and Blowholes, such closeness leading to a low-risk enjoyable experience. Provision of good accessibility is facilitated here by proximity of the site to the main road and to the stable although fragile physical conditions. Concrete paths winding in amongst the coastal forest and bush provide an easy walk, including wheelchair access, to view the rocks while bridges also allow visitors to get extremely close to the blowholes (Figure 14.2). The well-maintained tracks also help control visitor behaviour and ensure the karst system and surrounding plant life receive minimal disturbance. The management response here is essentially site harden- ing, a technique which appears to have been readily accepted by visitors who appreci- ated the access provided and did not comment adversely on any change to the natural conditions of the site which this involves. Operators in Paparoa reliant on the Dolomite Point track were also satisfied with general accessibility provided by the department and commented that the track is always well maintained for visitor use. The only issue noted from field observation, and then a relatively minor one, was that the circular nature of the track appeared to be causing some confusion for visitors not knowing which path to take.

In the glacier valleys of Westland National Park the normal problems caused by

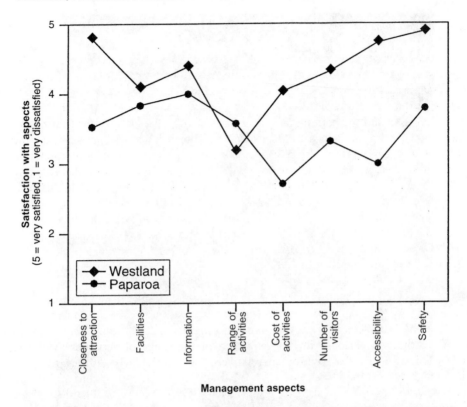

Figure 14.4. Levels of satisfaction with aspects of visitor management in Westland and Paparoa National Parks

severe weather acting on steep, unstable landforms have been compounded by the recession or advance of the glacier. During the last fifteen years the Franz Josef Glacier access road has been severely damaged on several occasions and despite expensive restoration works, is now about 1.5 kilometres shorter than before (DoC, 1989). The Fox Glacier access road also requires frequent maintenance. Visitors to Franz Josef are usually able to walk up the valley floor from the car park at the end of the access road, guided by ropes and markers, to view the glacier's terminal face (Plate 14.2). However changing conditions creating general safety concerns can periodically restrict access to the upper reaches of the valley creating major challenges for park managers.

Such an event occurred during the course of this study and in the period of peak summer visitation. Heavy rain in December 1997 and January 1998 contributed to a rockfall which demolished an information kiosk and cut vehicle access to the car park, adding an extra 20 minutes to the round-trip walk to the glacier. This was compounded soon after by high spring waters that made walking along the valley floor dangerous. These conditions necessitated a multifaceted response from the Department of Conservation. Access to the upper reaches of the valley was restricted and for several months in 1998 viewing by the general public was limited to a new tiered platform which DoC staff built on Sentinel Rock, the access track to which

Plate 14.2   Under normal valley conditions, park visitors have access right up to the terminal face of Franz Josef Glacier. (Photo: D. Pearce)

was upgraded. A second track was subsequently established to allow visitors to walk up the valley floor but this is only temporary until the new car park and main track to the glacier valley are finished. Episodical reconstructive work of this nature is clearly very demanding of resources.

Viewing the glacier from the Sentinel Rock platform, situated approximately one kilometre down the glacial valley from the ice and requiring a 5-minute walk uphill, was disappointing for some visitors, especially those who had visited the park before and knew the unique experience gained close-up. This no doubt contributed to the pattern of responses evident in Figure 14.4. Visitors who did not understand the physical environment of the park and the limitations which that imposes asked questions such as 'Why can't the managers of the park design paths around the side of the valley so we can get closer?' (Sowman, 1998, p. 103). This situation was exacerbated at times by the lack of information provided. Over the summer the department had apparently employed someone to stand at the base of Sentinel Rock and explain to visitors what had happened and a white board was also used. However, during the survey period for this research there appeared to be no information at all. Later, new information signs were erected along the access track explaining the location of the glacier, discussing the nature of the 'Well Prepared Visitor' and what is expected of visitors within the valley (Plate 14.3). By referring directly to the visitor, this sign is perhaps likely to be more eye-catching, causing visitors to stop and read the information related to their safety, ultimately providing them with a more satisfying experience.

Other than for experienced and appropriately equipped ice climbers, access onto the glacier itself is limited to those taking a day or half-day guided walk offered by one of the concessionaires (Plate 14.4). When general public access up the glacier valley is out, the concessionaire is still able to bring visitors up and onto the glacier as, in the words of the director of Franz Josef Glacier Guides, 'access to the glacier is our product' (Sowman, 1998, p. 103). His company has to be able to provide a safe and reliable service for its clients year round regardless of what is happening within the valley. An additional access track has therefore been constructed along the valley wall so his business can continue to operate when the valley floor is unusable. This notion of restricting general public access while allowing those with tour guides to venture beyond barriers also provides confusion to visitors. Failing to appreciate the experience and expertise which concessionaires offer to their clients, some unguided visitors assume that the risk cannot be high if others are going past danger signs and consequently proceed past barriers with little knowledge of the area.

Another issue arises over the granting of a concession to a second guiding company to operate on the glacier. This would provide visitors with a choice. However, as access routes on the ice are limited, matters relating to safety and the cutting and maintenance of steps are raised by the current concessionaires who, for reasons of visitor experience and safety, have on their own initiative limited the size and number of parties taken onto the ice each day.

Maintaining good visitor access to the glacier is therefore a challenging visitor management issue due to the dynamic nature of the park environment and one which requires an integrated set of responses involving the DoC staff, concessionaires and the visitors. These include: maintenance of physical access and facilities, provision of information, monitoring safety and development of an appropriate concessions policy. Other interrelated management issues also arise. Provision of air access is another response to opening the valley up to visitors but this also brings with it other considerations; aircraft noise may be a source of annoyance to other park users. Differences in accessibility between Westland and Paparoa highlight the need to take into account differences in the resource base, both in terms of opportunities and constraints in developing tourism in national parks.

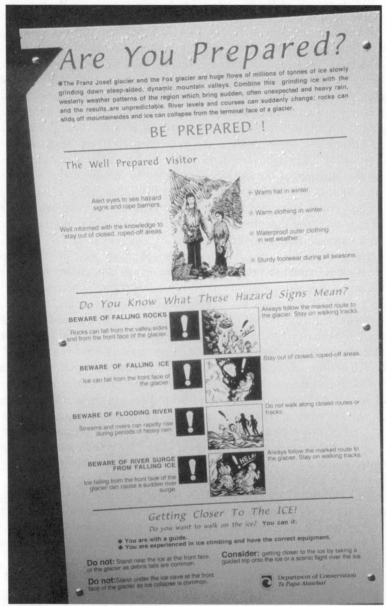

Plate 14.3 "The well-prepared visitor": effective information is an important aspect of visitor management. (Photo: M. Brosnan)

Conclusions

Visitor management in national parks is a complex and challenging activity due to the exceptional physical and/or cultural settings, the varied demands which arise in providing for a satisfying visitor experience while protecting the resource base, and the range of parties involved. Meeting these challenges requires not only developing

Plate 14.4 Guided glacier walks provided by a concessionaire enable access into the glacier itself. (Photo: M Brosnan)

greater specialised knowledge of particular facets of visitor management, whether this be better understanding of demand or improving specific management practices, but also bringing these together in a more comprehensive and integrated fashion. Figure 14.1 provides a basic conceptual framework though which this integration might be achieved and a broader picture of the processes at work examined. As the application of this framework to the study of visitor management in Paparoa and Westland National Parks has shown, general issues may be identified but a greater understanding of them necessitates close consideration of local factors and conditions and the use of a range of research methods.

References

Bamford D., Pharazyn C. and Bryant J., 1995, *Westland National Park: Review of visitor access to the glaciers*, Tourism Resource Consultants, Wellington

Booth, K.L., 1993, Recreation on public lands in New Zealand – past, present and future. *GeoJournal*, **29**: 299–305

Booth, K. and Peebles, C., 1995, Patterns of use. In *Outdoor recreation in New Zealand Volume One*, P.J. Devlin, R.A. Corbett and C.J. Peebles, eds, pp. 31–62, Lincoln University and Department of Conservation, Wellington

Buckley, R. and Pannell, J., 1990, Environmental impacts of tourism and recreation in national parks and conservation reserves. *The Journal of Tourism Studies*, **1**: 24–32

Burchfield, R., 1990, *The New Zealand pocket Oxford Dictionary*, 7th edition Oxford University Press, Auckland

Carter, B., 1996, Private sector involvement in recreation and nature conservation in Australia. In *National parks: private sector's role*, T. Charters, M. Gabriel and S. Prasser, eds, pp. 21–36, USQ, Toowoomba

Charters, T., Gabriel, M. and Prasser, S., 1996, *National parks: private sector's role*, USQ, Toowoomba

Corbett, R., 1995, Managing outdoor recreation. In *Outdoor recreation in New Zealand Volume One*, P.J. Devlin, R.A. Corbett and C.J. Peebles, eds, pp. 191–214, Lincoln University and Department of Conservation, Wellington

Department of Conservation, 1989, *Westland National Park management plan*, Department of Conservation, West Coast

Department of Conservation, 1992, *Paparoa National Park management plan*, Department of Conservation, Hokitika

Department of Conservation, 1996a, *Visitor strategy*, Department of Conservation, Wellington

Department of Conservation, 1996b, *West Coast conservation management strategy (WCCMS)* (draft), Vol. 1, Department of Conservation, Hokitika

Department of Conservation, 1996c, *Concession document*, Department of Conservation, Wellington

Eagles, P.F.J., 1996, Issues in tourism management in parks: the experience in Australia. *Australian Leisure*, **6**: 29–37

Espiner, S.R. and Simmons, D.G., 1998, A national park revisited: assessing change in recreational use of Arthur's Pass National Park. *New Zealand Geographer*, **54**: 37–45

Fennell, D.A. and Eagles P.F.J., 1990, Ecotourism in Costa Rica: a conceptual framework. *Journal of Park and Recreation Administration*, **8**: 23–34

Gunn, C.A., 1994, *Tourism Planning*, 3rd edition, Taylor & Francis, Washington, DC

Hall, C.M., Jenkins, J. and Kearsley, G., 1996, *Tourism planning and policy in Australia and New Zealand*, McGraw-Hill, Roseville, Australia

Hall, C.M. and McArthur S., 1996, *Heritage management in Australia and New Zealand*, Oxford University Press, Melbourne

Higham, J.E.S., 1996, Sustainable wilderness tourism: motivations and wilderness perceptions held by international visitors to New Zealand's backcountry conservation estate. In *Tourism planning and policy in Australia and New Zealand*, C.M. Hall, J. Jenkins and G. Kearsley, eds, pp. 75–86, McGraw-Hill, Roseville, Australia

Hundloe, T., 1996, The private sector and resource management in parks and protected areas. In *National parks: private sector's role*, T. Charters, M. Gabriel and S. Prasser, eds, pp. 37–53, USQ, Toowoomba

Jacob, G.R. and Schreyer, R., 1980, Conflict in outdoor recreation: a theoretical perspective. *Journal of Leisure Research*, Fourth Quarter, 368–380

Kearsley, G.W., 1996, Perceptions of social and physical impacts upon New Zealand's back country environments. In *Towards a more sustainable tourism. Proceedings of Tourism Down Under II*, G. Kearsley, ed., pp. 378–389, Centre for Tourism University of Otago, Dunedin

Kearsley, G., 1997, Tourism planning and policy in New Zealand. In *Tourism planning and policy in Australia and New Zealand*, C.M. Hall, J. Jenkins and G. Kearsley, eds, pp. 49–60, McGraw-Hill, Roseville, Australia

Le Heron, R. and Pawson, E., 1996, *Changing places: New Zealand in the nineties*, Longman Paul, Auckland

McArthur, S. and Hall, C.M., 1996, Visitor management. In *Heritage management in Australia and New Zealand*, 2nd edition, C.M. Hall and S. McArthur, eds, pp. 37–51, Oxford University Press, Melbourne

McKercher, B., 1996, Benefits and costs of tourism in Victoria's Alpine National Park: comparing attitudes of tour operators, management staff and public interest group leaders. In *Tourism planning and policy in Australia and New Zealand*, C.M. Hall, J. Jenkins and G. Kearsley, eds, pp. 99–109, McGraw-Hill, Roseville, Australia.

McNeely, J.A., Thorsell J.W. and Ceballos-Lascurain, H., 1992, *Guidelines: development of national parks and protected areas for tourism*, WTO/UNEP, Madrid, Spain

Pearce, D.G., 1992, *Tourist Organizations*, Longman, Harlow

Pearce, D.G. and Richez, G., 1987, Antipodean contrasts: national parks in New Zealand and Europe. *New Zealand Geographer*, **43**: 53–59

Pearce, D.G. and Simmons, D.G., 1997, New Zealand: tourism – the challenges of growth. In *Tourism and economic development in Asia and Australasia*, F.M. Go and C.L. Jenkins, eds, pp. 197–220, Cassell, London

Prasser, S., 1996, Foreword. In *National parks: private sector's role*, T. Charters, M. Gabriel and S. Prasser, eds, p. iii, USQ, Toowoomba

Sem J., Clements, C.J. and Bloomquist, P., 1996, Tourism and recreation management: strategies for public lands. *Parks and Recreation*, **31**: 92–104

Sowman, P., 1998, *The management of tourism in national parks: a comparative analysis of Westland and Paparoa*, unpublished MA thesis, University of Canterbury, Christchurch

Wilson, P.M., 1993, *Commercial wildlife tourism in the South Island: a comparative analysis*, unpublished MA thesis, University of Canterbury, Christchurch

15 Tourism, national parks and partnerships

HAROLD GOODWIN

Introduction

Nature, or nature-based, tourism encompasses all forms of tourism – mass tourism, adventure tourism, low-impact tourism, ecotourism – which use natural resources in a wild or undeveloped form – including species, habitat, landscape, scenery and salt and fresh-water features. Nature tourism is travel for the purpose of enjoying undeveloped natural areas or wildlife (Goodwin, 1996). Much of the debate about nature-based tourism has been aspirational and case studies have generally focused on particular initiatives, often ecotourism initiatives. There are a number of competing definitions of ecotourism, with no consensus having emerged over its definition. For at least 25 years the argument has been advanced that there could be a symbiotic relationship between tourism and conservation (Myers, 1972; Budowski, 1976; Philips, 1985). As Valentine (1992) has argued, ecologists and conservationists need to 'take control of the language being used in the name of 'ecotourism' and use it to benefit conservation and the maintenance of protected areas. For this purpose ecotourism is here defined as

> low impact nature tourism which contributes to the maintenance of species and habitats either directly through a contribution to conservation and/or indirectly by providing revenue to the local community sufficient for local people to value, and therefore protect, their wildlife heritage area as a source of income (Goodwin 1996, p. 228).

While this is an aspirational definition of ecotourism, aspiration is essential if change is to be made, and this definition identifies a particular agenda for change. If carefully managed at the destination level, tourism can offer diversified low-impact development (Goodwin, 1996). There is a great deal to be done if nature tourism is to make a net contribution to conservation and to sustainable development, providing significant livelihood opportunities for the communities who live in the vicinity of the national parks.

This requires that both the form and impact of nature tourism be managed to meet the definition of ecotourism. In and around national parks the tourism product needs to be reshaped so that a sustainable yield is generated for local communities *and* for conservation. No form of tourism is without environmental impacts and positive and negative consequences for local communities. Large numbers of nature tourists can quickly come to constitute a mass. If tourism in rural areas is not carefully managed it will not necessarily be compatible with diversified rural development and conservation objectives (see Nepal, Chapter 6). Not all forms of nature tourism serve the twin objectives of conservation and local sustainable development. It is protected area managers and conservationists, working with local communities and the tourism industry, who are generally best placed to manage nature tourism, to ensure that it is low impact, and that both local people and parks benefit significantly from it.

The key issue is the impact of the tourist on the local communities and on their environment. Whatever the motivation of the tourist, whether they see themselves as ecotourists or not, the key issue is the balance of their positive and negative impacts in the destination. It is through changing the tourist impacts in and around natural heritage attractions such as national parks that nature-based tourism may be turned into ecotourism, demonstrating that parks can be important generators of local sustainable economic development as well as funds for conservation. As Aylward and Freeman (1992, p. 413), cautioned 'If the revenues of ecotourism do not accrue to national park systems or local communities, there will be little economic incentive for investment in the recurring costs of conservation activities'.

National parks and tourism

Economic considerations

National parks have generally been considered as merit goods and priced accordingly. Charges for access to national parks, and for the use of accommodation and other facilities in parks, traditionally have been kept low in order to facilitate access to national heritage. Income maximisation has not been a policy objective and charges have been set by many governments often with social or educational objectives in mind. However, with national independence and the consequent democratisation of policy-making processes, the money available for the maintenance of protected areas has been squeezed by the pressure for increased expenditure on health, welfare and development among other government priorities in many countries, none more so than those in the developing world. The habitats and species of national parks have long been used to attract international visitors and to develop national tourism industries in countries rich in charismatic megafauna. However, the benefits of these assets have primarily been realised at the national level in foreign exchange revenues rather than at the local or destination level through increased employment and diversified economic development. Wildlife has been identified as a national asset (see Lilieholm and Romney, Chapter 10), but revenues from it have not been maximised either within national parks departments or in terms of local economic development.

The increase in international tourism has raised the issue of whether national governments should be subsidising the use of its natural heritage by more affluent foreign tourists. In a developing country, with limited budgets should parks be viewed as a public amenity or as a self-supporting enterprise which contributes to rural development? Undercharging for parks increases the cost to the national treasury of maintaining the parks estate and fails to maximise revenue, much of it in the form of badly needed foreign exchange. Child and Heath (1990, p. 223) posed the issues surrounding the funding of Zimbabwe's Wildlife Estate clearly:

> State-subsidised social services are justified in a developing country such as Zimbabwe, with its limited budget (and the many urgent calls on it), only for legitimate services... to disadvantaged elements in the community. It is thus important to decide whether the Estate is to be viewed as a public amenity or as a more or less self-supporting enterprise contributing as much as possible to rural development.
>
> Present pricing structures in the Estate favour foreigners and those Zimbabweans best able and probably most willing to pay more, i.e. more affluent citizens and foreign visitors.

The issue is whether or not international tourists (and affluent domestic tourists) make a 'fair' contribution to the costs of maintaining the habitats and species that they travel to see. In Zimbabwe (as elsewhere in sub-Saharan Africa) the World Bank has been pressing successfully for national parks departments to become reliant on the revenues that they generate from tourism and other activities.

In Zimbabwe, the Jansen Report was commissioned to recommend 'allocative' strategies which would enable the Department of National Parks and Wild Life Management to maximise revenue within 'limits determined by environmental and equity goals (Child and Heath, 1990, p. 24). Jansen's report was based on a number of principles. The access system should be more transparent, competition fostered, investment encouraged, and unfair competition avoided between the Estate (public) and the private sector. These objectives should be achieved with a framework established by environmental and equity criteria. Zimbabweans should not be denied access by prices set for foreign tourists as it is their heritage and Jansen asserted 'it is important to establish a lobby to ensure the continued existence and support of the Parks and Wildlife Estate'. As Jansen pointed out, it is Zimbabweans who bear both the direct fiscal burden and the opportunity costs of maintaining the Parks and Wildlife Estate and she advocated a 60 per cent discount for Zimbabwean citizens based on purchasing power parities. National parks are created in order to preserve areas of significant biodiversity value in a natural state, they are gazetted in order to conserve them, and adjudged important for conservation, yet local people are generally excluded and they lose access to resources which have traditionally contributed significantly to their livelihoods (see Nepal, Chapter 6). There are significant opportunity costs which protected areas place on their neighbours. There is increasing recognition that local people are important stakeholders with whom protected area managers must build cooperation. As McNeely (1994) points out, protected area managers cannot coexist long term with communities which are hostile to them. Tourism has been widely identified by protected area managers as one of the primary means whereby they can endeavour to provide opportunities for local people to derive economic benefit from their proximity to the park, thus offsetting the opportunity costs. McNeely (1993) reflects the new perspectives of protected area managers arguing that long-established human activity embracing cultural identity, spirituality, and subsistence practices has contributed to the maintenance of biodiversity. Biological and cultural diversity are often linked, thereby defining the tourism product and the management context for the protected area manager.

Examples from Africa, South-east Asia and India

This chapter draws on a Department for International Development (DFID) study (Goodwin *et al.*, 1997a–d) undertaken on tourism in and around Keoladeo National Park, Bharatpur, India; Komodo National Park, Indonesia and Gonarezhou National Park in the Southeast lowveld, Zimbabwe. The focus of this study was to identify the opportunities that exist in these settings to harness tourism for conservation and local economic development addressing some of the dynamics of the relationships between national parks, local communities and tourism.

The three DFID-funded case studies of Tourism, Conservation and Sustainable Development (TCSD) looked at the relationships between the conservation of habitats and species, the tourism which the parks attract and the economic and social impacts on communities which neighbour the conserved areas. The research focused primarily on national parks, but in the southeast lowveld of Zimbabwe the research included the conservancies, former cattle ranching land now being put back to conservation, and a major lodge development on communal land. The TCSD project focused on assessing the economic, social and ecological impacts of tourism in and around the parks to assess to what extent conservation and local communities benefited. Focus was on nature-based tourism, encompassing all tourists attracted to the park and to the surrounding area by natural habitats and species (often but by no means exclusively in national parks) and the industry that both brings the tourists and provides them with services.

Tourism opportunity and services provided: evidence from case studies

At Keoladeo significant numbers of local people find employment as guides and cycle-rickshaw/guides; licensed by the Park they can enter the tourism industry with relatively little capital (Table 15.1). At Komodo there are some supplementary tourist-escorting opportunities when the cruise ships arrive with large numbers of tourists. By contrast, in Zimbabwe it is very difficult for local people to become guides because of the dangerous game constraints and the high entry costs produced by the guide-training and licensing regulations. However, there is interest among members of the local community in providing wildlife-related tourism services for which there is demand among tourists. Asked whether their clients would be prepared to pay for a fully trained local guide around the Gonarezhou Park, all the German tour operators and two-thirds of the UK tour operators said that they would (Goodwin, 1998).

Most of these specialist guiding services could be provided outside national parks as could opportunities for tourists to learn more about the ways in which natural resources were harvested from the forest by local communities. In Gonarezhou, traditional hunting and the harvesting of wild honey and plants for culinary and medicinal purposes would be of interest to tourists. The Mahenye Community is

Table 15.1 The services respondents would be interested in providing for tourists

Service	%	Frequency of a 'Yes' response	Level of interest expressed by tourists (%)
Bush survival training	4.5	8	38.3
Boat trips on the river	9.0	16	18.7
Teaching wildlife tracking	11.8	21	48.6
Providing vegetables to lodges	11.8	21	N/A

Source: Goodwin *et al.* (1997d, p. 65)

Table 15.2 Foreign tourists' motivation for travel, ranking of 'most important' response

	Gonarezhou, Zimbabwe		Keoladeo, India		Komodo, Indonesia	
Culture	3	9%	1	45%	2	57%
Wildlife	1	66%	2	30%	3	7.4%
Landscape	2	20%	3		1	19%
Art & architecture	5		4		5	
History & archaeology	4		5		6	
Marine	N/A		6		4	7.4%
Markets and shopping	6		7		7	

Source: Goodwin *et al.*, (1997b, p. 69)

developing a traditional show village, situated close to Mahenye and Chilo Lodges to avoid tourist intrusion into the daily life of the Shangaan community and to maintain their privacy. The success of this venture will be dependent upon the effectiveness of the lodge management at Chilo and Mahenye in promoting these opportunities to their guests and of the Park in drawing the attention of visitors to the existence of this alternative accommodation. Shangaans will be employed at the show village to demonstrate aspects of their subsistence economy and of their culture, particularly dance and there will be opportunities for the sale of Shangaan art including baskets, pottery and wooden spoons. The Mahenye people plan to offer the opportunity for tourists to stay in the traditional huts in the show village and to offer a cultural experience (Goodwin *et al.*, 1997b, p. 185).

International tourists interviewed in and around the national parks were asked to rank the relative importance of different components of their motivation for travel and were also asked to identify the most important. The interviews were conducted when a recent wildlife experience could be assumed (see Table 15.2). Wildlife was ranked first in Zimbabwe, second in India and third at Komodo (the large monitor lizard, the Komodo 'dragon' is the major charismatic megafauna species) where only 7.4 per cent of international visitors rated seeing wildlife as their most important motivation for travel in Indonesia. In Africa the travel industry has given very little prominence to African culture and only 9 per cent of respondents considered it their most important reason for travel. By contrast in the two Asian parks, where the industry has placed its primary emphasis on culture, 45 per cent and 57 per cent of international travellers interviewed asserted that culture was their primary

Table 15.3 Potential interest in cultural services of residents and tourists

Service	%	Frequency of a 'Yes' response	Level of interest expressed by tourists (%)
Storytelling & theatre	5.1	9	10.3
Music & dancing performances	56.2	100	10.3
Tours around your village	61.2	109	14
Cooking a meal in your home	64.6	115	10.3
Selling hanicrafts in your village	74.7	133	10.3

Source: Goodwin *et al.*, (1997d, p. 65)

motivation for travel. There is considerable scope for building on the international and doubtless domestic, travellers' interest in culture in Africa in particular.

Recognising that there is very little of cultural interest currently offered to tourists in the southeast lowveld, local communities were asked what they would like to provide and tourists were asked what they would like to do if it were available to them (see Table 15.3). Care needs to be taken in interpreting these results as tourists were being asked about their propensity to purchase an experience currently not available to them and to which no prices were attached. However, the figures do suggest that there is scope for the development of some of these opportunities and that there are local people interested in providing these services, most of which would offer opportunities for the diversification of livelihoods and require relatively low investments of time and other resources, thus minimising risk.

The success of individual and community initiatives would depend in part upon the marketing and product development support provided by the tourism industry, local government and the park.

At the workshop in Keoladeo, local tour operators and hoteliers were all keen to see diversification of the local tourism product in order to increase visitor length of stay. Very few Park visitors are currently aware of nearby cultural attractions, such as the Deeg Palaces and the Bharatpur Fort, close by. Smt. Shruti Sharma, the Director of Keoladeo National Park, endorsed this strategy of using the Park as the primary attraction in the area to make visitors aware of the culture of Bharatpur, including Ganga Madir, the history of Aghapur village, folksongs and poetry about Lord Krishna and local myths; and to provide opportunities for local arts and craft workers to sell their cultural products.

Local cooperative initiatives of this kind also require the support of the international and domestic tour operators based in the tourist-originating countries and in the metropolitan centres, who largely control the industry. The decisions that determine the volume and character of tourism to a particular site are not made locally, but by people remote from the parks and the local communities which surround them. Foreign tour operators generally have a low level of commitment to particular destinations. The local destination remains relatively isolated from the international market, receiving tourists but not understanding or playing any part in controlling the terms on which, and the processes by which, they arrive.

National parks and sustainable development: local issues

As Din (1997) has argued, outside players exercise a pervasive influence on tourism development in destinations and local issues are given, at best, palliative attention. The tourism development process has focused on the needs of tourists and the development of products and services designed to attract and provide for tourists, with less attention being paid to the ways in which tourism might bring diversified economic development at the local level. The focus of policy has been on national revenues rather than on local economic development. The Brundtland Report (WCED, 1987) placed considerable emphasis on poverty alleviation in its advocacy of sustainable development. In the words of the World Commission on Environment and Development: sustainable development requires meeting the basic needs of all and extending to all the opportunity to fulfil their aspirations for a better life. A world in which poverty is endemic will always be prone to ecological and other catastrophes (WCED, 1987, p. 8).

Din (1997, p. 15) argues that the key questions are, who controls tourism at the destination, who should tourism be sustainable for? Some groups will gain and others may lose. For local communities the key issue is ... what good does change bring to their midst? What's in it for them? Tourism development that displaces or marginalises the original host community is more of a *misdevelopment* than development (Din, 1997, p. 161). The creation of a national park is often just such a misdevelopment, and can be an example of a local change that disadvantages local people. If their traditional uses of the land are criminalised, they lose gathering rights and hunters became poachers.

The international tourism market is a competitive and volatile one. As parks and local economies adapt to incorporate tourism as a significant income, their dependency on the international tourism market increases. This makes parks and local economies vulnerable to changes in the international market and to loss of confidence by tour operators and individual travellers. In the UK, NGOs like Tourism Concern and Voluntary Service Overseas (VSO) have been raising the issue of 'fair trade' in tourism, campaigning for consumers to be aware of the impacts, both positive and negative, of their holidays. VSO's WorldWise campaign has focused on how to get more out of a holiday emphasising how 'taking a closer look at the local culture can bring you closer to the people and their country in ways that benefit us all'. The WorldWise campaign also points out that many 'people travel to the most distant locations on earth and never eat, drink or shop outside their hotel'. The campaign literature asserts that 'at a local market you can buy direct from the craftspeople and see local traditions come alive. An experience for you. A livelihood for local people' (Tourism Concern, 1997).

Tourism is marketed internationally but is consumed at the point of production. There are opportunities for additional spending in the local economy to the benefit of local communities, if destination-level tourism can be managed to provide opportunities for diversified local economic development. International agencies and governments have been active in planning and promotion but the private sector has been the real engine of tourism development. Companies based in the tourist-originating countries dominate international tourism, while in the destination countries, the established entrepreneurs in the metropolitan centres dominate the national industry. It is at the destination level that the opportunities for local people to gain from this export industry need to be maximised (Goodwin, 1998). As Butler (1992) has argued, there is a lack of rational, objective evaluation of tourism in the context of sustainability from the perspective of the destination area. The challenge is to manage tourism at the local destination level to increase economic benefits to local communities and to enable them to have a say in the management of tourism in their place.

National parks as destinations

National parks are major attractions, bringing domestic and international tourists to rural areas which would not otherwise attract tourists. Growth in visitor arrivals at the three National Parks under consideration in the TCSD study (see Figure 15.1) was substantially above average international arrivals trend rates.

During the 1990s, the lines lie within a band showing a clear upward trend. The annualised growth rates between 1991 and 1995 are 7 per cent for Keoladeo, 15 per cent for Komodo and 10 per cent for Gonarezhou. Keoladeo is growing more slowly than the others, possibly a reflection of its well developed status (Goodwin *et al.*, 1997b, Vol. II, p. 19). These substantial flows of visitors create economic opportunities that are often not harnessed locally. Park officials have not traditionally seen their parks as tourist attractions and they are not equipped to maximise the benefits and revenue that can accrue to local communities and conservation from tourism. It is not argued here that national parks should be seen primarily as tourist attractions; conservation is their primary function. However, by not identifying the opportunities for local economic development and for increasing direct revenues to conservation, the potential benefits of tourism are not maximised.

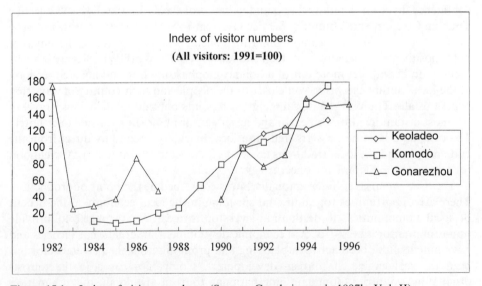

Figure 15.1.   Index of visitor numbers. (Source: Goodwin *et al.*, 1997b, Vol. II)

In rural areas, particularly in less-developed countries, alternative tourism is likely to be particularly appropriate. Alternative tourism is defined as likely to be small scale, locally owned with low import leakages and with profits reinvested locally (Gonsalves, 1987; Cater, 1993; Smith and Eadington, 1992). Advocates of alternative tourism, recognising that local people are affected by tourist development, seek to empower local communities about the forms of tourism which use their places and to ensure that local people gain significantly from tourism development. Tourism to many national parks is growing strongly, but the question remains, Who benefits? The challenge is to turn nature tourism into ecotourism by increasing direct revenues to conservation and to people in those local communities currently disadvantaged by their proximity to national parks.

The role of partnership in turning nature tourism into ecotourism

Turning nature tourism into ecotourism for the greater benefit of conservation and local people requires cooperation between the private sector, conservationists, and the local community in order to achieve balanced, diversified, sustainable tourism development. Tourism often reinforces socio-economic and spatial inequalities, but it could also be harnessed to bring sustainable local development though the localisation of benefits. The tourism industry is driven by demand, although marketing and promotion play a significant role in shaping both form and volume of that demand. But at the local destination level sustainability and the maximisation of local economic benefits requires a degree of supply-side management at the destination level. Advocates of ecotourism have enjoined tourists to 'leave only footprints'. The greater challenge is to maximise tourist spending in local communities in order that visitors can make a more significant contribution to the local economy, leaving more than footprints. The localisation of benefits, the creation of economic linkages and local employment, and the development of locally owned complementary products need to be addressed at the destination level with the active participation of local communities. It requires their empowerment.

The Rio Earth Summit in 1992 put partnership at the heart of achieving sustainable development through Agenda 21 and the subsequent series of summits on urban development, population, social development and gender have adopted a similar approach. Agenda 21 (Chapter 27) illustrated the need to activate a sense of common purpose on behalf of all sectors of society. It recognised that success would be dependent on all sectors participating in genuine partnership and dialogue, but accepted the independent roles, responsibilities and abilities of all parties.

Davies (1998) has argued that a partnership approach to development has proved effective in many parts of the world and demonstrates that it can be a mechanism for stability, peace and prosperity. Cross-sector working in private sector business, civil society and public sector institutions at local and national and international levels presents considerable challenges. At the Commission on Sustainable Development's discussions on tourism there was representation from government, the industry, trade unions and the NGOs. The local communities were not present. However, at the local destination level the direct involvement of local communities in the planning and implementation of tourism development is necessary if the aspirations for partnership approaches are to be achieved. At the core of successful strategies for developing and strengthening partnerships is the understanding and recognition of the benefits to all partners and the negotiation of a clear and shared set of partnership objectives. This approach is well geared to enable the resolution of conflict – economic, social and ecological – which arise in the tourism-development process. Tourism need not be a zero-sum game if a partnership approach can be implemented which recognises the different objectives of the major players, and if agreements can be negotiated and implemented.

The April 1999 Commission on Sustainable Development (CSD) considered Tourism and Sustainable Development and placed considerable emphasis on consultation and partnership at a local level in policy formulation, planning, management and the sharing of benefits. There was explicit reference to the eradication of poverty and to the inclusion of cultural approaches through music, art and drama. The success of the multi-stakeholder elements of the dialogue process on tourism at CSD resulted in an 'ad hoc informal open-ended working group on tourism' to look at the maximisation of benefits for indigenous and local communities and to build capacity for participation (Goodwin et al., 1998).

There is evidence that some tour operators are sympathetic to ideas of local community involvement in tourism and a levy on park admissions for local development. In surveys of UK and German operators conducted for the TCSD study, over 60 per cent of British tour operators strongly agreed that local people should be assisted in developing tourism-related businesses. When asked whether tourists visiting national parks should be charged a levy for a rural development fund, 36 per cent of German operators and 65 per cent of British operators agreed (Goodwin et al., 1997a, pp. 70–71).

Revenues for conservation

Park revenues are often below park operating budgets, and entrance (and other) fees are often below what visitors would be willing to pay. In Zimbabwe, at peak periods, the allocation of chalets in parks has, until recent changes, been decided by a bureaucratic rationing system, graphically demonstrating the existence of excess demand at current prices. In the TCSD study estimates of tourism-related park expenditure (ranging between 6.5 per cent and 12.7 per cent of the costs of maintaining these parks (Goodwin et al., 1998, p. 41) were compared with park visitor revenue. At Keoladeo visitors made a net contribution of 27 US cents per visit, while at Gonarezhou and Komodo each visit was subsidised by taxpayers to the tune of 17 cents and 4 cents, respectively (Goodwin et al., 1998, p. 43).

Surveys of visitor willingness to pay, using a contingent valuation method, revealed significant scope for increasing entrance charges for international visitors at all three parks. At all three parks, a doubling of price leads to an estimated fall in demand of no more than 21 per cent and at Keoladeo and Komodo the estimated fall was less than 10 per cent. As Table 15.4 shows, there is apparently considerable scope for increasing revenues for conservation by increasing admission charges, and

Table 15.4 Proportion of respondents willing to pay hypothetical increases in entrance fees, and the estimated change in total revenue

Proposed	Proportion of sample willing to pay (%)			Projected revenue as a proportion of current revenue (%)		
Entrance fee	Gonarezhou	Keoladeo	Komodo	Gonarezhou	Keoladeo	Komodo
Current	100	100	100	100	100	100
x2	79	91	93	158	182	187
x4	24	70	81	97	281	326
x8	8		62	65		495

Source: Goodwin *et al.* (1997b, p. 50)

there are other opportunities for increasing park revenues from guiding and other services, as well as from concession and lease fees.

At the workshops in Keoladeo and Komodo, incoming operators and local hoteliers agreed that there was considerable scope for increased entrance charges. Operators felt strongly that 'the rise in fees ... should be proportionate to the enhancement of the product experience.' They felt strongly that any increase ought to be staged and that it ought to be made clear what the increased revenue was being used for. A notice at the main gate and elsewhere making clear that the increased revenue was being used for conservation measures in the park or for local development projects would, in their view, significantly reduce the hostility likely to be engendered by entrance fee increases (Goodwin *et al.*, 1997a, pp. 51–53). Among Indonesian operators a fivefold increase in entrance fee was not considered a problem, although the feeling among some respondents was that the price itself was not as important as the way that the revenue was used. Eighty per cent of respondents said that a fee of Rp10 000 (US$4.33) would not affect their business, since this only represented 1–2 per cent of the cost of a typical package. This suggests that demand is even less elastic for package tourists than it is for independents (Goodwin *et al.*, 1997a, pp. 51–52).

In pursuit of increased revenues from tourism, park managers need to consider the purpose of the park(s) for which they are responsible and to balance a number of competing management goals. The most important goal will almost certainly be the maintenance of the ecological integrity of the park and the conservation of its habitats and species (see Boyd, this volume). Visitor fee income is generally supplementary rather than core, with very few individual parks in a position to become self-financing. A key objective may well be to build understanding of and support for, conservation amongst the domestic population. Dual-pricing systems facilitate access for nationals while enabling a revenue maximisation strategy to be applied to international tourists. The setting of park entrance fees is one aspect of the total management of national parks; it is a complex issue involving a number of trade-offs.

While increasing revenues from tourists visiting national parks is not a zero-sum game, a strategy of revenue maximisation may lead to increased conflict with local communities, if their opportunities to earn from tourism are reduced by changes in the visitor profile caused by changes in park entrance fees. The Keoladeo case study

Table 15.5 Proportion of respondents in Keoladeo National Park prepared to pay hypothetical increases in entrance fee by self-ascribed category of tourist

Fee		Self -ascribed category				Visits made	
RS/-	US$	All visitors (%)	Package tourists (%)	Independent travellers (%)	Backpackers (%)	3 or less (%)	4 or more (%)
50	1.43	91	97	89	87	91	91
75	2.14	81	94	78	70	82	76
100	2.85	70	87	69	52	72	52

Source: Goodwin et al. (1997b, pp. 52–53)

gives cause for caution when the willingness to pay data are analysed by self-ascribed category. Table 15.5 shows the impact of two-, three- and fourfold increases in fees for foreign visitors from the 1996 rate of 25Rs/. The impact on package tourists of a tripling in the admission charge is very limited, but they are least likely to stay in Bharatpur and they make very few purchases in the local economy. By contrast, independent traveller and backpacker responses suggest that they would be more markedly deterred from visiting, as would those staying longer and making multiple visits. Independent travellers and backpackers make more use of local owned and informal sector-provided services. The impact of entrance fee increases on the rickshaw operators and the guides would be to adversely affect their incomes. There would also be secondary revenue effects in the park itself, particularly on bicycle hire and use of the boat trips (Goodwin et al., 1997b). Park managers need to take such impacts into account when and if they have the opportunity to determine park fees at a local level.

National parks are important local tourist attractions. They create destinations in rural areas that might not otherwise attract significant numbers of tourists. The way in which national parks are managed for tourism will have significant effects on the opportunities for local communities to diversify their livelihoods and improve their standards of living by engaging with the tourists who come to their area. Park managers can encourage tourists to visit other natural and cultural heritage attractions in the area, to purchase sustainably produced art and craft products, and to enjoy complementary locally owned products, extending length of stay and increasing visitor spend in the local economy. Tourism is not the only development opportunity that may be available to local communities living adjacent to national parks, but that opportunity ought to be evaluated alongside others and to be pursued wherever appropriate.

Opportunities in tourism for local communities

As already suggested, there are a number of ways in which park managers, the tourism industry and local communities can work together to create more activities for domestic and international tourists in and around national parks, and by doing so increase the local economic benefits for the parks; or other conserved areas, local communities, and the local tourism industry. These include the creation of linkages between the tourism industry and the local economy, maximising local employment through skills development and other measures, the development of informal sector activities, infrastructure or planning gain, and, where common property ownership permits, local communities should be enabled to secure a stake in tourist development through leaseholds and joint ventures. The success of these kinds of initiatives is dependent upon the creation of a locally managed tourism strategy where park management, the industry and local communities work together to shape tourism to the advantage of local communities and conservation.

The Komodo case study reveals some of the problems to be overcome in developing forms of tourism which benefit the local community. At least 50% of the tourism revenues leak out of the local economy as a result of imports and non-local involvement in the tourism industry and as little as 1% reaches the communities most disadvantaged by living within the Komodo National Park, as the gateway communities of Labuan bajo and Sape are the main beneficiaries. Most of the tourism-related employment goes to young males, and most local people are excluded by lack of capital and skills (Goodwin et al., 1997c, pp. 105–107). There are very significant differences in the contributions to the local economy made by different categories of tourists to the Komodo National Park. The average cost of a cruise ship based visit to Komodo National Park was US$600, and the business was worth over US$6.5 million in 1996. While the visit to Komodo National Park was not the sole purpose of the trip, it was the primary purpose and only about 3 cents per cruise boat passenger accrued to the local economy. Package travellers spent about US$300 on a trip to Komodo, of which about US$52.5 (17.5%) was spent in the local economy. Independent travellers and backpackers spent an average of US$97 on their trip to Komodo, all of which was spent in the local economy (Goodwin et al., 1997c, p. 93). Managing the pattern of visiting to Komodo could significantly increase the value of tourism to the local economy. If the public ferry ceased calling at Komodo there would be a consequential increase in demand for small boat charters from Labuan bajo and Sape to the Park and an increase in overnight stays. Such a change would also advantage the Park by discouraging people from overnighting on Komodo.

Cruise ship passengers, safari groups and coach groups are all forms of 'all inclusive' enclave tourism. At the destination level it is important to resist the tendency of some tour operators to bypass local business opportunities and instead to create opportunities for tourists to interact with the local community. This can be done by creating and marketing opportunities for tourists to visit local markets and craft workers, to visit villages when hosted by members of the local community, and to encourage the development of complementary products like boat trips, guided walks and local cultural experiences.

A recent study for DFID concluded that linkages 'are frequently discussed but rarely seen, and are particularly important but difficult to develop' (Deloitte and Touche, 1999). At the local economy or destination level the development of linkages and local sourcing of goods and services by the tourism industry is one of the most significant ways in which leakages can be reduced. In the southeast lowveld of Zimbabwe the new conservancies have been considering what local linkages they can create to reduce leakages and to increase the local economic impact in order to strengthen the case for the change of land use from unsustainable cattle ranching to

Table 15.6 Tourism-related complementary enterprise development in the lowveld

	Zimsun Mahenye/ Chilo Lodges	Malilangwe Conservation Trust	Bubiana Conservancy	Chiredzi River Conservancy	Save Valley Conservancy
Supply of goods					
Curio manufacture	•	•	•		•••
Furniture manufacture			•		••
Manufacture and supply of building materials	•				•••
Uniform manufacture		•••	•		•
Food and vegetable production			•		•
Supply of services					
Game meat retailing and distribution			••		••
Provision of transport					•
Retailing and distribution of fuel wood					•
Complementary tourism enterprises					
Cultural tourism	•		•		•
Tourist accommodation	•				
Traditional show village	••				••
Community-based wildlife projects			•	•	•
Joint ventures					
Accommodation joint ventures		••			
Incorporation of resettlement of communal lands into conservancies			•	•	•
Wildlife ownership on Conservancy land earning dividends				•	•

• Idea has been discussed, •• Implementation has been commenced, ••• In Operation
Source: Goodwin *et al.* (1997d)

eco-based tourism based on wildlife. Table 15.6 shows the initiatives that have been discussed and the progress towards implementation in each enterprise in the lowveld.

Linkages will most easily be achieved where local technology can be used. The transferability of skills and hence local involvement is greatest where existing capital and know-how can be utilised. Tourism developers should be encouraged, wherever possible, to use and promote existing local modes of transport, accommodation and art and handicrafts, food production and preparations.

The development of the local informal sector has particular advantages in that it enables those without access to capital to access the opportunities presented by the local tourism market. Hotel and tour operators (local and international) can do a great deal to ensure that tourists are aware of the opportunities available in the local area to diversify their tourism experience. Local involvement in the tourism industry depends largely on access to the market. In many cases local benefits are maximised in the informal sector. Local skills and services are often maximised where the scale of capital investment is low. This aspect is sometimes neglected in tourism planning, and access to tourists by the informal sector is often restricted. Training in market research, understanding consumer tastes and product promotion may increase sales for small traders.

In Keoladeo and Komodo there was some awareness of the contribution that these kinds of linkages into the local economy could make to local economic development. However, there was little concrete discussion of how these linkages might be achieved. At Keoladeo the local guides and cycle-rickshaw driver/guides, and at Komodo the guides and charter boat operators, are examples of local people diversifying their livelihood strategies. The boat operators also fish, and many of the cycle-rickshaw drivers work in town in the low season.

As the analysis of the aspirations of local people and tourist demand in Tables 15.1 and 15.3 in the lowveld showed, there are other opportunities for the development of enterprises requiring low levels of capital investment. Zimbabwe Sun Ltd (Zimsun) leases communal land from the Mahenye community for safari lodge developments. They are committed to pay a minimum annual lease fee or a percentage of gross trading revenue rising from 8 per cent for the first three years, to 12 per cent for the final four years of a 10-year lease, paying whichever is the larger. The Mahenye Community benefits through a CAMPFIRE scheme (see Nepal and Lilieholm and Romney, this book), some of the revenue being used for community projects and some being taken as household income. The development of the Mahenye and Chilo Lodges has also brought planning gain and infrastructural development. A piped water supply and electricity both have now reached Mahenye Ward. The community dug the trench in which the pipe was laid, and Zimsun met the other costs. The electricity supply has been extended from the Zimsun properties into the village, with the community meeting the costs of extension to the village from its lease earnings. The road has been improved to service the Zimsun developments, and although this may have occurred anyway, it is a considerable gain to the community. Telephone lines have been brought from the Zimsun properties to the village and there are now a limited number of phones in Mahenye.

The Mahenye leasehold agreement specified that Zimsun should 'utilise, wherever possible, the work-force potential of the Mahenye Ward Community' (Goodwin et al., 1997d, p. 184). In March 1997 the Mahenye and Chilo Lodges were employing 63 per cent of their labour from the local community; and whilst only seven women were employed in the lodge, six of them came from the local community. The Chipinge Rural District Council and local community were both pushing hard for more local employment and for the training necessary for members of the local community to fill more skilled posts. This lease agreement points to the value of formal development and lease agreements in laying the basis for local employment and associated training. Local employment is greatest in the family-run enterprises, in the larger hotels and restaurants there is a tendency to bring in skilled labour from elsewhere. Without consistent efforts at the local level to insist on training local workers to fill tourism jobs employers will often prefer to engage experienced labour in order to reduce training costs. Government and NGOs can assist in meeting training needs but again it is effective local partnerships for tourism development that are required.

Conclusion

Although similar local economic development issues arose at each of the three locations discussed above, the specific solutions that were being articulated at the local level were specific to the destinations. There is a need to create and strengthen appropriate institutions based on partnerships at the local level between the private sector, local authorities and local communities and NGOs. Such partnerships are essential if the potential of tourism to national parks is to be captured for local economic development. Local concerns regarding tourism development and attempts to retain some of the revenues from tourism are often hampered by the lack of local representation at an institutional level (see Nepal, Chapter 6). Nature tourism, conservation and income generation often fall between the jurisdiction of several institutions and coordinated approaches involving all the stakeholders are rare. The multi-stakeholder approach envisaged in CSD will assist this process if it can be applied at the local level.

Appropriate planning structures would facilitate effective community participation in the tourism development process and provide a mechanism for capturing planning gain through infrastructural, employment and economic linkages. A planning process that addresses carrying capacity and sets limits of acceptable change is most likely to local communities an active influence over tourism development. It is through participatory forms of these technical processes, informed by traditional and local knowledge, that local communities can most effectively be empowered, and the environmental, social and cultural integrity of destinations maintained. Benefits will only be achieved through partnerships at the destination level. Park managers, hoteliers and tour operators need to work with local communities and local government to develop forms of tourism which bring sustainable local development and provide a richer experience for domestic and international tourists. Such partnerships will benefit both the host communities and the tourism industry, ensuring that more tourism dollars stay in the local community where they can make significant contributions towards the elimination of poverty, and ensure that local communities recognise the financial value which attaches to the conservation of their natural heritage, particularly through the institution of national parks.

Acknowledgements

This chapter draws on the results of a 3-year comparative collaborative research project funded by the Environment Policy Department of the Department for International Development. It involved people from local communities, national parks, universities, the tourism industry, government and NGO's in each country. They are acknowledged in the three country reports.

References

Aylward, B. and Freedman, S., 1992, Ecotourism. In *Global biodiversity*, B. Groombridge, ed., pp. 413–441, Chapman and Hall, London

Budowski, G., 1976, Tourism and conservation: conflict, coexistence or symbiosis? *Environmental Conservation*, **3**(1): 27–31

Butler, R.W., 1992, Alternative tourism: the thin end of the wedge. In *Tourism alternatives: potentials and problems in the development of tourism*, V. Smith and W. Eadington, eds, John Wiley, Chichester

Cater, E., 1993, Ecotourism in the Third World: problems for sustainable development. *Tourism Management*, **24** (2): 85–90

Davies, R., 1998, Managing business partnerships. In *Tools for mobilising the public sector, business and civil society as partners in development*, R. Tennyson, ed., pp. 3–6, Prince of Wales Business Leaders Forum, London

Deloitte & Touche, 1999, *Summary of a report on tourism and poverty elimination: untapped potential*, International Institute for Environment and Development and Overseas Development Institute, DFID, London

Din, K.H., 1997, Tourism development: still in search of a more equitable mode of local involvement. In *Tourism development, environmental and community issues*, C. Cooper and S. Wanhill, eds, pp. 153–162, John Wiley, Chichester

Goodwin, H., 1996, In pursuit of ecotourism. *Biodiversity and Conservation* **5** (3): 277–292

Goodwin, H., 1998, Sustainable tourism and poverty elimination: a discussion Paper for DFID/DETR Workshop on Sustainable Tourism and Poverty, 13 October 1998, London (unpublished)

Goodwin, H., Kent, I., Parker, K. and Walpole, M., 1997a, *The Tourism Conservation and Sustainable Development Report Volume I: Comparative report*, DFID, London

Goodwin, H., Kent, I., Parker, K. and Walpole, M., 1997b, *The Tourism Conservation and Sustainable Development Report Volume II: Keoladeo National Park, India*, DFID, London

Goodwin, H., Kent, I., Parker, K. and Walpole, M., 1997c, *The Tourism Conservation and Sustainable Development Report Volume III: Komodo National Park, Indonesia*, DFID, London

Goodwin, H., Kent, I., Parker, K. and Walpole, M., 1997d, *The Tourism Conservation and Sustainable Development Report Volume IV: The Southeast Lowveld, Zimbabwe*, DFID, London

Goodwin, H., Kent, I., Parker, K. and Walpole, M., 1998, *Tourism, conservation and sustainable development: case studies from Asia and Africa*, International Institute for Environment and Development, London

Gonsalves, P.S., 1987, Alternative tourism – the evolution of a concept and establishment of a network. *Tourism Recreation Research*, **12** (2): 9–12

Kemp, E., 1993, *The law of the mother: protecting indigenous people in protected areas*. Sierra Club Books, San Francisco

McNeely, J.A., 1993, Diverse nature, diverse cultures. *People and the Planet*, **2**(3): 11–13

McNeely, J.A., 1994, Protected areas for the 21st century: working to provide benefits to society. *Biodiversity and Conservation*, **3**: 390–405

Myers, N., 1972, National parks in savannah Africa. *Science* **178**: 1255–1263

Philips, A., 1985, *Tourism, recreation and conservation in national parks and equivalent reserves*, Peak Park Joint Planning Board, Derbyshire

Smith, V.L. and Eadington, W.R., 1992, *Tourism alternatives: potentials and problems in the development of tourism*, John Wiley, Chichester

Valentine, P.S., 1992, Nature-based tourism. In *Special interest tourism*, B Weiler and C.M. Hall, eds, pp. 105–127, Belhaven, London

World Commission on Environment and Development (WCED), 1987, *Our common future*, Oxford University Press, Oxford

16 Tourism and international parks

DALLEN J. TIMOTHY

Introduction

The aim of this chapter is to review the nature of international parks, and their role with respect to tourism, and to examine some of the challenges that face their designation and management. National parks and nature reserves have been protecting valued landscapes around the world since the 1800s. As an extension of this, a movement began early in the twentieth century in Europe and North America to establish international parks where protected areas meet on opposite sides of political boundaries. The idea was to bring governments and peoples together to cooperate in preserving ecosystems that straddle political lines. This movement has been praised by world leaders and environmental advocacy groups, but experience has revealed how difficult such an endeavour can be when international boundaries are involved and cross-national partnerships are required (see Marsh, Chapter 9).

International boundaries have traditionally acted as barriers to communication and interaction because their primary functions have been military defence or filters against people and goods arriving and departing. Recent improvements in international relations, however, have resulted in fewer protective measures being levied at national frontiers, and borders are now viewed in many parts of the world as places where people come together, not where they should be kept apart (Minghi, 1991). While this change has opened the way for better communications between administrators and more freedom for individuals in terms of travel, it is still difficult to incite enthusiasm among nations to cooperate on issues of conservation and even tourism.

Borderlands are becoming, or at least finally acknowledged as, important tourist destinations (Timothy, 1995b; Butler, 1996). International parks are one of the most prominent tourist attractions in border regions, and as such, by their very nature require some degree of cross-border coordination, which is necessary for sustainable transfrontier management. The following section describes the relationships between sustainability, resources, and cross-frontier partnership. The rest of the chapter examines the development of, and tourism within, international parks and the economic, political, and cultural challenges facing conservationists and decision makers in cross-national parklands.

Cross-border partnership, resources, and sustainability

In their discussion of sustainability, scholars have emphasised a form of tourism development and planning that advocates the long-term integrity of natural and cultural resources so that they will be maintained for continuous future use (Butler, 1999; Mowforth and Munt, 1998). Several principles, or goals, of sustainable tourism development have been identified by various scholars and organisations. In the natural environmental context these include preservation of ecological processes and protection of biodiversity. The human element has also come to the forefront of this debate as development principles, such as community involvement, cultural integrity, holistic planning, harmony, balance, integration, efficiency, and equity, have been promoted by tourism development scholars (Bramwell and Lane, 1993; Wall, 1993; Hall and Lew, 1998; Milne, 1998; Murphy, 1998).

Partnership in regional tourism planning is important regardless of its geographical context. Coordinated efforts between government agencies, different levels of administration, and the private and public sectors contribute to a better balance in resource use, infrastructure development, human resource management, and promotional efforts. However, in regions where natural and cultural resources lie across, or adjacent to, international boundaries, cross-border joint efforts are necessary if the principles of sustainability listed above are to be upheld and put into action. Natural ecosystems, and in many cases, cultural areas, are not confined within human-created boundaries. When this occurs, coordination between nations becomes particularly important (Timothy, 1998), although several border-related difficulties create obstacles to this type of interaction. These challenges will be discussed later.

There is a significant and growing literature on the methods and benefits of cross-border partnerships in regional planning and resource management (e.g. Dupuy, 1982; Hansen, 1983; Briner, 1986; Scott, 1993; Sweedler, 1994; Church and Reid, 1995). A newer, but just as important, line of research is now focusing on cross-frontier cooperation in tourism planning and development (Boyd, 1999; Leimgruber, 1998; Timothy, 1998, 2000; Wachowiak, 1994). Some writers, however, have pointed out that cross-national partnership may have negative effects, including political opportunism, reinforcement of existing power structures, harmful competition and rivalries between local authorities, and the bureaucratization of partnership processes (Church and Reid, 1996; Scott, 1998). Nevertheless, the potential benefits that might accrue from such cross-border partnerships are manifold. While the development and planning literature differentiate between cooperation and collaboration, collaboration being more integrated than cooperation (Timothy, 1999), the terms are used interchangeably throughout this chapter.

Since many cultural and natural resources are not bound by political lines, most conservation problems cannot be solved without the joint involvement of administrators in neighbouring countries. Cross-border cooperation in ecosystems management can help facilitate the standardisation of conservation controls on both sides of a border. This has the potential to offer protection of migratory species, water bodies, and scenic landscapes that cross boundaries. It also reduces the risk of fire and air pollution and allows fuller and easier enjoyment of recreational experiences (McNeil, 1990, p. 27). Cross-border collaboration also reduces the over-exploitation of resources on one side of a border – something that all too commonly results in severe conservancy problems in neighbouring regions (Ingram *et al.*, 1994). This action promotes the conservation, balance, harmony, integration, and equity principles inherent within sustainable development and allows for ecosystems to be managed holistically.

Another benefit of cross-border cooperation is a decrease in the costly and needless duplication of facilities and services, such as airports and hotels. Gradus (1994) remarked about this problem along the Israeli–Jordanian border where airports, highways, and utility services are replicated on opposite sides of the border only metres apart. Open accessibility could be improved with shared infrastructure development (Tenhiälä, 1994; Wachowiak, 1994). Transportation standards might also be maintained better with the internationalisation of infrastructure development, and communities and tourists on both sides of the border could utilise facilities and services on the opposite side, thereby producing an interdependent relationship. By working together on matters of infrastructure both parties can create similar conditions that will appeal to visitors and contribute to a sense of harmony and integration, as well as provide opportunities for a more efficient tourism system.

Marketing and promotion also benefit from cross-national collaboration (Wachowiak, 1994). With the publication and distribution of joint promotional materials, as well as concerted efforts in marketing research and planning, budgets on both sides of a border can be decreased and the differences spent on other important aspects of management such as conservation and infrastructure development (Timothy, 1999). Since broadcast media spill across national frontiers, more collaborative efforts to promote common destinations would increase efficiency and reach a larger and more diverse market (Clark, 1994).

Tolerance and understanding between administrative personnel and entrepreneurs might also be helped by joint endeavours (Tenhiälä, 1994). This is necessary to prevent disputes about concurrent national uses of internationally shared resources. According to Schrijver (1993, p. 28), international law declares that states are 'under an obligation to utilise resources equitably, which implies that the state should utilise its resources and environment in such a way that other states can utilise theirs in the same way'. Management systems that allow cross-border administration can also be created, which would allow a more holistic approach to be followed. This could be instrumental in bridging the political, cultural, and social gaps between officials on both sides.

International parks

In many border regions where natural and cultural heritage is worthy of conservation, international parks have been established. Figure 16.1 illustrates the widespread establishment of cross-national parks on every continent where international land boundaries exist. Most of the parks have been designated international by virtue of the fact that two national parks or other protected areas meet at an international boundary. For these parks to be sustainable, transfrontier cooperative efforts are vital.

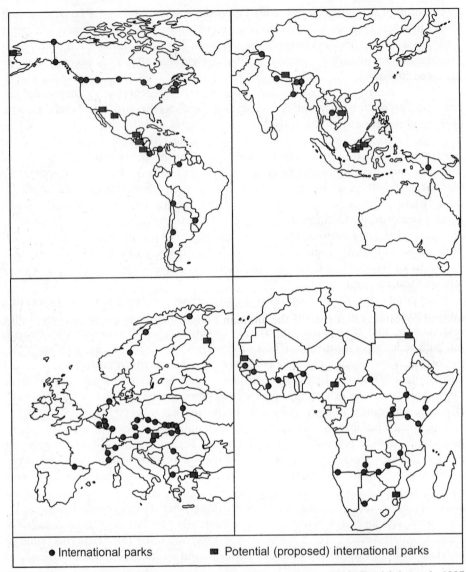

Figure 16.1. Locations of international parks. (Sources: Bonn, 1998; Denisiuk *et al.*, 1997; MacKinnon, 1993; Parent, 1990; Steffens, 1994; Systra, 1994; Thorsell and Harrison, 1990; Weingrod, 1994; Young and Rabb, 1992)

Czechoslovakia and Poland initiated the concept of international cooperation for the development of borderland parks. In 1925, the two countries signed the Krakow Protocol, which opened the way for the establishment of three international parks between 1948 and 1967. Among the earliest areas of cooperation between the six park managers were tourism and conservation research (Thorsell and Harrison, 1990, p. 6). In another early move (1932), legislative action on both sides of the USA–Canada border established Waterton-Glacier International Peace Park (IPP). This act of goodwill connected Waterton Lakes National Park, Canada (established

1895), to Glacier National Park, USA (established 1910). The primary aims of this union were to promote peace between neighbours and to conserve the natural environment on both sides of the border. In 1995, Waterton-Glacier International Peace Park was designated a UNESCO World Heritage Site. The summer of 1932 was an important time in the development of international parks, especially in North America. Only four weeks after the formation of Waterton-Glacier IPP, the International Peace Garden, also on the USA–Canada border in the province of Manitoba and the state of North Dakota, was established. Several additional borderland parks were paired during the 1960s, 1970s and 1980s in various parts of the world, and some were established in Central and Eastern Europe as recently as the 1990s (Thorsell and Harrison, 1990; Denisiuk *et al.*, 1997).

International borderlands seem to be ideal locations for national parks and other protected areas because their attributes are usually highly conducive to the establishment of nature reserves. Constituting the national periphery, except for a few notable cases like Canada, frontier regions are commonly remote and sparsely populated, and a general lack of government development typically renders them disadvantaged economically and relatively undisturbed. In the case of Eastern Europe, the old frontier zones associated with the 'iron curtain' contain some of Europe's most fascinating natural scenery and wildlife (Young and Rabb, 1992). The political conditions that created the 'no man's lands' that were established along the East–West divide and between the former socialist countries also created zones of untouched vegetation and wildlife habitats. Many of Central and Eastern Europe's national parks, for example, are located along national frontiers (Denisiuk *et al.*, 1997).

Westing (1993, p. 7) argues that at least several hundred of the nearly 7000 protected natural areas that existed in the mid–1990s are either adjacent to, or very near, national boundaries. Thorsell and Harrison (1990) identified 70 locations throughout the world where parks and other protected landscapes meet at international frontiers, and additional sites have been identified since then (see Table 16.1). Some of these bi- and tri-national reserves have been established in name as international parks through legislative action, and others are classified as international simply because they meet at an international boundary. While many international parks exist in name in a variety of places, few are governed by genuine jointly managed transborder entities as true cross-border parks. In this sense, even Waterton-Glacier, which is often cited as the prime example of this phenomenon (Lieff and Lusk, 1990), is not truly an international park. While the 1932 designation did link the two existing parks together symbolically, each maintains its individuality, is managed separately, and each country retains full sovereignty over its section (Scace, 1978; Lieff and Lusk, 1990).

Hundreds of other nature reserves lie adjacent to political boundaries but do not have protected counterparts on the other side. In some cases, neighbouring landscapes have been irreversibly modified by human actions either through habitation itself or by a purposeful deletion of natural resources in uninhabited regions. In these instances, the creation of binational nature reserves becomes difficult in ecological, political, and socio-cultural terms. However, as international relations have improved and as the global conservation movement has increased in strength, additional locations have been identified as potential cross-border parks by

Table 16.1   Existing international parks

Name of park(s)	Location	Name of park(s)	Location
The Americas			
Arctic-N. Yukon	USA–Canada	Amistad Intl. Park	Costa Rica–Panama
Kluane-St. Elias	Canada–USA	Los Katios-Darien	Colombia–Panama
Peace Arch Park	USA–Canada	Neblina	Venezuela–Brazil
Saget/Cascade-N. Cascade	Canada–USA	Sajama-Lauca	Bolivia–Chile
Waterton-Glacier	Canada–USA	Iguazu	Argentina–Brazil
Intl. Peace Garden	USA–Canada	Puyehue/Rosales-Lanin	Chile–Argentina
Quetico-Boundary Waters	Canada–USA	Los Glaciares-Bernado O'Higgins	Argentina–Chile
Roosevelt Campobello	Canada–USA		
Niagara Falls	Canada–USA		
Asia			
Khunjerab-Taxkorgan	Pakistan–China	Sundarbans	India–Bangladesh
Royal Chitwan-Udaipur	Nepal–India	Yot Dom-Preah Vihear	Thailand–Cambodia
Barnadi-Shumar	India–Bhutan	Samunsam-Hutan Sambas	Malaysia–Indonesia
Manas	Bhutan–India	Wasur-Tindu WMA	Indonesia–Papua NG
Africa			
Saloum	Senegal–The Gambia	Masaai Mara-Serengeti	Kenya–Tanzania
Bardiar-Niokola Koba	Guinea–Senegal	Virunga-Queen Elizabeth	DR Congo–Uganda
Mont Nimba	Côte d'Ivoire–Guinea	Volcanoes-Gorilla	Rwanda–Uganda
Comoé-Komoé Leraba	Burkina Faso–Côte d'Ivoire	Nyika	Malawi–Zambia
Pendjari-Arly	Benin–Burkina Faso	Lower Zambezi-Mana	Zambia–Zimbabwe
Parc 'W'	Niger–Benin–Burk. Faso	Victoria Falls-Mosi Tunya	Zimbabwe–Zambia
Radom-Yata Ngaya	Sudan–Cent. Afr. Rep.	Gemsbok Kalahari Gemsb.	South Africa–Botswana
Kidepo	Uganda–Sudan	Luiana-Caprivi	Angola–Namibia
Boni-Lag Bagdana	Kenya–Somalia	Luiana-Sioma Ngwezi	Angola–Namibia
Mkomazi/Umba-Tsavo	Tanzania–Kenya	Skeleton Coast-Iona	Namibia–Angola
Europe			
Anarjokka-Lemmenjoki	Norway–Finland	Sumava-Bayerischerwald	Czech Rep.–Germany
Stora Sjöfallet-Rago	Sweden–Norway	Sachsiche Schweiz	Germany–Czech Rep.
Femundsmarka-Rogen	Norway–Sweden	Karkonoski-Krkonose	Poland–Czech Rep.
Waddensee	Germany–Neth.–Denmark	Stowowe Mountains	Czech Rep.–Poland
Fagnes Eifel-Nordeifel	Belgium–Germany	Tatra Mountains	Slovakia–Poland
Germano–Lux. Nature Park	Germany–Luxembourg	Babia Góra	Poland–Slovakia
Belgian–Lux. Nature Park	Belgium–Luxembourg	Pieninski	Slovakia–Poland
Pfälzerwald-Vosages du Nord	Germany–France	Magura	Poland–Slovakia
		Bieszczady	Poland–Ukr.–Slovakia
Berchtesgaden-Hochkönig	Germany–Austria	Aggtelek-Slovak Karst	Hungary–Slovakia
Unterer Inn	Austria–Germany	Lake Ferto-Neusiedlersee	Hungary–Austria
Stelvio-Swiss	Italy–Switzerland	Djerap-Cazanele	Yugoslavia–Romania
Vanoise-Gran Parasido	France–Italy	Mikra Prespa-Galicia	Greece–Macedonia
Argentera-Mercantour	Italy–France	Belovezhskaya-Bialowieza	Belarus–Poland
Ordessa-Pyrenées Occid.	Spain–France		

Sources: Denisiuk *et al.* (1997); Thorsell and Harrison (1990); Timothy (1999a)

Table 16.2 Examples of Potential (proposed) international parks

Name of park(s)	Location	Name of park(s)	Location
The Americas			
Bering Straits (Beringia)	USA–Russia	La Ruta Maya	Mexico–Belize–Guatemala
Gulf of Maine Atlantic	Canada–USA	La Fraternidad	Guat.–Hont.–El Salvador
Big Bend-Sierra del Carmen	Mexico–USA	Intl. Protected	Nicaragua–Costa Rica
		Area for Peace	
Organ Pipe Cactus-proposed sites	USA–Mexico		
Asia			
Sagarmatha-proposed site	Nepal–China	Pulong Tau-Sungai Kayan	Malaysia–Indonesia
Kouprey protection area	Laos–Vietnam–Cambodia	Gunung Bentang-Lanjak Entim	Indonesia–Malaysia
Kayan Mentarang-Pulong Tai	Indonesia–Malaysia		
Africa			
Djoudj-Diaouling	Senegal–Mauritania	Oban-Korup	Nigeria–Cameroon
Elba Mountains	Egypt–Sudan	Kruger-proposed site	South Africa–Mozambique
Europe			
Evros River Peace Park	Greece–Turkey	Danube	Austria–Hungary–Slovakia
Paanajärvi-proposed site	Russia–Finland		

Sources: Bonn (1998); Denisiuk *et al.*, (1997); MacKinnon (1993); Steffens (1994); Systra (1994); Thorsell and Harrison (1990); Young and Rabb (1992)

governments and other interest groups. In several locations, discussions and negotiations have begun and in more advanced cases, legislative action has already been initiated on one or both sides of the border. Some of these sites are illustrated in Figure 16.1 and Table 16.2.

Talks are under way to establish a tri-nation nature reserve on the borders of Cambodia, Vietnam, (Cresswell and Maclaren, Chapter 17) and Laos. Several endangered animal species are indigenous to the area, and all three countries agree that their protection is warranted. Tourism is viewed as being a positive result of the designation on the Vietnam and Laos sides of the border, but guerrilla warfare is still a real danger in the proposed Cambodian sections of the park (MacKinnon, 1993). Ambitious efforts are still in progress along the Danube River at the point where Austria, Hungary, and Slovakia meet. A remarkable floodplain ecosystem at this location includes dozens of islands, oxbow lakes, fragile forests, and pristine wetlands. Environmentalists in all three countries are pushing hard for widespread public acceptance of this proposed tri-national park (Young and Rabb, 1992). Similar actions are stirring along the USA–Mexico border where American and Mexican officials in the early 1990s attempted to come to an agreement on a jointly managed international park along the Rio Grande River. Officials at Big Bend National Park (USA), which is already a major tourist destination in Texas, desire that park to be linked to a corresponding national park on the Mexican side, which has yet to be formed. The ultimate goal is to enact a symbolic link between the two sides, in much the same way that Waterton and Glacier are linked. However, in this case, it is hoped that a joint management council will evolve eventually. Such a council would create a forum to solve common problems, communicate each park's concerns and plans to each other, and initiate joint programmes. The Mexican government has tentative plans to preserve nearly half a million hectares of mountainous land adjacent to Big Bend National Park for this purpose (Parent, 1990; Steffens, 1994).

Perhaps one of the most ambitious endeavours is a proposed Bering Strait international park (Beringia) between the USA and Russia. This effort began in 1987 as discussions between Soviet and US officials opened up the possibility of a jointly operated natural and cultural park spanning the 128-kilometre distance between the two countries across the Bering Strait (Brown, 1988). In recognition of the region's common human cultures and unhindered flow of wild plants and animals, the goal of the dialogue is to create an international heritage park that will protect Beringia's land and wildlife and at the same time accommodate the cultural life of its native peoples (Graham, 1991, p. 44). In June 1990, Presidents Bush and Gorbachev endorsed an agreement that would allow the establishment of the Beringian Heritage International Park. Although, with the dissolution of the former Soviet Union in 1991, much government attention in Russia has been diverted away from the project towards more pressing economic concerns. Nonetheless, the project has not fallen by the wayside, and proponents, particularly in the US National Park Service, are pushing the idea forward. Several other such potential international parks are under consideration in the Americas, Asia, Africa, and Europe (Figure 16.1).

Types of international parks

Three types of international parks have been identified by Timothy (1999) based on their spatial relationship to the international boundary and their management structures (Figure 16.2). The first type includes parks that lie directly on the borderline itself and usually function as one entity. As mentioned earlier, few examples of this type exist anywhere in the world. The International Peace Garden on the USA–Canada boundary is perhaps the best example of this, and according to

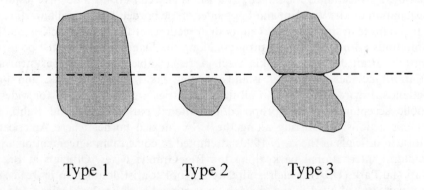

Type 1   Type 2   Type 3

Figure 16.2.   Three spatial types of international parks

Thorsell and Harrison (1990), the 'W' Park in Benin, Burkina Faso, and Niger was approaching this status in the early 1990s as proposals were under way to establish a single tri-national authority to manage the park and to raise funds for its operation. The International Peace Garden is privately owned and operated as a single and complete entity by International Peace Garden Incorporated (IPG Inc.), which is comprised of a 20-member board of directors and whose membership is divided equally between Canadians and Americans. Management and general operations are headed by the park's executive director, who delegates responsibilities over various park matters (e.g. personnel, grounds maintenance, publicity) to six committees composed of board members and hired staff. Ownership of the US lands is held by the state of North Dakota in trust for the express use of IPG Inc. On the Canadian side, lands were allocated from Manitoba's Turtle Mountain Forest Reserve in trust for the express use of IPG Inc. as well. Funding comes from the federal government of Canada (but not from the USA), various state and provincial government sources on both sides, gate receipts, camping fees, concessions, and building rentals. The park is loosely affiliated with the US National Park Service in the sense that it does receive assistance in management plan formulation and other administrative support. It is not affiliated with Parks Canada (Timothy, 1999).

The second type includes parks that lie entirely in only one country but are adjacent to the border, and these can also be classified as international in some rare instances, such as when they are jointly managed or financed by both adjacent countries. Roosevelt Campobello International Park (RCIP) is a good example, and one of the few, of the second type. RCIP was established in 1964 by treaty between Canada and the USA as a memorial to US President Franklin D. Roosevelt, who was a key player in both countries' twentieth-century histories and who spent many summers at the Roosevelt family vacation home on Campobello Island, New Brunswick. Although the park lies entirely within Canada, adjacent to the US border, both countries are equal partners in its management and operations (Roosevelt Campobello International Park Commission, nd). The park is owned by the RCIP Commission, which received the Roosevelt property as a gift from its owners in 1964. The Commission is composed of three Canadian representatives, three American representatives and three alternates from each country. The chair of the Commission alternates every two years between Canadian and US representatives. To assist the executive secretary, who oversees everyday operations, eight subcommittees have been formed among members of the Commission to address various management needs, such as finance, restoration, marketing, natural areas, and handicap accessibility. Unlike the International Peace Garden situation, funding for the RCIP is derived almost entirely from the two federal governments on an equal, on-par basis. Like the International Peace Garden, the RCIP is not part of the US National Park system but is loosely affiliated with the agency in administrative terms for planning assistance (Timothy, 1999).

The third type of international park is where two contiguous protected areas lie adjacent to each other on opposite sides of the border but function as individual and separate entities. With the exception of the few examples mentioned above, nearly all the remaining transnational parks throughout the world fall into this category. Waterton-Glacier is an excellent example of this type of international entity. As mentioned earlier, Waterton Lakes National Park and Glacier National

Park are owned and managed separately under the jurisdiction of each nation's park service. This has resulted in two management systems working side by side along an international frontier. In the USA, the park is managed by a superintendent who relies on four sub-committees to assist in daily matters. The superintendent of the Canadian park is assisted by five sub-committees. The place of Waterton Lakes in the Canadian national parks system is much more complex than that of Glacier, which lies under the indirect supervision of the US Department of the Interior (Timothy, 1999). No common commission exists to manage operations within Waterton-Glacier, although several informal, local arrangements have been made for cooperation between the two sides in matters of joint firefighting, search and rescue operations, and constant communications about public safety warnings, weather conditions, and trail closures (Lieff and Lusk, 1990). There is no cross-border funding for park operations at Waterton-Glacier.

Timothy's (1999) study shows that the more integrated the two sides of an international park are in relation to the border, the higher the level of cooperation will be. Parks in category one above are most likely to experience the greatest degree of cross-border cooperation at a national level as well as at a local level. Parks in the second category tend to be more often affiliated with national-level cooperation with few local initiatives, owing to the fact that the park lies entirely within one country. Parks in category three experience few national-level joint efforts. Rather, most coordination between the two sides is informal and based on park-level memorandums of understanding.

Another useful way of classifying international parks is by the type of heritage they are mandated to protect – natural, cultural, or both. In addition to areas of natural value, cultural heritage conservation areas also exist, or are being planned, in borderlands, and many are classified as international parks. For example, a master plan for the Jordan River valley has been drafted and includes provisions for a transboundary cultural heritage park between Israel and Jordan (Lippman, 1994). Similar arrangements have already been operationalised along the USA–Mexico border where the Los Caminos del Rio binational heritage trail winds back and forth across the boundary (Sánchez, 1994). Likewise, the Chamizal National Memorial (USA) lies adjacent to the Chamizal Federal Park in Mexico. Both sides commemorate the 1963 peaceful resolution of a boundary dispute between the two countries, and one proposal suggests linking the two sections under the name of Chamizal International Peace Park (National Park Service, 1986).

Though it may at first appear to be easy to categorise parks into natural and cultural preserves, the distinction between the two is not always clear. For example, while the primary purpose of the Roosevelt Campobello International Park is to protect the historic buildings and material culture associated with the Roosevelt family on Campobello Island, the park's natural areas have become a nature reserve and the job of managers has come to include preserving the natural environment in the same relatively pristine state that existed when the Roosevelts vacationed on the island. Other binational parks exist whose primary function is to conserve element(s) of the cultural heritage, while the natural setting is of secondary importance. The Chamizal Monument-Park mentioned earlier is a good example of this. Furthermore, several of the parks listed on Table 16.1 were formed primarily as nature preserves but have since taken on a secondary role to protect the cultural environment as well.

Ownership also provides another way of viewing international parks. Although the vast majority of binational protected areas are comprised of nationally owned lands, some international parks have been established by lower-level authorities (Odegaard, 1990), such as states or provinces (e.g. Peace Arch Park), for precisely the same reasons that national-level parks are metaphorically fused with their cross-border counterparts: conservation of nature and culture, and to commemorate international goodwill and cooperation. Much less common is private or semi-private ownership, such as the International Peace Garden and Roosevelt Campobello. These are sometimes referred to as quasi-public because they are not publicly owned, but not entirely private either, owing to their dependence on government administrative and financial assistance.

Tourism in international parks

National parks represent one of the most important types of tourist destination in the world. Most experienced travellers are aware of the American canyonlands, the African game parks, and the European mountain preserves. Likewise, by extension, international parks have become important global destinations, such as Waterton-Glacier, Iguazu Falls, and Masaai Mara-Serengeti, which attract millions of tourists from around the world. Other lesser-known international parks feature more prominently as destinations for domestic tourists and foreign visitors from countries within the region or as ancillary attractions for global tourists who are already in that area for other purposes. This second type is most common among the parks listed in Table 16.1. It is likely that difficult access, often caused by their specific locations on political and natural frontiers, is a major factor in most international parks being considered secondary attractions.

Table 16.3 demonstrates annual visitor numbers at three international parks in North America. Waterton-Glacier International Peace Park is one of the most important tourist destinations in the USA and Canadian mountain west, drawing approximately 2 million tourists to the American side and nearly 400 000 to the Canadian side every year. Visitors to this park come from all over the world, and many consider it to be their primary destination (Lieff and Lusk, 1990; Parks Canada, 1996). On a more regional level, more than 200 000 people visit the International Peace Garden each year primarily from the American mid-west and the Canadian prairies, although international visitation from further afield is significant (Mayes, 1992). The Garden is particularly popular with youth for its music and athletic camps, which attract hundreds of young people from around the world every summer. Annual visitor numbers at Roosevelt Campobello range from 110 000 to 150 000, which is a significant count given that the park is only open 20 weeks per year from May to October. Most visitors are from the eastern United States and Canada, although travellers from other parts of North America and overseas are part of the market base as well. Visitors from far afield generally visit as part of a group tour in conjunction with other destinations in the region (Roosevelt Campobello International Park Commission, nd).

Table 16.3 Tourist numbers at three international parks

Year	Number of tourists	Year	Number of tourists

Waterton-Glacier International Peace Park[a]

	Waterton		Glacier
1985	N/A[b]	1985	1 580 620
1986	N/A	1986	1 579 191
1987	N/A	1987	1 660 737
1988	N/A	1988	1 817 733
1989	338 157	1989	1 821 523
1990	353 908	1990	1 987 000
1991	344 028	1991	2 096 966
1992	345 662	1992	2 199 767
1993	344 453	1993	2 141 704
1994	389 510	1994	2 152 989
1995	364 740	1995	1 839 518
1996	346 574	1996	1 720 576
1997	370 733	1997	1 708 877

International Peace Garden

1985	177 300	1992	209 345
1986	183 600	1993	215 625
1987	187 400	1994	222 093
1988	186 000	1995	218 036
1989	191 580	1996	211 495
1990	197 327	1997	205 151
1991	203 247		

Roosevelt Campobello International Park

1985	131 477	1992	138 950
1986	148 678	1993	135 842
1987	153 939	1994	132 551
1988	160 369	1995	122 682
1989	162 881	1996	111 431
1990	144 678	1997	121 530
1991	151 327		

[a] Each park enumerates visitors separately and some people are counted twice since they visit both sides of the park
[b] Prior to 1989, a different counting system was used in Waterton National Park

Sources: Personal Communication with superintendants at Waterton Lakes National Park, Glacier National Park, International Peace Garden and Roosevelt Campobello International Park

If relations are good between the countries in which an international park is located, crossings by tourists from one side to the other can usually be done with relative ease. Since the designation of an international park usually requires some measure of benevolence between neighbours, in the majority of cases tourists are permitted to enter both sections of a park. This possibility brings potential economic benefits to both sides of the border and allows tourists to view the protected area in its entirety. For some tourists, viewing the attraction from both sides of the border, and even seeing the border itself, can be a highlight of the visit (Timothy, 1995b). This is apparently the case at Waterton-Glacier where, according to a study by Parks Canada (1996), approximately half of the visitors to the Canadian park also visited the American park on the same trip. In most cases crossing a frontier requires formalities to be followed, but in some parks, passage across the border can go unhindered and unregulated (e.g. Peace Arch Park and the International Peace Garden).

Challenges

Although extensive partnership efforts have been successful in creating cross-border parks, their creation and continued management are not without problems. International parks confront the same types of challenges that most protected areas face, including law enforcement, funding, research, staff training, as well as the effects of destructive agricultural practices, illegal hunting (see Dearden, Chapter 12), and the depletion of forests and other natural resources. However, their location at international boundaries creates a range of unique obstacles that are typically not encountered by most other parks and protected areas.

Cultural and political differences

Cultural and value differences on opposite sides of a border can create chasms between neighbours that are difficult to bridge. This depends, however, on the degree of difference and the willingness of each side to work at cooperation. These efforts are much easier when symmetrical interests and values are present on both sides of a border (Blatter, 1997). In some instances language barriers can be so great that joint efforts become difficult or curtailed altogether (Saint-Germain, 1995).

Differences in administrative practices and organisation also have the potential to create insurmountable constraints to international partnership. Realising common goals in borderland parks is difficult when agencies in each country, whose responsibilities include environmental protection and/or tourism development, have contrasting mandates and opposing views of natural resources. For example, park and forest management agencies in the USA and Canada have traditionally been at odds with each other. In the USA, 'the Park Service strives to preserve the natural environment while allowing recreational activities, and the Forest Service seeks to balance multiple uses of the land with recreation. In [Canada], the agencies are more polarised. While the Ministry of Parks functions much like the U.S. Park Service, the Forest Ministry operates solely for the purpose of resource extraction' (Weingrod,

1994, p. 29). (*Editors' note*: there is no Ministry of Parks in Canada. Canadian national parks are administered by Parks Canada, which is within the Federal Heritage Canada Ministry.)

Problems also arise when different levels of government that are responsible for various aspects of planning and conservation meet at international frontiers. In Mexico, parks and preserves are ordinarily administered by states instead of the national government, and the US borderlands are administered by states and federal agencies that do not always agree. The Fish and Wildlife Service, Bureau of Land Management, the National Parks Service, Bureau of Reclamation, Customs, and the Immigration and Naturalization Service, as well as the Mexican states of Sonora, Chihuahua, and Coahuila all have an interest in what occurs along the border (Steffens, 1994, p. 36).

Political traditions in most areas have dictated that all levels of international negotiations are the rights and responsibilities of central governments (Gaines, 1995). This has produced a situation wherein local authorities have few or no rights to enter into agreements with their cross-border neighbours unless they have received prior authorisation from the central government (Dupuy, 1982; Hansen, 1983). According to Gaines (1995) and Hansen (1983), this is unfortunate because the capacity to implement conservation and tourism policies and programmes usually works best on a local level, even if public authority and adequate resources are largely in control of central governments, because the basis of mutual understanding and trust necessary for transfrontier collaboration at the national level is often very weak (Gaines, 1995, pp. 444–445). In contrast, the relatively close economic and social ties within border communities frequently foster opportunities for cross-border cooperation. This is a particularly important concept in international parks since residents are more likely to be familiar with local natural and cultural environments than are bureaucrats from an often distant and detached national capital.

Sovereignty and territoriality

Countries jealously guard every fraction of national space, and sovereignty is generally viewed as absolute state control of territory. This explains why state boundaries and territory have been at the centre of nearly every war that has been fought throughout history. Many of these conflicts have been started over seemingly diminutive and insignificant areas, some even as small as a few metres or hectares.

Truly integrated international parks, even under friendly conditions, are difficult to achieve because the parties involved know that they will be required to give up some degree of sovereignty in the name of collaboration (Blake, 1994). This means that partial control over a portion of national space will be in the hands of some bilateral body, thereby diminishing absolute territorial sovereignty. Nations do not generally favour being told what to do on their own territory (MacKinnon, 1993, p. 83).

Border formalities and fortifications

As alluded to earlier, immigration and customs restrictions are usually required for travel between sections of an international park. Depending on the degree of strictness in border-crossing requirements, people may not be able, or desire, to visit both sides. This is particularly true if crossing requires a visa or invasive searching procedures. Some people may be deterred from crossing, even when formalities are minimal (Timothy, 1995a). In terms of park functions, customs barriers can avert the free flow of goods between sides. This prevents the standardisation of equipment and products offered for sale to tourists, and immigration restrictions hamper staff exchanges, which are particularly useful for research, interpretation, and building understanding. For example, for many years, customs and other border difficulties plagued relations between Argentera National Park (Italy) and Mercantour National Park (France), both of which had a tradition of cooperation, particularly in terms of scientific research and joint promotion (Rossi, 1990). However, with the abolition of most frontier formalities between members of the European Union, this situation will likely continue to improve.

As this European example demonstrates, border-related issues commonly take priority over conservation needs in frontier regions. National governments appear to be more keen on preventing illegal migration and controlling the inflow of goods than they are on protecting the environment and establishing cooperative relations. Regarding international parks, one American official stated:

> For every agency that wants to encourage the greater flow for [*sic*] wildlife, another agency wants to build 14-foot walls to keep immigrants and drugs out. All of our conservation problems are affected by social problems: drugs, illegal immigration, the language barriers ... If we don't make progress with illegal immigration and drug traffic – which will continue to be difficult to resolve – we won't make progress on conservation issues. We need to be working on all of these issues together (quoted in Steffens, 1994, p. 36)

Border fortifications are a major hindrance to cross-frontier park management. Defensive demarcation methods, such as high fences, walls, and minefields are not conducive to establishing international parks. These barriers not only prevent the flow of people, they bisect ecosystems, thereby altering animal migration and feeding patterns, and they scar the natural landscape. Furthermore, mines and dangerous construction materials (e.g. barbed wire) kill and maim unsuspecting wildlife. Poor international relations usually result in these types of border fortifications, whose primary function is either military defence or to keep undesirable people out and citizens in. In the case of South Africa and Mozambique, the frontier is fortified by an electrified barbed wire fence (Blake, 1993). There is talk now of establishing an international game park between the two countries (Bonn, 1998) where Kruger National Park meets protected lands on the Mozambique side of the border. For these efforts to be successful, the physical nature of the border will certainly have to be altered so that the ecosystem can heal and become a borderless range for wildlife.

Even in borderlands where friendly neighbours meet, methods of boundary demarcation can create difficulties in international park management. Along the USA–Canada border, for example, law and the International Boundary Commission require that the border be clear of all cultural structures and tall vegetation 3 metres wide on either side of the line. This requires the use of clear-cutting and herbicides that keep the 6-metre cleared swathe free of trees and large bushes along the entire boundary. Unfortunately this includes Waterton-Glacier International Peace Park. Conservationists abhor the idea of destroying part of a functioning ecosystem for the sake of marking the limits of national sovereignty. In the words of a former park superintendent on the American side, 'Maintenance of this artificial scar between the two parks is incongruous with the concept of an International Peace Park and hinders the goal of preserving a naturally functioning ecosystem' (quoted in Gilbert, 1996, p. 26).

Differing levels of development

Contrasts on opposite sides of a border are particularly evident when developing country meets a developed country. Different levels of economic development are difficult to balance when it comes to park protection, because in Third World countries it is often difficult in incite enthusiasm for conservation when much of the population is concerned with basic survival (see Cresswell and Maclaren, Chapter 17) (Norton, 1989). International cooperation is made difficult in these instances because most less-developed nations are more concerned with domestic problems, such as unemployment and poverty, than they are with international issues (Timothy, 2000). Imbalances occur when one country has the resources and knowledge to devote to park designation and management but its neighbour does not. As Parent (1990, p. 33) suggests,

> Like Mexico itself, the Mexican park system is still developing. Mexico does not have the resources to staff and manage its parks as intensively as in the United States. Unlike the United States, Mexico cannot give such strong emphasis to environmental preservation. Instead, it must compromise more with economic development for the local people.

Different levels of development sometimes produce varying environmental standards between neighbouring countries. Where pollution is uncontrolled on one side of a border, conservation efforts and tourism development are necessarily influenced on the other side (Steffens, 1994). On the Mexico–USA boundary 'polluted surface runoff, unimpeded by the border, threatens the health of residents on both sides' (Ingram et al., 1994, p. 29). For example, sewage and industrial waste from Tijuana (Mexico) flows directly into the Pacific Ocean and is carried northward with the ocean currents, which contaminates coastal and ground waters south of San Diego (USA). Warning signs have been erected on the beaches by California officials, and the Border Field State Park, which lies adjacent to the Mexican border, is often closed, its beaches unusable for recreational and tourism purposes.

Marginality

Early in the 1960s, Mexico's government invested millions of dollars into the northern frontier zone for economic and infrastructure development, urban renewal, and cultural preservation (Dillman, 1970). Mexico is, however, not the norm in this respect. Frontier zones are usually viewed by decision makers as marginal and unimportant in their modernisation and economic development efforts. Typically, the more populated and industrious interior is favoured. This leads to a lack of administrative support and funding for developing international parks (Blake, 1993; Korona, 1995), even if support exists on the other side. Peripherality also leads to the marginalisation of border residents' concerns during policy development. Thus, it is not surprising that national and state policies are often at odds with border needs and priorities (Ingram *et al.*, 1994, p. 30).

Conclusion

Complete cross-frontier integration in managing international parks is a lofty goal that is rarely achieved. The challenges discussed above create social, economic, and political conditions that prevent total integration in most instances, and often even basic collaboration. Nonetheless, cross-border partnership is essential for such endeavours to succeed, and these efforts are essential for transfrontier protected areas to be sustainable.

Westing (1993) believes that transfrontier reserves improve relations between adjacent countries at both national and local levels. Even when central governments refuse to bend to pressure by altering political will and boundary restrictions, local initiatives between managers and borderland communities can be instrumental in creating a sustainable international park through cross-border cooperation. It is generally at the local level that the best solutions to problems are found and obstacles to international park management overcome.

The purpose of international parks is not simply to protect and manage the environment; all national parks have this as one of, or their primary, goals. Equally important, and what makes international parks unique, is their other primary role – to promote peace and harmony between nations. Tourism, together with resource conservation, has the potential to be the largest peace-promoting movement in human history by building understanding between cultures and peoples (Var and Ap, 1998, p. 44).

McNeil (1990, p. 25) argues that the creation of binational protected areas does not need to wait for peaceful conditions, nor for agreeable partners on both sides of a boundary. Instead, 'these parks can precede, lead to, and result in, as well as help to maintain, peace among nations and communities'. The efforts to develop international parks along the old East–West European borders are viewed by many as earnest attempts not only to conserve a rapidly changing European natural environment, but also to foster reconciliation between two formerly hostile socio-political systems (Young and Rabb, 1992). The new countries that comprised the former Soviet Union do not appear to have inherited many nature reserves, but as Blake (1993, p. 44) suggests, working towards the creation of transnational parks would be valuable in confidence building between states along their new international frontiers.

According to Young and Rabb (1992, p. 37), in terms of parkland management, many people and governments 'now realise that peaceful and sustainable coexistence is possible only if borders cease to be dividers'. As one commentator expressed:

Why not seed the borderlines of the world with peace parks and gardens, nature preserves, and wilderness areas that encourage cultural and physical development of youth, respect for and appreciation of wildlife and irreplaceable landscapes? These border peace parks are precious places where peoples share and where they celebrate what they share: history, culture, beliefs, landscape (MacLeod, 1988, quoted in Lieff and Lusk, 1990, p. 48).

It is clear from the preceding discussion that existing international parks play an important role in peace and conservation efforts globally, and many more potential parks have yet to be established. As the role of political boundaries becomes less of a dividing line and more a line of integration (Minghi, 1991), as in the case of the European Union, it is likely that more international parks will be established because many of the challenges that are unique to them will diminish or vanish altogether.

References

Blake, G.H., 1993, Transfrontier collaboration: a worldwide survey. In *Transfrontier reserves for peace and nature: a contribution to human security*, A.H. Westing, ed., pp. 35–48, United Nations Environment Programme, Nairobi

Blake, G.H., 1994, International transboundary collaborative ventures. In *Political boundaries and coexistence*, W.A. Gallusser, ed., pp. 359–371, Peter Lang, Berne

Blatter, J., 1997, Explaining crossborder cooperation: A border-focused and border-external approach. *Journal of Borderlands Studies* 12(1/2): 151–174

Bonn, C., 1998, Peace parks. *Country Life* 192(47): 72

Boyd, S.W., 1999, North–South divide: the role of the border in tourism to Northern Ireland. *Visions in Leisure and Business*, 17(4): 50–71

Bramwell, B. and Lane, B., 1993, Sustainable tourism: An evolving global approach. *Journal of Sustainable Tourism*, 1(1): 1–5

Briner, H.J., 1986, Regional planning and transfrontier cooperation: the Regio Basiliensis. In *Boundaries: transborder interaction in comparative perspective*, O.J. Martinez, ed., pp. 45–53, University of Texas, Centre for Inter-American and Border Studies, El Paso

Brown, W., 1988, A common border: Soviets and Americans work to create a joint park in the Bering Strait. *National Parks*, 62(11): 18–22

Butler, R.W., 1996, The development of tourism in frontier regions: issues and approaches. In *Frontiers in regional development*, Y. Gradus, H Lithwick, eds, pp. 213–229, Rowman & Littlefield, Lanham, MD

Butler, R.W., 1999, Sustainable tourism: a state-of-the-art review. *Tourism Geographies*, 1(1): 7–25

Church, A. and Reid, P., 1995, Transfrontier co-operation, spatial development strategies and the emergence of a new scale of regulation: the Anglo-French border. *Regional Studies*, 29(3): 297–306

Church, A. and Reid, P., 1996, Urban power, international networks and competition: the example of cross-border cooperation. *Urban Studies*, 33(8): 1297–1318

Clark, T., 1994, National boundaries, border zones, and marketing strategy: A conceptual framework and theoretical model of secondary boundary effects. *Journal of Marketing*, 58: 67–80

Denisiuk, Z., Stoyko, S. and Terray, J., 1997, Experience in cross-border cooperation for national parks and protected areas in Central Europe. In *National parks and protected areas: keystones to conservation and sustainable development*, J.G. Nelson and R. Serafin, eds, pp. 145–150, Springer, Berlin

Dillman, C.D., 1970, Recent developments in Mexico's Northern Border Program. *Professional Geographer*, 22(5): 243–247

Dupuy, P.M., 1982, Legal aspects of transfrontier regional co-operation. *West European Politics*, 5: 50–63

Gaines, S.E., 1995, Bridges to a better environment: building cross-border institutions for environmental improvement in the U.S.–Mexico border area. *Arizona Journal of International and Comparative Law*, **12**(2): 429–471

Gilbert, R., 1996, Growing down a wall: One barrier yet divides Waterton-Glacier International Peace Park. *The Rotarian*, 26–27, March

Gradus, Y., 1994, The Israel–Jordan Rift Valley: A border of cooperation and productive coexistence. In *Political boundaries and coexistence*, W.A. Gallusser, ed., pp. 315–321, Peter Lang, Berne

Graham, F., 1991, U.S. and Soviet environmentalists join forces across the Bering Strait. *Audubon*, **93**(4): 42–61

Hall, C.M. and Lew, A.A., 1998, The geography of sustainable tourism development: an introduction. In *Sustainable tourism: a geographical perspective*, C.M. Hall and A.A. Lew, eds, pp. 1–12, Longman, Harlow

Hansen, N., 1983, International cooperation in border regions: An overview and research agenda. *International Regional Science Review*, **8**(3): 255–270

Ingram, H., Milich, L. and Varady, R.G., 1994, Managing transboundary resources: Lessons from Ambos Nogales. *Environment*, **36**(4): 6–38

Korona, K., 1995, The border should help cooperation, not block it. *International Affairs*, **6**: 92–94

Leiff, B.C. and Lusk, G., 1990, Transfrontier cooperation between Canada and the USA: Waterton-Glacier International Peace Park. In *Parks on the borderline: experience in transfrontier conservation*, J. Thorsell, ed., pp. 39–49, IUCN, Gland

Leimgruber, W.A., 1998, Defying political boundaries: transborder tourism in a regional context. *Visions in Leisure and Business*, **17**(3): 8–29

Lippman, T.W., 1994, Israel, Jordan agree to plan joint ventures. *The Washington Post*, 8 June, 28

MacKinnon, J.R., 1993, An Indochina tri-state reserve: The practical challenges. In *Transfrontier reserves for peace and nature: a contribution to human security*, A.H. Westing, ed., pp. 77–85, UNEP, Nairobi

MacLeod, J., 1988, Peace parks on the borderline: Canada and United States. Paper presented at the International Federation of Landscape Architects World Congress, Boston

Mayes, H.G., 1992, The International Peace Garden: A border of flowers. *The Beaver*, **72**(4): 45–51

McNeil, R.J., 1990, International parks for peace. In *Parks on the borderline: experience in transfrontier conservation*, J. Thorsell, ed, pp. 23–38, IUCN, Gland

Milne, S.S., 1998, Tourism and sustainable development: the global-local nexus. In *Sustainable tourism: a geographical perspective*, C.M. Hall and A.A. Lew, eds, pp. 35–48, Longman, Harlow

Minghi, J.V., 1991, From conflict to harmony in border landscapes. In *The geography of border landscapes*, D. Rumley and J.V. Minghi, eds, pp. 15–30, Routledge, London

Mowforth, M. and Munt, I., 1998, *Tourism and sustainability: new tourism in the Third World*, Routledge, London

Murphy, P.E., 1998, Tourism and sustainable development. In *Global Tourism*, 2nd edition, W.F. Theobald, ed., pp. 173–190, Butterworth-Heinemann, Oxford

National Park Service, 1986, *General management plan, development concept plan: Chamizal National Memorial, Texas*, National Park Service, US Department of the Interior, El Paso

Norton, P., 1989, Archaeological rescue and conservation in the North Andean Area. In *Archaeological heritage management in the modern world*, H. Cleere, ed., pp. 142–145, Unwin Hyman, London

Odegaard, C.H., 1990, Parks for peace. In *Parks on the borderline: experience in transfrontier conservation*, J. Thorsell, ed., pp. 89–93, IUCN, Gland

Parent, L., 1990, Tex-Mex Park. *National Parks*, **64**(7/8): 30–36

Parks Canada, 1996, *1994 Waterton Lakes National Park: exit survey final results*. Parks Canada, Western Region, Calgary

Roosevelt Campobello International Park Commission, nd *Roosevelt Campobello International Park*, RCIPC, Campobello Island, NB

Rossi, P., 1990, Rapport sur la collaboration entre le Parc Naturel de L'Argentera (Italie) et le Parc National du Mercantour (France). In *Parks on the Borderline: Experience in Transfrontier Conservation*, J. Thorsell, ed., pp. 63–71, IUCN, Gland

Saint-Germain, M.A., 1995, Problems and opportunities for cooperation among public managers on the U.S.–Mexico border. *American Review of Public Administration*, **25**(2): 93–117

Sánchez, M., 1994, *A shared experience: the history, architecture and historic designations of the Lower Rio Grande Heritage corridor*, Texas Historical Commission, Austin, TX

Scace, R.C., 1978, *Waterton-Glacier International Peace Park, story line document*. Parks Canada Western Region, Calgary

Schrijver, N.J., 1993, Sovereignty and the sharing of natural resources. In *Transfrontier reserves for peace and nature: a contribution to human security*, A.H. Westing, ed., pp. 21–33, UNEP, Nairobi

Scott, J.W., 1993, The institutionalization of transboundary cooperation in Europe: recent development on the Dutch–German border. *Journal of Borderlands Studies*, **8**(1): 39–66

Scott, J.W., 1998, Planning cooperation and transboundary regionalism: implementing policies for European border regions in the German–Polish context. *Environment and Planning C*, **16**(5): 605–624

Steffens, R., 1994, Bridging the border. *National Parks*, **68**(7/8): 36–41

Sweedler, A., 1994, Conflict and cooperation in border regions: an examination of the Russian–Finnish border. *Journal of Borderlands Studies*, **9**(1): 1–13

Systra, J., 1994, The Paanajärvi National Park: the international dimension. *International Affairs*, **6**: 29–33

Tenhiälä, H., 1994, Cross-border cooperation: key to international ties. *International Affairs*, **6**: 21–23

Thorsell, J. and Harrison, J., 1990, Parks that promote peace: A global inventory of transfrontier nature reserves. In *Parks on the borderline: experience in transfrontier conservation*, J. Thorsell, ed., pp. 3–21, IUCN, Gland

Timothy, D.J., 1995a, International boundaries: New frontiers for tourism research. *Progress in Tourism and Hospitality Research*, **1**(2): 141–152

Timothy, D.J., 1995b, Political boundaries and tourism: Borders as tourist attractions. *Tourism Management*, **16**(7): 525–532

Timothy, D.J., 1998, Cooperative tourism planning in a developing destination. *Journal of Sustainable Tourism*, **6**(1): 52–68

Timothy, D.J., 1999, Cross-border tourism resource management: international parks along the US–Canada border. *Journal of Sustainable Tourism*, **7**: in press

Timothy, D.J., 2000, Tourism planning in Southeast Asia: Bringing down borders through cooperation. In *Tourism in Southeast Asia: opportunities and challenges*, K.S. Chon, ed., The Haworth Press, Binghamton, NY

Var, T. and Ap, J., 1998 Tourism and world peace. In *Global Tourism*, 2nd edition, W.F. Theobald, ed., pp. 44–57, Butterworth-Heinemann, Oxford

Wachowiak, H., 1994, *Grenzüberschreitende Zusammenarbeit im Tourismus: eine Analyse grenzüberschreitende Massnahmen entland der westlichen Staatsgrenze der Bundesrepublik Deutschland zwischen Ems-Dollart und Baden-Nordelsass-Südpfalz*, Europäisches Tourismus Institut, Trier

Wall, G., 1993, Towards a tourism typology. In *Tourism and sustainable development: monitoring, planning, managing*, J.G. Nelson, R.W. Butler and G. Wall, eds, pp. 45–58, Department of Geography, University of Waterloo, Waterloo, ON

Weingrod, C., 1994, Two countries, one wilderness. *National Parks*, **68**(1/2): 26–31

Westing, A.H., 1993, Building confidence with transfrontier reserves: the global potential. In *Transfrontier reserves for peace and nature: a contribution to human society*, A.H. Westing, ed., pp. 1–15, UNEP, Nairobi

Young, L. and Rabb, M., 1992, New park on the bloc. *National Parks*, **66**(1/2): 35–40.

17 Tourism and national parks in emerging tourism countries

C. CRESSWELL AND F. MACLAREN

Introduction

Tourism has been heralded as an economic development nostrum for countries trying to emerge from situations of internal conflict or global economic dislocation. Cambodia and Vietnam are examples of developing countries dealing with issues of political instability and lack of civil order that view tourism as a means of attracting much-needed foreign currency and investment. One form of tourism being promoted is nature-based tourism, which has been defined in the tourism literature as responsible travel to natural places which conserves the environment and sustains the well-being of the local people (Valentine, 1992; Boo, 1990; Mowforth and Munt, 1998), with economic returns acting as incentives to conserve natural areas and their ecological components. Also, nature-based tourism can promote improved ecological planning and management by encouraging a more interdisciplinary and integrated approach.

This chapter examines the conditions and issues affecting the development of national parks in emerging countries, and assesses Cambodia's and Vietnam's particular circumstances in fostering nature-based tourism in national parks. For the purposes here, the term nature-based tourism rather than ecotourism is used, as ecotourism has expanded into many different connotations that imply it being any form of tourism that is 'environmentally friendly' instead of being merely sensitive to the natural environments being visited. Ecotourism, however, will be included in references obtained from outside sources.

An appropriate socio-economic description for emerging nations is the label 'least developed country' (LDC). The term was originally applied by the United Nations in 1971 to describe the poorest and most economically weak of the developing countries, facing economic, institutional and human resources problems, often compounded natural and man-made disasters. The debt of many LDCs is growing and may equal or exceed their gross domestic product, thereby hindering attempts to halt socio-economic decline, reactivate development and set these countries on a path of sustained growth. According to the United Nations, Cambodia is classified as one of thirty-six current LDCs, while Vietnam with its application of home-grown economic renovation policies in 1989, known as *doi moi*, rests just above that group.

'Emerging' in this chapter also refers to those countries which were formerly closed to foreign investors and travellers, or beset by conflict. Cambodia, Laos, Myanmar and Vietnam can hence be considered as 'emerging', while North Korea falters. These countries then choose or are forced to link to the global economy, for trade and foreign currency purposes. Heavily indebted countries must undergo International Monetary Fund Structural Adjustment Programme preconditions, including being integrated into the global economy, deregulating and liberalising their economies, shifting from an agriculture-based economy, and liberalising their financial sector (de Chavez, 1999).

Nature-based tourism

The Pacific Asia Travel Association (PATA) stated that the Pacific Asia region is one of the fastest-growing regions in terms of tourism with an annual average growth rate of 11.3 per cent (PATA, 1995; Cork, 1993; McKay, 1997). Asian countries, however, are handicapped with limited economic bases and institutional resources. In hopes of stimulating economic growth, generating employment and boosting living standards through foreign exchange, many countries are seeking to develop and actively promote tourism.

Travellers are becoming more discerning when choosing their destinations. Tourism sites that are known to be insensitively developed are more likely to be avoided (FNNPE, nd; Cork, 1993). This has stimulated the development of more 'environmentally friendly' specialised forms of tourism such as nature-based tourism. Nature-based tourism is the only industry allowed to develop in many of world's great natural sites. It will only survive if natural resources are protected – thus the industry must contribute to the conservation of the natural resource base. It also requires the support of local people if to survive – local communities must play a role in its development and management and secure a fair share of its benefits.

By providing economic benefit through the diversification of local economies in impoverished areas of growing populations and limited natural resources, nature-based tourism related employment can offer alternatives to current activities, lessening subsistence resource use and land uses that may be explotive (Murphy, 1985; Whelan, 1991; Cork, 1993). There can also, however, be unrealistic economic expectations. If the potential tourism market is small, significant local or governmental investment in tourism development may be unjustified. There are also justifiable fears that new economic globalisation scheme, will further enable transnational corporations to gain access to ecologically sensitive areas and biological resources and accelerate the reduction of biodiversity. As a result, local communities may lose land use and resource rights and the natural environment suffer (Pleumeron, 1999).

The General Agreement on Trade and Services (GATS), signed in Morocco in 1994, established a legal and operational framework for the gradual reduction of barriers in the international trade in services. With regard to tourism, GATS makes it easier for transnational and foreign tour operators and travel agencies to invest in developing countries. This also means that protection of local tourism industries would be construed as unfair practice, and thus eliminated. Tourism revenues from these foreign-owned tour companies would be transmitted to head office overseas, rather than being kept in the local community (de Chavez, 1999).

Nature parks under pressure

Tourism to natural areas in developing countries has been steadily increasing. In rapidly industrialising countries, such as Malaysia and Thailand, a new urban middle-class seeks out natural areas for recreation and refuge from a bustling city life (Le and McNeill, 1995). National parks are indispensable to environmental conservation and can also contribute to sustaining human societies. The World Commission on Environment and Development (WCED, 1987) concluded that the protection of species and ecosystems is a prerequisite to sustainable development.

Tourism to natural areas can result in a number of costs and benefits. Nature-based tourism on its own is not a panacea to the threatened environments of the world or to rural poverty, but it can be one tool for sustainable development (see Boyd, Chapter 11). The potential costs include environmental degradation, erosion of local culture and socio-economic instability. The potential benefits are generation of revenues for protected areas management, environmental education and recreation for tourists, and jobs and community projects for local people (Boo, 1992; Lindberg, and Hawkins, 1993; Mowforth and Munt, 1998).

Nature-based tourism to an unspoilt, pristine wilderness may be 'internally contradictory', because 'in order to generate substantial revenue the number of tourists has to be large. That implies a greater impact on the local culture and the environment, fewer controls and, with more foreign involvement, more foreign currency leakage' (Pleumaron, 1994). This assessment is insightful but tourism to natural areas is inevitable and increasing in volume, therefore, efforts should be made to maximise the potential positive impact of nature-based tourism. From another critical standpoint, nature-based tourism development, particularly with its emphasis on wilderness protection through the creation of parks and reserves, is largely serving the interests of the privileged upper-middle classes, mainly First World tourists and scientists. National parks and tourism conflicts have been argued to include associating conservation with colonialism, with some protected areas secured for the purposes of providing raw materials for the imperial infrastructure, passing control of common lands to the state, and uncertainty whether the actual beneficiaries of national parks are tourists not local inhabitants (Colchester, nd)

In general, much of the local spending by tourists in terms of food, transportation, lodging and park entry fees goes to the central government or politically favoured concessionaires. Much of the inbound tourist spending leaks out to international operators organising tours for adventure seekers. Popular national park destinations often see tourism revenues outstripping their operating budgets. For example, in Khao Yai National Park, Thailand, tourism revenue is estimated at US$5 million, which is one hundred times the operating budget. Little of that amount goes to local people (Wells and Brandon, 1992).

Even if the vast conservation benefits potentially available from nature tourism could be realised, it is important to remember that only a small minority of protected areas attract significant numbers of visitors. The required characteristics of sites to attract large numbers of tourists include spectacular scenery, large mammals, uniqueness, reasonable access and developed infrastructure. The proportion of most countries' protected areas for which large-scale tourism is viable is extremely small (Wells and Brandon, 1992).

National parks and tourism development in Cambodia

Cambodia has undergone a period of civil conflict since the ascension to power of the Khmer Rouge (KR) in 1975. The whole population was indoctrinated into forced labour in the countryside as the Pol Pot-led Khmer Rouge initiated 'Year Zero' in 1975, to build a totally independent agrarian-based nation-state. Pol Pot pushed for agricultural development which led to widespread deforestation. The extreme restriction on food during and after the Pol Pot regime caused people to eat almost anything, including wildlife to supplement their diet (IDRC, 1993). The soldiers who were later involved in the containment of Khmer Rouge forces also relied on wildlife for their diet and the consequent lack of control over hunting led to the rapid decline of Cambodia's wildlife population. The forested areas along the Thai borders provided the first source of income to sustain both guerrilla and government armies, through extensive logging, despite a moratorium on the exporting of timber. Conversely, landmines, civil unrest and banditry have meant that extensive tracts of forest and natural habitats have, in a sense, been protected from development and agricultural encroachment. The KR, despite signing the Paris agreement, continues to control about 5 per cent of the country, mainly along the south-west and north-west borders, and therefore, warlike threats still exist and represent barriers to tourism development.

Current status of tourism development

Emerging from the disruptive events of the past twenty-five years, Cambodia is now undergoing a dynamic transitional period towards a market economy, with an environmental focus on promoting sustainable development. Obstacles to overcome include a shifting governmental structure, a lack of interministerial cooperation, informal decision-making powers and only recently established natural resource use policies and strategies.

Cambodia is considered a new, undiscovered venue on the Asian travel circuit and is still in an exploratory stage of tourism development, with relatively small numbers of international visitors arriving and few existing tourism sites. A total of 186 333 foreign visitors arrived in 1998, 14.8 per cent lower than the previous year's 218 843 and well off the 1996 peak of 260 489 (Yates, 1999). The Angkor Wat temple complex in Cambodia's north-western Siem Reap region is the country's leading destination and was designated as a World Heritage Site by UNESCO in 1994. The Cambodian government is only beginning to respond to this international market by providing and upgrading visitor facilities and services. According to the country's First State of the Environment Report (RGC, 1994) revenues from tourism are expected to be a major, if not the largest, potential source of foreign exchange in the country (Cork, 1993). Domestic travel is also fluctuating. During the first eight months of 1998, overall numbers were down compared to the same period in 1997 from (166 652 to 124 708). This was due to the political problems and regional economic depression. The country's turbulent history eliminated many opportunities for its people to explore their homelands and learn about their ancestor's culture and connections with nature, but many Cambodians, particularly from Phnom Penh, are enjoying their new found freedom and are now seeking to escape to nature and relaxation.

The current status of national parks

Cambodia has a long history of creating protected areas. It was in 1913 that the forest surrounding Tonle Sap Lake was first protected against cutting (IDRC, 1993). On 23 December 1924, the French Colonial administration in Cambodia established the first National Park in South-east Asia, Angkor Wat, of 10 700 hectares to protect the landscape surrounding the temples. During the French Administration, 16 more sites were protected and are listed as Protected Natural Sites and Monuments (IDRC, 1993). In 1960, King Sihanouk nominated the *Kouprey* (a wild cattle) as the national animal, and six wildlife reserves were established and managed. The plan was to convert them to national parks but the conflict with the Khmer Rouge prevented this transition.

Between 1975 and 1993, international consultants proposed revisions to the system of protected areas to make them more representative of the ecosystems in Cambodia. Due to security issues, however, in-depth ground surveys were not completed. In 1993, a Royal Decree classified 18 per cent of the country under different levels of protection. This placed Cambodia in first place among Asian countries in terms of the percentage of territory protected as wildlands (ETAP, 1997). Protected areas have been catalogued according to the IUCN classification system as follows: 62 per cent as Wildlife Sanctuaries (Category I) for the purpose of nature conservation and research, 23 per cent as National Parks (Category II) for nature conservation, research, education and recreation, 3 per cent as Protected (Cultural) Landscapes (Category X) for cultural and scenic assets preservation, research and recreation and, 12 per cent as Multiple-Use Areas (Category VIII) for nature conservation and sustainable development (ETAP, 1997).

There is draft legislation for a 'Policy, Organisation and Administration of a National Protected Areas System' which states that two special protection categories would be added: Strict Nature Reserves for scientific purposes, and Buffer Zones for the promotion of sustainable activities supporting the development of local communities and a better integration and acceptation of the core protected area (IDRC, 1993). To date there is not a single protected area, among the 23 listed by Royal Decree, which has an effective management system in place. Since early 1997, however, the National Parks Office (NPO) has been developing the concept of coordinated planning and management of a cluster of four national parks in southern Cambodia (Ream, Kep, Bokor and Kirirom) within a common park management structure.

There are two legal instruments in place concerning protected areas: the Royal Decree (Kret) concerning the Creation and Designation of Protected Areas and the Law on Environmental Protection and Natural Resource Management. The Royal Decree, promulgated in November 1993, established a National Protected Areas System comprising 23 designated protected areas under four categories: seven national parks; ten wildlife sanctuaries; three protected landscapes; and three multiple-use management areas. It allocates management and administration of the National Protected Areas System to the Ministry of Environment (MoE) in collaboration with other competent institutions. In practice, however, the MoE has assumed the sole leading role for planning and managing the parks but has delegated these responsibilities to the Department of Nature Conservation and Protection (DNCP).

A National Parks Office (NPO) has been established with the DNCP to develop and implement park strategies. The 23 areas were preserved for six years from illegal logging, but in the past two years there has been large-scale and consistent military logging operations within most parks and only the most isolated remain intact.

The Law on Environmental Protection and Natural Resource Management, proclaimed December 1996, grants the responsibility for environmental protection and natural resource management to the MOE in collaboration with other ministries and institutions. Preah Sihanouk National Park was inaugurated in March 1995 as the country's first national park, hereinafter known as Ream. It constituted the first major step towards development of the protected areas system. A draft management plan for Preach Sihanouk Park, for example, was developed in conjunction with the IUCN to integrate biodiversity conservation with the land use and resource needs of the local communities.

The principal objectives of the Ream management plan are:

- to enhance the capacity of the government and local communities to effectively manage the park for the conservation of its natural value;
- to enhance the access and use of the park for tourism, recreation and environmental education;
- to increase the options for sustainable livelihoods and income generation in local communities living in and around the park (RGC, 1994a).

Park management was relegated to the Kompong Som Provincial Environment Department (PED) with five rangers to patrol the park. When IUCN support ended, in late 1995 the effectiveness of ranger patrols were greatly reduced, and there are now no regular patrol programmes for the park. There is currently no budget from the national government for the operation of Ream specifically.

The MoE's aim is to have a presence inside parks and within surrounding communities so that they can raise people's awareness about the existence and purpose of parks as well as work with them to develop a more sustainable system of park resource use. Land speculation within the park boundaries and migration to settlements (further encroachment of settlers into parks) in buffer zones may become impossible to deal with, unless a genuine MoE presence is soon established. In Ream, there is rapid development in Kompong Som Town (rapid growth in buffer settlements) and ongoing illegal incursion into the park by settlers. There are no clear laws or rules regarding land and resource use. The UNDP report (1997) stated that, with military concurrence and possible protection, in May 1997, there were reports of substantial illegal road construction through the middle core of Ream. As well, the unmanaged use of park resources threatens the parks' biodiversity, especially marine fisheries and mangrove ecosystems on which local communities are dependent for their livelihood (uncontrolled resource exploitation in and near the park).

The second National Park, Preah Suramarit-Kossomak National Park at Kirirom (Kirirom), was established in 1995 (McDowell, 1995).

National parks management

The Royal Government of Cambodia established the Ministry of Environment (MoE) in July 1993 which has lead responsibility for national park management. As in most of the Asia–Pacific region, however, the MoE has extremely limited operational capabilities and political influence due to the desperate need for rapid economic development and the perception that this conflicts with good environmental management. Interministerial cooperation is virtually non-existent because of lack of financing and attempts by individual ministries to gain entire ownership of projects, and because the political factions that form the ministries that have, until recently, been blood enemies. Cooperation among ministries will be essential for effective management of the country's national parks and tourism. There is minuscule budget allocation for each of the parks. Park management plans will require significant resources (in the order of several million dollars) in order for plans to be implemented. This is compounded by the fact that the MoE has no effective strategy to manage the system of national parks and Cambodian staff need training in park management techniques.

The MoE lacks experience to directly manage and implement a demonstration project and thus needs assistance from international organisations. It also does not have reliable financial control mechanisms, nor has it demonstrated capacity for managing and reporting on the use of funds to support such projects. Cambodian law requires internationally donated funds to be managed through the Ministry of Finance, thus overhead costs from the MoF are charged against projects (UNDP, 1997).

There is a need to recruit, train and deploy a ranger force. The effective development and management of tourism in a national parks system will be affected by the operational capacity of the ministries. Due to the lack of educated and trained citizens in Cambodia, a low level of technical and managerial capacity exists within each ministry (le Billon, 1994). Inadequately and inappropriately trained personnel and management within the ministries limits essential experience in policy and regulation formulation, implementation and enforcement. Many bureaucrats and mid-level government staff are not familiar with elementary policy making and project management principles. In addition, many civil servants have not been appropriately placed within government according to their experience (le Billon, 1994, p. 47).

There have also been a number of timber concessions granted by the state of Cambodia to foreign companies, many of them located in protected areas. Environment officials in Cambodia say illegal logging in the national parks has increased dramatically. Loggers are able to take advantage of Cambodia's political instability. Armed operators are said to be taking advantage of the political confusion, cutting down valuable tropical hardwoods in the Bokor National Park – once proposed as a UNESCO World Heritage Site because of its rich plant and animal life.

Locally, the necessities of incomes for the rural poor combined with the lack of forest management, promotes small-scale logging and fuel collection. In every corner of the country there are small groups that organise illegal traffic. Local, provincial and or national authorities often support them, often heavily armed and backed by local army forces or KR guerrillas. There are also land disputes regarding park and buffer zone boundaries. Park boundaries need to be demarcated and land ownership conflicts within the park need to be resolved. Traditional property and land ownership relationships were upset when the KR regime took control of the country in 1975. Following this period land was distributed to each household and collection production operated until the mid-1980s. By the late 1980s certain resources such as sugarpalm trees and lotus ponds became private property. Local governmental officials have also sold land to outside interests (including fishing, forestry, mining interests) (RGC, 1995). The absence of clear management within the country's system of protected spaces has major implications for tourism development.

Tourism development in national parks

As stated in the Ministry of Tourism's (MoT's) *Tourism development policies and strategies* report, the natural environment has been targeted as the focus for tourism development long term because it is envisaged to have the potential to create jobs, generate foreign exchange and spread benefits (e.g. infrastructure and economic development) to many rural areas. Tourism promotion is a priority of the Royal Government (RGC, 1994a). The MoE s First State of the Environment Report (RGC, 1994b) stated that ecotourism has the potential to become a key strategy for the tourism sector. The concept of nature-based tourism has been introduced as a possibility for revenue generation and conservation for protected areas management, and is included in the IUCN's draft management plans for the country's first two protected areas.

The national government has expressed its desire to explore the socio-economic and biodiversity conservation potentials of nature-based tourism, but recognise that nature-based tourism sites will require integrated plans to provide for future site development and on-going management (RGC, 1994a; Cork, 1993). Nature-based tourism sites exist throughout Cambodia but have been developed with little planning and are not regularly managed.

A preliminary assessment of ecotourism potential in Kirirom and Ream was completed in 1997. Ream is expecting a growth in tourism. Since it is close to Sihanoukeville (which receives 40 000 visitors annually with each staying for 2–3 days at a time), the provincial tourism and environment authorities are positive about development, and the site has a good attraction base (beaches, mangrove forests, isolated islands, reef diving, snorkelling, and nature trails).

National parks, and tourism development in Vietnam

Threatened biodiversity and actual loss

Vietnam's protected areas represent 3 per cent of the country's land surface, or 11 000 km^2. The country's forest cover, however, has dropped from 43 per cent in 1943 to 19 per cent today. Remote sensing data indicates that only 2 million hectares of natural primary forests remain. These are being reduced at the rate of 100 000 hectares to 200 000 hectares yearly. During the Vietnam War, 72 million litres of herbicides including Agent Orange, Agent White, and Agent Blue were sprayed on 16 per cent of southern Vietnam's land area, including 10 per cent of the inland forests and 36 per cent of the mangrove forests. More than 2 million hectares of forest and farmland were lost to defoliation and bombing (WWF Vietnam, 1996).

Despite this loss, more than 10 per cent of the world's animals, birds, and fish and over 40 per cent of special-use plants are found in Vietnam. The latest survey in Vietnam shows that this country is home to 12 000 species of flora, of which about 7000 have been named. Of these 7000 named species, 2300 are used as foodstuffs, 3200 are herbs, and more than 200 are species such as hardwoods with high commercial value. In addition, Vietnam has about 275 mammal species, 800 bird species, 180 reptile species, 80 amphibian species, 2470 fish species and 5500 insect species (VNN, 1998).

For various socio-economic reasons, many Vietnamese ecosystems have been over-exploited for decades, including evergreen forests, mangrove forests, wetlands and sea areas, resulting in decreased economic potential and lowered environmental protection and losses to the gene pool. In 1991, Vietnam started a programme of research on forest resources and began discovering changes in the ecological system. The state is taking different measures to stop the destruction of Vietnam's biodiversity by gradually cutting back timber exploitation from natural forests to under 300 000 cubic metres per year by the year 2000.

Five causal factors account for most extinctions: habitat destruction, habitat fragmentation, overkill, invasive species and secondary effects cascading through an ecosystem from other extinctions. In the case of habitat fragmentation, species are doomed by consigning them to small, island-like parcels of habitat surrounded by an ocean of human impact and then subjecting them to the same jeopardies (small population size, acted upon by environmental fluctuation, catastrophe, inbreeding, bad luck, and cascading effects) that make island species especially vulnerable to extinction (Quammen, 1998).

The Vu Quang area has already yielded several spectacular wildlife finds. This includes the discovery of the Saola (*Pseudoryx nghetinensis*) or Vu Quang ox in 1992, and a deer-like animal known as the giant muntjac (*Megamuntiacus vuquangensis*) in 1994, the first discoveries of new large mammal species since the Okapi (*Okapia johnstoni*) in 1910. Other species that have been found in Vu Quang include Edwards pheasants (*Lophura edwardsi*) in 1996 – a species thought to be extinct – and a 20–25-centimetre fish of the *Crossocheilus* genus family in 1996 (WWF Vietnam, 1996). As a result of these spectacular wildlife findings in Vu Quang, the WWF and Ha Tinh Province's Forestry Department launched the Vu Quang Conservation Project in 1994. The 5-year project recognises that protecting the reserve also means addressing the needs of the 30 000 people living in and around the reserve. There is a need to create job opportunities and develop economic alternatives to resource exploitation as these are seen as key to conserving Vu Quang (WWF Vietnam, 1996). The Vietnamese government has since enlarged the Vu Quang reserve and imposed logging and hunting bans.

Species in other areas are not so fortunate. Collectors have made such impacts on turtles in countries like Vietnam and Laos that it can be impossible to find a single turtle even in ideal habitats in national parks and remote preserves. Studies of actual export numbers corroborate the evidence for large-scale exportation of these turtles. According to reports from *Traffic*, a wildlife trade-monitoring programme, more than 240 tons of turtles, representing more than 200 000 individual turtles, left Vietnam each year for sale in China in 1994 (Yoon, 1999).

Wildlife conservation within Vietnam's national parks

The Ministry of Forestry is responsible for the management of forest lands in Vietnam, which according to the 1991 Forestry Resource Protection and Development Act covers the three following categories of forests: protection forest (critical watersheds and wetlands), special-use forests (wildlife sanctuaries/national parks) and production forests.

Vietnam now has 105 natural conservation parks, including 10 national parks, 61 natural reserves, and 43 environment and historic and cultural sites. These natural conservation parks cover an area of 2.09 million hectares (VNN, 1998). Between 1965 and the early 1990s, the total area of national forests has declined at an estimated rate of 350 000 hectares per year, from about 40 per cent to 26 per cent of total land area. It was estimated that only 8.8 million hectares of land was under natural forest cover in 1993.

Within these forests, there are 365 endangered animal species in Vietnam. According to the government's Biodiversity Action Plan, 'In Vietnam, 28 per cent of mammals, 10 per cent of birds and 21 per cent of reptiles and land amphibians face extinction. From 1970 to 1994, the tiger population has dwindled from 3000 to about 200, and the rhino population from 300 to about 25' (WWF Vietnam, 1996). Vietnam's subsequent signing of the Convention of the International Trade of Endangered Species (CITES) in 1994 also meant that the government could start implementing legislation that would help to combat the high levels of cross-border trade.

In 1992, the World Bank introduced the concept of integrated conservation development projects (ICDPs). These projects attempt to ensure the conservation of biological diversity by reconciling the management of protected areas with the social and economic needs of local people (Wells and Brandon, 1992). ICDPs focus on three operational areas: protected area management, buffer zones, and local social and economic development. The establishment of the natural conservation parks entails restricting or even banning the local residents' use of resources in these regions, while ignoring the requirements, desires, and even traditional customs of residents. The effectiveness of natural resource protection depends on settling existing problems in buffer zones around natural parks.

An example of forest protection is provided by local people in Ha Tinh Province's Ky Anh District. After receiving education on the importance of forest-based resource, Ha Tinh farmers have worked to protect the Ke Go upstream forest and rare wild animals living in this forest from deforestation and even extinction. Effectiveness of natural resource protection improves once authorities solve problems in the buffer zones around national parks and reserves (VNN, 1998).

Current status of tourism development in Vietnam

Since opening its doors to tourism in the post-*doi moi* era, Vietnam has become a popular adventure tourism destination. However, comparatively few visitors venture off the beaten track to the north-west mountainous region. Stunning scenery, fascinating pre-and post-colonial history and a population of ethnic minority groups is likely to make this one of Asia's key tourist destinations within the near future. Many tourists, however, have found the country expensive despite the widespread poverty, and suffering from poor infrastructure and too persistent 'touting' of tourists. Expensive tourist visas – US$50.00 each at the Vietnamese embassy in Paris, for example – little overseas promotion about the country, a lack of resorts for the mass tourist market and the absence of private sector initiative currently handicap the industry (VNN, 1999a).

Vietnam saw a dramatic increase in tourism arrivals in the first half of the 1990s. By 1995 overseas visitors numbered 1.3 million with a turnover of approximately US$540 million, a tenfold increase over 1990 (VNN, 1996). Hanoi combines tourist figures with total arrivals, including business and official visitors, ending up with a figure of 1.5 million in 1998 compared to 1.7 million in 1997 (VNN, 1999b). The *Vietnam Economic Times* reported that return foreign tourists in 1998 amounted to only 1 per cent of total arrivals, although Vietnam's tourist department insists the figure is more than 10 per cent. Official figures obtained by Reuters show less than 600 000 foreign tourists visited in 1998, down from 690 000 the previous year, a drop the government blamed on Asia's economic crisis.

Controlling the way a country is perceived internationally at any point in time is one of the most difficult problems confronting a developing nation. Tourism is an international industry dominated by multinational companies and for many developing countries it is difficult to maintain control over such development. In order to avoid such a situation in Vietnam, tourism has been placed under the direct control of the Office of the Prime Minister, a status shared only with the oil and gas industries, and all foreign tourism investment projects must be joint partnerships with Vietnamese companies (Biles *et al.*, nd).

The government identified tourism as one of three major thrusts in its national economic development strategy in 1990 (Vo Nhan Tri, 1990). In 1992 the Vietnam National Administration of Tourism (VNAT) was established to focus energy and determination on 'boosting tourism development and turning the traditionally passive business into a business increasingly corresponding to the country's great potential' (VNAT, 1995). The government has restricted overseas marketing and advertising to state-run tourism companies with international licences. This has meant a heavy reliance on the promotion of Vietnam as a tourist destination by foreign tour operators.

These agents have tended to focus more on leisure, cultural and educational tourism, whereas the Vietnamese authorities, state-run travel operators and hotels have tended much more to link tourism with business travel. This latter form of tourism is significant: it was estimated that 35 per cent of visitors who arrived on tourist visas in 1994 were combining trade and market exploration with their visit (Campbell, 1994). The recommendations of the World Tourism Organisation reinforced the priority given to this 'business-class' tourism strategy by the Vietnamese tourism authorities in the mid-1990s (VNN, 1999b). Following WTO recommendations, the 1995 master plan for national tourism development identified three regions for focused tourism expansion. These were a northern region covering Hanoi, Hai Phong, Ha Long and Dien Bien Phu; a central region covering Da Nang and Hue; and a southern region encompassing the Nha Trang, Da Lat, Ho Chi Minh City and its surroundings, Vung Tau and the Mekong Delta (VNAT, 1995).

National parks and tourism in Vietnam

Vietnam is rich in cultural and historical sites and abounds in sites of natural beauty, endemic with exotic wildlife, including Halong Bay, Sapa, Bich Dong, Cuc Phuong National Park, and the Mekong Delta. Nam Cat Tien National Park is a good example of a protected area rich in rare birds which can be easily seen in beautiful surroundings.

Vietnam is particularly rich in cultural diversity, with 54 ethnic groups. These ethnic peoples, many of them tribal hillpeople, attract foreign, and domestic visitors, as in Thailand. Although some hillpeople have received some economic benefits from being guides or providing lodging, their cultures have also been impacted by the tourists.

A 'stakeholders' approach is one that promotes the local peoples' sense of ownership of their area and any ecotourism projects ongoing in their region. Local people are encouraged to make investments in projects, such as planting trees, managing nurseries, patrolling the forest, and setting up guest lodges. In some cases community participation in conservation of a national park could be rewarded by a contribution to a community development programme, revolving loan fund, or granting privileges in access to some park resources (see Nepal and Goodwin, this book). Unfortunately, nature-based tourism has not always led to eco-development. The lack of integration of conservation and development objectives can cause degradation of the resource base and reduce tourism potential and possible economic benefits from tourism. The causes for this include lack of commitment by government bodies and the fact that tourism is promoted by large-scale interests from outside the area. The most obvious problem is the exclusion of local people from the planning process.

Vietnam's natural areas must be assessed according to specific criteria, including quality of natural features, ecosystem resiliency, and carrying capacity for tourism and accessibility. Ba Vi National Park, for example, has a lower biodiversity conservation value than the Vu Quang nature Reserve – whose biodiversity is of international importance – but Ba Vi also has a high potential for tourism due to its beautiful vistas, waterfall, ruins, and its proximity to Hanoi. The Cuc Phuong National Park, just over 100 kilometres south of Hanoi, was established in 1962 as Vietnam's first protected area. This 220-km^2 area contains approximately 180 km^2 of relatively undisturbed subtropical and tropical evergreen forest, and remains one of the largest forests in the north-west of Vietnam. Tam Dao's 2 hours' proximity to Hanoi means that guest houses and hotels are full at the weekends (McRae, 1999).

Bach Ma National Park also has high tourism potential; it offers spectacular views of Hue and Danang cities, and the ocean is accessible as the park entrance is only 5 kilometres from Highway 1. Well-planned and managed accommodations and services could support many tourists with little detriment to forests and wildlife. Bach Ma also has high biodiversity value, but most of its species are represented in other protected areas. Taking a comprehensive, country-wide view of the situation it is more prudent to develop Bach Ma for tourism rather than more vulnerable areas such as Cat Loc, Vu Quang or Phu Mat.

Vietnam's protected areas, however, have limited accessible wildlife attractions, for tourism compared to parts of Africa or India or the Galapagos, where large numbers of large mammals can be seen easily (see Lilieholm and Romney and Weaver, this book). Although Vietnam is home to two of the only seven large mammals discovered to science in this century, no scientist or tourist has ever seen either of these animals in the wild. The only habitat for Javan rhinoceros (*Rhinoceros sondaicus*) on mainland South-east Asia is the forest of Cat Loc Reserve in Lam Dong Province, but researchers have been unable to see this small remaining rhino population and it is doubtful if many tourists would ever get to see them. Even if Cat Loc's Javan rhinos were easily accessible (as are Indian rhinos in Nepal), tourism development might still be inappropriate for the fragile forest and wetland ecosystem of Cat Loc. The rhinos and their habitat must be studied carefully before any conclusions can be drawn. The rhino population is estimated at only 9–15 and their survival is not ensured (Le and McNeil, 1995). Although the Saola, a shy forest-dweller, seldom seen even by scientists, has become a flagship species for conservation of Vu Quang Nature Reserve, it too will not become a big attraction for tourists.

Birds could be an attraction for serious ecotourists, for example, since Vietnam has many rare and endemic bird species. According to a survey by BirdLife International, Vietnam contains three endemic bird areas (areas with two or more birds entirely restricted to them), namely Dalat Plateau, the Annamese Lowlands and the Southern Vietnamese lowlands. The birds of the forest area around Ho Ke Go in Ha Tinh province have already attracted foreign bird tour companies from the UK and the USA (Eames, 1993). Although the number of birders is small, they usually pay more than typical tourists, especially to see such rare and restricted range birds. In this case, the guides also participate in the conservation project, regularly patrolling the habitat of rare birds.

Assessing tourism development in national parks in emerging tourism countries

Using the Cambodia and Vietnam examples as benchmarks, emerging tourism countries face a number of opportunities and threats in developing nature-based tourism in national parks. A simple SWOT analysis summarises these considerations.

Strengths

Tourism in national parks in countries beginning to develop tourism and enter the international tourism scene have certain strengths and advantages. Appropriate tourism can:

- Offer cultural and ecological diversity
- Promote the conservation of rare, indigenous flora and fauna
- Enhance foreign exchange earnings and promote socio-economic development including sustainable human societies.

Weaknesses

It is clear from the previous discussion that there are problems and weakness faced by countries such as Cambodia and Vietnam in developing tourism of any type, but particularly tourism in national parks. These include:

- Civil unrest, political issues, lack of enforcement and tourists forced to take risks
- Lack of infrastructure
- Generic developing country issues (e.g. poverty, disease, lack of financial resources, over dependence on mega-development projects, lack of a skilled workforce, uncontrolled exploitation on the natural resource base).

Opportunities

Despite such problems, the potential in many countries is considerable:

- Emerging countries are often starting in tourism from a very small base so can learn from elsewhere. Cambodia and Vietnam are in unique positions with the opportunity to build upon the experience of other nations when developing environmentally sensitive and socio-economically feasible resource management park strategies. They can learn from the mistakes of other countries and incorporate preventative proactive management strategies rather than relying on reactive mitigation measures.
- Factors such as globalisation, increasing world peace, new aspects of tourism, increases in travel to remote parts of the world, and global support for sustainable development all make Cambodia and Vietnam likely to benefit from nature-based tourism. Internally, nature-based tourism can enhance attitudes towards the conservation of endangered species.

Threats

It would be naïve, however, to suggest there are no difficulties or dangers in such development:

- Tourism is predominantly controlled in tourist-originating developed countries. As a result, there is a need for stronger institutional structures in destination countries if tourism is to play an appropriate role in economic development. Parks are already centres of institutional strengths, and thus they can play a role in national tourism development.
- It is necessary to resist the common general pressures exerted by globalisation, cultural exploitation, and trade in endangered species.
- Governments eager to generate the foreign exchange often cover up the true risk of travel, i.e. the actual degree of safety that travellers are afforded in destinations because of desire to generate tourism revenues.
- As well as growing numbers of visitors to nature reserves and wildlife sites can have adverse consequences for the environment, such as the disturbance of sensitive species and habitats resulting from tourism infrastructure (visitor centres, trail systems, car park development).

In light of the foregoing, three critical points must also be addressed where nature-based tourism is developed in order to support rural development and conservation objectives. Governments must have well-defined conservation objectives and priority areas gazetted for conservation. Just as a national park cannot be totally exposed to market forces, so tourism attractions should also be regulated and carefully managed. A common pitfall of nature-based tourism is the tendency to compromise the integrity of a natural tourism attraction to reach a broader range of consumer needs and types. Natural areas must be identified and prioritised for their tourism potential and masterplanning must be carried out. This process is analogous to the type of planning that goes into the management of a national park and it must be realised that not all areas are equally suited for tourism development. Finally, local people must be involved as partners in the process of planning and managing tourism projects to ensure their needs are recognised and incorporated into developments.

Conclusion

In the past, many governments have over-estimated their ability to manage natural resources and ignored local capacities and traditional management systems. The aim of sustainable tourism should be to supplement and complement local lifestyles and cultures rather than control them. Tourism development will inevitably lead to change in the resident community as it cannot be developed in social isolation from the local community (see Nepal, Hall and Goodwin, this book). Absence of local involvement can lead to resentment and divided support for the tourism development as the communities are directly affected by the development economically, physically and socially. By empowering people to mobilise their own capacities, individuals are encouraged to become 'social actors' rather than 'passive subjects' and thus, have some control over projects that can affect their lives (Murphy, 1985). Operational frameworks need to integrate local authorities and communities into management plans and local residents must actively participate in on-going management. In such a way, local support for national park objectives can be expanded.

Cambodia and Vietnam are eager to rebuild and stabilise themselves and see tourism as a means to generate future economic growth. Complications involving intransigent rebel groups (in Cambodia), the unsustainable extraction of natural resources, dangers from war detritus (in Vietnam and Cambodia), competing bureaucracies, and meagre treasuries are placing natural areas and their tourism potential under threat. By moving towards a more orderly civil society and establishing conservation management frameworks in its four national parks, Cambodia is is making cautious strides towards the retention and promotion of its natural heritage.

Cambodia and Vietnam are in positions to carry out tourism planning, which includes the involvement of local people, before the tourism industry becomes too unmanageable. Government tourism policies and investment priorities and regulations can be set up before tourism reaches other sensitive national park areas. In Vietnam there are problems, however, in building a nature-based tourism industry around new or rare species, which may be very difficult to observe in their natural habitat. Efforts must be made to restrict access to some park areas to prevent the trampling of flora that have not yet been properly recorded.

Tourism as an engine of economic development in national parks represents a choice between resource extraction or conservation. Given the perilous state of their economies, difficulties of civil society, and citizens' limited access to economic resources, national governments such as those of Cambodia and Vietnam must weigh options carefully in terms of the sustainability of natural heritage versus the economic needs of residents.

References

Biles, A. Lloyd, K. and Logan, W.S., nd, *Tiger on a bicycle: the growth, character and dilemmas of international tourism in Vietnam*, (in press)

le Billon, P., 1994, *Protected areas in the Kingdom of Cambodia: report on initial phase*, File No. 93–506100-01, International Development Research Centre, Cambodia

Boo, E., 1990, *Ecotourism: the potentials and pitfalls*, World Wildlife Fund, Washington, DC

Boo, E., 1992, *The ecotourism boom: planning for development and management*, World Wildlife Fund, Washington DC

Campbell, D., 1994, Saigon has the right mix. *Travel News Asia*, 21 November to 4 December

de Chavez, R., 1999, Globalisation and tourism: Deadly mix for indigenous peoples. *Third World Resurgence*, No. 103

Colchester, M., nd, *Salvaging nature: indigenous peoples, protected areas and biodiversity Conservation*, United Nations Research Institue for Social Development, Geneva

Cork, C., 1993, *Community-managed ecotourism: a feasibility survey on Phnom Baset, Cambodia*, University of Calgary Faculty of Environmental Design, master's degree project, Calgary

Eames, J., 1993, *Conservation of biodiversity in the Annamese Lowlands and the Dalat Plateau, Vietnam: preliminary report on Spring 1994 fieldwork*, BirdLife International, Ministry of Forestry, Hanoi

Environmental Technical Advisory Programme (ETAP), 1997, *ETAP/MoE Park Management Demonstration Project: the Initial management of Preah Sihanouk National Park, draft report*, Phnom Penh, Cambodia

Federation of Nature and National Parks of Europe (FNNPE), nd, *Loving them to death? Sustainable tourism in Europe's nature and national parks*, FNNPE Sustainable Tourism Working Group

International Development Research Centre (IDRC), 1993, *Meeting the global challenge: themes and programs of the International Development Research Centre*, IDRC, Ottawa

International Union for the Conservation of Nature (IUCN), 1984, *Threatened protected areas of the world*, IUCN Commission on National Parks and Protected Areas, Gland

Le, Van Lanh and MacNeil, J., 1995, Ecotourism in Vietnam: prospects for conservation and local participation. Paper presented at the Hanoi National Conference on National Parks and Protected Areas of Vietnam, 23–24 February

Lindberg, K. and Hawkins, D.E. (eds), 1993, *Ecotourism: a guide for planners and managers*, The Ecotourism Society, North Bennington, VT

McDowell, R., 1995, King Heralds opening of Kirirom Park. *The Cambodia Daily*, 6 July, pp. 1–2

McKay, S., 1997, Asia-Pacific air travel to boom. *The Age*, 15 July

McRae, M., 1999, Tam Dao – sanctuary under siege. *National Geographic*, June

Mowforth, M. and Munt, I., 1998, *Tourism and sustainability: new tourism in the Third World*, Routledge, London

Murphy, P.E., 1985, *Tourism: a community approach*, Methuen, London

Pacific Asia Travel Association (PATA), 1995, *Annual report*, PATA, San Francisco, CA

Pleumoron, A., 1994, The political economy of tourism. *The Ecologist*, **24**(4)

Pleumoron, A., 1999, Tourism, globalisation and sustainable development. *Third World Resurgence*, No. 103, March

Quammen, D., 1998, Planet of weeds. *Harper's Magazine*, **297**(1781)

Royal Government of Cambodia Ministry of Environment, Department of Nature Conservation and Protection (RGC), 1995, *Baset integrated conservation and development: feasibility survey: project report written by the Baset Working Group*, B. Herod, ed., IDRC, Phnom Penh Cambodia

Royal Government of Cambodia, Ministry of Tourism (RGC), 1994a, *Tourism development policies and strategies*, Phnom Penh, Cambodia

Royal Government of Cambodia, Ministry of Environment (RGC) 1994b, *Cambodia: first state of environment Report*, prepared in collaboration with the Cambodia Environmental Advisory Team (UNDP/OPS), Phnom Penh, Cambodia

United Nations Development Programme (UNDP), 1997, UNDP Project Document, *Preah Sihanouk National Park Management Demonstration Project*, Phnom Penh, Cambodia

Valentine, P.S., 1992, Nature tourism. In *Special interest tourism*, B. Wieler and C.M. Hall, eds, pp. 105–127, Belhaven Press, London

Vietnam National Administration of Tourism (VNAT), 1995, *Master plan of Vietnam tourism development period 1995–2010*, VNAT, Hanoi

Viet Nam News (VNN), 1996, 'Socio-economic plan for 1996' No. 2 (January/February)

Viet Nam News (VNN), 1998, Scientists suggest ways to protect natural resources. 3 April

Viet Nam News (VNN), 1999a, A new picture of rural Viet Nam. 13 March

Viet Nam News (VNN), 1999b, Lam Dong fears collapse of prestige tourist project. 16 March

Vo Nhan Tri, 1990, *Vietnam's economic policy since 1975*, Institute of Southeast Asian Studies, Singapore

Wells, M. and Brandon, K., 1992, *People and parks: linking protected area management with local communities*, The World Bank, Washington, DC

Whelan, T. (ed.), 1991, *Nature tourism: managing for the environment*, Island Press, Washington, DC

World Commission on Environment and Development (WCED), 1987, *Our common future*, United Nations, New York

World Wide Fund for Nature Vietnam (WWF Vietnam), 1996, *Vietnam country profile*, WWF, Gland

Yates, D., 1999, Tourists barely dipping toes into Vietnam. *Reuters*, 21 May

Yoon, C.K., 1999, Turtles vanish in black hole: soup pots and pans of China. *New York Times*, 4 May

Electronic references

Australian National University Coombs Library: Vietnam Science, Technology and Environment Page
    http://coombs.anu.edu.au/~vern/avsl.html

Conservation Monitoring Centre: Biodiversity Profile of The Socialist Republic of Viet Nam
    http://www.wcmc.org.uk/infoserv/countryp/vietnam/index.html

Douc Langur Project Information
    http://www-rohan.sdsu.edu/faculty/lippold1/info.htm

Where do you want to go birding today – Vietnam
    http://www.camacdonald.com/birding/asiavietnam.htm

Sao la, Pseudoryx, Vu Quang Ox
    http://www.pathcom.com/~dhuffman/saola.html

Species Under Threat: Vu Quang Ox
    http://www.panda.org/resources/publications/species/underthreat/vuquangox.htm

Viet Nam's Development Path & Implications for Natural Resource Degradation
    http://gurukul.ucc.american.edu/ted/papers/doc2.htm#env

Vietnam Parks and Reserves
    http://coombs.anu.edu.au/~vern/parks.html

Part Four:
Future Context

R.W. BUTLER

This concluding part of the book represents both a contemporary overview of parks and tourism and a futuristic gaze at possible relationships between tourism and parks in the next century. The first chapter is by Gordon Nelson, one of the most prolific researchers and writers on national parks over the last three decades. Nelson builds on a wealth of personal experience garnered from much fieldwork in national parks, particularly the western parks of Canada, to present a personal review of issues arising from the joint development of parks and tourism, with particular reference to North America. Expanding earlier discussions to include Mexico, he reviews the nature of the issues arising over the years from the combination of tourism and other pressures on national parks, and some of the responses in terms of planning approaches and concepts such as ecotourism and sustainable development. In so doing, he provides an appropriate overview which re-emphasises some of the issues discussed in more detail in the preceding chapters. Proceeding through a review of environmental and human dimensions, he moves on to discuss issues relating to policies and institutional arrangements, and concludes with a review of planning, management and decision making in the three systems of parks. He sees the successful combination of tourism and parks being dependent upon a wider approach to planning which incorporates regional and ecosystem dimensions and much more consideration of civics and community values.

The concluding chapter by Butler looks to the future in the context of tourism and national parks, by reviewing past trends and developments and suggesting scenarios and options along which that relationship might progress. He notes that barring catastrophic events, tourism will almost certainly continue to grow and that tourism in national parks will not only remain a significant problem to management, but most likely will become *the* major issue in national parks in many countries in the decades ahead. He argues that there would be great political as well as economic and social difficulties in attempting to severely restrict or prohibit tourism use of national parks in general, and notes the impossibility of ever removing all evidence of tourism use of parks. The current pattern of incremental development and impact is not feasible nor desirable for the future of either tourism or national parks. Butler argues for greater local variation in response to the problems faced and acceptance of the reality and likely permanence of tourism in most national parks. The differences in attitudes towards tourism by local and non-local groups in many countries are likely to continue and need to be addressed on a long-term basis. Tourism in national parks, Butler argues, will continue to be dynamic, involving both new forms of tourism and new parks, and a wide range of management philosophies and approaches will be needed to deal successfully with an even broader range of issues and problems in the future. He concludes that in many cases national parks need tourism as an ally in a positive and complementary relationship in order to ensure their continued maintenance in the decades ahead. The political and economic contributions of tourism to national park survival should be able to outweigh the environmental costs through the use of appropriate and effective planning and management.

18 Tourism and national parks in North America: an overview

J. G. NELSON

Introduction

Tourism is increasingly seen as an important economic force locally, nationally and internationally. It also makes people aware of changing cultures, societies and environments and helps justify and support national parks as well as other institutions. National parks and other protected areas conserve water, plants, animals and the natural systems underpinning human and other life on earth, as well as offering opportunities for tourism and related activities. Both tourism and national parks can, however, be seen as interfering with one another as well as with other economic and social activities. In other words, they inflict costs as well as benefits on individuals, communities and the state (Mathieson and Wall, 1982; McNeely, 1988; Butler, 1991; Ishwaren, 1994; Nelson, 1996a, b; Nelson and Serafin, 1997). Planners are interested in maximising the benefits and minimising the costs of both tourism and protected areas. Exploring this challenge in broad strategic terms is the main purpose of this chapter.

The focus is on tourism and national parks in North America: in Canada, the USA and Mexico. As a region, the three countries share mountains, such as the coast ranges and the Rockies, as well as lowlands such as the Great Plains. They also share plant and animal life. Wolves and grizzlies move across their borders. Vast continental migrations are part of the life cycle of songbirds, waterfowl and insects such as butterflies. The three countries also share large ocean systems such as the Gulf Stream, the Labrador Drift and the California Current.

The USA, Canada and Mexico do, however, differ considerably in cultural or human terms. Their people speak different languages, have different histories, economies, and social and political systems. As we shall see, the three countries also tend to differ in the way the people relate to nature and/or the environment. Indeed in these three countries, tourism and national parks can generally be understood in terms of the relations between humans and the environment.

Environmental dimensions

We can begin with environment, a term that increasingly in recent years has given way to concepts such as **ecosystem** (Gauthier, 1993; Woodley, S., 1993). This term has relatively precise scientific definitions of interacting parts of the natural world – species, associations, communities, trophic levels, landscapes and the like, as well as animal movements, habitats, and the life cycle. The term ecosystem is also associated with certain concepts, hypotheses, theories or approaches, intended to lead to greater understanding of how nature or the natural environment works. One image is of a relatively stable system, succeeding slowly to an end or climax state or landscape, unless interrupted by fire, disease, volcanic eruptions or other irregular disturbances. On the other hand, many ecologists today no longer subscribe to the idea of relatively gradual succession but rather to the idea of patch or pulse dynamics in which disturbances by fire, disease, earthquakes and other processes are seen to occur in a more or less regular fashion. The resulting landscape consists of a mosaic of patches of different ages and origins rather than a generally similar association, community or climax.

Such ecological or ecosystem concepts, hypotheses or theories are of growing importance to planners, geographers and decision makers, including those concerned with understanding and dealing with tourism and its effects (Moss, 1988; Lindberg and Hawkins, 1993). In this context, some particularly relevant ideas or approaches include island biogeography, biodiversity, ecological health or integrity, stress–response theory, landscape ecology, biological conservation and bioregions.

Island biogeography refers to species behaviour which tends to occur when a natural community or ecosystem is isolated from other systems. Detailed studies of Pacific and other islands have shown that the number of species decline at a more or less regular or predictable rate depending on factors such as island size and the degree to which populations of species are able to be enhanced by migrations from other areas. Numerous attempts have been made by scientists, planners and managers to apply this theory to terrestrial situations where populations are isolated or fragmented into relatively small areas by agriculture and other human activities.

Biodiversity is generally used to refer to differences in nature such as in species or habitat. High biodiversity has come to be associated with the resilience or capacity of species, communities or ecosystems to survive in the face of fire, pollution or other natural or cultural disturbances.

Stress–response theory provides a framework for understanding the interactions between the elements and processes in an ecosystem. A stress is seen as a force applying pressure to the elements and processes in a system, leading to changes or responses that in themselves are neither good or bad. However, humans may view the results as healthy or unhealthy depending on how they value parts of the system or the system as a whole. Stresses can lead to the decline or extinction of valued species or communities. Examples are the infestation known as 'red tide' and trampling or disturbance by swimmers, snorkellers or scuba divers, both of which damage or destroy coral reefs.

Landscape ecology focuses on the extent to which natural systems have been divided or fragmented by agriculture, roads or other development, into patches of varying size, shape and distribution. In accordance with island biogeography and other theory, fragmentation is seen as likely to increase the isolation of patches, thereby leading to a reduction in the capacity to maintain species and habitats and to a decline in biodiversity.

Biological conservation generally refers to the use of ecosystem science in planning, management and decision making. In the strictest sense, this includes scientific attempts to identify the minimum population levels and habitat sizes needed to conserve valued species, notably major predators such as the wolf. Studies in Banff National Park, for example, have shown that the range needed by the wolf tends to be very large, exceeding the size of the park, which is about 2500 square miles. The results of such studies have led to very large scale ecosystem planning initiatives. An example is the Yukon to Yellowstone or Y2Y project which encompasses much of the Rocky Mountain region of Canada and the central and northern United States.

The concept of the **bioregion** has roots not only in science but also in human spirituality. In the words of Thomas Berry, a scholar and theologian, 'the earth presents itself to us not as a unknown global reality but as a complex of highly differentiated regions caught up in the comprehensive unity of the planet itself' (Berry, 1990, p. 163). Bioregional thinking is being applied to an increasing number of areas. The Wildlands Project involves planning for very large areas in northern New England and the Maritimes of Canada, as well as the Sky Islands and other mountainous regions in the south-western United States and northern Mexico.

It is important to note that the foregoing concepts, theories and approaches are all evolving and interacting with one another as they unfold into a much richer blend of ecosystem science and associated planning. However, the whole process is marked by numerous uncertainties (Cardinall and Day, 1998) that are vexing to ecologists as well as planners, managers and decision makers. They wish to apply ecosystem science rather precisely to different kinds of areas and situations so that management regimes can consider activities such as tourism on the one hand, and nature conservation on the other. The concepts and the boundaries of ecosystems are, however, leaky. Species, communities, watersheds and other aspects of nature are difficult to capture solely in terms of current theory, concepts and approaches and caution is in order. These ideas will be discussed later, after reviewing the human dimensions of tourism and national parks.

Human dimensions

The human dimensions of tourism and national parks are not as well grounded in science, theory and systematic understanding as are the natural or environmental dimensions. In fact, a general framework or human ecological model of these dimensions and their interactions with nature has not been agreed. The theoretical and conceptual linkages among or across the dimensions are in consequence not well developed.

In this chapter, three broad concepts, or sets of general attributes, are used to define what it means to be human while remaining a part of the natural world. Each concept helps to explain how humans respond to the natural environment and to one another as individuals and groups. The three are the *psycho-social*, the *policy and institutional*, and the *technological* characteristics typical of all humankind. They have been used previously by the author (for example, Nelson *et al.*, 1978) and represent the cultural, that is the spiritual or emotional, the technical and the other learning that distinguishes humans from the rest of the world. In this sense, the terms culture and human often are used more or less interchangeably. The three broad concepts or categories will now be discussed briefly with reference to their applicability to tourism and national parks.

The psycho-social

The human individual not only conceives of himself or herself as alone but also interactively, as a member of groups that make up the human family. Personal and group experiences are to some degree separate and to a considerable degree intertwined. Individual knowledge, perceptions, attitudes and values reflect to some degree the experience and outlook of the individual and to some degree, the experience and influence of family, neighbourhood, tribe, community, school and other groups and organisations. These psycho-social attributes are applicable to the understanding of tourism and national parks, as well as to related planning, management and decision-making. In North America, the results vary among the three countries of Mexico, USA and Canada.

While recognising that considerable variability occurs in all three countries and that many basic changes are ongoing, some broad generalisations can be made. The people of Mexico, while still tied to family, to the community and to the Church, especially in rural areas, are becoming increasingly incorporated into North American and global trade and economic patterns. Mexicans are, however, still preoccupied with meeting their basic needs while aspiring increasingly to the high level of consumerism and the distinct managerial, professional or corporate status typical of Canada or the USA. The individual and the social outlook in Mexico consequently tends to be more utilitarian with regard to the perception and use of the natural environment than in the USA and Canada. The land and the sea are perceived more in terms of resources, work, and economic opportunity than as wild or natural areas with recreational opportunities in the sense more applicable in the USA and Canada.

One consequence is that Mexicans see their environment – as well as their cultural heritage – in terms of a very strong interest in tourism, foreign exchange, and economic development. Recent tourism receipts are at the level of 19 per cent of export earnings (Ceballos-Lascurain, 1996). Tourism earnings in the USA and Canada are not nearly so high in proportion to other sources of export income. One result of the strong Mexican interest in tourism as a major source of income and development has been a strong historic and current focus on mass tourism. Over the last three to four decades large hotels, resorts and tourist facilities have opened throughout Mexico, notably on the coasts of the Pacific Ocean and the Gulf of Mexico. These resorts attract millions of visitors each year from the USA, Canada and other countries and have been developed with a large market and foreign earnings understandably in mind. Less attention has been paid to the effects of tourism on the people and the environment. Many wetland and other wildlife habitats have been changed or destroyed, as have many villages and human communities.

In recent years, however, individual, group and government sensitivity to the social and natural environment has increased in Mexico. A government tourism development branch (FONATUR) now assists local people in dealing with the effects of development. This offers some advantages but more interest needs to be shown in alerting, training and assisting local people to plan for development and engage in the benefits as it proceeds. In this context, the Mexican government has made recent efforts to gain greater understanding of how this might be done. A number of meetings and conferences have been held to consider potentially promising alternatives such as ecotourism, a term coined by a Mexican, Héctor Ceballos-Lascuráin (1996).

In Canada and the USA, the degree of reliance on tourism and particularly mass tourism as a major means of economic development has been less than in Mexico, partly because of their more diverse and developed economies and partly because of rather different perceptions, attitudes and values. In the USA, for example, the idea of the wild and the wilderness has been valued since at least the early part of the nineteenth century when people travelled to the Adirondacks, the Catskills and Niagara Falls to enjoy the sublime, beauty and wildness of nature. Growing interest in wild places led to the idea and the creation of national parks in Yellowstone, Yosemite and other areas in the late nineteenth century (see Boyd and Butler, this book).

From the beginning, however, relations between tourism as a business and the conservation of natural or wild systems were uneasy. As a business, tourism interests saw nature as a resource to be used to achieve high levels of visitation and revenue. In contrast, the citizen-driven conservation or wilderness movement increasingly saw nature or wild places as best conserved and left alone. Tourism activities, especially as business, came to be seen as a growing threat to the isolated qualities of wilderness. By the 1960s these perceptions, attitudes and values led to the very large membership of influential advocacy groups such as the Sierra Club and the US National Parks and Conservation Association. They also led to the US Wilderness Act and to legal protection for wilderness as essentially areas untrammelled by humans whose only presence is transitory. This kind of thinking led to moves to exclude technology from areas set aside for wilderness purposes, including backcountry shelters and other facilities for bikers, campers and other tourists. Nature and the wild were increasingly valued for their own sake, setting a backdrop for the later development of 'deep ecology' and bioregional thought and practice. All this greatly increased the tensions and conflicts between tourism and nature and wilderness conservation.

In Canada tourism developments tended to parallel those in the USA. Travel to distant wild places was valued. As in the USA, in the nineteenth century railroads such as the Canadian Pacific promoted national parks for their tourism potential and have operated hotels and tourism programmes there ever since. Large-scale citizen interest in, and support for, nature and especially for wilderness did not express itself in the form of conservation organisations until well into the twentieth century. Civic interest in the idea of wilderness in Canada was not sufficient to lead to the creation of any major relevant non-government organisation until the Canadian National and Provincial Parks Association in the 1960s. At that time the Sierra Club and other large US conservation groups also came to Canada.

Influential people like J. B. Harkin, an early director of the Canadian National Parks, were strong spokesmen for the US idea of wilderness in Canada and was responsible, to some degree, for its introduction in government policy and practice

(Nelson and Butler, 1974). But Harkin also saw tourism as a handmaiden for conservation. He saw it as earning income and as leading visitors to appreciate and become supporters of nature conservation and the national park idea. He also supported some large-scale development in the national parks, for example the construction of the Banff–Jasper highway through the heart of the Canadian Rockies in the 1930s.

One basic reason for Canadians' slowness in taking up the wilderness idea was the perception of the forest and outlying areas as 'the bush'. This was the place of the *coureur de bois*, the fur trade, logging and mining. The forests and the hinterland were home for harvesters and of the resources needed to supply goods and services for development in the metropole. This was an essentially utilitarian rather than a preservationist or wilderness point of view.

The foregoing situation is complicated by the position taken by the native people or First Nations of Canada. In many cases in recent decades, Canada has been making its first attempts to settle native demands for compensation and redress for the loss of lands, access to resources and economic opportunities in the past. The First Nations people tend to have a utilitarian attitude to nature and wilderness areas. Many claim little or no affinity with the southern idea of wilderness which they see as applying more to the city than the forest or the tundra. The wilderness of the average Caucasian Canadian is homeland for the native people. The civilisation of the city is to many First Nations people a wild, awesome and often lonely place. First Nations wish to regain control of their lands and ultimately of their well-being (see Hall, Chapter 5). This situation is not necessarily favourable to either tourism or wilderness. Oil production or other activities have been pushed by First Nations on their remote northern lands. On the other hand, they have also supported national parks as part of recent agreements with government. However, in these parks, hunting and traditional activities tend to be favoured and roads and facilities for tourism often frowned upon.

Technology

At a basic level, technology can be defined as the organised use of knowledge for human purposes. Technology has played a strong role in tourism for centuries. Advances in watercraft and seafaring laid the foundation for the travel of the curious and the pleasure seekers from Europe to Africa, the Pacific, and other parts of the world in the eighteenth and nineteenth centuries. The railroad and the automobile opened up North America to settlement and eventually to tourism. The development of medicines made it possible for visitors to sojourn in distant lands in the nineteenth century. Advances in equipment have continued to provide access for increasing numbers of people to a growing range of recreational and tourism activities throughout the world including biking, sailing, camping, climbing, hang-gliding and river rafting. It is technology that has largely made it possible for tourism to intensify and to spread into ever more remote areas including national parks.

It is also technology which is a major threat to the social and natural environments that are attractive to tourists. Jet planes, airports, rapid ground and water transport and advanced gear and supplies make it possible for thousands of hikers and backpackers to penetrate the high Sierras of northern California and other mountains systems in the USA and, to a growing extent, in Baja California and the Sierra Madres of Mexico. It is advanced technology that has led to the development of huge ski resorts for hundreds of thousands of visitors in the formerly forbidding winters of the high country of Colorado, Utah, British Columbia and Quebec.

Such changes and their effects on people and communities are well illustrated by development in Mexico (Burford, 1997) or trekking in Thailand (Dearden, 1993) or the Himalayas. However, these effects are also quite noticeable in many parts of North America. Examples are villages which have become ski resorts in the west or towns and villages in growing cottaging areas such as the southern shore of Georgian Bay, Ontario where close to 30 per cent of the population is over 65 and retired.

The effects of tourism on the natural environment are complex, interactive and wide-ranging. They include air and water pollution, solid waste disposal, noise and aesthetic degradation. Various attempts have been made to classify these effects in ways that are helpful to general understanding, and to planning, management and decision-making (Lindberg and Hawkins, 1993; Ceballos-Lascuráin, 1996; Nelson, 1996b).

These effects are of particular concern when they occur in or near national parks and other protected areas where the major purpose is wilderness or nature conservation. However, government agencies and groups within Mexico have been less actively concerned than have similar agencies and groups in Canada and the USA. Of basic importance here is the fact that, over the years, national parks in Mexico have been created predominantly for recreation and tourism. This contrasts with the situation in Canada and the USA where the historic interest has been more in a dual mandate, or what might be called a balance between recreation and tourism and nature conservation.

Certain national parks highlight the environmental concerns in the USA and Canada. These include the Great Smokies, Yosemite, Shenandoah, and Banff (Nelson, 1994). The spread of recreational and tourism technology has been mapped for Banff National Park (see Nelson, 1994). In such cases, internal pressures on the park environment are exacerbated by growing pressure from recreation, tourism, logging, mining and other developments outside their boundaries (Figure 18.1).

Policies and institutional arrangements

Policies and institutional arrangements refer to the sets of activities and arrangements that provide direction or guidance for human actions (Nelson *et al.*, 1978). These include laws, guidelines, agencies, goal-setting, budgeting, communication, education, and other processes and procedures. Policies and institutional arrangements refer to the internal, as well as the external, dynamics of agencies and groups involved in tourism, national parks and other activities. In Mexico, tourism planning and development is a basic responsibility of the federal agency known as FONATUR (Long, 1993). This agency is mainly focused on tourism as a form of economic development, although it is concerned with mitigating unwanted effects on the social and natural environments. At the federal level in Canada and the USA, no agency seems to be charged with prime responsibility for tourism planning and development. In Canada, a Canadian Tourism Commission, consisting of a mix of

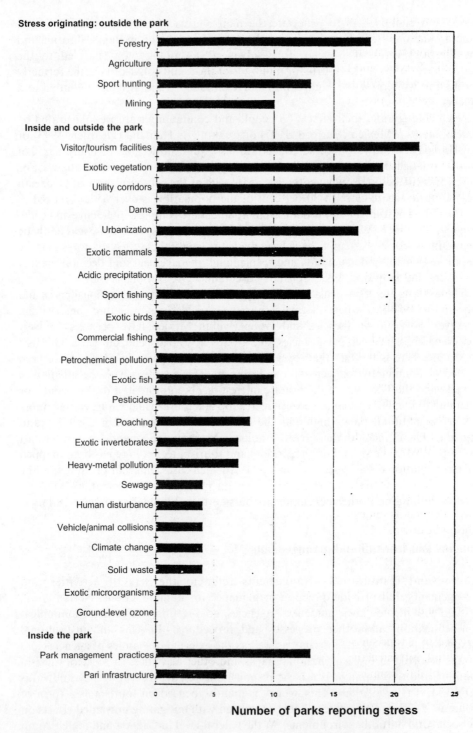

Figure 18.1. National parks in Canada reporting significant ecological impacts from various human stresses. (Source: Nelson, 1996b)

government and the private sector, was appointed by the federal government in 1995 to promote tourism. In all three countries, some responsibility for tourism lies with public land management agencies such as the Department of Forestry, the Fish and Wildlife Service, and the National Parks Service in the USA and the Parks Canada Agency and the Wildlife Service in Canada. A generally comparable situation applies at the state and provincial levels, although any mandate for tourism usually is part of a wider portfolio such as tourism, culture and communications. The status and structure of tourism also tends to rise and fall with the economy, governments, the party in power and other influences.

As a result of these policies and institutional arrangements, tourism tends not to be a major political force in the USA and Canada although it is more so in Mexico because of the heavier reliance on tourism income in that country. In all three countries, tourism is heavily promoted by the private sector, notably large hotel, travel and other corporations with big investments in the field. These corporations and the many middle to small businesses characteristic of tourism all traditionally tend to put pressure on governments to develop more infrastructure for tourism in national parks and other public lands where many of the transportation, resource management and other costs can be borne by government.

In this regard, the Canadian Tourism Commission has recently been making a stronger case for the economic importance of tourism in Canada. The Commission recently published a report on how the tourism industry affected Canada's economy between 1986 and 1996. According to the study, tourism shows: (1) a long-term revenue growth trend of almost 2 per cent per year despite ups and downs for the national economy and the industry; (2) job creation at nearly twice the rate of Canadian business; (3) employment rising by 69 100 to reach 489 200 jobs by the end of 1996; (4) the creation of another 13 100 jobs in other industries during that period; and (5) big revenue gains by travel agencies at 224.6 per cent (*Toronto Globe and Mail*, 10 May 1999, p. B3). The returns from US and other international visitors ($13.7 billion) was, however, less than the $15.6 billion that Canadians spent travelling to other countries, yielding a travel or trade deficit of $1.9 billion (*Toronto Globe and Mail*, 10 May 1999, p. B3). The industry and government tend to see this trade deficit as undesirable in the national balance of payments sense, needing to be brought down.

The proposed major solutions both involve growth (*Toronto Globe and Mail*, 10 May 1999, p. B3). The first is to encourage more international tourism to Canada, and the second is to encourage Canadians to do more of their travel at home. Yet for many years, voices within and outside tourism have been calling attention to the often undesirable social and environmental effects of tourism growth throughout North America. According to Butler (1993), tourism and tourists tend to change or evolve in a tourism area over time. These changes are associated with changes in facilities, infrastructure, means of access and the resources required to sustain new types of development. In many cases, these changes represent a change from what Butler calls authenticity to artificial, from indigenous to imported, from low density to high density, from low energy consumption to high energy consumption, from locally controlled to externally controlled, and from sustainable or renewable to unsustainable and non-renewable (Butler 1993, p. 32).

Wall (1993) has made comparable observations about the changes that ensue from tourism growth. He has stressed the importance of assessing the effects of tourism on the environment and society and has developed assessment frameworks and approaches for preventing or mitigating undesirable effects (Mathieson and Wall, 1982). Wall has also argued that if tourism is to be a sustainable activity, a typology will be needed to facilitate matching tourism types with economic, social and environmental factors or conditions for planning, management and decision-making purposes. More fundamentally, he argues for the need to move away from consideration of tourism as an undifferentialist phenomenon or activity to thinking about and planning in terms of different types of tourism.

In recent years, concerns about tourism growth and effects have been increasing generally. One focus of interest in dealing more effectively with adverse effects is the concept of *sustainable development* (see Boyd, Chapter 11). Wall (1993) gives a definition of sustainable development as it arises from work and extensive formal and informal discussions with the people of Bali, Indonesia. This Balinese-based approach to sustainable development is more culturally and socially oriented than views of the concept in North America of Europe. Yet it appears to be appropriate in numerous contexts, for example, Mexico, the US Southwest, Northern Canada and among native people – if applied with sensitivity not only to the environment but local ways of life.

Another concept that has been advanced to help deal with tourism and its effects is *ecotourism*, another rather general notion that has been defined and applied in various ways in various places (Ceballos-Lascuráin, 1996; Nolan, 1999; Tenneson, 1998; Ross and Wall, 1999). Others have noted the general nature of concepts such as ecotourism and have suggested that they will not address the unwanted effects of tourism if applied in name only. Nelson (1994) for example, has pointed out that conservation management of the kind now advocated under the name of ecotourism has been a part of policy in Banff and other national parks in North America for decades. Yet his research shows that the use of this concept has been associated with the widespread dissemination of tourism facilities and activities throughout much of the park during that time. He consequently calls for consistent and careful application of impact assessment procedures for tourism policies, programmes and projects, and for life cycle, ethics and civics approaches to planning, management and decision making.

At this point we can turn from the policies and institutional arrangements that apply to tourism to those that apply to national parks and protected areas in Mexico, the USA and Canada. These policies and arrangements are very complex in all three countries. Policies and institutional arrangements apply at various levels of government including the federal, state or provincial and the municipal. Private organisations are also increasingly active in the protected areas field in all three countries.

An excellent overview of the Mexican situation has been provided by Salcido (1995), who notes that Mexico's wealth in biodiversity is recognised world-wide. It encompasses an array of natural communities and ecosystems ranging from those of the tropics to the deserts of Northern Mexico. Salcido points out that this richness has suffered deterioration at an accelerating rate in recent years, largely because of exploitive activities arising from debt and other economic difficulties faced by Mexico during that time. He concludes that management of protected areas in

Mexico is still incipient and has serious deficiencies; legally there is a system but in reality none exists.

Salcido reports that more than 670 protected areas of various kinds have been created at the federal and state levels. However, according to him, these figures reveal only the extent of the paperwork that has gone into establishing protected areas under more than 150 categories and names throughout Mexico and the figures do not reflect what is truly being protected. A summary of the federal-level protected areas that have been established 'on paper' in Mexico is shown on Table 18.1.

According to Salcido, the protected area field in Mexico also lacks the planning, research and training programmes designed for protected areas as well as the professional input that is needed to develop an effective natural areas system. Salcido sees some hope in recent government moves such as the establishment of a Ministry of Natural Resources and Fisheries (SEMARNAP) but concludes by saying that the future of protected areas is uncertain.

In contrast to Mexico, a comprehensive and effective national parks and protected areas system is in place throughout the USA and is especially strong at the federal level. The Department of Interior houses the national parks, the forest reserves and the fish and wildlife refuges that are the main elements of the system. The Department also administers the 1960s Wilderness Act which provides for special legal status for wilderness in all these types of protected areas as well as in lands administered by the Bureau of Public Land (BLM). Hundreds of federal protected areas are in operation across the USA. These are supplemented by state systems of varying quality, including those of California's with laws providing for special designation of wilderness.

The US national park and protected area system is a highly political as well as a diverse administrative system. Large non-government organisations such as the National Park and Conservation Association, the Sierra Club, the Wilderness Society and the World Wildlife Fund are powerful watchdogs and lobbyists who push for improved policies and practices in an ongoing and vigorous manner. The US governmental system also allows much greater freedom and opportunity to individual elected members of the House of Representatives or the Senate in

Table 18.1   Summary of federal-level Mexican protected areas

Management category	Number of areas	Extent (ha)
Main categories of SINAP		
Biosphere Reserves	17	6 759 264
Special Biosphere Reserves	18	738 725
National Parks	60	824 653
Natural Monuments	3	13 023
Marine National Parks	2	386 006
Areas of Protection for Natural Resources (terrestrial and aquatic wildlife)	5	1 391 355
Other protected areas (beaches)	18	33 305
Research Stations	2	749
Subtotal, main categories of SINAP	125	10 147 082 (5.07% of national territory)

Source: Salcido (1995)

preparing and pushing for their own legislation, policies, practices, funding and ideas for national parks. Many park and other conservation initiatives have come about in this manner and in ways which would not be possible in the Mexican or Canadian political systems which are more centrally driven by the president and the prime minister, respectively.

The US national parks are part of a family of protected areas programmes that offer various recreation and tourism opportunities, and conservation efforts. This evolving family includes national monuments, national preserves, national seashores, wild and scenic rivers, riparian conservation areas and national heritage areas. The system involves various ownership arrangements, as well as various ways of cooperating with other federal, state and local government agencies and with private organisations and groups.

This array of arrangements in turn allows for many different opportunities for tourism, including mass tourism, adventure tourism, ecotourism and heritage tourism. The results can be favourable to both tourism and conservation. However, they have been associated also with many conflicts and conservation challenges. A well-known example is the extensive construction of facilities for recreation and tourism in Yosemite National Park, California, with adverse effects on environmental quality, notably on the floor of the main valley. Another example is snowmobiling in Yellowstone National Park. This activity started gradually but now attracts thousands of users from ever larger areas, causing major air pollution on numerous winter weekends. Zoning systems, environmental impact assessment and other procedures have been developed in Canada, the USA and other countries such as Australia in attempts to protect against such developments and conditions (Buckley, 1999). Very few analyses of the use and effectiveness of these zoning systems, impact assessment and other policies and procedures are known, at least in the public sense (Dearden and Berg, 1993; Cahn and Cahn, 1995; Sellars, 1998).

After 1985, the US National Parks Service (NPS) added 31 new national parks, reaching a total of 370 protected areas of various kinds by 1995. At this time, visits to the NPS areas had grown to 270 million annually. At this time also, budgets were cut to meet political concerns about national debt and the size of government spending overall. The US NPS appropriations for 1996 fell 6.6 per cent from 1995 (Reynolds, 1995, p. 23) and these budget problems continue today. The result is growing disrepair of bridges, buildings, pollution control facilities, trails, and firefighting equipment. Interpretive programmes 'long believed to be the key ingredient to an aware, interested and involved public' have been reduced. Employee training and development programmes have been cut.

More fees have been introduced by the national parks to gain revenue. Efforts also are underway to increase returns from food concessions and other sources. This greater emphasis on revenue generation is a growing concern because it could result in more environmental damage as well as less access to the park by lower-income groups. A US National Accounting Office report depicts national parks at a crossroads and as needing serious corrective measures including one or more of the following: (1) increased financial resources; (2) reduction in the number of units in the national park system; and, (3) reduction in the level of visitor services (Reynolds, 1995, p. 72). The last two possibilities would certainly have negative effects on recreation and tourism and should be a significant concern for the tourism industry.

Policies and institutional arrangements for national parks and other protected areas in Canada are in some ways similar and in some ways different than those in the US (Nelson, 1997; Vogelsang, 1998). Canada has a well-established system of national parks that has been developed to represent its different natural regions. (Parks Canada, 1994). About 35 terrestrial national parks have been created to date with many natural regions remaining to be represented. Despite major efforts, only a few marine parks – or what are now called national marine conservation areas – have been created. The protected areas system is not as wide-ranging and adaptive in Canada as it is in the USA. At the federal level, counterparts to national recreation areas, national seashores, national monuments, and national heritage areas do not exist in Canada. This reduces the federal government's flexibility to provide more explicitly for recreation and tourism while working for different levels and types of conservation. Moreover, Canada still has a long distance to go in developing a large independent and influential NGO system comparable to that in the USA.

At the outset of the development of national parks in North America in the late nineteenth century, the Canadian government saw tourism as having a stronger place in national parks than nature conservation, whose stature has developed gradually to the present day. To this end, the government assisted with the development of townsites and other centres for businesses and the people serving tourists in national parks. The USA did not support such townsites and centres in national parks and controlled tourism services more effectively through concessions licensed by the federal government. In recent years, the Canadian government has given residents of Banff townsite powers of local government. Such arrangements have led to more wide-ranging and intense tourism and associated environmental effects in Canada than in US national parks (see also Dearden, Chapter 12).

Like the USA, financial and general support for national parks and other protected areas in Canada has also been cut by the federal as well as provincial governments. The national parks budget has been reduced by about 40 per cent in the last several years. Measures similar to those in the USA have also been introduced, including more and higher fees, and greater acceptance of commercial activities and revenue generation. Again, the concerns are the potential damage to the ecosystem and the natural resources of parks. Equity in access to national park opportunities by people of lower incomes is also a concern in Canada.

In Mexico, the USA and Canada – as well as other countries – tourism, therefore, is an increasing challenge to national parks but so also are the logging, mining and other exploitive activities conducted around them (Buckley and Pannell, 1990; Gauthier, 1993; Salcido, 1995; Nelson, 1996a, b, 1997; Burford, 1997; Wang and Miko, 1997; Tenneson, 1998). As population growth and economic development have proceeded during the last few decades, these pressures have moved closer and closer to park boundaries. As island biogeography, landscape ecology and other ecosystem theory indicates, park ecosystems cannot be sustained in the form of fortresses or islands separate from surrounding lands, waters and the dynamic atmosphere. Wolves, bears and other animals move across boundaries, as do rivers and polluted air. Mining, logging, tourism and other developments outside the boundaries, coupled with tourism and related developments inside, threaten the long-term well-being of parks and their regions.

In this context, tourism pressures and effects are important current and potential influences on the sustainability of park ecosystems. However, they are also part of the larger problem of how to conserve nature in Canada and the USA in the face of a growing consumer society and ongoing economic development. This challenge has led to a growing interest in what is called 'greater park ecosystem' and 'ecosysterm conservation planning' in the USA and Canada respectively (Nelson and Skibicki, 1998). The ecological health of the parks depends on land use and conservation policies and practices outside as well as inside them. The wildlife, water conservation and other ecological services provided by the parks are also of vital importance to sustainable development of surrounding lands and waters. In Canada this has led to a requirement that each national park prepare an ecosystem conservation plan which addresses ecological and land use policies and practices inside and outside the park. This plan builds not only on the ecological but also on the communication, negotiation, and human dimensions of planning, management and decision making. One major result has been calls for changes in attitude and behaviour on the part of all those concerned with tourism in national parks. Thus, tourism personnel are being urged to recognise the challenge and take it more deeply into their understanding, their attitudes and their ways of doing things.

According to Stephen Woodley (of Parks Canada):

> Tourism in parks and protected areas is currently an industry with environmental impacts just like any other industry. Until it redefines its role, it should be regulated as a polluting industry.... The tourism industry must become an environmental watchdog and advocate, not only for the purpose of image but for the purpose of sustainability. The tourism industry must work to develop products that are appropriate to both the setting and ecosystem of parks and protected areas. As an industry it must not only accept but actually promote limits to both the type and scale of tourism activities in parks and protected areas. Finally the industry should work with protected area managers to ensure that whole ecosystems are protected and not just the areas within park boundaries (Woodley, S., 1993, p. 94).

Planning, management, decision-making

The big question is how all these changes are to be made or come about. In posing the question in this way, the search is not so much for a list of desirable, ethical guidelines or other practices of the kind frequently advocated for park and protected area staff, tourism personnel, or tourists themselves (Lindberg and Hawkins, 1993; Scace, 1993; Ceballos-Lascuráin, 1996). Rather the question is put in a fundamental way to signal that we need to consider major modifications to the more directed or corporate types of planning and management that have predominated in the fields of tourism, and parks and protected areas in the past.

To promote desirable increases in cooperation, communication, and inter-organisation learning, we need more interactive and adaptive approaches of a civic as well as a directed, corporate or managerial kind (Faludi, 1973; Hudson, 1979; Briassoulis, 1989). Professional planners and managers have recognised the ways in which classical objective-driven planning by an organisation tends to close out other stakeholders and to be rather insensitive to changes in the operational environment (Etzioni, 1973; Friedmann, 1973). Newer approaches such as *adaptive and integrated resources management* are more promising in bringing stakeholders together early and throughout planning, management and decision-making (Holling, 1978; Margerum and Born, 1995, Margerum, 1997). Such approaches also tend to deal better with 'surprises' and uncertainty. In this respect, management is envisioned as a series of experiments which can be monitored, assessed and adapted as considered necessary. Yet, like classic rational or corporate planning, these approaches still tend to focus on concepts such as mandate and on the idea of lead and supporting agencies or groups. These approaches do not seem to be as open and encouraging to interaction among different agencies and groups as they might be. Nor do they seem to leave much room for stronger roles in planning, management and decision making by non-government organisations. These would be especially important in circumstances in which public and private groups and individuals with different values, interests and goals might communicate, negotiate and work together as, for example, in monitoring and assessing environmental change in a local or 'home' environment and in the process increasing overall knowledge and civic response capacity (Fisher and Urey, 1981; Chipeniuk, 1993).

In this context, agencies and groups will have to move beyond organisationally directed planning into the wider world of civic decision making (Nelson and Serafin, 1994; Cardinall and Day, 1998). The new system will have to recognise explicitly that order and control are generally not possible in the complex, pluralistic and dynamic fields of tourism and national parks and protected areas (Nelson, 1994). These fields involve many different people and a variety of groups of different size, form, purpose and values. To understand, control and direct such a system is exceedingly difficult and beyond any models or approaches relying primarily or solely on science and on formal professional planning and management. Science and professionalism are necessary but not sufficient to the task. More socially inclusive, transactive, or interactive and adaptive planning and decision making are needed.

Another very promising way forward is *regional planning*. Interest in it has risen and fallen over the years and suffered from the emergence of directed, corporate or sectoral planning in the 1960s, 1970s and 1980s. Interest has revived, however, for a variety of reasons, including the new scientific underpinnings offered by the development of ecosystem science.

Regional planning has advantages in complex, pluralistic and dynamic situations like those applying to tourism or national parks today. First, regional planning involves identifying and working within a given geographical area of interest. Such areas can be defined in terms of various measures or criteria, including ecological, social and economic ones of the kind being considered in this chapter. Second, understanding a region involves both the natural and human histories of an area, and their interaction, again a significant attribute in terms of our topic. Third, understanding a region involves considering a range of interacting variables, factors, or fields, although focus can be placed on a given topic or relationship such as tourism or parks and protected areas. Fourth, comprehending a region involves considerable understanding of the laws, policies, agencies, groups, and other institutional arrangements that have worked to guide land use, communities, economies and ecosystems to their present state. This kind of understanding makes us aware of arrangements that have been used in the past, to what effect, and how they could be built upon and augmented in future.

Some examples of relevant regional planning arise primarily from government and include the Ecosystem Conservation Plans for Canadian National Parks (Nelson and Skibicki, 1997) and the California Desert Protection Act passed by the US Congress in 1994 (Cunningham and Burke, 1996). The Desert Protection Act brings together numerous federal, state and local agencies as well as private groups around planning, managing and deciding upon the interaction among increasingly destructive recreation and tourism policies and practices, mining and other land uses, and nature conservation in the southern deserts of California. Approaches such as Ecosystem Conservation Planning and the Desert Protection Act arise from a science-based understanding of the natural environment and a broad civic approach to planning and decision making. Both of these examples are still unfolding, however, and it is too early to judge how well they will work from the standpoint of tourism, parks and protected area and other interests.

A third example – the Yellowstone to Yukon Bioregion (Y2Y) – arises largely from the efforts of private or non-government groups (Locke, 1997). The Y2Y involves a huge area with many diverse natural characteristics and human dimensions. The NGOs involved in the Y2Y use scientific theory and methods, for example the identification of corridors and gaps between the protected areas which are seen as the basic framework for the conservation and sustainable development of the bioregion. The NGOs also use civic processes such as assemblies or 'rendezvous' of many organisations, groups and individuals to build interaction and support while not necessarily providing specific direction.

As a final example, the biosphere reserve approach has been used with considerable success in some areas and holds promise for others (Baumgartl, 1997). One instructive case is the Great Smokies Biosphere in the southern Appalachian region of the USA. This biosphere has been built on interaction among many federal, state and local governments as well as private groups, universities and schools. We need careful assessments of these regional approaches and their effects as a basis for addressing the interactions among tourism, protected areas and other land uses more effectively for as many involved interests, agencies, groups and individuals as possible. In this respect, regional planning is a handmaiden for local stewardship initiatives which can be seen as linking the conservation programmes of parks and protected areas more effectively with other land uses and interests in an area or region of concern where such interests can include tourism (Brown and Mitchell, 1997).

Acknowledgements

I would like to thank the many people in government and the private domain who helped me with my work on tourism and national parks over the last three or four decades. They are unfortunately too numerous to mention here, and include many students who worked with me on these and other projects. I would especially like to thank Ken Van Osch and Heather Fraser who prepared the manuscript and Dr Patrick Lawrence who prepared the References. I am especially grateful to the Social Sciences and Humanities Research Council of Canada for supporting much of my research over the years.

References

Baumgartl, H., 1997, The potential role of biosphere reserves in piloting effective cooperative management systems for heritage, landscape and nature conservation. In *National parks and protected areas: keystones to conservation and sustainable development*, J.G. Nelson and R. Serafin, eds, pp. 187–191, Springer-Verlag, Berlin

Berry, T., 1990, *The dream of the earth*, Sierra Club Books Paperback Edition, Sierra Club, San Francisco

Briassoulis, H., 1989, Theoretical orientations in environmental planning: an inquiry into alternative approaches, *Environmental Management*, **13**(4): 381–392

Brown, J. and Mitchell, B., 1997, Extending the reach of national parks and protected areas: local stewardship initiatives. In *National parks and protected areas: keystones to conservation and sustainable development*, J.G. Nelson and R. Serafin, eds, pp. 103–116. Springer-Verlag, Berlin

Buckley, R., 1999, Tools and indicators for managing tourism in parks. *Annals of Tourism Research*, **26**(1): 207–209

Buckley, R. and Pannell, J., 1990, Environmental impacts of tourism and recreation in national parks and conservation reserves. *Journal of Tourism Studies* **1**(1): 24–31

Burford, T., 1997, *Backpacking in Mexico*, Bradt Publications, Bucks, UK, and The Globe Pequot Press, Inc., Old Saybrook, CT

Butler, R.W., 1991, Tourism, environment and sustainable development. *Environmental Conservation*, **18**(3): 201–209

Butler, R.W., 1993, Tourism – an evolutionary perspective. In *Tourism and sustainable development: monitoring, planning, managing*, J.G. Nelson, R.W. Butler and G. Wall, eds, pp. 27–44, Department of Geography Publication Series, No. 37, University of Waterloo, Waterloo, ON

Cahn, R. and Cahn, P., 1995, Policing the policy. *National Parks*, **69**(9–10): 37–41

Cardinall, D. and Day, J.C., 1998, Embracing value and uncertainty in environmental management and planning: a heuristic model. *Environments: A Journal of Interdisciplinary Studies*, **25**(2,3): 110–125

Ceballos-Lascuráin, H., 1996, *Tourism, eco-tourism and protected areas*, IUCN, Gland

Chipeniuk, R., 1993, Vernacular bio-indicators and citizen monitoring of environmental change. In *Tourism and sustainable development: monitoring, planning, managing*, J.G. Nelson, R.W. Butler and G. Wall eds, Department of Geography Publication Series No. 37, University of Waterloo, Waterloo, ON

Cunningham, B. and Burke, D., 1996, *Hiking California's desert parks*, Falcon Press Publishing Co., Helena and Billings, Montana

Dearden, P., 1993, Cultural aspects of tourism and sustainable development: tourism and the hill tribes of Northern Thailand. In *Tourism and sustainable development: monitoring, planning, managing*, J.G. Nelson, R.W. Butler and G. Wall, eds, pp. 165–178, Department of Geography Publication Series, No. 37, University of Waterloo: Waterloo, ON

Dearden, P. and Berg, L., 1993, Canada's national parks: a model of administrative penetration. *The Canadian Geographer*, **37**(3) 194–211

Etzioni, A., 1973, Mixed scanning: a third approach to decision-making. In *A reader in planning theory*, A. Faludi, ed., Pergamon Press, New York

Faludi, A. (ed.), 1973, *A reader in planning theory*, Pergamon Press, Oxford

Fisher, R. and Urey, W., 1981, *Getting to yes: negotiating agreement without giving in*, Penguin Press, New York

Friedmann, J., 1973, *Retracking America: a theory of transactive planning*, Anchor Press, New York

Gauthier, D.A., 1993, Sustainable development, tourism and wildlife. In *Tourism and sustainable development: monitoring, planning, managing*, J.G. Nelson, R.W. Butler and G. Wall, eds, pp. 97–109, Department of Geography Publication Series No. 37, University of Waterloo, Waterloo, ON

Holling, C.S., 1978, *Adaptive environmental assessment and management*, John Wiley, New York

Hudson, B.M., 1979, Comparison of current planning theories: counterparts and contradictions. *Journal of the American Institute of Planners*, **45**(4): 389–398

Ishwaren, N., 1994, The role of protected areas in promoting sustainable development. *Parks*, **4**(3): 2–7

Lindberg, K. and Hawkins, D.E., 1993, *Ecotourism: a guide for planners and managers*, The Ecotourism Society, North Bennington, VT

Locke, H., 1997, The role of Banff National Park as a protected area in the Yellowstone to Yukon Mountain corridor of Western North America. In *National parks and protected areas: keystones to conservation and sustainable development*, J.G. Nelson and R. Serafin, eds, pp. 117–124 Springer-Verlag, Berlin

Long, V., 1993, Techniques for socially sustainable tourism development: lessons from Mexico. In *Tourism and sustainable development: monitoring, planning, managing*, J.G. Nelson, R.W. Butler and G. Wall, eds, pp. 201–208, Department of Geography Publication Series No. 37, University of Waterloo, Waterloo, ON

Margerum, R.D., 1997, Integrated approaches to environmental planning and management. *Journal of Planning Literature*, **11**(4): 459–475

Margerum, R.D. and Born, S.M., 1995, Integrated environmental management: moving from theory to practice. *Journal of Environmental Planning and Management*, **38**(3): 371–391

Mathieson, A. and Wall, G., 1982, *Tourism: economic, physical, and social impacts*, Addison-Wesley Longman, London

McNeeley, J.A., 1988, *Economics and biological diversity*, IUCN, Gland

Moss, M., 1988, *Landscape ecology and management*, Polyscience Publications Inc., Montreal

Nelson, J.G., 1993, Are tourism growth and sustainability objectives comparable? Civics, assessment, informed choice. In *Tourism and sustainable development: monitoring, planning, managing*, J.G. Nelson, R.W. Butler and G. Wall, eds, pp. 254–268, Department of Geography Publication Series No. 37, University of Waterloo, Waterloo, ON

Nelson, J.G., 1994, The spread of ecotourism: some planning implications. *Environmental Conservation*, **21**(3): 248–255

Nelson, J.G., 1996a, How much is enough? Banff and the Bow Valley corridor. *Heritage Canada* September/October: 5–9

Nelson, J.G., 1996b, Outdoor recreation and tourism. In *State of Canada's Environment 1996*, Government of Canada, Ottawa, pp. 116–128

Nelson, J.G., 1997, The status of the Heritage Estate in Canada and Ontario in protected areas in our modern world. *Parks Canada Ecosystem Science Review Reports*, No. 005, 135–142

Nelson, J.G. and Butler, R.W., 1974, Recreation and the Environment. In *Perspectives on Environment*, I. Manners and M. Mikesell, eds, Association of American Geographers, Washington, D.C.

Nelson, J.G. and Serafin, R., 1994, Improved monitoring and assessment for environmental decision-making. In *Public issues: a geographical perspective*, J. Audrey, and J.G. Nelson, eds, pp. 391–412, Heritage Resources Centre and Department of Geography Publication Series, University of Waterloo, Waterloo, ON

Nelson, J.G. and Serafin, R., 1997, *National parks and protected areas: keystones to conservation and sustainable development*, Springer-Verlag, Berlin

Nelson, J.G. and Skibicki, A., 1997, *Georgian Bay Islands National Park ecosystem conservation plan*, Heritage Resources Centre, University of Waterloo, Waterloo, ON

Nelson, J.G. and Skibicki, A., 1998, Some approaches to planning for greater park ecosystems in Ontario, Canada. *Salzburger Geographische Arberten*, Bandsz 9–23

Nelson, J.G., Butler, R. and Wall, G. (eds), 1993, *Tourism and sustainable development: monitoring, planning and managing*, Department of Geography Publication Series No. 37, University of Waterloo, Waterloo, ON

Nelson, J.G., Needham, R.D. and Mann, D.L. (eds), 1978, *International experiences with national parks and related reserves*, Department of Geography Publication Series, University of Waterloo, Waterloo, ON

Nolan, S., 1999, Ecotourism: too much of a good thing? *The Globe and Mail*, 10 May: A19

Parks Canada, 1994, *Guiding Principles and Operational Policies*, Ministry of Supply and Services Canada, Ottawa

Reynolds, J., 1995, National parks in the United States: an overview of current conditions. *The George Wright Forum*, **12**(4): 22–29

Ross, S. and Wall, G., 1999, Ecotourism: towards congruence between theory and practice. *Tourism Management*, **20**: 123–132

Salcido, G.P.R., 1995, Natural protected areas in Mexico. *The George Wright Forum*, **12**(4): 30–38

Scace, R.C., 1993, An ecotourism perspective. In *Tourism and sustainable development: monitoring, planning, managing*, J.G. Nelson, R.W. Butler and G. Wall, eds, pp. 59–82, Department of Geography Publication Series No. 37, University of Waterloo, Waterloo, ON

Sellars, R.W., 1998, Science or tradition? *National Parks*, **72**(1–2): 29–40

Tennesen, M., 1998, The road less travelled. *National Parks* **72**(5–6): 28–31

Vogelsang, R., 1998, National parks in Canada: tourism and nature conservation. *Die Erde*, **128**: 139–157

Wall, G., 1993, Towards a tourism typology. In *Tourism and sustainable development: monitoring, planning, managing*, J.G. Nelson, R.W. Butler and G. Wall, eds, pp. 45–58, Department of Geography Publication Series No. 37, University of Waterloo, Waterloo, ON

Wang, C.-Y. and Miko, P.S., 1997, Environmental impacts of tourism on US national parks. *Journal of Travel Research* **36**(1): 31–36

Woodley, A., 1993, Tourism and sustainable development: the community perspective. In *Tourism and sustainable development: monitoring, planning, managing*, J.G. Nelson, R.W. Butler and G. Wall, eds, pp. 134–147, Department of Geography Publication Series No. 37, University of Waterloo, Waterloo, ON

Woodley, S., 1993, Tourism and sustainable development in parks and protected areas. In *Tourism and sustainable development: monitoring, planning, managing*, J.G. Nelson, R.W. Butler and G. Wall, eds, pp. 83–96, Department of Geography Publication Series No. 37, University of Waterloo, Waterloo, ON

19 Tourism and national parks in the twenty-first century

R.W. BUTLER

Introduction

As the world enters the third millennium, national parks are well into their second century. The idea of establishing a system of protected areas for a range of purposes, of which tourism (and recreation) is often a major feature, is not only well established, but has received strong endorsement with the general acceptance of the principles of sustainable development. National parks were one of the few specific area discussed in the Brundtland Report (WCED, 1987) related to the issues and problems discussed in this book, although the emphasis there was clearly upon the conservation function of such park systems. As earlier chapters (in particular, Boyd and Butler, Booth and Simmons, Hall, Parker and Ravenscroft, and Dearden) have clearly shown, tourism (and its counterpart, recreation) has always been a major feature of national parks in most countries, and in the more recently established systems is likely to assume even greater significance (see the chapters by Goodwin and Cresswell and Maclaren). The problems implicit in and created by the use of parks for tourism and recreation purposes are not likely to diminish in the future, but in fact, for the reasons discussed in this book, are almost certain to increase in importance and complexity. This chapter proceeds by reviewing the future role of tourism and national parks at a general level in the context of the general framework discussed in the introductory chapter, and discusses the issues which are likely to threaten the already difficult relationship between tourism and national parks in the future.

To call for a review of the relationship between protected areas in general, and national parks in particular with the leisure industry should not be interpreted as a call for a change in current relationships. Many national parks systems have performed amazingly well in terms of juggling their twin (and often multiple) mandates of protection and providing tourism and recreation opportunities. That there have been undesirable impacts upon the ecosystems of some national parks (see Dearden's chapter on Banff for a good example) because of tourism-related development is unfortunately inevitable, although none the less regrettable. To attempt to delete the tourism role of national parks, either unilaterally or globally, is not only unrealistic but would almost certainly be counter-productive to the parks movement as it would remove a great deal of public sympathy and support for the parks concept. While the scientist and the academic may appreciate the need to preserve and protect large areas of the earth's surface (land and water) for ecological reasons (including species maintenance, species diversity, gene pools and even human mental benefit), and while the public, at least in some countries, may also subscribe to such a viewpoint in general, to attempt to keep the public from enjoying parks such as Yellowstone, Banff, Mount Cook and others would not only result in considerable opposition but could even cause changes in legislation to change the functions of national parks or 'delist' some parks. It might be difficult at the present time, given the nature, scale and permanence of impacts in such parks, to justify their retention as national parks on the basis of preservation alone. Certainly they do not represent, unfortunately, pristine unimpaired ecosystems throughout parts, if not much, of their surface areas. In some systems, where significant permanent populations live within park boundaries (the UK is the obvious example, as noted by Ravenscroft and Parker, but such a situation exists in other countries elsewhere in Europe, in Africa and in Australasia) the concept of preservation of ecosystems as the only objective for such park systems is clearly unrealistic and unobtainable.

In looking to the future, therefore, it is difficult to see beyond a continuation of the problems which are currently facing national parks as they attempt to fulfil their multi-functional role. Despite the ongoing series of resource conflicts discussed by Dearden and other authors in this book, it is not unrealistic to anticipate that it will be tourism which will cause most national parks the greatest difficulty in the future. Tourism shows no signs of decreasing, indeed all prognostications suggest that it will continue to grow in the future throughout the world (WTO, 1999). The factors which have given rise to the great expansion of tourism over the past century are likely to be those which will lie behind its expected continued expansion in the next. Greater affluence, greater free time, improved mobility, greater freedom to travel and improved infrastructures are all likely to remain positive trends in the future. While the absolute rate of growth of tourism may decline and there may be fewer significant innovations such as the jet aircraft and the package holiday, doubtless other innovations and improvements will appear. The apparent increased interest in and concern for the environment (Mowforth and Munt, 1998) is likely to manifest itself in a greater desire to visit impressive and significant landscapes such as those found in national parks, thus placing even greater pressures on the accessible parks than at present.

If this is correct the management problems and techniques to solve them discussed earlier by Vaske, Donnelly and Whittaker, and Sowman and Pearce are likely to be at best only partial and temporary responses. It is probably not overly pessimistic to say that the most popular national parks such as Yellowstone, or Banff, will not be able to withstand even slightly increased visitation rates without major changes in the way they are managed and the experience they offer having to be introduced. One cannot see a happy and universally acceptable solution to these pressures. Even in parks such as Masai Mara, Galapagos, or Sagarmatha (Everest), where actual visitation is much less than at the most popular parks in North America and elsewhere, major problems are already present in terms of impacts on wildlife and vegetation (see Lilieholm and Romney, Weaver, and Nepal, this book).

Future scenarios

A number of possible scenarios arise, none of which are particularly attractive if one is concerned over parks continuing to meet fully their complex and often contradictory mandates. The first would be for national parks to severely reduce or even totally exclude tourist visitation from all or parts of their areas. A second would be for some parks to cease to have a primary protection mandate and instead place their emphasis on providing tourism and recreation opportunities, similar to the National Recreation Areas of the US system. A third alternative is to 'sacrifice' parts of national parks to development in the hope of saving the remaining, often signficantly larger areas (this third option is currently being practised in many parks throughout the world on a purely pragmatic if unstated basis). In reality all these scenarios present problems rather than solutions to park authorities. In the first case, any or all of these scenarios may be counter to the legislation and stated policies of the park systems and would be unlikely to go unchallenged in most countries. Second, while the third scenario has the apparent advantage that it would keep most parties somewhat satisfied, in reality, over the long term, the pressures from tourism and recreation would inevitably increase as they have done for the last century and a quarter and the area devoted to related activities and developments would inevitably increase. This has been the pattern in most North American parks (see Nelson, Chapter 18) and can be seen in the more popular parks in many other parts of the world.

To prohibit or severely restrict pleasure use of national parks is highly contentious and difficult to implement. The use of zoning systems in operation in many park systems can go some way towards prohibiting access by recreation users to parks, but it is rare for zoning to prohibit entry of visitors to anything but extremely small portions of parks. Rather this method of management tends to restrict the creation of facilities and means of access, and by so doing keep numbers relatively low. Only in parks which have few visitors for the most part have those responsible been able to impose the kind of capacity limits and numbers described by Vaske, Donnelly and Whittaker as operating in Gwaan Hada or Brooks. Only perhaps, in remote parks which receive relatively few visitors whose primary interest is wildlife, or in parks in which traditional cultures still exist and are important, are such measures likely to win and retain general support among visitors.

In the case of parks that are heavily developed and have a wide range of facilities and which have received large numbers of visitors for most of their existence, it will be much harder to impose realistic capacity limits, let alone remove facilities in an attempt to restore habitat. The likelihood of the removal of the Banff Springs Hotel, the ski facilities at Sunshine and Lake Louise and much of the permanent population of Banff townsite is somewhat unlikely to say the least. Yet without such drastic action, little can be achieved in Banff to restore the park, or at least the Bow Valley, to anything like the state which it was at when the park was established. The actions recently decided for Banff, as outlined by Dearden (Chapter 12) were not without controversy and opposition. The continued presence of townsites, ski facilities, hotels and other tourist facilities within parks, and with them the traffic jams of Yellowstone and Yosemite, the air traffic within Grand Canyon, and the daily procession of tourist boats to the Great Barrier Reef from Cairns only serve to increase demand, paradoxical though that may appear.

However, the fact that tourists keep coming to such popular parks means that money can be made and jobs created, and in many peripheral areas and in less-developed countries these are likely to take priority over more abstract issues such as species diversity and ecosystem maintenance. To many governments centrally located far from such parks the willingness of tourists to continue to visit these parks, despite, for the most part, a gradual decline in their environmental purity, means that further development and expansion of tourism is not only possible, but profitable in the broad sense. It is not only governments far from the parks which are relatively insensitive to park protection needs compared to the expansion of tourism. In many areas local residents and regional or state/provincial governments are equally or even more keen to see tourism (and sometimes other land uses) developed in national parks for financial and employment reasons. In Alberta provincial organisations have long opposed the restrictions on developments in the Rocky Mountain National Parks in Canada and argued for many changes, including ones as extreme as removing specific areas from the parks to allow tourist development to their full potential (Alberta Chamber of Commerce, 1971). While such views may not be expressed as strongly three decades later, there is still concern over restrictions on developments in the parks.

It is a fascinating although perhaps somewhat disturbing feature of national park planning and development that it is often local communities and local governments who are the most vocal supporters of the development of tourism in national parks in their locality, and it is frequently the federal parks agency (whatever its form may be) and national or international NGOs which are the strongest opponents of further development in these parks. On the international scale it is even more troublesome to witness that this pattern is often repeated, with developed world organisations protesting and opposing tourism and other developments in national parks in less-developed countries. One cannot help but feel uneasy that countries which established national parks with high and praiseworthy ideals a century or more ago are now somewhat guilty of criticising other communities for following their own examples. Namely, establishing parks for a combination of reasons, but wanting and needing to see those parks help support their economies and populations and therefore allowing considerable and varied development within their boundaries. Looking back at the role of tourism in the establishment of parks in North America and Australasia (Boyd and Butler, Booth and Simmons, Hall, and Dearden, this book), one can see a similar pattern being repeated elsewhere at an even faster rate.

To break that pattern, if it is to be broken, requires a different approach. Unfortunately what we are seeing in many national parks today is a process of incremental and unidirectional change, caused in many cases by tourism and recreation. If current trends continue, then this process will not only continue also but is likely to increase at a faster rate. The management actions discussed by Vaske, Donnelly and Whittaker, as noted above, are at best 'holding actions', delaying but not ultimately preventing further change and negative impacts on the environments of the parks in which they are being introduced. Too many factors lead inevitably to too many visitors and too many inappropriate uses of national parks.

To successfully introduce and operate a policy which would place the protection function of national parks clearly ahead of the public enjoyment and economic development options requires not only significant political courage but a willingness to face likely opposition from more than tourism proponents. Parks Canada has gone some way in this direction by placing a higher priority on ecological integrity than on use of national parks in Canada in its 1994 National Parks Policy but has not placed prohibitions on the entry of tourists to any parks (Parks Canada, 1994). To ban only tourists from vulnerable park ecosystems, or even entire parks would almost certainly be strongly opposed from many quarters, and the identification of tourists as the only problem in national parks is for the most part inaccurate and indefensible. Agricultural, forestry, mining and scientific interests also cause impacts and change in national parks (Dearden, Chapter 12), as do transportation, water, military and communications activities. To allow *any* inappropriate and harmful activities in national parks weakens greatly the case for excluding tourism. At an individual level the impact of a scientific researcher is often very considerably greater than that of a tourist, and much scientific research is undertaken within national parks for reasons of convenience and logistics rather than environmental necessity or potential management benefit. The transfer of results and the use of the results of the research undertaken is often minimal. Only in recent years has pressure from NGOs caused scientific research operations in Antarctica to be more environmentally sensitive (Hall and Johnston, 1995). In some cases it has been tourist and media concerns which have brought about changes in behaviour. Thus a prohibition on tourist entry to specific parks or parts of parks should only be introduced in conjunction with similar bans on entry for other reasons, unless there are truly crucial reasons why exemptions should be made. Such exemptions should be few and very much the exception to the general rule.

Such a policy of exclusion, however, can only work in conjunction with restoration, if the goal of such a policy were to return the parks to their natural 'original' ecosystems and processes. Here managers would enter a potentially endless minefield of moral and ethical issues which cannot be discussed fully here but which do need attention. The re-introduction of species extinct to specific parks may cause greater problems than the absence of that species, especially if reintroduction takes place into an environment significantly changed from that which existed at the time of extinction. Introducing bison or wolves into the North American national parks over which they once roamed, is likely to create a large number of problems within the parks and in adjacent areas. Even the maintenance of this traditional species can cause problems. In the case of Wood Buffalo National Park in Canada parks officials are planning to exterminate the original herd because of the risk of contamination of stock on cattle farms adjoining the park with brucelosis.

The introduction of wolves into US national parks has already created considerable controversy, not unrelated to the unfortunate and inacurate image of the animals in western folklore. Wolves are not likely to remain in a park but to hunt beyond park boundaries and come into contact with farmers and other residents in surrounding areas (Nelson, Chapter 18). The inevitable result has been claims of damage and harm to stock and humans and calls for hunts and extermination. In the absence of predators, bison or buffalo are likely to reach excessive numbers and need controlling if they are not to have severe effects on vegetation, in the same way that elk have done in the relative absence of large predators in Banff National Park (a situation artificially created almost a century ago). As noted earlier, parks are dynamic living environments and their development does not stop because one or more species disappear. Adjustments are made, niches are filled, and environmental processes continue, sometimes with changes of which we are unaware. The way back is rarely clear if even attainable, and the wisdom and appropriateness of attempting to put the clock back needs considerably more discussion. The 'era' approach to park management has generally been abandoned in favour of an evolutionary and 'hands-off' approach as the virtual impossibility of halting processes of vegetation succession and evolution itself have been appreciated (Conservation Foundation, 1972; Nelson and Butler, 1974).

Tourism pressures, however, are often in favour of maintaining what is felt to be the appropriate or 'right' appearance and environment of parks. In the UK this is a particular problem faced by many rural areas, not just those in national parks, where the national consciousness has a vision of what rural England should look like. The fact that it may be a somewhat false vision based on art, literature, nostalgia and the media in all forms from film makers to Christmas card producers is almost irrelevant. Any attempt at a restoration of the English landscape would face major problems of determining which landscape, real or imagined, and for which period of English history, restoration should be attempted, apart from the impracticality of such a task. Even restoring the Galapagos Islands flora and fauna to a 'pristine' state would be difficult, if not impossible, given that Darwin did not give a perfect and full picture of the islands, and the rationale for reproducing a pre-Caucasian or pre-human environment for human satisfaction is somewhat perverse.

New markets

The appeal of national parks for tourism was traditionally based on the inherent natural attractions of these parks, the scenery and wildlife in particular (Boyd and Butler, Booth and Simons, Hall, this book). In the past few decades there is no doubt that the gradual development of facilities has resulted in attracting a wider market, including skiers, golfers, fishermen, and those interested in more sedentary and urban pursuits. While in principle there is nothing wrong in such a broadening of the market and the user population, in practice this has often resulted in new and significant impacts upon the environments of parks, as well as major increases in total numbers of visitors. The practice of utilising national parks in tourism promotion material is as old as the parks themselves (Hart, 1983) but in recent years such promotional material is reaching a much wider audience, many members of which are not familiar with either the concept or role of national parks or the particular countries advertising. The result is a potential mismatch of demand and supply, or putting it in another way, visitors coming to parks expecting to engage in activities and to find facilities which are inappropriate for national park purposes. One result is for parks authorities to allow participation in activities and to develop facilities to meet and satisfy the expressed demand. Another result is disappointed visitors, which can ultimately result in changes in park policy and/or management if authorities wish to maintain tourist numbers and expenditures. Either result can spell problems in terms of maintaining a park's ecological quality and diversity.

The appearance of new forms of tourist activities in the last decade or so, for example hang-gliding and parasailing, heli-skiing, snowmobiliing, mountain biking and off-road vehicle use, all pose new threats to park environments. In most cases these uses are not specifically covered in park policies or legislation and the tendency is for users to try to gain access to parks for these activities until prohibited. Parks, especially in the developed world, are, therefore, under constant threat from new forms of tourism, some at least of which are not compatible with traditional park protection mandates or sustainable development principles (see Boyd, Chapter 11). Threats from new forms of tourism are not confined to those forms dependent upon technology alone. Large and rapid increases in numbers of ecotourists and other forms of tourism related to the natural environment have resulted in greatly increased pressure on interior backcountry areas of national parks in many regions of the world, areas which previously were rarely visited by tourists. Rare or unique species or features have attracted people to parts of the world formerly not popular with tourists, including islands such as Galapagos, the Himalayan peaks, and the jungles of Asia (see Weaver, Nepal, and Cresswell and Maclaren, this book). While the wildlife parks of Africa have long been popular with a limited number of visitors, in the last two decades numbers have increased markedly with the establishment of ecotourism, photo-safaris and other forms of tourism (see Goodwin, and Lilieholm and Romney, this book). There are no signs that such forms of tourism will not continue to increase in popularity and new forms emerge, unless the world suffers severe economic or political instability at a global level. New markets are therefore a two-edged sword for national parks. On the one hand, they represent increased support and financial return for the systems, but, on the other, increased and varying impacts on the environment and conflicts for management.

New areas

It is tempting to say that there are now few new areas to be established as national parks. It is perhaps true to say that there are few new systems of national parks to be established in the world, but there is a considerable way to go before all systems can claim to be complete. Many systems are established on the basis of representing not only spectacular landscapes but also representative examples, and thus considerable expansion of some systems is still necessary. While representative, as opposed to spectacular, landscapes may not be as attractive to tourists, in reality, the designation of an area as a national park is likely to attract tourists almost regardless of the nature of the landscape. National park designation carries with it baggage and implications such that it is likely to be assumed to be worthy of visitation by virtue of its very designation. This can be problematic when designation was given to prevent impact from over-use and visitation in the first place!

Of all the new areas in the world which warrants national park status, Antarctica is probably pre-eminent, but because of its international rather than national status such designation is not possible at present. It may be that one or more international parks, as discussed by Timothy (Chapter 16), may be established, but that too is unlikely. Rather, as Marsh (Chapter 9) notes, special areas with management policies may be designated in lieu of national parks. The world is likely, therefore, to see two types of expansion of national parks. One is through the completion of existing systems, sometimes through what may be regarded at present as unconventional means, to accommodate other land uses where new parks are not in virgin wilderness. The other is through the establishment of new systems of national parks, which may run the full gamut of landscapes. Of all countries not currently having a national parks system, Scotland is probably the most surprising. Recent government pronouncements and the creation of a Scottish Assembly, along with a measure of devolution in 1999, may see this situation rectified. National parks in Scotland are likely to be in remoter parts of the country, protecting some of the most scenic areas, especially those under tourism and recreation pressure, but not necessarily following policies of representation or visitor needs. As has almost always been the case, in Scotland, as elsewhere, political pressures from interested parties are likely to be the determining factors in the ultimate selection of areas rather than ecological significance, landscape vulnerability or tourist need. Be that as it may, the creation of national parks in Scotland will represent another signficant step in completing a world system of national park systems.

Heritage tourism

Visitation to national parks can reasonably be regarded as a form of heritage tourism, since one of the major roles of national parks is protection of the natural heritage of a country. Whether visitors see themselves as being heritage tourists, ecotourists, or sightseers probably says more about the over-abundance of categories of tourism than it does about the purposes of the parks. Many national parks contain built or cultural heritage within their boundaries, however, and thus are clearly heritage attractions in more than the 'natural' heritage sense. In the Canadian system, as well as national parks, there are national historic parks, heritage rivers, and canals, while the US system has even more components (see Nelson, Chapter 18).

There remains an interesting area of research to pursue with respect to the relative roles of national parks and World Heritage Sites. One might argue that in some cases the systems duplicate one another, and while they may have different primary functions and purposes, there can be made a strong case for closer integration of their establishment, management and use. World Heritage Sites are, or have the potential to be, major tourist attractions. They face many of the same problems as national parks in terms of visitor numbers, pressures for change and the creation of additional, sometimes inappropriate, facilities, and confusion over their roles. Where the two systems overlap, for example the Rocky Mountain parks in Canada, it is not clear whether there are mutual benefits or problems arising. As the world tourism market is expanding in terms of interest in heritage tourism, this set of problems is likely to increase in severity and frequency, and national parks may experience even more visitation where they have cultural and built heritage features to offer the visitor as well the natural heritage which has traditionally been their major attraction.

Relationships

The relationship between tourism and national parks in most countries is both sensitive and complex. In many countries, particularly the oldest ones in terms of national parks systems, tourism has always been so intertwined with the establishment and early operation of the parks that they are probably inseperable in the public's mind. In some cases, such as Yellowstone and Banff, tourism was one of the key reasons for the parks' establishment and it would be a legitimate question to ask why these parks should be preserved if not for tourist purposes. They do not represent pristine wilderness any more and one might argue quite strongly that it is only the tourism value that justifies the maintenance of national park status to such areas. Of course, a strong case can be made for their protection on environmental grounds, but probably not any stronger than for protecting areas which adjoin but are outside of the park boundaries. It is precisely their tourism, and hence their historic heritage, which makes them unique and therefore appropriate for protection. Clearly such remarks do not apply to unique and relatively recent additions to national park systems such as the Great Barrier Reef Marine National Park in Australia. Where a park is protecting a unique natural feature such as the Reef, the Grand Canyon, or the Galapagos, it is hard to argue that tourism values should equal those of the environment. However, even in such situations, maintenance of some level of tourism visitation may be essential to obtain revenues to maintain protection over the park and to generate political support for the park's protection from other resource uses. As recent events have shown in Northern Australia, however, even widespread positive publicity over the attractions and significance of an area such as Kakadu National Park may not be sufficient to prevent resource exploitation being allowed (in this case in the form of mining).

In parks systems such as that of Canada and the USA, where representativeness of landscape and ecology is a key factor in the selection of new national parks, the selection of many of the older parks would often be hard to justify now if they were not already part of the system. Their initial selection represented compromises, political whims and economic pressures at the respective times of their creation, and it is precisely because they are popular tourists attractions that there appears to be support for their maintenance. New parks in remote inaccessible locations draw far less support, especially if their establishment threatens indigenous peoples' rights or potential economic gain from mineral or other resource exploitation. Parks officials are well aware of the political and economic realities of national park establishment, management and maintenance and it is generally a credit to their adaptiveness and political acumen that the parks in their care have been maintained in the way that they have. The battles which they have been fighting are not new ones, almost a century ago Harkin (commissioner of Canada's national parks) walked a thin line between park protection and tourist and other use (Nelson, 1982). Without the pioneer efforts of individuals such as Harkin and the compromises which they had to make to meet the multiple and often contradictory mandates which they were given, many of the early systems would have been in far worse state than they are today.

The role that tourism pressures and tourist needs and preferences should play in the development of national park policy and management has not been satisfactorily resolved. Such a role has, inevitably, to vary from country to country and perhaps even from park to park. Important though tourism may be in terms of often much-needed income and employment, unless such benefits can be maintained over the long term, which normally means maintaining the attractions which represent the reasons for tourists visiting the destination, then it should not have high priority. To allow any land use or resource activity to radically change a national park and its environmental integrity for short-term gain is surely unacceptable as we enter the third millennium. The battles to establish national parks have often been hard won and should not be sacrificed at the altar of short-term gain. In arguing thus in many ways one is arguing for sustainable development, in the sense that the principles of that doctrine include taking a long-term view, only allowing development in the present which does not preclude appropriate development in the future, which takes into account and protects natural processes, and which places a high priority on local populations and their needs. Unfortunately as noted earlier, there are often differences between what are expressed as local needs and global needs or preferences, particularly with respect to tourism and national parks.

Sustainable tourism, or what passes for that activity, is not necessarily the answer (see Boyd, Chapter 11). Tourism can never be sustainable, just as no single sector in isolation can ever be fully sustainable or independent (Butler, 1997: Wall, 1997). We have only one complete system, the global one, and even that is dependent on external sources for energy and light for many processes. It would be a mistake of considerable magnitude, in this author's opinion, to assume that sustainable tourism will solve the many and severe problems of tourism in national parks. Certainly, tourism operated along sustainable development principles would be infinitely preferable in national parks, as elsewhere, to tourism which is not operated on such principles, but that is rarely the issue. We have high-impacting, intensive tourism in a considerable number of parks involving large numbers of tourists and large amounts of money, in terms of investment and expenditures, and large numbers of people in employment. It is that form of tourism which needs the greatest attention, in order to make it more sustainable and less impacting on park environments. To ignore that and to allow or promote further development of tourism of an environmentally friendly or 'sustainable' form in national parks is to worsen the problem, not to improve it. It may be appropriate to allow, in some areas in some parks, more tourism development, and one would hope that that development, whether it be for small numbers of ecologically and culturally sensitive tourists or for larger numbers of relatively uninformed tourists simply interested in seeing the features of a particular national park, would always be on sustainable development principles. If such principles are not followed in national parks, there is little hope that they can be followed elsewhere in the world.

Problems

Many of the problems which need addressing have been illustrated earlier in this book. Of all the areas which tourism visits, national parks are generally the ones which are most vulnerable to unwanted impacts and change, and it becomes vitally important that research addresses the issues of carrying capacity and environmental impacts from tourism and related uses in a much more intensive manner. The research and management responses discussed by Vaske, Donnelly and Whittaker (Chapter 13) illustrate the type of work which is urgently necessary. Unfortunately much research in national parks is aimed at ecological study, which while possibly assisting interpretation and wildlife management, does very little to help the management of human use of the parks. Very few park authorities undertake extensive research on human behaviour in national parks, and yet most of the problems which management faces results from human use, misuse or over-use. As the majority of national parks employees, and particularly researchers have a natural science background and training, this focus is not surprising, and one cannot argue that their ecological research is unimportant. However, one can argue strongly that it must be balanced by an equivalent research focus on human activity and impact within national parks if exisiting and future problems are to be resolved and avoided.

A second area needing attention is the study of the relations between the tourism and recreation functions of national parks and their other functions. Most national park mandates and legislation include some references to tourism (recreation, enjoyment, leisure) but apart from general 'motherhood' statements qualified by terms such as 'reasonable' and 'appropriate', there is normally little exploration and explanation of how what are quite often diametrically opposed functions are supposed to function effectively within the same system. The framers and creaters of legislation have often made a difficult job almost impossible in terms of strict compliance with policies and legislation for park managers, particularly those in the field. The result is inevitably compromise and often individual variations within a system which can weaken the overall integrity of a system. Park managers can reasonably expect those above them to give them adequate tools and powers to do the job they are supposed to do, and among such tools should be clear guidelines on the relative priorities of tourism and other functions of parks. One cannot expect the problems outlined by Cresswell and Maclaren (Chapter 17) to disappear overnight from countries wracked by war and political turmoil, but similar problems occur in many other countries, even if in a less blatant manner. Confusion and lack of clear direction is a common problem in many countries with respect to the relative roles of tourism and conservation in national parks. It cannot and should not be solved on the ground in specific parks, but reather at the system level.

Neither can this problem be resolved by restrictions on certain types of accommodation in parks or by locating tourism and related developments outside parks, particularly if users of such developments then continue to enter and use the parks in virtually the same manner as if they were staying within parks. This author has long argued that the simple provision of accommodation within national parks is not the problem it is often made out to be (Butler, 1985). A well-designed and located hotel, operating under strict environmental controls, can be much less intrusive and damaging to the environment than a poorly located and inefficient campsite, yet some systems still allow only camping within parks and not permanent accommodation for visitors. In small parks no accommodation may be much more appropriate, but in larger parks there seems no ecological or other rationale for allowing camping and not other forms of accommodation. The only justification for this policy would appear to be a long irrelevant belief that people who camp are somehow more appropriate or more deserving (by way of energy expended or discomfort suffered?) of being able to stay overnight within a national park than those who enjoy the comforts of a hotel or lodge. While early users of national parks may have had to camp to be able to stay in national parks, contemporary users can utilise mobile homes and tents with facilities which far exceed those of some lodges.

A second aspect of this problem can be seen in the areas surrounding some national parks. The development of accommodation and other facilities adjoining the boundaries of national parks is hardly an improvement over having such facilities the other side of the boundary. Indeed, the problem may be aggravated by the fact that controls on such developments may be much less outside the park, thus environmental impacts and densities of developments may be much greater than if the developments were within parks. In most cases, as in the example of Canmore (Dearden, Chapter 12), many of the visitors to such developments simply enter the adjoining park as day visitors, often with as many if not more severe impacts, particularly related to transportation, than if they had been staying overnight in the park. A similar situation exists in Queensland, where, wisely, little development of a permanent nature has been allowed on the Great Barrier Reef Marine National Park itself, but day visitation is considerable, even excessive in some locations, by visitors staying in resorts such as Cairns.

While such situations are rarely international in nature, that is, the development is normally within the same country (state/province/region), some of the issues discussed by Timothy (Chapter 16) about the irrelevancies of boundaries to tourist travel and the need for cooperation across boundaries are particularly relevant. Much greater attention needs to be paid to ensuring that areas adjoining national parks do not become either inadequate and inappropriate substitutes for unwanted developments within the parks, i.e. dumping grounds from national parks, nor locations for excessive development designed to take advantage of national parks without any responsibility for impacts resulting within the parks. Neither type of development should be acceptable or allowed to occur.

Conclusions

In reviewing the contributions in this book it is clear that national parks face major problems for the future. Many of these are related, directly or indirectly, to tourism. The use of parks for tourism is as old as the parks themselves and over the past century and a quarter has become a well-established fact. It is extremely unlikely, with very few exceptions, that such use will not continue into the future, almost certainly at an increased level. To prevent the use of parks for tourism would be to betray one of the founding principles of the parks systems, and would almost certainly place a number of systems in great financial jeopardy. As noted above, such a move would also weaken very considerably the political support which many national park systems appear to share among their respective populations. One may argue a strong case that the survival of national park systems as we know them today depends very much upon the continuation of a positive relationship between tourism and the parks. While it is clear from the chapters in this book that this relationship, in its many forms, is far from perfect, and that tourism creates a number of often severe problems for some systems or individual parks, to extinguish this relationship would most likely create far more severe problems for parks (and other areas, which would then experience relocated increased tourism pressures, without the controls and management which park authorities have). The relationship between tourism and national parks will never be an easy one, but for the mutual well-being of both partners, the relationship must not only continue, but become more symbiotic if parks are to continue to perform their multiple functions into the third millennium.

References

Alberta Chamber of Commerce, 1971, Brief submitted to Public Hearings on Rocky Mountain National Parks, Edmonton, Alberta, April, 1971

Butler, R.W., 1985, Tourism and heritage use and conservation. In *Heritage for tomorrow: Proceedings of the Canadian Assembly on National Parks and Protected Areas*, Volume 5, R.C. Scace and J.G. Nelson, eds, pp. 60–72, Ministry of Supply and Services, Ottawa

Butler, R.W., 1997, Modelling tourism development: evolution, growth and decline. In *Tourism, development and growth: the challenge of sustainability*, S. Wahab and J.J. Pigram, eds, pp. 109–128, Routledge, London

Conservation Foundation, 1972, *National parks for the future*, Conservation Foundation, Washington, DC

Hall, C.M. and Johnston, M. 1995, *Polar tourism: tourism in the Arctic and Antarctic regions*, John Wiley, Chichester

Hart, E.J., 1983, *The selling of Canada: the CPR and the beginnings of Canadian tourism*, Altitude Press, Banff

Mowforth, M. and Munt, I., 1998, *Tourism and sustainability: new tourism in the Third World*, Routledge, London

Nelson, J.G., 1982, Public provision of rural recreation opportunities: Canada's national parks, past preent and future. In *Recreational Land Use: Perspectives on its Evolution in Canada*, G. Wall and J.S. Marsh, eds, pp. 41–61, Carleton University Press, Ottawa

Nelson, J.G. and Butler, R.W., 1974, Recreation and the environment. In *Perspectives on environment*, I. Manners and M. Mikesell, eds, Association of American Geographers, Washington, DC

Parks Canada, 1994, *Guiding principles and practices*, Ministry of Supply and Services, Ottawa

Wall, G., 1997, Sustainable tourism – unsustainable development. In *Tourism, development and growth: the challenge of sustainability*, S. Wahab and J.J. Pigram, eds, pp. 33–49, Routledge, London

World Commission on Environment and Development (WCED) 1987, *Our common future*, Oxford University Press, Oxford

World Tourism Organisation (WTO), 1999, *Yearbook of tourism statistics*, Madrid: World Tourism Organisation, Madrid

Index

The index covers all chapters, but not reference lists. Tourism and national parks, the principal topics of the book, are classified under definitions and other headings. Terms are arranged word-by-word, where spaces precede letters in filing order, so 'market policy' precedes 'marketing'. A figure within an entry is indicated by the letter 'f' after the locator, a plate by the letter 'p', a table by the letter 't'.